T0326452

International Business –
Baltic Business Development

This volume represents research papers prepared in conjunction with the Colloquium „Baltic Business Development" which was held at Tallinn University of Technology on 19th of June 2012, and was organised by Tallinn School of Economics and Business Administration with support of the Baltic-German University Liaison Office, Riga, and Hamburg University of Technology, Germany.

Baltisch - Deutsches
OCHSCHULKONTOR
BALTI-SAKSA KÕRGKOOLIDE BÜROO BALTIJAS–VÂCIJAS AUGSTSKOLU BIROJS BALTIJOS ŠALIŲ IR VOKIETIJOS AUKŠTŲJŲ MOKYKLŲ BIURAS

The book was published with support from the Baltic-German University Liaison Office from funds of the German Academic Exchange Service (DAAD).

This collection of studies provides information, opinions, and research that should be of value to practitioners, academics, and students.

Editorial and Scientific Committee
Professor Dr. Üllas Ehrlich
Professor Dr. Wolfgang Kersten
Professor Dr. Tatajana Muravska
Professor Dr. Gunnar Prause
Professor Dr. Urve Venesaar
Professor Dr. Joachim Winkler

The contributions have been double blind peer reviewed.

Copy Editors: Marika Kirsspuu and Kim Kabelitz

Gunnar Prause / Urve Venesaar / Wolfgang Kersten (eds.)

International Business – Baltic Business Development

Tallinn 2013

Bibliographic Information published by the Deutsche Nationalbibliothek
The Deutsche Nationalbibliothek lists this publication in the Deutsche
Nationalbibliografie; detailed bibliographic data is available in the internet at
http://dnb.d-nb.de.

Library of Congress Cataloging-in-Publication Data
Baltic Business Development (Colloquium) (2012 : Tallinn)
  International business : Baltic business development, Tallinn 2013 / Gunnar
Prause, Urve Venesaar, Wolfgang Kersten (eds.).
    pages cm
  "This volume is the collection of the research papers presented at the colloquium
  "Baltic Business Development", which was held in Tallinn on 19th of June 2012"–
Preface.
  ISBN 978-3-631-63816-3
  1. International business enterprises–Baltic States–Congresses. 2. Baltic
States—Commerce–Congresses. 3. Baltic States–Foreign economic relations–
Congresses. I. Prause, Gunnar. II. Venesaar, Urve. III. Kersten, Wolfgang. IV.
Tallinn School of Economics and Business Administration. V. Title.
  HD2877.75.B35 2012
  658'.04909479--dc23

                                        2013034973

ISBN 978-3-631-63816-3 (Print)
E-ISBN 978-3-653-03785-2 (E-Book)
DOI 10.3726/978-3-653-03785-2

© Peter Lang GmbH
Internationaler Verlag der Wissenschaften
Frankfurt am Main 2013
All rights reserved.
PL Academic Research is an Imprint of Peter Lang GmbH.

Peter Lang – Frankfurt am Main · Bern · Bruxelles · New York ·
Oxford · Warszawa · Wien

www.peterlang.de

Table of Contents

Preface

This volume is the collection of the research papers presented at the colloquium "Baltic Business Development", which was held in Tallinn on 19th of June 2012. The colloquium was organised by Tallinn School of Economics and Business Administration of Tallinn University of Technology in cooperation with Hamburg University of Technology.

The colloquium has been supported by the Baltic-German University Liaison Office. This generous support has helped to bring together academics and specialists from business and academic areas for an exchange of their knowledge and experience. The aim of the colloquium was to provide a forum for discussions of issues related to the assessment of business development in the Baltic Sea Region (BSR) coinciding with the end of the German Presidency in the Council of Baltic Sea States (CBSS) in June 2012. The colloquium was honoured by the appearance and the presentation "The Baltic Sea Region at the end of the German presidency of the Baltic Sea Council" of his Excellency the German Ambassador in Estonia Mr. Christian-Matthias Schlaga.

The colloquium provided the participants a great platform for establishing contacts, promoting cooperation within joint projects and research networking and for disseminating knowledge and experience on international business and university - business interaction in the frame of the Baltic Sea Strategy and the Agenda EU2020.

The colloquium was placed in the environment of the 3rd international conference "Economies of Central and Eastern Europe (ECEE)" also organised by Tallinn School of Economics and Business Administration. Within the ECEE conference the colloquium focused on "International Business in the Baltic Sea Region", which is reflected by the accepted papers covering the three topics: Logistics in the BSR; Organizational Development; Business Management and Marketing.

A special feature of the colloquium was the Round Table Discussion on the issue "University-Business Cooperation in the Frame of the Baltic Sea Strategy and the Agenda EU2020", which brought togehter leaders of business organisations, representatives from responsible government institutions, and research and education specialists. During the discussion between the Round Table participants - Wolfgang Kersten, Allar Korjas, Mait Palts, Gunnar Prause, Piret Treiberg and Urve Venesaar - new models and experiences about university-business cooperation as one important pillar for business development and the implementation of the Baltic Sea Strategy and the Agenda EU2020 in the Baltic Sea Region have been discussed.

We gratefully acknowledge on behalf of colloquium participants the support of the Organizing Committee as well as the Scientific and Editorial Committees of the colloquium and the ECEE conference. A special thank we want to give to Marianne Kallaste of the Tallinn School of Economics and Business Adminsitration, for their efforts to make this event efficient and enjoyable.

The present book contains papers which have been peer-reviewed under the supervision of the Editorial and Scientific Committee. The main copy editing was done by Marika Kirsspuu and Kim Kabelitz whom we want to thank on behalf of all participants.

The Editors

Competitiveness of Companies – Logistics in the Baltic Sea Region

Wolfgang Kersten[1], Meike Schroeder[1], Caroline Singer[1] and Mareike Boeger[1]

Abstract

The Baltic Sea Region (BSR) is one of the most dynamic regions in the European Union (EU). Differences in logistics play a major role in this issue. In this area, no comparable analyses and investigations have been made until recently. The aim of this paper is to describe the status quo and the development needs of manufacturing and trading companies as well as logistics service providers in the BSR. First, the paper explains the influence of core competencies on the competitiveness of companies. In practice, the outsourcing of services often results from the creation of core competencies due to the bundling of specific resources. Second, the findings of an empirical logistics study as part of the EU project LogOn Baltic are presented. Selected regions are compared with respect to the logistics costs and the outsourcing of logistics services. Last, development needs in logistics are described.

JEL classification codes: O57, R, R1, R11, R4.

Keywords: competitiveness, outsourcing, resource based view, logistics services, logistics costs, development needs, Baltic Sea Region

1. Introduction

Due to the dynamically changing business conditions, companies from nearly all industry sectors have been facing high cost pressures recently. In order to reduce costs, manufacturing and trading companies take measures such as outsourcing transportation. However, since the level of costs is already very low in this area, companies start to realise that further cost reductions are not possible anymore. Thus, there is a growing demand for external logistics services beyond transportation such as inventory management and increasingly also individualised service packages, raising the question of which logistics function should be outsourced in the trade-off between cost reduction and high service level requirements.

In different countries companies are in dissimilar states of the described outsourcing process. Their development needs and business threats vary. The aim of this paper is to analyse the status quo of logistics outsourcing in regions with

---

1   Hamburg University of Technology

different economic backgrounds and environmental conditions. In the following, empirical results will be presented which were gathered as part of the EU project called "LogOn Baltic – Developing Regions through Spatial Planning and Logistics & ICT Competence". The purpose of LogOn Baltic was to present solutions improving the interplay between logistics & ICT competence and spatial planning, on the one hand, and strengthening small and medium-sized enterprises' (SMEs) competitiveness in the BSR, on the other hand. The following regions – represented by research institutions, logistics and transport associations, development agencies and regional authorities – participated in the project: Estonia, Latvia, Lithuania, Poland (Pomerania), Germany (Southern Metropolitan Region of Hamburg and Wismar Region), Denmark, Sweden, Finland and Russia (St. Petersburg Region) (LogOn Baltic 2008; Kersten et al. 2007a).

In the remainder of this paper, the theoretical background is first provided for outsourcing decisions, namely the resource based view (RBV) of the firm. Afterwards, the empirical results of the above-mentioned study are presented in three sections: target group and sample as well as survey design, status quo and development needs in logistics as a whole. Finally, the paper closes with conclusions and a short outlook.

2. The Resource Based View

The logistics field is influenced by ongoing trends like individual and heterogeneous customer demands, shorter product life cycles, technological innovations, strong competition and dynamic changes in the environment. Companies which have so far always developed, produced and distributed products independently, now often add less value to the product than before and realise even more; they form part of globally distributed supply chains. As a consequence, they are forced to reduce their costs and to focus on core competencies. Activities and services that do not belong to their core activities have to be outsourced.

In connection with the sustainable competitive advantage of companies and the outsourcing of services, the resource based view is often referred to as an explanatory model in the business literature. According to Penrose (1995), resources include all "tangible things", such as buildings, machinery and raw materials, but also "intangible things", namely the staff's technical and management capabilities.[2] Instead of deriving the demand for resources from the market, the available resources are exploited and experiences are broadened.

---

2   The contributions were first published in 1959. Kristandl and Bontis (2007) derive a common definition for intangibles from the resource-based view analysing various definitions from different fields in the literature.

Based on Penrose's works, Wernerfelt applies Porter's five forces model to diversified companies and explores under which circumstances a resource yields a high return in a long-term perspective. He defines "resource position barriers" as partially analogous to entry barriers. Furthermore, Wernerfelt observes that companies have to strike a balance between the exploitation of existing resources and the development of new resources (Wernerfelt 1984; Porter 1998).

In contrast to Penrose, Barney (1991) distinguishes between three categories of firm resources, i.e. physical capital resources, human capital resources and organizational capital resources. On the assumption that strategic resources are heterogeneous and immobile, he discusses four attributes which resources must have in order to generate a sustained competitive advantage. They have to be valuable, rare, inimitable and not substitutable.

Prahalad and Hamel (1990) demand similar properties from core competencies in a company: Core competencies have to provide potential access to markets, must contribute to the customer benefits of the end product and have to be difficult to imitate. The authors distinguish between core competencies providing a basis for core products which on their part generate end products. In their view, the unique combination of production capabilities with technology enables the generation of competitive advantages. However, Stalk *et al.* (1992) expand this perspective by the special capabilities along the value chain as a bundle of processes. The resulting core competencies represent the outstanding and long-lasting capabilities leading to a high customer value.

The creation of core competencies through bundling specific resources often leads to the outsourcing of services. Continuously pushed by globalization, increasing requirements, by rising complexity of processes and products and susceptibility to risks, companies choose outsourcing in order to meet these challenges. Complexity and risks can be controlled or even reduced by transferring logistics services to professional value added partners. Other reasons for logistics outsourcing, for example, can be to achieve an increased flexibility and personal productivity or to improve services and to benefit from the use of new technologies (Kersten and Koch 2007; Koch 2011). However, one of the most frequently mentioned reasons for the outsourcing of logistics services is the reduction of logistics costs.

In the following it is demonstrated that reducing logistics costs belongs to one of the main motives when it comes to the outsourcing of logistics services within the Baltic Sea Region.

3. Empirical Results of the Logistics Study in the Baltic Sea Region

The empirical activities of LogOn Baltic compare the existing logistics services and competencies to the logistics needs in the participating regions, enabling the development of perspectives and action plans for strengthening logistics competence. In each region, a logistics survey, an ICT survey and expert interviews were conducted. In the following, the results from the logistics survey are analysed.

In the following, the target group and sample as well as the survey design are described.

3.1 Methodology: Target group and sample

The logistics survey has by far been the largest survey conducted in the BSR in the field of logistics. It was mainly carried out as a web-based survey in the first quarter of the year 2007. The e-mails sent out to target companies contained a link leading to a website where the participants could directly answer the questions. In order to increase the response rate, two reminders were sent at two-weekly intervals (Kersten et al. 2007c). Post and telephone were used as complementary measures in some regions. The response rate varied from about 2% in Hamburg to about 14% in Finland. In Mecklenburg-Vorpommern, personal interviews were used to collect data. In addition, the link to the survey was published on the websites of the participating institutions and in newsletters of regional logistics associations to broaden the data base.

In total, more than 1,200 companies participated in the study, the number of respondents varying from about 80 in Pomerania/Poland to about 330 in Southwest Finland. 38% of the respondents can be characterised as manufacturing companies, 33% represent the trading industry and 29% belong to the group of logistics service providers. Thus, a broad picture of the perspectives from users as well as from logistics services providers is guaranteed.

In addition to the industry sector, the respondent companies were also categorised according to the company size. Micro, small or medium-sized enterprises (SMEs) depending on the turnover are defined by the European Commission (2012) as follows:

- Micro companies: €0–2 million turnover
- Small companies: €2–10 million turnover
- Medium-sized companies: €10–50 million turnover

More than 90% of the 1,200 respondents can be classified as SMEs. The distribution of participants supports the objective of the LogOn Baltic project to evaluate the needs in order to strengthen the competitiveness of SMEs in particular.

3.2 Survey design

The survey targeted at three company types: manufacturing companies, trading firms and logistics service providers, whereas the first two groups represented customers of logistics services. The aim of this explorative study was to evaluate the internal situation of companies – especially of SMEs – with respect to logistics, but also to the companies' views of their regional business environment. The same questionnaire was used for all regions. The first part of the survey contained identical general questions for the three types of companies, while the second part included specific questions pertaining to the type of the responding company.

The five major topics of the survey were as follows:

- Current logistics costs and their development
- The need for further competence development
- Outsourcing – today's situation and the expected future development
- The operating environment – an assessment of the regional advantages and disadvantages
- A self-assessment of the companies' logistics activities and to what extent they are coordinated with customers and suppliers.

The following sections encompass the first three of the afore-mentioned topics.

3.3 Logistics costs of manufacturing and trading companies

The four major logistics cost elements examined in the survey are related to transport, warehousing, inventory and administration. All costs were given as percentages of the turnover. For each category, a drop down menu was used, ranging from 0–40% at intervals of 1%. Companies indicating an amount of costs equal to 0% or greater than 40% were excluded from the sample for plausible reasons.

The *overall logistics costs* in the investigated regions mostly vary from 8% to 14% of the turnover of the participating companies (see Fig. 3.1). Only Mecklenburg-Vorpommern deviates from this bandwidth; here, the logistics costs account for more than 20%. An important reason is the structure of the enterprises since the region is dominated by micro to small companies rather than small to medium-sized companies in other regions. In addition, logistics costs vary substantially between different industries and the products are predominantly relatively low-value goods. Another surprising result is that the logistics costs of Southwest Finland are among the lowest third of all regions. Previous studies often came to the conclusion that due to the large distances between cities and the small population density, logistics costs are significantly higher in Finland than in other countries (Klaus and Kille 2007). At least for Southwest Finland, this does not seem to hold true. The area around the city of Turku is one of the most densely populated regions in Finland with a well-developed infrastructure.

No significant differences can be observed regarding the *composition of logistics costs* between the regions (see Fig. 3.1). In general, transport costs account for the largest part of the logistics costs, followed by inventory costs. However, in terms of the logistics performance of the regions analysed – measured by the percentage of perfect order fulfilment – an advantage of the Western EU countries can be recognized (Kersten et al. 2007a; Ojala et al. 2007).

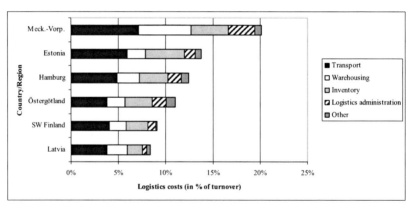

Fig.1:   *Comparison of logistics costs and their composition of manufacturing companies as a percentage of turnover; Source: Kersten et al. 2007a; Ojala et al. 2007*

In addition to the level of costs, companies were asked about their expectations regarding the future development of costs. Here, the evidence seems to be clear: in all regions except St. Petersburg, more than 50% of the companies from the manufacturing sector believe that their logistics costs will rise in the next years, particularly in the field of transportation. There are several *reasons for the estimated rise in transportation costs*: The increasing oil price is the strongest reason why they may go up, as the main factor influencing the fuel price is the cost of crude oil. Furthermore, taxes such as the petroleum tax are an uncertain cost factor. In addition, the development of highway toll systems makes transport more expensive in Europe.

A rather operational reason for higher logistics costs are more customer-oriented approaches to logistics involving higher flexibility, smaller batch sizes and more frequent shipping of goods. These solutions also attribute to higher inventory carrying costs in the future, although companies try to reduce logistics costs with lean management methods. The latter methods as well as outsourcing lead to higher risks in the supply chains and therefore a greater urgency about disruption management systems. The implementation of these systems may in turn result in a decrease in inventory carrying costs, which is anticipated for example by more than 10% of the responding companies in the Hamburg Region. Outsourcing is an efficient measure which companies adopt aiming at the reduction of transportation costs, but increasingly at inventory and warehousing costs as well.

3.4 Outsourcing of logistics services

As explained before, companies have to adapt their business strategies and activities to the changing environment. The comparison of logistics costs in section 3.3 has shown that transportation costs account for the largest part. One possibility to reduce logistics costs is to outsource transportation, because the transportation function does not belong to the core activities of manufacturing and trading companies. These resources saved may be used for improving the existing core competencies, described in section 2.

In the survey, companies were asked up to which percentage different functions are outsourced to external companies. The answers were grouped into three categories: 0%, 1%–75% and over 75%. *National and international transport services* combined show the highest share of outsourcing. Concerning national transport services, the logistically further developed regions rank the highest, with the majority of manufacturing and trading companies outsourcing more than 75% of all inland transport services to external service providers (see Fig. 2). The Baltic States are in the middle of the range, whereas St. Petersburg and Mecklenburg-Vorpommern rank the lowest. In the latter region, only 20% of the companies indicated that they outsource inland transport more than 75%.

However, a completely different result is shown when it comes to outsourcing of other logistics services such as *IT services*. These services are performed by the companies themselves to a much greater extent. In addition, the ranking of the regions differs. Estonia is the leader with respect to the outsourcing of IT services, since 17% of the companies indicated they outsourced more than 75%

of IT services. This is not surprising when considering the high acceptance of information and communication technologies in Estonia in general.

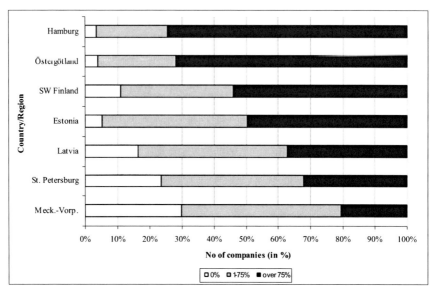

Fig.2:   *Share of outsourced national transportation services by manufacturing and trading companies; Source: Authors' illustration*

Figure 3 exemplarily shows the outsourcing ratio of different kinds of services for the Southern Metropolitan Region of Hamburg.

Transport, reverse logistics and freight forwarding are the most commonly outsourced logistics operations in the surveyed companies (Kersten et al. 2007b). On average, about 75% of the companies in Hamburg declared that more than 75% of their domestic as well as international transportation are handled by an external service provider. About 20% of the companies stated they outsourced 1%–75% of their domestic transport (15% of the companies for international transport respectively). In these areas, manufacturing companies generally do not see their core competence and thus they do not lose any know-how when outsourcing them. In addition, transportation, freight forwarding, and reverse logistics are areas that have a long history of expertise in the world of logistics service providers. Since the main criteria for outsourcing decisions are usually cost factors, these functions are outsourced to third parties.

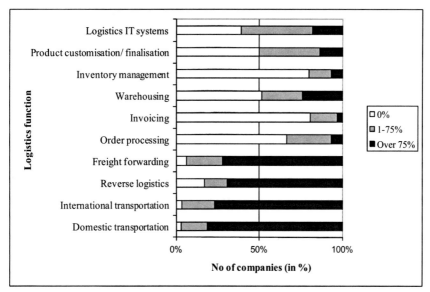

Fig.3:   *Outsourcing of different logistics functions by manufacturing and trading companies in the Southern Metropolitan Region of Hamburg; Source: Kersten et al. 2007c*

The survey shows that companies spend a relatively small amount on third party warehousing as well as inventory management, and they particularly prefer to keep control of their own operations (product customisation and logistics IT systems). This holds even truer for invoicing and order processing. As these activities mean direct customer contact, companies are unwilling to leave this field to service providers to a large extent.

Recently, however, prices for logistics services in many cases dropped to a very low level with two consequences: first, manufacturing and trading companies cannot further reduce their transportation costs. They have to find new ways to increase their competitiveness by reducing costs in other areas, such as inventory and warehouse management, and/or increasing the quality of their goods. Second, and correspondingly, logistics service providers cannot only compete in pricing but more in extending their range of services and in offering high-quality services.

3.5 Development needs for manufacturing and trading companies

The status quo described above showed that the same tendencies concerning the transportation costs and the willingness to outsource logistics services exist in nearly all Baltic Sea Regions. Therefore, it is now analysed if the requirements for competencies are expected to develop similarly in the regions. For this purpose, the development needs for manufacturing and trading companies as well as the biggest threats for logistics service providers are illustrated.

In order to face the future developments, the participating manufacturing and trading companies were asked to estimate their most important development needs in the field of logistics within their companies. In all regions, the reduction of costs was mentioned as one of the three *development needs* for the respondent companies, in both Eastern as well as Western European regions. The second most important one was the improvement of customer services. In addition, the development of information systems and the selection of logistics service providers were named as the main development needs. In Hamburg, the increase in transparency of the supply chain ranked in the top 3 as an interorganizational aspect.

The afore-mentioned development in market and competition changes the industry and the tasks of co-workers. As a result, some qualification requirements will become more important during the next years. If companies aim at staying competitive for a longer period they have to eliminate and to prevent existing deficits in qualification with the help of qualification measures. A lack of qualified and well-trained employees is the reason for the bottleneck in the German trade and service industries in 80% of the cases. This deficit evolves into an incremental brake, which can only be released through targeted education and training (Kersten et al. 2007a).

Companies have to analyse the bottlenecks in their day-to-day business caused by the lack of qualified and well-trained executives. Figure 3.4 shows the findings of the areas in which manufacturing companies see the most urgent needs for competence development of their personnel in the regions of Hamburg, St. Petersburg and Estonia.

The requirements for competence development vary to a surprisingly large extent in manufacturing companies. In the region of Hamburg, the needs for personnel competence in strategic planning (about 45%) and in operational activities (about 30%) are quite high. The knowledge of supply chain flows and networks (nearly 20%) seem to be important, too. In Germany, there is a huge variety of logistics networks, ranging from very simple locally oriented chains with only few participants to chains operating internationally and connecting companies all over the world. Working within these networks and handling of the supply chain flows requires good knowledge in strategic planning and management.

In St. Petersburg, the developments show reverse tendencies. The need for competencies in rather operational activities is quite high (about 60%), while strategic (about 35%) or even inter-organizational activities (about 5%) are regarded as less important. The values of the Estonian responses rank between those of the Hamburg and the St. Petersburg region. However, all regions show that the development of language skills is considered of minor importance.

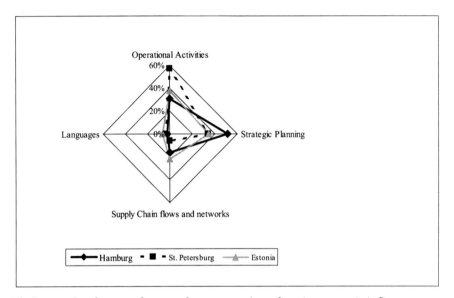

Fig.4:　　Development of personnel competence (manufacturing companies); Source: Kersten et al. 2007a

After presenting the development needs of manufacturing and trading companies, in the following the focus is set on the most important threats of logistics service providers.

3.6 Development needs for logistics service providers

Logistics service providers were asked in which areas they see the biggest *threats* for their business in the future which they need to counteract. Figure 5 exemplarily illustrates the findings of the regions Hamburg, St. Petersburg and Estonia. Increasing costs of service provision were regarded as the biggest threat in all three regions. This corresponds to the answers of the manufacturing companies mentioned in the previous section, which regard the reduction of costs as one of the main development needs in the future. Logistics companies have to take this particular need into account, because costs are one of the most important reasons for selecting a logistics service provider.

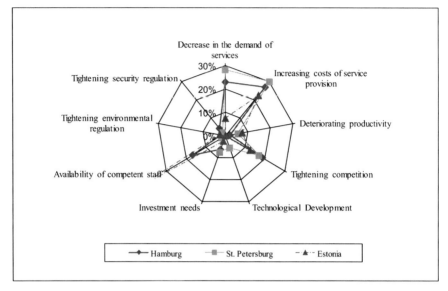

Fig.5:   *Estimation of the biggest threats for logistics service providers; Source: Kersten et al. 2007a*

In both regions, Hamburg and St. Petersburg, the decrease in demand for services was ranked the second largest threat. However, in Estonia, one of the growing logistics markets of the Baltic Sea Region, this was not seen as a big menace. Another problem which was considered in all three regions was tightening competition, which can be a direct consequence from less demand on the one hand and cost pressure on the other hand. Furthermore, new competitors entering the market as a consequence of the EU enlargement and globalization can be seen as a hazard. Tightening competition in general makes it harder to pass costs on to customers.

Like manufacturing and trading companies, logistics service providers noted that the availability of skilled personnel could be a problem, particularly in Estonia and in Hamburg. This poses a serious challenge (Kersten et al. 2007a).

The need for qualified employees in the field of logistics was confirmed by the empirical findings of two studies: One has been conducted by the *Suederelbe AG* and the other one has been conducted by the Institute of Business Logistics and General Management at Hamburg University of Technology. The studies show that there is a need for higher educated employees in logistics in the Metropolitan Region of Hamburg since 2005. Until 2011, this need has increased while the need for lower educated employees in logistics in the Metropolitan

Region in Hamburg has decreased (Suederelbe AG 2011; Kersten & Schröder 2012).

By contrast, the deteriorating productivity in connection with tightening security and environmental regulations, as well as rapid technological development or investment needs have not been characterised as threats in the near future.

4. Conclusions and Outlook

The aim of this paper was to describe the status quo and the development needs of manufacturing and trading companies as well as logistics service providers in the BSR. The resource based view is frequently mentioned in connection with a sustainable competitive advantage of companies and the outsourcing of services since the latter often results from the creation of core competencies by bundling specific resources. One of the main objectives of the outsourcing of logistics services is the reduction of logistics costs. Within the scope of the EU project LogOn Baltic, the logistics survey examined to what extent the strategy is pursued in selected regions of the BSR. The overall logistics costs account for 8% to 14% of the turnover of the participating manufacturing companies with an upward trend and with transport costs representing the largest share. This tendency enforces outsourcing of logistics services even more. It became apparent that transport, reverse logistics and freight forwarding are currently the most commonly outsourced logistics functions.

The analysis of future development needs shows that the reduction of costs, the improvement of customer services, the development of information systems and the selection of logistics service providers are most important to manufacturing and trading companies. Qualification requirements for the staff are expected to become more significant depending on the region. The biggest threats to logistics service providers are the increasing costs of service provision, on the one hand, and the decrease in demand for services as well as tightening competition, on the other hand.

The results show that the trend towards outsourcing logistics services is continuously growing and logistics service providers have to prepare for the specified future challenges in order to remain competitive in the long run. Furthermore, end customers increasingly demand more individualized products and services which they also reflect in the decreasing demand for more individualized logistics services.

Further research is needed in order to compare the results gained within the study presented in this paper with future results. This can be done by carrying out a longitudinal analysis. Hence, potential changes of the results over time and their reasons may be observed and investigated further.

References

Barney, J. 1991. Firm Resources and Sustained Competitive Advantage. *Journal of Management*, Vol. 17, No. 1, pp. 99–120.

European Commission 2012. Small and medium-sized enterprises (SMEs) – what is a SME? Available from http://ec.europa.eu/enterprise/policies/sme/facts-figures-analysis/sme-definition/index_en.htm, accessed May 10, 2012.

Kersten, W. and Koch, J. 2007. Motive für das Outsourcing komplexer Logistikdienstleistungen (English translation: Reasons for outsourcing complex logistics services). in: W. Stölzle, W., J. Weber, E. Hofmann and C.M. Wallenburg, (Eds.). *Handbuch Kontraktlogistik (English translation: Handbook contract logistics)*, Weinheim: Wiley-VCH, pp. 115–130.

Kersten, W., Boeger, M., Schroeder, M. and Singer, C. 2007a. *Developing Regions through Spatial Planning and Logistics & ICT competence – final report.* As part of the publication series of the EU project LogOn Baltic, Turku School of Economics, report No. 1:2007, Turku.

Kersten, W., Ojala, L., Schroeder, M. and Singer, C. 2007b. Innovative Regional Development for Logistics and ICT – The Baltic Sea Region Example. In: W. Kersten, T. Blecker and C. Herstatt (Eds.). *Innovative Logistics Management – Competitive Advantages through new processes and services*, Berlin: Erich Schmidt Verlag, pp. 343–359.

Kersten, W., Schroeder, M. 2012. *Qualifikationsforderungen in der Logistik – Anforderungen am Standort Hamburg (English translation: Qualification in logistics – challenges for the Hamburg Region).* Published soon.

Kersten, W., Schroeder, M., Singer, C. and Boeger, M. 2007c. *Logistics Survey in the Southern Metropolitan Region of Hamburg.* As part of the publication series of the EU project LogOn Baltic, Turku School of Economics, report no. 30:2007, Turku.

Klaus, P. and Kille, P. 2007. *Top 100 in European Transport and Logistics Services. Market Sizes, Market Segments and Market Leaders in the European Logistics Industry.* 2nd edition, Hamburg: Deutscher Verkehrs-Verlag.

Koch, J. 2011. *Qualitätsmanagement in Logistikunternehmen: eine empirische Untersuchung (English translation: Quality management in logistics companies: an empirical investigation).* Lohmar: Eul Verlag.

Kristandl, G., Bontis, N. 2007. Constructing a definition for intangibles using the resource based view of the firm. *Management Decision*, Vol. 45, No. 9, pp. 1510–1524.

LogOn Baltic 2008. Key Objectives. Available at http://info.tse.fi/logonbaltic/uudetsivut/logonbaltic.asp, accessed May 10, 2012.

Ojala, L., Solakivi, T., Hälinen, H.-M., Lorentz, H. and Hoffmann, T. 2007. *State of Logistics in the Baltic Sea Region – Survey Results from Eight Countries.* As part of the publication series of the EU project LogOn Baltic, Turku School of Economics, report no. 3:2007, Turku.

Penrose, E.T. 1995. *The Theory of the Growth of the Firm.* 3rd edition, Oxford, New York, Athens: Oxford University Press.

Porter M.E. 1998. *Competitive Advantage: Creating and Sustaining Superior Performance.* New York: Free Press.

Prahalad, C.K. and Hamel, G. 1990. The Core Competence of the Corporation. *Harvard Business Review*, May-June, pp. 79–91.

Stalk, G., Evans, P. and Shulman, L.E. 1992. Competing on Capabilities: The New Rules of Corporate Strategy. *Harvard Business Review*, March-April, pp. 57–69.

Suederelbe AG 2011. Logistik-Arbeitsmarktmonitoring 2010 *(English translation: Logistics – monitoring of the labour market), Hamburg: Suederelbe AG.*

Wernerfelt, B. 1984. A Resource-Based View of the Firm. *Strategic Management Journal*, Vol. 5, No. 2, pp. 171–180.

Financing Logistics Facilities by Applying Public Private Partnership Models: Solutions for the North-East European Area

Joachim R. Daduna[1]

Abstract

Logistics facilities are of increasing importance for the design and development of efficient logistic structures, because they constitute an essential element to control the flow of goods especially in multi-modal processes. As these facilities should not only be viewed under economic aspects but also under regional planning and structural aspects, it is appropriate to include public institutions in this context. Financial participation enables these to engage actively in the planning and design process of such investment decisions with the objective of realizing public interests. In the following basics of private financing models will be discussed at first. Subsequently existing and potential applications of Public Private Partnership (PPP) concepts will be presented. On this basis possible approaches are developed and critically discussed with a view to the developments in the North-East European area.

JEL classification codes: R14, H44

Keywords: Logistics facilities, freight villages, city logistics, public private partnership

1. Introduction

The availability of a sufficiently large *traffic infrastructure* is essential for *functioning market structures* and *sustainable economic growth*. Already Launhardt (1885) realized that (...) the improvement of means of transport (...) is dangerous for expensive goods as the most effective of all protective duties, the protection of bad roads, is getting lost. Rammler (2003) refers to (...) transport infrastructures (...) which in a way are the skeletal and neural system of the modern industrial growth society. For these reasons (putting aside a few exceptions) providing the transport infrastructure is only seen as one of the core tasks within the scope of the *general public services* (see e.g. Aberle 2009). In addition, it is also an (political) instrument of structural and spatial development planning, not only on a national level (see e.g. Stender-Vorwachs 2005; Gather et al. 2008) but increasingly also within the *European Community* (EC) (see e.g. Dionelis and Giaoutzi 2008). Thus, the development of cross-border transport infrastruc-

---

1   Berlin School of Economics and Law, *Badensche Str, 52, 10715 Berlin, Germany,* phone: +49 30 30877 1114, fax: +49 30 30877 1199, e-mail: daduna@hwr-berlin.de

ture is a main element of cohesion policies even though the underlying strategic direction here is controversial.

Core elements are the *Pan-European* corridors which were defined in 1994 (see e.g. HB-Verkehrsconsult and VTT, 2005; Vinukurov et al. 2009) in order to meet changing demands in the *Central* and *Southeast European Regions*. These corridors have to ensure connections both to the former EC territory (westbound) and to the *Russian Federation* (eastbound). On the basis of traffic flows and developments forecasted as well as by bearing in mind political objectives regarding the realization of a (future) common European economic area, specific *transport corridors* were developed which must build the backbone of highly efficient transport structures including the (partly realized) structures of the *Trans European Transport Network* (TEN-T) (see e.g. Baird 2007; Stratigea et al. 2008; Dionelis and Giaoutzi 2008; de Ceuster et al. 2010). Major focus is put here on terrestrial systems of *road* and *rail transport* as well as *freight transport* on *inland waterways* (see e.g. Notteboom 2007; Rohács and Simongáti 2007). In the maritime field, the *Short Sea Shipping* (SSS) (see e.g. Ng 2009; Paixão Casaca and Marlow 2009; Styhre 2009; Daduna 2012) as well as the *River Sea Shipping* (RSS) are considered as the main transport modes (see e.g. Kaup 2008; Radmilović et al. 2011).

However, problems on all levels increasingly arise in public *infrastructure financing* due to the *limited public budgets* so that the possibility of financing with private funding is discussed as an alternative (see e.g. Daduna 2009). But such an approach is controversial for different reasons with respect to transport and budget policy. This concerns models with a use-dependent refinancing, but also pre-financing models that are designed with long-term repayments by public-law authorities. Hereby, the criticism aims at the extensive transfer of risk at public expense and also at budgetary matters of a (de facto) shifting of capital expenditures into the following budget years caused by the (long-term) fixed payments (see e.g. Mältsemees 2009). These lead to the restriction of fiscal decisions of the parliaments elected at later points in time, which is seen as a violation of the budget authority which ground in constitutional regulations. However, the same effects occur with public borrowing for which repayments have to be made in the following periods, so that public financing factually has the same effects.

The financing of *logistics infrastructure*, for example freight traffic facilities as well as trans-shipment and storage facilities, is completely different. Here, it is mostly about private investors who are in charge of the financing and realization but who also bear the economic risk. Operating such facility can be carried out by the investor itself or also by an operating company. Excluded in this case are facilities that are directly integrated into to particular (public) traffic networks, as for example *rail freight terminals* or (*deep*) *sea* and *inland ports* which are developed and operated within the scopes of an overall network system and hence are also integrated in these financing structures.

Logistics facilities do not only constitute important elements of efficient *supply chains*, but also have to be viewed as *spatial* and *structural planning instruments*. From here the question arises to what extend a stronger collaboration between *public-law authorities* and the corresponding (*logistical*) *companies* make sense in this market segment to develop sustainable structures in freight transport. In this context, *Public Private Partnership* (PPP) *concepts* do play an important role (see e.g. Allen et al. 2010). Those are often seen (to some extend highly undifferentiated) as the perfect solution of the problems of public budgets, but are continually doomed as a highly dangerous evil from an ideologically oriented point of view.

2. Theoretical Considerations of Logistics Facilities

Logistics facilities as *transport nodes* do not only form origin and destination points of *transport flows* within transportation networks, they also constitute the basis for *precisely organizing* the flow of goods. Here, the focus is put on structuring *multi-modal transport chains* within inter- and transcontinental supply chains (see e.g. Panayides and Song 2008; Rodrigue and Notteboom 2009; Rodrigue et al. 2010). The facilities have differing *functionalities* and *dimensioning* which are mainly based on economic structures and the available transportation infrastructure. Here, it is focused on bi-modal and tri-modal links of different means of transport as well as (in an extended view) on the provision of warehousing, distribution and (logistics-related) services (see e.g. Grundey and Rimienė 2007; Jaržemskis 2007).

A framework (based on the *traffic-related* functions) of the following (*maritime* and *terrestrial*) facilities can be assumed:

o *Seaport container terminals* (SCT) with an *international* hub function and multi-modal links (see e.g. Notteboom 2008; Roso et al. 2009; Rodrigue and Notteboom 2010; Daduna 2011), for example within *trunk* and *feeder networks*. With respect to the North-East European area, the SCT of the *North Range* with the ports Antwerp, Rotterdam and Hamburg, which are dominating the region, are in the foreground.

o *Regional* and *local* SCT in *short sea shipping* (SSS) with usually geographically limited hinterland, which are the dominating form in the Baltic Sea region.

o *Inland ports* with a regional and local function, and if applicable, with a connection to the *river-sea shipping* (RSS).
o *Hinterland terminals* with a supra-regional function (as for example in the form of MegaHubs with the focus on rail / rail trans-shipments) (see e.g. Alicke 2002; Rodrigue 2008; Limbourg and Jourquin 2009; Daduna 2011).
o *Regional* and *local trans-shipment terminals* in (*bi-* and *multi-modal*) *freight transport*, especially in view of the access to rail freight transport.

The efficiency of these facilities depends largely on the trans-shipment techniques applied, especially relating to time and cost aspects. It is problematic to be able to satisfy the logistical requirements because an investment volume is necessary, by which the amortization cannot be guaranteed in local and regional facilities due to the low trans-shipment volume (see e.g. Woxenius 2007). Through this, the potential rail / road trans-shipment possibilities are limited and hence the access to rail freight transport. This has negative effects on a stronger market penetration of multi-modal transport.

By including additional functions, such as warehousing, distribution and services, in the design of logistics facilities (primarily with respect to logistical hinterland structures), the following basic types, including a hierarchical graded structure, are of relevance (see e.g. Nobel 2004; Wermuth and Wirth 2005; Grundey and Rimiené 2007; Nathanail 2007; Higgins et al. 2012):

o (*Central*) *freight villages* with supra-regional (and international) significance (see e.g. Nobel 2004; Ballis and Mavrotas 2007; Rall 2008), which (should) form the basis for an European-wide interconnected network structure of freight transport.
o (*Regional*) *freight villages* which are suitable for a geographically-limited aggregation and disaggregation of flows of goods (see e.g. Tanaguchi et al. 1999). This could be also *Dedicated Warehouses* (see e.g. Nobel 2004), which could be operated for example by service providers on behalf of retail trade companies
o *City-Terminals*, *Urban Distribution Centres* (UDC), and *Urban Consolidation Centres* (UCC) linked to a local-oriented distribution within bigger cities as well as within agglomeration areas (see e.g. Yang et al. 2005; van Duin et al. 2010; Allen and Browne 2010). The main objective here is (in conjunction with city logistics concepts) to extensively use bundling effects and to allow for a customer-oriented provision of goods.

In practice, the (basic) forms with a largely clear distinction that have been listed above are usually not given. One of the main causes for this is the very complex objectives which are associated with freight facilities. This is, among other things due to the particular interests of the parties involved (and the parties affected) (see e.g. Nobel 2004). For this reason, functional and spatial-related facilities have to be assumed with a view to the respective structural framework. This particularly refers to the issue of generating synergy effects, for example, by *spatial linkages* of hinterland terminals for multi-modal (road/rail) freight transport with other logistical facilities. Those facilities are characterized by functionally linking of transportation, warehousing and logistical services. Similar developments can be also observed in the area of SCT (see e.g. Gouvernal et al. 2011).

This short overview about logistics facilities demonstrates a large variety of different types which constitute the basis for a situation-based development. As mentioned above, the provision of part of these facilities is a field of responsibility of public-law authorities, as it is the case for rail freight terminals and ports. The other part (of mostly privately provided and operated facilities) offers significant potentials for cooperative approaches due to the complex influencing factor. Like that, the influence of public-law authorities when deciding for a location out of traffic and structural considerations is of big significance for the community. The objective of this paper is therefore to demonstrate what PPP applications really mean to be and in what way the use of those financing models are possible and reasonable. In order to illustrate the existing options the potentials of PPP solutions are presented with the help of suitable examples.

3. Approaches to Private Sector Financing

Both in scientific debate and in practice, there are a couple of financing models that are private sector oriented and which can be used for example in conjunction with the construction and improvement of transport infrastructure and logistics facilities. Essential aspects are the degree of privatization, meaning to what extend there are changes in the ownership structures (like real estate of the public sector) and how cooperation between the public sector and private companies that act on the market is working in form and content. It is distinguished between (see e.g. Rösch 2007) an *assets privatization* (e.g. the sale of public real estate) and the *material, functional*, and *formal privatization*. A critical analysis shows that only in connection with a functional privatization, cooperation in conjunction with private sector financing forms is possible. In the case of asset privatization as well as material privatization, a complete (legal) shifting to a private sector based structure takes place. Referring to a formal privatization the *legal form* only changes and the form of public-law ownership remains (see e.g. Daduna 2009).

The main types of functional privatization have very different structures (see e.g. Daduna 2009; Alfen and Berckhahn 2012). Here, three approaches are in the foreground with respect to the financing of measures in the field of transport infrastructure and logistics facilities:

o   Pre-financing models:
    This is about private pre-financing of investment measures for which the contractor (and in some cases also the concessionaire) assumes the project planning as well as its realization (see e.g. Stender-Vorwachs 2004; Aberle 2009). The basic responsibility remains with the public-law side, later the public authorities are also responsible for operation and maintenance. Hence, investment measures are only planned and realized by private contractors.
    The payments for the services provided are made by the public contracting authorities at fixed rates over an appropriate period of time. Therefore, this model is also called hire-purchase model. The approach of leasing and fund financing models are similar but taking additionally into account fiscal aspects (see e.g. Stender-Vorwachs 2004). However, the effectiveness of these models is considered to be critical (see e.g. Haßheider 2005). Two essential points are the transfer of risks which will be rolled over to the government as well as legal aspects in conjunction with the (de facto) shifting of investment expenditures to later budget periods (see e.g. Mältsemees 2009). Especially the later point is controversial on the political level.
o   Operator models:
    Here, not only the planning and realization are in the hands of private companies, but also operations and maintenance. The refinancing of the investments as well as the covering of running costs are usually carried out under concession contracts with the help of respective user fees (see e.g. Stender-Vorwachs 2004; Haßheider 2005; Aberle 2009). In that context, Koenig et al. (2004) talk about a correlation of concession models where the operator model is limited to cases where the revenues of the operator are not considered to be user fees. In exchange, a fixed operational fee over a defined period is being charged. The fundamental responsibility of the tasks in question remains with the State in that case. However, after the expiration of the defined useful life, the facilities that have been built based on the project become public property. For this reason, it is talked about as Build-Operate-Transfer (BOT) model. In some cases, the property right is transferred to a (private) contractor, so that this is called Build-Operate-Own (BOO) model. For both types, the risk is on the operator

side, but in many cases it can be reduced by possibilities of hedging with compensation payments and exit options.

o Public Private Partnership models:
PPP approaches that can be applied in different forms (see e.g. Budäus 2006; Daduna 2009; Alfen and Berckhahn 2012), are based on mixed financing of measures where private companies and public-law authorities cooperate (see e.g. Koenig et al. 2004; Ziekow 2006; Oppen and Sack 2008; Aberle 2009). The starting point is usually the formation of an (project) association. Here, the shares are preponderantly in the hands of private investors. Due to the participation of public-law authorities, state interference is guaranteed. Under certain circumstances this interference can be very extensive because of a blocking minority. This approach is to be understood in terms of a (functional) partial privatization (see e.g. Koenig et al. 2004, p. 357) of public services in connection with the transfer of tasks without time-related limitations. The objective is to refinance private investments through user fees, for example by a (project-related) charging. Different examples for PPP solutions in the field of transport infrastructure are explained for example by Kamella (2006) and Daduna (2009). For such approaches which can be conceptualized in different ways, a conjunction with case-specific operator models is appropriate (see above).

When considering the structure of the three depicted models, it becomes clear that with the pre-financing and the operator models, no cooperation in the proper sense is taking place. In these cases, it is more a principal / agent relation which is based on defined contractual relationships. The influence on the public-law side is limited to the *invitation to tender* (which is generally legally binding) and the *contracting* as well as the *monitoring* of the service provision. Within the scope of existing design possibilities, the current market situation can also impose restrictions, meaning that the invitation to tender has to be marketable so that a contractor can be found. In case of deficiencies in fulfilling the contract, it can be interfered and sanctions can be imposed as agreed in the contract.

PPP models in contrast (given the respective contractual design) offer significantly higher possibilities for the public-law side to be able to proactively participate. However, certain general conditions should be given so that such a solution can be realized successfully. For this reason, the following section is about some aspects of planning and designing PPP solutions as well as their advantages and disadvantages.

4. Feasibility Considerations

The involvement of public institutions in PPP solutions has to be generally seen as a political decision. However, this does not mean that the feasibility under economic aspects becomes less important. It is to be examined whether and to what extend the political objectives can be realized. The following aspects play an essential role here (see e.g. Daduna 2009):

- o Analysis of the *market structure*: First of all, it has to be found out if there are appropriate market segments available because if these are lacking PPP solutions cannot be implemented.
- o Definition of the *scope of service*: the necessary services have to be identified, where in many cases the assignment to the public or to the private sector is included.
- o Compilation of the *specification of services* (as a preliminary *requirement specification document*): Description of the required services which are *functional* and *result-oriented* (in terms of specific targets).
- o Deciding on the *risks-sharing*: Determination and evaluation of all possible *risks* and *allocation* between the contracting partners under the aspect of (partner-based) *risk minimization*.
- o Designing the *financial agreements*: Configuring the form of financing and assigning the services to be rendered.

The success of a PPP project is largely dependent on this preliminary work as the errors do not only have negative financial effects during that phase but also impair the acceptance of this form of participation, especially on the political level. In conjunction with the preliminary work *opportunities* and *risks* have to be taken into consideration as well. This has to be done from the point of view of the public-law institutions and private companies (see e.g. Krasemannn 2008; Rufera 2009).

- ■ *Opportunities* for public-law institutions:
  - o Access to private (risk) capital in financing the project.
  - o A more efficient (and accelerated) realization of the project and of the service provision as well as the use of externally generated economies of scale.
  - o Access to external know-how and participation in external innovation.
  - o Depoliticization of decision processes.
- ■ *Risks* for public-law institutions:

o Conflicting goals and management due to diverging interests of the cooperation partners.

o Disadvantages due to asymmetric information in favour of the private partners.

o Bankruptcy risk of the private companies.

o Loss of direct (political) intervention.

o Negative results are at the expense of the public side.

■ *Opportunities* for private companies:

o Access to new markets in connection with the possibility of risk spreading by diversification.

o Possibility to increase sales volume and profit.

o Improvement of cooperation with the public administration and an enhanced public image.

■ *Risks* for private companies:

o Conflicting goals and management due to diverging interests of the cooperation partners.

o Disadvantages due to asymmetric information in favour of the public-law institutions.

o Risk of financial loss and bankruptcy risk.

o Loss of image if the PPP project fails.

This brief comparison of opportunities and risks on the part of cooperation partners demonstrates that the decision-making processes are difficult for all parties involved as the risks are generally hard to estimate. Furthermore, no general statement can be made as too many case-specific influences are to be taken into consideration.

5. Application of Public Private Partnership Approaches in Traffic Infrastructure and Logistics Projects

Concession models in the form of BOT solutions are currently being applied in private financing in the field of *traffic network infrastructure*. These apply especially to the construction and development of highways (see et al. Beckers, 2005; Jacob and Schröter 2009; Sack 2011) as well as of special constructions for road traffic (see e.g. Kamella 2006). As the paper is about cooperation models (see above) this market segment will not be further discussed.

In conjunction with the financing of logistics facilities BOT models can be applied in principle. However, this does not always make sense, especially with respect to the design of the operational processes. Therefore, PPP solutions are suitable at this point as they also make the influence of public-law institutions on the operational processes possible. The so far successful implementation of a *partial privatization* at the Hamburg Airport is one example of a PPP approach. In that case the objective was (see e.g. Kamella 2006) to finance and to realize the extension of the existing airport infrastructure with new terminals and the construction of a link to the city train system (see Fig. 5.1). The underling structure of that financing model (and the resulting ownership structure of the operating companies) is shown in Fig. 5.2. In the area of (international) air traffic further examples for PPP solutions, which were developed for different reasons, can be found. This is about companies of the construction industry (as for example Hochtief AirPort (HTA) with participation in the airports of Athens, Budapest, Düsseldorf, Sydney and Tirana) or financial investors (as for example the *Macquarie Airport Group* (MAG) with participation in the airports of Brussels, Copenhagen und Sydney) (see e.g. Graham 2008).

Fig. 5.1:   *Examples of infrastructure extensions at the Hamburg Airport*

Similar solutions exist by now also in the *port industry* (see e.g. Vining and Boardman 2008), even though this is about logistics facilities, the establishment and operation of which are to be assigned to the public-law area of responsibility resulting from a traditional perception.

This basic structure of a PPP approach is also suitable for the realization of logistics facilities where planning, financing, construction and operation are conducted on a private sector level. In the foreground here are *logistics facilities* with warehousing and transshipment function (see e.g. Tsamboulas and Kapros 2003; Grundey and Rimienė 2007; Du and Bergqvist 2010; Higgins et al. 2012), especially those that are in connection with the design of *multi-modal transport processes*. Of special interest in this context are *supra-regional* and *regional freight villages* (see e.g. Boile et al. 2009; Schulte 2009; Kampf et al. 2011; Sack 2011) as well as UCC, UDC, and City-Terminals (see e.g. Di Bugno et al. 2007; Russo and Comi 2010).

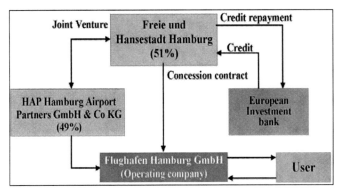

Fig. 5.2:   *Structure of the PPP model of the Hamburg Airport project*

One example of a freight village that was realized in Germany on the basis of a PPP concept is the *Güterverkehrszentrum* (GVZ) Bremen, which went into operation in 1984. The city of Bremen has been involved as co-partner with a blocking minority of the GVZ *Entwicklungsgesellschaft mbH* Bremen (GVZ-E). The GVZ-E was the project management organization (and owner of the infra-structure) because of which the city was part of all strategic decisions. Like this, the (political) objectives of the public-law side which affected areas such as structural, traffic, and economic development can be brought into decision pro-cesses. Due to the cooperative structure it is guaranteed that also the interests of industry and retail trade are sufficiently taken into consideration with the GVZ-E simultaneously. The operation is in the hands of an operating company which has been founded as a private company. The GVZ Bremen is now one of the most important facilities in Europe and an important node within the interna-tional logistics infrastructure. Figure 5.3 shows the facilities with the tri-modal linking to means of transport.

The application of PPP concepts for the construction of GVZ is today very common, not only in Germany but also in Austria, Denmark, France and Italy (see e.g. de Cerreño et al. 2008; Boile et al. 2009). It has been demonstrated that the positive results that have been achieved so far can be used as a starting point for more PPP solutions in that field.

Fig. 5.3:   Tri-modal freight village GVZ Bremen (Germany)

The second form of logistics facilities which are suitable for PPP concepts are examples in the area of city logistics (see e.g. Russo and Comi 2008; Benjelloun and Crainic 2009). It is primarily about a more efficient and ecological reasonable design of inner-city freight deliveries. In the foreground here are UCC and UDC as well as *City-Terminals*. Regardless of the question whether and to what extent a functional differentiation exists or whether it is about a semantic discussion, the same objectives have to be assumed. The task is to find solutions that make sense, that offer an acceptable compromise between the diverging interests of retail trade and the municipality and at the same time satisfy the expectations of the customers.

The basic structures of cooperation are not very different from the one that has been established in conjunction with the establishment and the operation of the freight villages. However, the impact of public-law institutions is significantly higher here as in addition to the location planning problems also the design of the traffic-related framework is a major factor that allows for more efficient processes. Moreover, the number of companies involved in retail trade could be quite high, which is due to the small-scale retail trade in inner-city centres. The objective is to avoid *traffic-related obstructions* that arise due to freight transport and to reduce the incurring emissions by bundling delivery trips. The problems here are less of a quantitative nature as the percentage of delivery traffic is relatively low; they are more about the impairment of traffic flow due to the stopping trucks within the delivery processes. Figure 5.4 gives an impression of this problem.

Fig. 5.4:   *Examples of obstructions of traffic because of inner-city delivery traffic*

These examples show clearly what the *traffic-related problems* that have to be taken into account in this context are. Appropriate *administrative measures* can be taken against such traffic violations involving the obstruction of third parties. This, however, does not necessarily lead to an efficient and sustainable solution in the long run.

The central point of classical city logistics concepts is the use of bundling effects to obtain economic but also ecological advantages. Due to insufficient cooperation between retail trade and logistics service providers on the one hand and the public-law institutions on the other hand deficits arise in the implementation. Even if the steps taken make sense from a *traffic-administrative point of view*, contra-productive developments may arise. As studies have shown, regulating measures of the road and traffic authorities do not lead to the desired impacts on the economic and ecological efficiency of delivery processes.

In the first place, this is about introducing *delivery time slots* as well as *size restrictions* (in terms of the permitted total weight) for the vehicles being used in delivery traffic (see e.g. Browne et al. 2008; Quak and de Koster 2009; Dablanc 2011; Gevaers et al. 2011; Quak 2011). That is why the time slots determine an increase in the number of trips required and hence also for the vehicles applied. The same effect results from size limitations so that based on appropriate framework conditions these various effects accumulate. In addition to higher cost, an increase in the environmental pollution can be observed (see e.g. van Rooijen et al. 2008; Quak and de Koster 2009). The effects are in contrast to the actual objectives which are connected to concepts of city logistics. It follows that only a closer cooperation of all parties involved can offer the necessary basis for an efficient and sustainable development, also in connection with PPP solutions (see e.g. Russo and Comi 2o11).

6. Potential Applications in the North-East European Area

The experiences arising so far from the use of PPP solutions, especially in the west- and southern European area, have proven that this form of financing traffic infrastructure as well as logistics facilities is a suitable approach. For this reason it makes sense to transfer the use of such financing models also in northeast European areas, as (see e.g. Lindholm and Behrends 2012) there is a need to undergo structural changes. Prioritized can be two fields of applications: development of *freight villages* and integration in designing *city logistics concepts.*

Concerning the development of freight villages the major objective is an efficient control of (domestic and international) flows of goods especially in connection with the seaport hinterland traffic (see e.g. Palšaitis and Bazaras 2004; Daduna 2011; Daduna and Prause 2011) through the Baltic ports. In this context it appears not only useful but indispensable to focus the planning processes on the economic region of the Baltic Sea area. When designing these concepts one should not only look at the mentioned area but also the linking with the neighbouring regions must be considered. The responsible public-law institutions are called in these cases because that kind of logistics facilities has to be connected to the traffic infrastructure in an appropriate manner. Doing this at least a *bimodal* or better a *tri-modal linkage* should be available. Regarding the structural differences in the respective areas hierarchically differentiated facilities (see above) may be considered.

The discussion about city logistics has regained attention after some years of relative negligence (see e.g. Vaghi / Percoco 2011). An important reason is the multiple efforts for revitalizing urban centres also to increase the attractiveness of those areas not only for the own inhabitants but also for customers from the surrounding regions. Furthermore, in many cases touristic concepts play a role, especially for cities with a *historical nucleus* as presented by Di Bugno et al. (2007) with the example of Lucca in Italy (see Fig. 6.1). Similar structures are in historical cities in the Baltic area, for example Narva, Tallinn (see Fig. 6.2) or Tartu.

Fig. 6.1:   *Arial view of the historic city centre of Lucca (Italy)*

Fig. 6.2:   *Arial view of the historic city centre of Tallinn (Estonia)*

Here it is essential to develop facilities (see above) designed for the individual situation, allowing a better *supply* (and *disposal*) of the shopping sites and a contribution to traffic reduction. Integrated traffic concepts for the *commercial traffic* and for *motorized individual traffic* (residential traffic, shopping traffic, etc.) are necessary. An additional task is the reorganization of *warehousing* in the urban retail trade by removing parts of the goods stocked at the shopping sites to central warehouses in suburbs or beyond the urban district.

Starting point for the realization of efficient and sustainable solutions must be cooperation of all actors involved, local authorities, local retail trade and local logistic service providers whereas the PPP model may be the appropriate solution. If a consequent realization is achieved, there are benefits for all parties involved not only in terms of economy but also ecologically.

7. Opportunities and Limitations

With a view to the role of logistics facilities, a number of (not always conflict-free) objectives which often result from the diverging interest of the parties involved have to be taken into consideration in constructing such facilities. Especially the commercial considerations of private companies are in contradiction with the specifications of public-law institutions with respect to the spatial planning-related design. Therefore, it has to be taken into account that the selection of location of such facilities cannot and should not only be identified under *economic aspects*, also *spatial* and *structural policy* aspects have to be included. To be able to enforce these requirements, the insertion of public influence has to primarily take place in conjunction with the decision of a location, also in view of the case-specific required traffic infrastructure. A possible (and politically useful) approach is to bring the required area into (PPP-oriented) cooperation. Here it is also beneficial to keep the direct financial burden of the public budgets in such a contribution kind of relatively low.

Looking at the structural design of the PPP approach, two (formally and legally) different basic models can be distinguished. An important aspect is the question of who holds the responsibility for the operational implementation of the operational processes of the service provision:

- Founding an independent company (as a joint venture with public-law participation) which is responsible for the planning, construction and maintenance of the *infrastructure* (as the owner) as well as for the *operational processes*.
- Founding an *infrastructure company* (as a joint venture with public participation) which is (solely) responsible for the financing as well as for the construction and maintenance. The operational processes are carried out by an (independent) operating company which gets a timely limited contract within the scopes of an invitation to tender.

Under certain circumstances the first variant could be problematic due to competition regulations if the newly founded company holds a monopoly in a defined market area. This problem does not occur with the second model as the responsibility for the infrastructure and the operational processes are formally and legally separated and the operator is selected during the bidding process.

The establishment of logistics facilities on the basis of PPP models has to be considered as a useful solution for the development and design of supra-regional as well as regional and local logistics infrastructure. This holds especially true for freight villages (see e.g. Boile et al. 2009) as well as for UCC, UDC, and City-Terminals because these facilities relate to the main problem areas. However, it cannot be assumed that by applying PPP solutions, all projects always have a positive outcome. In practice, it is actually the case that not all projects can be realized with success (see e.g. Vining and Boardman 2008; Leruth 2009) like possible risks might be (under certain circumstances also systematically) underestimated to be able to push projects through on a political level. This leads to the problem that the risks are not sufficiently taken into consideration for the required economic feasibility studies and hence it comes to misjudgements. Critical in this case are the following aspects:

- Risks in the (technical) implementation (by exceeding the cost or by faulty construction) which can be, among other things, due to insufficient project management.
- Financial risk in case of changes on financial markets, for example (negative) changes of capital costs.
- Wrong estimation of demand (with negative effects for user-dependent re-financing).
- Risks due to changes of the political framework, for example if there is a change of (domestic) political power relationships and target structures or in case of disturbances in international (political and economic) cooperation.

In addition, the *complexities* of the *cooperation structures* should be mentioned as they often are *potential sources of conflict* that should not be underestimated. An important reason could be the diverging interests of the cooperation partners, especially those between public-law institutions, on the one hand, and private (market-oriented) companies, on the other hand. Such a situation in turn can lead to higher *transaction costs* which overcompensate the (financial) benefits that are actually expected in case of cooperation projects. To prevent conflict situations to happen it is mandatory to fix the contractual agreements in a sufficiently detailed manner, especially with respect to the approach to possible conflict situations.

8. Conclusions and Outlook

Also in the coming years a significantly increasing demand in freight transport is to be expected. Due to these anticipated developments it is absolutely mandatory to provide an efficient infrastructure *in time*, meaning that the necessary measures have to be taken now as their realization usually covers a longer period of time. The reasons for that are to be found especially in the very lengthy planning and approval processes and less in the technical implementation. Affected by this is not only the construction of *transport mode-related network infrastructure* but increasingly also the realization of *logistical facilities*. Those form an integral part for an efficient design and control of (domestic and international) flows of goods (see e.g. Kabashkin 2007) and are hence absolutely necessary.

To be able to secure the capability of traffic and logistics infrastructure, the participation of the public-law institutions (in that case governmental level) is an indispensable prerequisite. In the foreground here is supra-regional (and in many cases also trans-border) coordination in the design of structures, which usually cannot be ensured due to the diverging interests of the parties directly involved.

As the responsibilities in the field of network infrastructure are indisputably seen as a task of the state (in services of general interest), the field of logistics facilities is very much characterized by private structures. From a legal perspective, it does not make sense that public-law institutions get active as service providers on the logistics market, therefore other forms of insertion of influence have to be found.

As this paper has shown, the application of PPP models is a possible solution. Even though this is controversial on a political level, also in view of budget matters, necessary measures can be carried out with this form of cooperation between the public-law side and private companies. This applies especially to the combination of the superior traffic-related policy objectives with the structural and economic requirements so that the sustainability of logistical structures can be ensured. Nevertheless, PPP solutions are in no respect a financial panacea, even though it is always tried to give that impression. Therefore, each single advantage and disadvantage from the point of view of the parties involved has to be examined and evaluated to be able to take the necessary decisions on these grounds.

References

Aberle, G 2009. *Transportwirtschaft*. 5., überarb. u. erg. Aufl., Munich / Wien: Oldenbourg.

Alfen, H.W. and Barckhahn, S. 2012. PPP and infrastructure. In: Just, T. and Maennig, W. (Eds.). *Understanding German real estate markets*, Berlin/Heidelberg: Springer, pp. 387–403.

Alicke, K. 2002. Modelling and optimization of the intermodal terminal Mega Hub. *OR Spectrum*, Vol. 24, pp. 1–17.

Allen, J. and Browne, M. 2010. Sustainable strategies for city logistics. In: McKinnon, A., Cullinana, S., Browne, M. and Whiteing, A. (eds.): *Green logistics – Improving the environmental sustainability of logistics*, London et al.: KoganPage, pp. 282–305.

Allen, J., Browne, M. and Woodburn, A. 2010. Integrated transport policy in freight transport. In: Givoni, M. and Banister, D. (eds.). *Integrated transport – From policy to practice*, London / New York: Routledge, pp. 75–95.

Baird, A. J. 2007. The economics of Motorways of the Sea. *Maritime Policies & Management*, Vol. 34, pp. 287–310.

Ballis, A. and Mavrotas, G. 2007. Freight villages design using the multicriteria method PROMETHEE. Operational Research, Vol. 17, pp. 213–232.

Beckers, T. 2005. Die *Realisierung von Projekten nach dem PPP-Ansatz bei Bundesfernstraßen.* Diss., Fakultät Wirtschaft & Management der Technischen Universität Berlin.

Benjelloun, A. and Crainic, T.G. 2009. Trends, challenges, and perspectives in city logistics. *Buletinul AGIR*, Vol.14, No. 4, pp. 45–51.

Boile, M., Theofanis, S. and Strauss-Wieder, A. 2009. *Feasibility of freight villages in the NYMTC region (Task 3 – Description of how a typical freight village works)*. Study prepared for the New York Metropolitan Transport Council by the Center for Advanced Infrastructure and Transportation / Rutgers University New Jersey (http://www.nymtc.org/project/freight_planning/frtvillage/frtvillage_files/task_3_report_april_2009f2.pdf / 27 dec 2012).

Browne, M., Allen, J., Nemoto, T., Visser, J. and Wild, D. 2008. City access restrictions and the implication for good deliveries, In: Taniguchi, E. and Thompson, R.G. (eds.). *Recent advances in city logistics*, Amsterdam et al.: Elsevier, pp. 17–35.

Budäus, D. 2006. Public Private Partnership – Kooperationsbedarfe, Grundkategorien und Entwicklungsperspektiven, In: Budäus, D. (ed.). *Kooperationsformen zwischen Staat und Markt*, Baden-Baden: Nomos, pp. 11–28.

Dablanc, L. 2011. City distribution, a key element of urban economy – Guidelines for practitioners, In: Macharis, C. and Melo, S. (eds.). *City distribution and urban freight transport – Multiple perspectives*, Cheltenham / Northampton, MA: Edward Elgar, pp. 1–336.

Daduna, J.R. 2009. Public Private Partnerships – Zwischen Wunschdenken und Realität. In: Daduna, J.R., Haid, S., Walther, M. and Zeitzen, M. (eds.). *Puplic Private Partnership – Erfahrungen, Erfolge und Perspektiven*, St. Augustin / Berlin: Konrad-Adenauer-Stiftung e.V, pp. 13–84.

Daduna, J. R. 2011. Importance of hinterland transport networks for operational efficiency in seaport container terminals. In: Böse, J.W. (ed.). *Handbook of Terminal Planning*, New York et al.: Springer, pp. 381–397.

Daduna, J. R. 2012. Short sea shipping and river-sea shipping in the multi-modal transport of containers (to appear in: *International Journal of Industrial Engineering – Theory, Applications and Practice*).

Daduna, J.R. and Prause, G. 2011. Korridorbildung als Grundlage leistungsfähiger Transportketten im Ladungsverkehr, In: Ivanov, D., Kopfer, H., Haasis, H.-D., and Schönberger, J. (eds.). *Dynamics and sustainability in international logistics and supply chain management*, Göttingen: Cuvillier, pp. 28–40.

De Cerreño, A.L.C., Shin, H.-S., Strauss-Wieder, A. and Theofanis, S. 2008. *Feasibility of freight villages in the NYMTC region (Task 1 – Inventory of planning resources)*. Study prepared for the New York Metropolitan Transport Council by the Center for Advanced Infrastructure and Transportation / Rutgers University New Jersey

(http://www.nymtc.org/project/freight_planning/frtvillage/FrtVillage_files/Task%201%2
0Report%209-11-08FINAL.pdf / 22 may 2012).

de Ceuster, G., Voge, T., Chen, M., de Kievit, M., Laird, J., Koh, A., Sessa, C., Enei, R. and
Mascellaro, R. 2010. *Trans-European transport network planning methodology – Final
report*. Report for European Commission DG MOVE; TREN/R1/350-2008 lot2.

Di Bugno, M., Guerra, S., Ambrosino, G., Boero, M. and Liberato, A. 2007. A centre for eco-
friendly city freight distribution – Urban logistics innovation in a mid-sized historical
city in Italy
(http://srvweb01.softeco.it/LIFECEDM/_Rainbow/Documents/City%20Logistics%20200
7%20-%20Crete%20-%20CEDM%20Paper.pdf / 12 may 2012).

Dionelis, C. and Giaoutzi, M. 2008. The enlargement of the European Union and the emerging new TEN transport patterns. In: Giaoutzi, M. and Nijkamp, P. (eds.): *Network strategies in Europe – Developing the future for transport and ICT*, Aldershot / Burlington:
Ashgate, pp. 119–132.

Du, J. and Bergqqvist, R. 2010. Developing a conceptual framework of international logistics
centres. Paper presented at the 12th World Conference on Transport Research (WCTR),
July 11-15, Lisbon Portugal.
(http://intranet.imet.gr/Portals/0/UsefulDocuments/documents/03065.pdf / 10 May 2012).

Gather, M., Kagermeier, A. and Lanzendorf, M. 2008. *Geographische Mobilitäts- und Ver-
kehrsforschung*. Berlin / Stuttgart: Bornträger.

Gevaers, R., van der Voorde, E. and Vanelslander, T. 2011. Characteristics and typology of
last-mile logistics from an innovation perspective in urban context. In: Macharis, C. and
Melo, S. (eds.). *City distribution and urban freight transport - Multiple perspectives*,
Cheltenham / Northampton, MA: Edward Elgar, pp. 56–71.

Gouvernal, E., Lavaud-Letilleul, V. and Slack, B. 2011. Transport and logistics hubs – Sepa-
rating fact from fiction. In: Hall, P., McCalla, R. J., Comtois, C. and Slack, B. (eds.). *Integrating seaports and trade corridors*, Farnham / Burlington: Ashgate. pp. 65–79.

Graham, A. 2008. *Managing airports – An international perspective*. 3rd ed., Amsterdam et
al.: Butterworth-Heinemann / Elsevier.

Grundey, D. and Rimiené, K. 2007. Logistic centre concept through evolution and definition.
Engineering Economics, Vol. 54, No. 4, pp. 87–95.

Haßheider, H. 2005. *Die Bereitstellung überregionaler Straßeninfrastruktur*. Göttingen:
Vandenhoeck & Rupprecht.

HB-Verkehrsconsult GmbH and VTT Technical Research Center of Finland 2005. *Pan-
European transport corridors and areas status report*. Project N° TREN/B2/26/2004 European Commission DG Energy & Transport (Final Report).

Higgins, C.D. / Ferguson, M. / Kanaroglou, P.S. (2012). Varieties of logistics centres – Developing a standardized typology and hierarchy. 91st *Annual Meeting of the Transportation Research Board*, January 22–26, 2012, Washington D.C. (http://www.docs.trb.
org/prp/12-3874.pdf / 03 may 2012).

Jacob, D. and Schröter, N. 2009. Bedeutung von PPP für ein modernes Infrastrukturmanage-
ment im öffentlichen Sektor. In: Pechlaner, H., von Holzschuer, W. and Bachinger, M.
(Hrsg.), *Unternehmertum und Public Private Partnership*, Wiesbaden: Gabler, pp.
109–136.

Jaržemskis, A. 2007. Research on public logistics centre as a tool for cooperation. *Transport*, Vol. 23, No. 3, pp. 202–207.

Kabashkin, I., 2007. Logistics centres development in Latvia. *Transport*, Vol. 22, No. 4, pp. 242–246.

Kamella, H. 2006. *Erfolgsfaktoren und Bewertungsmöglichkeiten von PPP-Projekten für Verkehrsinfrastruktur.* (Gutachten im Auftrag des Deutschen Verkehrsforums) Berlin.

Kampf, R., Průša, P. and Savage, C. 2011. Systematic location of the public logistics centres in Czech Republic. in: *Transport* 26, pp. 425–432.

Kaup, M. 2008. Functional model of river-sea ships operating in European system of transport corridors – Part II. *Polish Maritime Research*, Vol. 15, No. 4, pp. 3–11.

Koenig, C., Kühling, J. and Theobald, C. 2004. *Recht der Infrastrukturförderung.* Heidelberg: Recht und Wirtschaft.

Krasemann, D. 2008. *Public Private Partnership – Rechtliche Determinanten der Auswahl und Konkretisierung von Projekten als Public Private Partnership.* Hamburg: Kovač.

Launhardt, W. 1885. *Mathematische Begründung der Volkswirtschaftslehre.* Neudruck der Ausgabe Leipzig (Scientia) Aalen 1968.

Leruth, L.E. 2009. Public-private cooperation in infrastructure development – A principal-agent story of contingent liabilities, fiscal risks, and other (un)pleasant surprises. *Network and Spatial Economics* (Online first: DOI 101007/s11067-009-9112-0).

Limbourg, S. and Jourquin, B. 2009. Optimal rail-road container terminal locations on the European network. *Transportation Research* (Part E), Vol. 45, pp. 551–563.

Lindholm, M. and Behrends, S. 2012. Challenges in urban freight transport planning – A review in the Baltic Sea region. *Journal of Transport Geography*, Vol. 22, pp. 129–136.

Mältsemees, S. 2009. Die Bedeutung von PPP für die regionale wirtschaftliche Entwicklung in Estland. In: Pechlaner, H., von Holzschuer, W. and Bachinger, M. (eds.), *Unternehmertum und Public Private Partnership*, Wiesbaden: Gabler, pp. 246–268.

Nathanail, E. 2007. Developing an integrated logistics terminal network in the CADES. *Transition Studies Review*, Vol. 14, pp. 125–146.

Ng, A.K.Y. 2009. Competitiveness of short sea shipping and the role of port – The case of North Europe. *Maritime Policies & Management*, Vol. 36, pp. 337–352.

Nobel, T. 2004. *Entwicklung der Güterverkehrszentren in Deutschland.* Diss., Institut für Seeverkehrswirtschaft und Logistik (ISL) Bremen.

Notteboom, T. E. 2007. Inland waterway transport of containerised cargo – From infancy to a fully-fledged transport mode. *Journal of Maritime Research*, Vol. 4 (2), pp. 63–80.

Notteboom, T. 2008. Bundling of freight flows and hinterland network developments. In: Konings, R., Priemus, H. and Nijkamp, P. (eds.): *The future of intermodal freight transport – Operations, design and policy*, Cheltenham / Northhampton, MA: Elgar, pp. 66–88.

Oppen, M. and Sack, D. 2008. Governance und Performanz – Motive, Formen und Effekte lokaler Public Privat Partnerships. In: Schuppert, G.F. and Zürn, M. (eds.): *Governance in einer sich wandelnden Welt*, Wiesbaden: VS Verlag für Sozialwissenschaften, pp. 259–281.

Paixão Casaca, A.C. and Marlow, P.B. 2009. Logistics strategies for short sea shipping operating as part of multimodal transport chains. *Maritime Policy & Management*, Vol. 36, pp. 1–19.

Palšaitis, R. and Bazaras, D. 2004. Analysis of the prospectives of international transport and logistics centres in Lithuania. *Transport*, Vol. 19, No. 3, pp. 119–123.

Panayides, P. M. and Song, D.-W. 2008. Evaluating the integration of seaport container terminals in supply chains. *International Journal of Physical Distribution and Logistics Management*, Vol. 38, pp. 562–584.

Quak, H.J 2011. Urban freight transport – The challenge of sustainability, In: Macharis, C. and Melo, S. (eds.). *City distribution and urban freight transport – Multiple perspectives*, Cheltenham / Northampton, MA: Edward Elgar, pp. 37–55.

Quak, H.J and de Koster, M.B.M. 2009. Delivering goods in urban areas – How to deal with urban policy restrictions and the environment. *Transportation Science* Vol. 43, pp. 211–227.

Radmilović, Z., Zobenica, R. and Maraš, V. 2011. River-sea shipping – Competitiveness of various transport technologies. *Journal of Transport Geography*, Vol. 11, pp. 1509–1516.

Rall, B. 2008. Güterverkehrszentren. In: Arnold, D., Isermann, H., Kuhn, A., Tempelmeier, H. and Furmans, K. (eds.): *Handbuch Logistik*. 3., neu bearb. Aufl., Berlin et al.: Springer, pp. 778–781.

Rammler, S. 2003. Güter, Gleise und Gewinne – Soziologische Anmerkungen zur Wachstumslogik des modernen Güterverkehrs. In: Verein Deutscher Ingenieure (VDI) (ed.): *Gesamtverkehrsforum 2003*, Düsseldorf: VDI, pp. 21–36.

Rösch, A. 2007. *Das A-Modell im Bundesautobahnbau*. Frankfurt a. M. et al.: Lang.

Rodrigue, J.-P. 2008. The Thruport concept and transmodal rail freight distribution in North America. *Journal of Transport Geography*, Vol. 16, pp. 233–246.

Rodrigue, J.-P. and Notteboom, T. 2009. The terminalization of supply chains – Reassessing the role of terminals in port / hinterland logistical relationships. *Maritime Policy & Management*, Vol. 36, pp. 165–183.

Rodrigue, J.-P., Debrie, J., Fremont, A. and Gouvernal, E. 2010. Functions and actors of inland ports – European and North American dynamics. *Journal of Transport Geography*, Vol. 18, pp. 519–529.

Rodrigue, J.-P. and Notteboom, T. 2010. Comparative North American and European gateway logistics – The regionalism of freight distribution. *Journal of Transport Geography*, Vol. 18, pp. 497–507.

Rohács, J. and Simongáti, G. 2007. The role of inland waterway navigation in a sustainable transport system. *Transport*, Vol. 22, pp. 148–153.

Roso, V., Woxenius, J. and Lumsden, K. 2009. The dry port concept – Connecting container seaports with the hinterland. *Journal of Transport Geography*, Vol. 17, pp. 338–345.

Rufera, S. 2009. Chancen und Risiken von öffentlich-privaten Partnerschaften (Public Private partnerships) aus Sicht der öffentlichen Hand, In: Pechlaner, H., von Holzschuer, W. and Bachinger, M. (eds.), *Unternehmertum und Public Private Partnership*, Wiesbaden: Gabler, pp. 81–108.

Russo, F. and Comi, A. 2010. A classification of city logistics measures and impacts. *Procedia Social and Behavioral Science*, Vol. 2, pp. 6355–6365.

Sack, D. 2011. Governance failures in integrated transport policy – On the mismatch of 'competition' in multi-level systems. *German Policy Studies*, Vol. 7, No. 2, pp. 43–70.

Schulte, C. 2009. *Logistik – Wege zur Optimierung der Supply Chain*. 5, überarb. u. erw. Aufl., München: Vahlen.

Stender-Vorwachs, J. 2005. *Staatliche Verantwortung für gemeinverträglichen Verkehr auf Straße und Schiene nach deutschem und europäischem Recht*. Baden-Baden: Nomos.

Styhre, L. 2009. Strategies for capacity utilization in short sea shipping. *Maritime Economics & Logistics*, Vol. 11, pp. 418–437.

Stratigea, A., Giaoutzi, M. and Koutsopoulos, C. 2008. European policy aspects of network integration in the TEN transport. In: Giaoutzi, M. and Nijkamp, P. (eds.): *Network strategies in Europe - Developing the future for transport and ICT*, Aldershot / Burlington: Ashgate, pp. 169 – 187.

Taniguchi, E., Noritake, M., Yamada, T. and Izumitani, T. 1999. Optimal size and location planning of public logistics terminals. *Transportation Research* (Part E), Vol. 35, pp. 207–222.

Tsamboulas, D.A. and Kapros, S. 2003. Freight village evaluation under uncertainty with public and private financing. in: *Transport Policy* 10, pp. 141–156.

Vaghi, C. and Percoco, M. 2011. City logistics in Italy – Success factors and environmental performance. In: Macharis, C. and Melo, S. (eds.): *City distribution and urban freight transport – Multiple Perspectives*, Cheltenham / Northampton, MA: Edward Elgar, pp. 151–175.

van Duin, J. H. R., Quack, H. and Muñuzuri, J. 2010. New challenges for urban consolidation centers – A case study in the Hague. *Procedia Social and Behavioral Sciences*, Vol. 2, pp. 6177–6188.

van Rooijen, T., Groothedde, B. and Gerdessen, J.C. 2008. Quantifying the effects of community level regulation on city logistics, In: Taniguchi, E. and Thompson, R.G. (eds.). *Recent advances in city logistics*, Amsterdam et al.: Elsevier, pp. 351–399.

Vining, A.R. / Boardman, A.E. 2008. The potential role of public-private partnerships in the upgrade for port infrastructure – Normative and positive considerations. *Maritime Policy & Mangement*, Vol. 35, pp. 551–569.

Vinokurov, E., Dzhaddraliyev, M. and Shcherbanin, Y. 2009. *The EurAsEC transport corridors*. MPRA-Paper No. 20908: (http://mpra.ub-uni-muenchen.de/20908 / 20 Apr 2012).

Wermuth, M., Wirth, R. 2005. Modelle und Strategien des Güterverkehrs. In: Steierwald, G., Künne, H. D. and Vogt, W. (eds.). *Stadtverkehrsplanung – Grundlagen, Methoden, Ziele*, 2, neu bearb. u. erw. Aufl., Berlin et al.: Springer, pp. 296–326.

Woxenius, J. 2007. Alternative transport network designs and their implications for intermodal transhipment technologies. *European Transport*, Vol. 35, pp. 27–45.

Yang, Z., Liu, C. and Song, X. 2005. Optimizing the scale and spatial location of city logistics terminals. *Journal of the Eastern Asia Society for Transportation Studies*, Vol. 6, pp. 2937–2946.

Ziekow, J. 2006. Public Privat Partnership als zukünftige Form der Finanzierung und Erfüllung öffentlicher Aufgaben. In: Hill, H. (ed.): Die Zukunft des öffentlichen Sektors, Baden-Baden: Nomos, pp. 49-60.

Air Cargo Outlooks of Regional Airports in the Baltic Sea Region: the Cases of Tallinn and Katowice

Tarvo Niine[1], Gunnar Prause[1], Ene Kolbre[1] and Bartosz Dziugiel[2]

Abstract

The air cargo market is forecasted to recover from the recent global downturn. However, the air cargo market is dynamic and the average growth rate does not guarantee success for every region, let alone every airport. Furthermore, the Eurozone crisis and underlying social and political issues are raising the question how much EU economy can sustain its relevance in the global economy.

This paper focuses on two airports in the Baltic Sea region: Tallinn and Katowice – with comparable volume, small catchment area and similar economic environment. In the framework of Interreg IV project Baltic.AirCargo.Net, stakeholders of selected airports were interviewed in 2011. The aim was to identify the local realities to find ways how to improve services for local customers as well as to benefit the airport itself and reach higher volumes, capacity utilization and profitability. The presented analysis of local strengths and development issues offers an input for optimal management decisions and help for defining future outlooks.

JEL classification codes: R40

Keywords: air cargo market outlooks, Baltic Sea Region, Tallinn airport, Katowice airport, belly cargo, RFS, airport strategies, air transport environment.

1. Introduction

Air cargo has always been a special business – offering the fastest delivery times over medium and long distances, but especially across continents. To utilize the speed factor to the maximum extent, airline networks are continuously expanding, making air industry more flexible compared to maritime transport, although not nearly as agile as road transport on reacting to demand changes. Alongside economic growth, the main demand drivers in the world are globalization, liberalization and lean inventory strategies (Senguttuvan 2006). Air cargo market is mostly driven by expansion of outsourcing and offshoring (Kleindorfer and Visvikis 2007). Rapid integration of world markets and demand for customized products has pushed air cargo to dominance in the 21st century market place

1 Tallinn School of Economics and Business Administration, *Akadeemia tee 3, 12618 Tallinn, Estonia*

2 Institute of Aviation, *Al. Krakowska 110/114, 02-256 Warsaw, Poland*

(Kasarda and Green 2004). According to Senguttuvan, air cargo business has three imperative roles in the global economic scenario, namely: 1) global sourcing – the speed and consistency helps manufacturers to lower inventories and optimize supplier base; 2) launching new products – global demand, instant information transfer and shorter product life cycles make air cargo favourable for global product launches; 3) satisfying customers' expectations – increasing demand for time-sensitive products has made manufacturers view the speed of air cargo much more as a selling point rather than cost (Senguttuvan 2006).

Approximately half of the world air cargo is carried by passenger airlines, known as „belly cargo", whereas the other half is freighter traffic, either scheduled or chartered, and integrator services. For intercontinental passenger lines, cargo transport can account for up to 40–50% of revenue (Hellerman 2006). The belly cargo concept, although great for space utilization and profit, means that part of the air cargo supply is driven by another market. The air cargo market is often clustered into service segments. For example, integrated parcel services are usually treated as a special segment both due to their pricing and guarantees provided by international network (Hertwig and Rau 2010). However, in some situations the borders are not clear. In conventional belly cargo, the service has almost never had a brand for the customer to be loyal to nor to recommend – the calculations all come down to speed and cost ratio. Also, the competition between modes, especially over short-to-medium distances, is increasingly tough, assuring that while the clients and forwarders are presented with more options than ever before, the market for air cargo service providers is demanding and cruel and transport services have become more substitutable (Heusener and Von Wichert 2002). An additional problem in that regard is the environmental aspect working against air cargo both in customers' as well as policy makers' heads (Schaecher 2011).

The air cargo sector volumes largely depend upon international trade situation, which often highly correlates with GDP. From the data of latest decade, global exports (by volume and value) have outpaced production volumes, which in turn have outpaced economic growth; still, air cargo growth trumps all (Kasarda et al. 2006). It has been often observed how air transport sector is the first to react to the changes in economic climate. This is a useful tool for predicting short-term economy changes.

Traditionally, most renowned market forecasts for air cargo come from leading aircraft manufacturers Boeing and Airbus. In 2009, world industrial production fell 9%, world GDP fell 2.1% and air freight volumes dropped 11.3% globally. Still, air cargo was one of the quickest sectors to recover. In the long run, Boeing is forecasting steady growth in world economy by 3.2% per year up until 2029 (Boeing 2010). Boeing expects world cargo volumes to increase roughly twice as fast – on average 6.0% yearly, compared to estimated 4% increase in world industrial production. For nearly four decades, air cargo traffic has expanded more than twice the rate of GDP growth. Boeing has suggested air cargo won back some clients from maritime shipping (Ibid.). However, this is in contrast with data between 2000 and 2008 when air cargo share in total freight transport fell from 2.8% to 2%, which was partially attributed to mode shift from air to sea (Morrell 2011, p. 23). A more modest forecast has been put forward by Airbus experts, expecting the average long-term world air cargo market growth of 5.1% (Airbus 2011). The current short-term outlook is positive. In a survey in April 2012 with international cargo business leaders, 43% were expecting improvement over the year. The IATA airline business confidence index reflects the same (Aircargonews.net 2012).

The future of air cargo traffic in Europe should be viewed in three most important segments: Europe-Asia (9.2% of world tonnage), Europe-North-America (6.6%) and intra-Europe traffic (3.6%). Boeing expects Europe-North-America traffic to increase 4% per year, with better outlooks for European exports than the other way around (Boeing 2010). Intra-Europe traffic is special due to high share of express services in the volume. In the past 20 years, intra-Europe freighter traffic has continuously decreased to give way to road transport. The fastest growing segment in intra-EU market is road-feeder services (RFS), with scheduled frequency going up 19% per year in 2005–2010. For intra-Europe market in general, forecasted long-term growth is 3.6%, mostly due to new member states' demand (Ibid.).

In EU, the total cargo volume is about 13 million tonnes with the main airports situated in Central Europe. The top 4 EU air cargo airports – Frankfurt, London, Amsterdam and Paris – are responsible for about half of all handled air cargo inside the EU (EU Transport 2011). Leading airports near the Baltic Sea are Copenhagen (#16 in the 2009 Europe cargo volume list with approximately 1/10 of volume of Frankfurt) and Helsinki (#18) (Ibid.). The south side of Baltic Sea is far more behind with only Warsaw on the border of TOP50. The cargo volume in the Baltic Sea region accounts for less than 5% in the total European air cargo volume.

This paper analyses the cargo market situation in airports of Tallinn, Estonia and Katowice, Poland. The airports share many similarities. Tallinn airport is the main airport in Estonia, geographically located very close to Helsinki (about 100km across the Gulf of Finland). Tallinn served around 2 million passengers, 40,000 flight operations and 20,000 tonnes of cargo in 2011 (Tallinn airport 2011). Katowice is located in southern Poland, is the 3rd largest airport in Poland in passenger traffic, served 2.54 million passengers, around 29,000 flight operations and around 12,000 tonnes of cargo in 2011 (Katowice airport 2011).

Both airports are operating as spokes feeding to larger hubs. Both airports have faced significant growth over the last decade. Research project Baltic.AirCargo.net (BACN) set out in 2009 to understand the development perspectives of airports in the Baltic Sea region and suggest improvement strategies. The selected airports in the regions were studied through structured expert interviews. This paper draws upon the data collected from stakeholders of Tallinn and Katowice airports, including airport officials, airline representatives and sales agents, forwarders, larger cargo clients and public authorities. The aim of the paper is to analyse cargo outlooks in these airports and to assist in optimal management decisions at airports, with research questions directed to understanding the situation and comparing the views of stakeholder groups. The following section presents a literature review on notable trends on air cargo market. The third section presents the approach used by the authors in the expert interviews and the fourth section deals with the most relevant findings.

2. Air Cargo Trends, Development Issues and Outlook

Air cargo has in the past been mostly a secondary consideration for passenger airline operators. However, the increasing cargo volumes have also called out for the need to carefully managing cargo capacity and revenues (Kasilingam 1997). Today, belly cargo is often the difference between route profitability and loss (Schaecher 2011). If historically the air cargo pricing was based on marginal cost and no separate focus on cargo operations, the last decade has changed it considerably as a number of operators consider air cargo increasingly as a revenue enhancing product, often differentiated through innovative marketing (Dewulf et al. 2011). Otto has suggested that in most cases, air cargo accounts for between 5–25% of airlines revenues, with international Asian airlines having the leading share (Otto 2005).

Paul Hertwig and Philipp Rau have pointed out that competitive pressure in air cargo industry, also from other transport modes, and higher fuel cost demand efficiency improvements from air carriers resulting in trends towards larger aircrafts, where the demand allows. The flexibility lost with larger aircraft must be compensated with better capacity and network planning. According to authors, capacity utilization risk and price risk are the most important operational risks for the air cargo service providers. Focusing on improved capacity planning and booking allows mitigating both risks (Hertwig and Rau 2010). ICAO statistics shows that over the last decade, airfreight weight load factor has increased from 59% in 2001 to 66% in 2010 across all scheduled services (ICAO 2011).

Air cargo market is continuously influenced by various factors and constraints from economic aspects of fuel prices and supply and prices of competing modes to environmental regulations, force majeure (volcanic ash or Japanese earth quakes as recent examples), labour issues, curfews, security threats, policy constraints etc. For example, the European Union has, in its recent transport white paper, set long-term goals to 40% of use of sustainable low carbon fuels in aviation and at least 40% cut in shipping emissions by 2050 as well as making considerable efforts to shift 50% of medium distance intercity passenger and freight traffic from road to rail and waterborne transport – a shift which will certainly have a negative effect on medium distance aviation as well (White Paper on transport 2011).

Additional layer of dynamics for air cargo market is presented by regional and general changes in trade (price changes, policies, quotas, currency fluctuations etc). Furthermore, political instability is a constant threat to air cargo lifeline – oil production (Schaecher 2011). As a result of various factors, air cargo yield decreased by one percent in the 2000s (Boeing 2010), which has increased competitive pressure as well as supply and induced overcapacity problems. One of the results of such competition is that service providers have actively been searching for ways how to differentiate themselves from the competition and one of the profitable ways has been to introduce own premium express services (Heusener and Von Wichert 2002).

One relevant development issue in air cargo business today is moving towards paperless supply chains. IATA eFreight concept denotes the vision of paperless freight transport processes where an electronic flow of information is linked to the physical flow of goods. The main reason for such innovation is the cost of paperwork in global supply chains (IATA 2012). Another advantage of eFreight would be to save time, improve data accuracy and avoid exception management by entering data once and accurately (Schaecher 2011). By the end of 2011, e-Freight was live in 430 airports (around 80% of total tonnage). A crucial aspect of eFreight is regulatory compliance – the solution has to meet all authority control requirements for provision of documents and data. IATA vision includes close to 100% market coverage for eFreight already in 2015 (IATA 2012).

In the new speed-driven, globally networked economy, individual companies are no longer the effective competing units. Rather, competitive advantage resides in networks of globally dispersed firms whose integrated supply chains often use air cargo (Kasarda and Green 2004). Another trend that the air industry is facing is heading towards more concentrated market structure. In 2008, eight largest air cargo carriers accounted for 37% of world air cargo traffic (Hertwig and Rau 2010). It can be said that this allows for better network optimization and less fluctuations and overreacting in trying tobalance demand with aircraft and route supply. The air cargo market dynamics has been described as a sum of turbulence and consolidation (Delfmann et al. 2005). Consolidation is also the main trend that Doganis predicts in the book "The Airline Business", pointing out the takeovers of KLM by Air France and Swiss by Lufthansa as examples (Doganis 2006). Doganis explains it as two parallel developments: growing consolidation into larger companies and growing consolidation into larger alliances (Ibid.).

Doganis has presented a holistic overview of the future shape of the airline industry as a result of consolidation and progressively relaxed regulatory controls. The market is expected to consist of three distinct types of airlines. First, each of the major world regions will see the emergence of a smaller number of long-haul network dominators – large airlines with 2–3 mega-hubs, linked to similar network dominators across globe to offer efficient global service. Their focus will be on long-haul and they will pull out of shorter-haul market due to increasing competition from the low-cost segment, although on dense routes and more business oriented routes the competition will remain. The low-cost passenger segment (no cargo involved) is expected to consolidate similarly to a few companies per region and some current low-cost operators will either collapse or be merged, but the segment will still be the fastest growing one with 15–20%. Low fares will push incumbent network airlines to abandon many of their traditional routes and low cost model will occupy most of regional short-haul. The third sector is niche carriers. On passenger side, there will be some national carriers that are able to survive (many will not), will be operating on point-to-point short-to-medium distance segment, with some cargo, but that will not be as important as to network dominators due to distance factor. Other airlines are likely to be parts of regional alliances (Doganis 2006, pp. 287–291).

Chiavi has pointed out that airfreight forwarding is a key driver in globalization and that through the second half of the 20th century, airfreight business has evolved from a niche product to a global service integrated into 3PL providers' one-stop shop business model. Looking into future, Chiavi foresees increased capital investment in the developing regions with lower labour cost, but is much less optimistic about the EU airfreight future and hints the 15 old European countries seem to be the losers mostly due to higher labour rates and less flexible cost structures (Chiavi 2005).

Senguttuvan has noted that a bottleneck from the client point of view is speed – not only down to flight frequencies and fast handling, but also customs operations. It has been observed that in customs clearance times, the economies of Asian region are similar to other developing economies but taken together developing countries customs are significantly slower than customs in developed countries. The typical European and North-American airport has customs cleared in a day, whereas from a sample of Asian airports, customs took on average 3.7 days (Ibid.). Kasarda and Green are on a similar position by pointing out that three critical policy levers can be applied to enhance the air cargo situation: air service liberalization (based on the nine freedoms of air), improving customs quality and reducing corruption. The authors suggest that passenger travel liberalization is much ahead of cargo services as most of the bilateral agreements on air transportignore modern supply chain practices such as door-to-door delivery and even the majority of "Open skies" agreements do not allow the 7th freedom, domestic cabotage from international carriers.

Concerning customs, it has been estimated that up to 20% of transit time and 25% of transit costs are spent in/on customs clearance (OECD 2002). In a 2003 survey by the International Logistics Quality Institute, 48% of 800 shippers said they are extremely concerned with customs practices (The International Logistics Quality Institute 2003). To quantify their assumptions, Kasarda and Green took estimates for customs performance, perceived corruption level and air market liberalization from 63 countries and analysed correlation with freight volumes and GDP. The data show that the extent of liberalization correlates strongly to GDP per capita and that quality of customs and low corruption level contribute to greater economic development statistically significantly and that the positive effects of liberalization remain significant even after accounting for other two factors. The authors conclude that air liberalization, based on its facilitating effects on country connectivity and resulting passenger and cargo flows play a causal role in fostering trade and development (Kasarda and Green 2004).

Delfmann et al. have brought attention to the observation that whereas airlines have encountered the importance of strategic decision-making for a long time, this is only slowly beginning to transcend to airports and their organizations (Delfmann et al. 2005). Whereas airlines have basically all the major parameters of competition at their disposal (product features, price differentiation, customer segmentation, advertising etc), with regulations being applied only occasionally, airports and airport operators are still in some cases seen as local monopolies and are limited in their actions, hinting that one of the development bottlenecks is the lack of strategic planning at many airports.

There is potentially a notable effect from air cargo development to the local economy. One of the main reasons for it is that air freight and integrated services are critical to time-based competition, which is the frontier challenge in many industries, and that air freight is connecting supplier and consumer markets across the world allowing supply chains to reap benefits of local cost optimization (Ibid.). There have been many metropolitan areas developing massively through air cargo. For example, in Dubai the free trade zone is cashing in the benefits of the location between Europe and Asia and along strong passenger hub has also established a notable air cargo volume (Senguttuvan 2006). Alongside liberalization and other political measures to induce air cargo supply, airfreight facilities are also playing an important role in attracting fast-growing high value-added industries. Airport effect on the economy has been described with a model of four impact channels:

• Airports generate economic activity as an investment factor.
• Airports function as an economic factor, which is the result of the services in the airport (airport operators, airlines and secondary services such as shops).
• Eventually airports unfold economic effects as a location factor (catalytic effects). This is reflected in productivity gains, market expansions, cost re-ductions and also fostering of structural change and settling of companies, all leading to employment and synergy.
• This welfare growth is counteracted by losses through damages caused by air traffic (noise, air pollution and effects on public health and climate change risk), which also have to be considered in an airport economic assessment.

Based on this, Baum suggests that the location factor has been neglected in the literature compared to direct benefits and negative externalities and that only a part of this effect can be quantified through statistics (Baum 2005).

Additionally, Senguttuvan has suggested a five-pillar model to evaluate the competitive situation of an airport system in the region:

1. Spatial factors – the regional development around the airport, trade zones, logistics centres, aviation related industrial complexes and other facilities, their capacity and utilization – all enabling growth of an airport.
2. Facility factors – the level of airport facilities and expandability of facilities to augment the handling capacity.
3. Demand factors – the level of origin-destination demand of traffic volumes for hub-spoke network development.
4. Service factor – types of services offered, the level of these services and air-port charges.
5. Managerial factor – economic considerations such as airport operating costs, productivity and revenue structure (Senguttuvan 2006).

It is not perfectly clear where political, environmental and social issues af-fecting airport operations as well as demand for air cargo, such as negative ex-ternalities and administrative regulations, but also liberalization and corruption rate, would fit in this model. Based on their relative importance these factors would perhaps be best to present as a separate pillar or pillars instead.

3. Methodology

The aim of this research is to identify relevant issues at air cargo market and development perspectives of Tallinn and Katowice airports. As shown in the literature review, the air cargo market is rather dynamic with various on-going trends and a number of potential bottlenecks blocking the progress. The scope of the matter hence calls for a qualitative approach rather than quantitative. There are also a few specific issues with quantitative approach in the case of studying local airports, which ought to be mentioned here. First, the strong correlation between expected economic growth and air cargo volumes is not working well in small scale, such as Tallinn and Katowice airports. For example, between 2006 and 2008, the volumes through Tallinn essentially doubled yearly (10,361 t in 2006, 22,764 t in 2007 and 41,867 t in 2008), whereas in 2008 the Estonian economy was already in decline. In the case of Tallinn it was not export, transit cargo is the real volume generator accounting for over 75% of the volumes. Most of this transit comes from a small number of clients and they are routed through Tallinn due to almost a single factor – a suitable site in EU close to Russian market. So the volumes rely on business success of few clients, which cannot be predicted with conventional means. For Estonian air cargo exports though the volumes correlate with GDP. However, a small and open economy such as Estonia is rather vulnerable to outside effects making it more difficult to predict. Furthermore, structural changes in the economy are often called out, which for our purposes increases planning uncertainty.

The wide-angle qualitative approach is also the most suitable for Katowice. One of the reasons is the early stage of market development around the airport, which limits exploiting full potential demand for air cargo services. This inability is, among other issues, a result of inhibitory effect of certain legal regulations and not optimal accessibility to the airport. Additionally, local airport investments are partially financed from the European Structural Funds focused on improvement of the European Transport network coherency, which means the growth is not that strongly related with economic growth. Therefore, although economic indices such as GDP correlate with air freight volume handled on the territory of Poland very well, this does not guarantee satisfactory accuracy in studying the case of only Katowice Airport.

In the case of small airports, the geographical context is crucial to understand the alternatives. A shared characteristic of the two airports is the proximity to other airports. Tallinn airport is situated only 100km from Helsinki airport across the Gulf of Finland. In Tallinn's case, this means that a notable share of air cargo leaves Estonia not on an airplane but rather on RFS to Helsinki (or also in many intercontinental cases to mega-hubs such as Frankfurt or Amsterdam). There is also an option to carry cargo to air hubs by conventional road transport bypassing home airport entirely, which does not appear under any statistics as air cargo and therefore would distort quantitative market overview. Another nearby airport is located only 300 km from Tallinn – Riga, which is number one in passenger traffic in the Baltics with 5.1 ml passengers in 2011 (Riga airport 2012).

Katowice Airport location factor is characterised by vicinity to the largest regional airport in Poland, Cracow Airport, with the straight-line distance less than 70 km between the two. This has resulted in market division. Based on re-cent observations it can be said that Katowice Airport, due to a lack of opera-tional constraints and distance to populated areas, is becoming an attractive gate to the region for air cargo operators. Also, from regional point of view, less competitive conditions for passenger transport allow to offer better conditions to charter line operators and some low cost carriers (LCC), whereas traditional air-lines and most of the LCCs prefer to operate through Cracow Airport, which is serving more populated areas. The two airports are in tough competition for car-go – pure cargo in Katowice Airport and belly cargo in Cracow. Furthermore, another important competitor for Katowice Airport is Frankfurt – good road connections allow the 700km trucking to be an attractive solution for cargo compared to relatively weaker offer of the regional airport.

To identify the regional air cargo situation in general, structured expert in-terviews were arranged with a number of different stakeholders from airport to forwarders and from airlines to public authorities. In Tallinn, 12 interviews with 12 air cargo sector representatives in 10 organisations took place in winter 2011/12 with around 19h of recorded data. In Poland, the cargo situation analy-sis included 10 interviews held with representative of Katowice Airport man-agement, air-cargo service providers and representatives of regulatory and R&D institutions.

The expert interviews were structured and based on a wide array of potential issues, bottlenecks and viewpoints. The starting point was the model of five general aspects of airport development as referenced above (Senguttuvan 2006), with modified and added aspects from other regionally relevant areas. By large, the logic of these five aspects could be divided simply as demand and supply side with the specific topics adding viewpoints to both. The following are the factors included as "areas of interest" in the conducted expert interviews.

- Demand – the characteristics of clients, needs, cargo types, industries, etc.
  - Customer's priorities (speed, cost, reliability etc.)

- o Geographical attractiveness – property market, logistics infrastructure, regional business environment development
- o Competition to air cargo from other transport modes
- o Potential contacts with international clients, with emphasis on Asia and Russia, business relations and institutional setup
- o Positive externalities
- Supply – available service options, quality and cost of alternatives etc.
  - o Strengths and weaknesses of local air cargo, future trends
  - o Quality and capacity of facilities, expandability
  - o Willingness to cooperate and topics for joint development
  - o Competition on the local air cargo market, service economy
  - o Comparison to adjacent regions/airports and their services
  - o Workforce skills and competences, education quality
  - o Local authorities support and policy, expectations from authorities
  - o Negative externalities

Structurally, all these topics of the interviews were divided into 6 chapters: regional air cargo situation, regional development, business connections, skills and competencies, location and property quality, and future outlooks.

It must be added that infrastructure and property topics affect both demand and supply. More specifically, 3L model was used for studying the spatial aspects of the local environments. According to 3L approach, the success of real estate development depends on three factors: location, location, and location (Peiser 2003, p. 127). It means that property quality and value are characterised by location, which should be studied on three hierarchy levels: 1) macro location, 2) micro location and neighbourhood, and 3) site. Macro location for our case is a general air cargo service area regardless of the administrative borders. Micro location and neighbourhood are analysed by indicators that characterise the area in close proximity to the airport and site level indicators characterise the actual property (airfield) in question.

In relationship between air cargo sector and property quality, the applied approach presents four factors, covering important relations and dependencies. The key point of such approach is that all the factors have to contribute to facilitate development – i.e. the air cargo sector realities and perspectives must support property market and property market has to facilitate the enablers for growth.

The four main relations are:

1. Air cargo sector influence on property development – how and to what extent does the current state of regional air cargo sector influence industrial property market and infrastructure developments.

2. Property influence on air cargo sector development – how does the current situation in industrial property market and existing infrastructure as well as their potential influence the development of air cargo sector.

3. Property and infrastructure quality as essential components for clients' location decisions – how proximity to airport and good infrastructure support might win air cargo sector new clients from other transport modes.

4. Sustainability of property solutions and decisions made in the airport influence area – how important is the sustainability aspect in property to stakeholders (locations, constructions methods, management costs, energy consumption, development projects) and does it attract air cargo clients.

The general purpose of evaluating the quality of property at air cargo location is to find out whether the current situation is working more as an enabler for area and sector development or does it represent a bottleneck to growth instead.

In data analyses, similar viewpoints were identified and adjoined and opposing viewpoints were contrasted. To allow for comparison of Katowice and Tallinn, we are presenting a SWOT analysis of both airports. Based on the collected information we can then identify realistic development scenarios for both airports and conclude with pointing out key development areas for the regions.

4.   Results

4.1.   Findings about Tallinn Airport

Tallinn airport serves cargo clients from all over Estonia. The leader in Estonia's air cargo exports is components for electronics industry. The leading destination appears to be Asia, with North-America and South-America following. It was noted, however, that there is not enough detailed market information due to lack of statistics on RFS and the fact that various forms of RFS have by far the biggest market share combined, added on top of it cargo that is exported to air hubs by road without flight number, making export quantities actually flying out of Tallinn „a tip of the iceberg". In many cases it makes economic sense to arrange transport via Tallinn airport on RFS rather than to make arrangements in, for example, Frankfurt, where costs as well as time delays might be an issue.

In local airport statistics, real air cargo import volumes are not known as by far the most of the „import" is actually multimodal transit cargo unloaded in Tallinn from freighter and loaded onto a truck headed for Russia. Another issue with statistics is that the market is so small that an additional export client with continuous cargo demand has a considerable impact, making the existing statistics fluctuate notably. To improve the market overview, better statistics would be, according to most stakeholders, beneficial; however, "flying trucks" are counted at cargo handlers, but they are not particularly interested to share their information as it is sensitive to business success. Also, there is a question how to define the scope of RFS.

The Estonian air cargo export market is estimated to be led by RFS exports (mostly via Helsinki and Frankfurt), followed by integrator services (TNT, DHL), with belly cargo a third and diminishing segment. This is in contrast to other airports in the Baltics. For example, Riga airport has more belly cargo (more airlines, more destinations), but supposedly much less RFS (some volumes being loaded onto RFS from Tallinn to Frankfurt). From the viewpoint of belly cargo, the local airline has felt notable changes in cargo market characteristics over the past decade, which can be attributed to local developing economy, the effect of structural changes and better economic integration, the latter also causing a modal shift from short-distance air (destinations such as Germany or Sweden) to road transport. For example, after Estonia accepted the Schengen agreement, the air cargo flows between Estonia and Germany dropped a considerable amount. There are two sides of such modal shift, one supporting this trend, another opposing it. The first is that forwarders have wider access to information and can therefore offer service quality that meets clients' actual needs better and allows for a better quality/price ratio. The counterpoint of an airline operator is that forwarders in general have often a good reason to be biased and favour road transport to air transport even if it is not optimal to a given client, as it can offer better resource utilisation for the company. Furthermore, forwarder has more flexibility in offering a price to a customer that can beat the airlines offer (provided that the marginal cost for transport was rather low for both solutions).

The modal shift is additionally supported by growing consolidation capabilities of road haulers, which means that road price is more comparable and the airline has the speed advantage mostly only on across continent distances. Finally, the integrator business model is also increasing its share. The competition from the road sector is more affecting smaller and regional airlines and Estonian Air is definitely regional in that sense, operating cargo on about ten main routes, most of which are in tight competition with road transport. Such a shift has contributed to Estonian Air business decisions to purchase some of the new airplanes with notably smaller cargo space. Furthermore, Estonian Air feels they need to find the ways to reach end customers directly and overcome the barriers of traditional business model. One vision could be to better cater for small shipments in a more express-service fashion, outsourcing the last leg to local carriers. On closer and more frequent routes, such as Stockholm and Copenhagen (4-5 flights per day) this could offer even faster service than integrators (usually one flight per day).

The catchment area of Tallinn airport is entire Estonia, with furthermost clients locating over 300 km from the airport. This distance is not an issue for customers as the airport is still only a couple of hours away, compared to RFS delay, which can be a day (to Helsinki) or more (to Frankfurt). Inside Estonia, location does not matter when talking about transport times, nor does airport proximity play a notable role in most of the locating decisions. There are many options in the form of industrial parks around Tallinn so that space and available infrastructure is not a bottleneck for potential new air cargo clients and interviewees were mostly on a position that the region has notable potential to attract new exporting customers and mark the airport as „moderately developing". For stakeholders located outside airport, only macro level location is an important factor in picking location. When it comes to micro location, Tallinn airport location as well as near logistics infrastructure is seen as sufficient for current service with some investments needed for increasing demand (road access, traffic management). There are no notable neighbourhood restrictions. In general the nearby property market is attractive. Estonian air cargo sector doesn't need large scale property development outside airport premises, whereas the current state of industrial property market serves as an enabler for air cargo growth potential. The property potential on airport premises is analysed to sustain long-term growth.

From transit point of view, it appears that Tallinn airport is in a reasonably good position, noting that today on world scale some large hubs have reached their capacity and that is giving more chances to smaller airports. The interviews suggest that Tallinn is used in Asia-Turkey-Russia route (the main volume generator) as a closest EU airport with good quality and reliable customs operations along with quick handling – in contrast to some of the experiences from Russian airports (both concerning operator and custom issues). The risk for Tallinn airport in that regard is Asian customs union, which means some cargo targeted for Russian market might be routed through Kazakhstan instead.

Stakeholders have suggested that Tallinn could take care of some supply chains currently routed through Finland or Sweden, mostly Scandinavian distribution of goods of Asian origin. It appears that lately there have been business talks with some such clients and although there is no "big fish" caught yet, some interviewees remained optimistic about the prospect. The current handling infrastructure might be a bottleneck in larger volumes, but Tallinn Airport is ready to expand.

The main issue with Asian flights is the financial risk that the local stakeholders don't dare to take and cooperation with Asian airlines is sought instead. Also from forwarders point of view, while theoretically cargo clients' orders for Asia could be consolidated and space booked on a freighter leaving Helsinki, this model so far does not exist on the market because no one wants to take the volume risk, claiming that such risk should be taken by an airline.

On Asian front, Estonian government has lately been successful in forming cooperation agreements with Singapore and Qatar. Also, the marketing of Tallinn Airport and Estonian Air has increased notably in the last year and directors of both organizations are making bold statements concerning near future Asian links. It has been suggested that while Finnair will remain the leader in Asian operations, there is still room in the growing market for new airlines and Tallinn shares one of the advantages of Helsinki, being one of few EU capital cities that is in a single-crew flight reach from main Asian locations. The suitable destinations would be second rank towns not currently covered with direct EU flights.

In evaluating the overall situation of Tallinn airport, the underlining tone was positive – Estonia is logistically well integrated to Europe and performance meets most insider expectations. Interviewees were usually more focused on describing local enablers than bottlenecks (such as competitive workplace culture contrasted with, as expected, Southern Europe, but surprisingly even closest neighbours). Another optimistic view was noticeable on airport negative externalities. Although Tallinn airport is rather special in being located less than 10 minutes away from town centre, it is not seen as important issue even in optimistic growth scenarios. The interviewees pointed out that the locals are used to the noise, which is improving and would only get worse if regular large freighters were taking off regularly, which is not expected. It was also noted that Estonians apparently don't have the West-European mindset to even think about such topics.

Two bottlenecks were still identified, the first from the operations level – flexibility of customs. Although regular customs service is seen as quick and smooth (and air cargo enabler), it has been noted in some problem cases the investigation and decisions take too much time. The second issue, from the strategic level, is EU regulations. According to Tallinn airport, many regulations, such as airport charges directive and regulations of work conditions for crew, are missing the goal of making the industry more competitive, to take on the increasing competition from Asian carriers. In other requirements, such as slot regulation, there is too much bureaucracy, which has increased cost for Tallinn airport. It was noted that the goal could have been achieved with lower costs for smaller airports. The EU regulations, however, are not a specific problem to Tallinn airport, but to EU aviation in general.

Similarly, the Eurozone crisis is seen as the main threat to air cargo, although potentially a crucial one. However, estimations of the effect varied greatly and some were also dismissive. Sector representatives were mostly focused on issues they see on a daily basis and which they can influence. The low frequency of some RFS lines is one issue for Estonian air cargo export. The capacity of cargo operations in Tallinn airport is not seen as a bottleneck in the long run with airport having expansion plans ready whenever demand calls. Tallinn airport will remain a single-runway airport, but with room to increase flight operation frequency more than twofold (current peak rate is one operation in 3 ml) and passenger capacity ceiling is 8 million, compared to record 1.9 million in 2011. One recent innovation for passenger growth in Tallinn airport is cooperating with cruise ships to offer "intermodal cruises". However, in the same time, Riga airport expects growth up to 20 ml yearly passengers. Cargo wise, Tallinn is leading Riga by 40% (first quarter of 2012) and is expected to retain the lead in Baltics. While catching up with Helsinki airport remains unrealistic for Tallinn (cargo volumes differ by 4x, passenger numbers by 7.5x), the local forecast is at least comparable if not more optimistic than EU air cargo general forecast. The critical success factor is Asian flights, but even without them, modest growth is expected.

To summarise, the most notable strengths and weaknesses of Tallinn air cargo are presented in Table 1 below.

Table 1: Main strengths and issues of Tallinn air cargo according to stakeholders

Tallinn air cargo strengths	Tallinn air cargo weaknesses
1. Expansion plans, government support, no notable restrictions	1. Close proximity to already internationally established Helsinki airport
2. Industrial property market and infrastructure supports air cargo development	2. High competition from road transport, shrinking belly cargo market
3. Good location to facilitate handling future transit from Asia	3. Transit volumes depend on few large customers
4. High operating speed and mostly quick customs service	4. Low frequency of some RFS routes

The effect of air cargo on Estonian economy, all things considered, is still rather marginal, at least compared to expected volumes and potential of ports. Still, the current government is making efforts to attract Asian airlines and Tallinn airport is mostly satisfied with government support in the big picture. Tallinn airport is one of the few state-owned organizations in Estonia that has had its earned profit reinvested into development throughout the company history. It is hoped that better flight connections also induce economic growth. While transit growth will not bring much more than income for airport and operators, increasing destinations support local entrepreneurship development, create jobs, attract more tourists and enable better and more efficient mobility for local population.

4.2. Findings about Katowice airport

Poland did not historically have strong incentives for air cargo development. Highly restricted export and transportation policies resulted in favoured development of railroads. The niche of typical air cargo clients was mostly served by road transport. Market liberalization implemented in 2005 was expected to result in unconstrained development of the sector, limited only by the demand and supply capacities. Today in Poland it is clear that there are some artificial obstacles limiting the growth. Total volume of cargo handled at Polish airports in 2010 was equal to 81 thousand tonnes (Civil Aviation Office 2011). Despite the noted significant and constant growth of the sector, there is a common opinion that progress should be even faster. The opinions indicate that many goods transported to or from Poland are handled at Frankfurt, Vienna or Prague, which entails unnecessary costs. Some reasons pointed out in the interviews are, amongst other, lack of intermodal possibilities other than air–road in Poland, poor road system, relatively high cost of rail transport and the most important VAT regulations causing necessity of extra operating capital commitment during import. In short, the competitive position of air transport is strong and significant growth is noted, but there are also many obstacles to be removed.

The estimated catchment area of Katowice airport is about 35 thousand km^2 or a distance of 150 km around the airport. Good location of the airport in relation to its main customers was brought forward on many occasions. All interviewees located in the airport vicinity pointed that location of the clients is satisfactory, while respondents located near other Polish airports, such as Warsaw, evaluated airport location as intermediate or even too far, making extra transport time from airport to client an important consideration for cargo clients. The answers indicate the important advantage of Katowice localization over Warsaw. For many clients of air cargo, access to the airport is high priority when locating their facilities. The distance to the airport is not considered as a significant factor for most of the surveyed air cargo stakeholders.

Results of the interviews, as well as economic indicators, lead to the conclusion that Katowice area offers moderately attractive conditions for business development. Silesia Region, where the city of Katowice is located, is one of the most developed in Poland. Although road infrastructure in Katowice Airport neighbourhood was evaluated as optimal for air cargo service, road surface conditions as well as road network extension were pointed out as most common logistical weaknesses in Poland. Perhaps it results from the belief that with European funds the road system will be also expanded in future. Silesia region is estimated to have notable potential to attract new air cargo customers. Also, a number of new clients have recently moved close to the airport. Regarding the future clients, the majority of them are believed to locate near the airport. This indicates a better environment for air cargo development in Katowice in comparison to other airports such as Warsaw, where prospects are not so optimistic both in terms of road infrastructure and general potential of the region. Business activity related to air transport is supported by creating a "Special Economic Zone" serving preferential conditions for enterprise development, which carries an important value in Silesia region especially. Together with a good land transport system this is an important source of demand for air transport served at Katowice Airport.

Poland as a central European country is located on one of the main global transit routes. Silesia region and Katowice airport are in the neighbourhood of one of the largest industrial zones in this part of the continent. According to one stakeholder, there are about 700 enterprises as active clients of air cargo (30% of them in automotive industry) and more than 11 million of inhabitants located in the airport catchment area. It means substantial potential demand, which is currently met by a hub in Frankfurt and airport in Prague, Vienna or Budapest. Increasing economic attractiveness of southern Poland for industrial property development together with easier access to global air transport will lead to further growth of Silesia finalised in becoming the largest, beside German, industrial unit in Central-Eastern Europe. Large numbers of automotive and pharmaceutical manufacturers are located in the catchment area, which reaches the northern part of the Czech Republic as well as Slovakia. Additionally good and rapidly developing road infrastructure in the airport proximity, as well as low prices and opportunities to create various intermodal concepts should be mentioned. As the most significant weaknesses, air cargo stakeholders pointed to poor road infrastructure outside the Silesia region, monopoly on supply of fuel to airport resulting from infrastructural restrictions and necessity of extra capital commitment during import of goods. These issues are caused by impractical regulations. Interestingly, close proximity to Cracow airport was not considered as a weakness by interviewees. The reason is the distinct market division between the airports.

In the opinion of interviewees, integrators are the main players in the air cargo sector in the region. As a rule, LOT Polish Airlines is notable with two direct transatlantic freight routes. Also a significant market share is held by quite large number of small and medium-sized enterprises, which are, in many cases, highly specialised and separately play a marginal role. Competition between large and small companies and among the groups appears to be dense. LOT tries to enter the global air freight transport market operating from Katowice Airport and develops slowly but steadily with rather optimistic future. The market stakeholders are expressing willingness to cooperate for development. The common interests are mostly related to regulations. Additionally, the intercontinental LOT Polish Airlines all-cargo routes from Katowice airport can be considered as an illustration for cooperation directed to developing global air transport in Poland.

Experts were also asked about current trends influencing air cargo in near future. Globalization, international cooperation, e-commerce development, market liberalization, increase of constraints due to environmental issues and decreasing unit volume of goods and increasing value were mentioned.

One of the notable strengths of Katowice Airport is location in micro scale. Remote from the agglomeration, the unpopulated area was seen by experts as optimal for air cargo service. The same opinion was expressed in terms of shape and size of the plot. The growing volume of cargo handled implies necessity for infrastructure expansion. Currently, in the framework of airport master plan, new commercial buildings are under construction. The opinions regarding airport facilities and expandability seem to confirm the belief that airport infrastructure development will be growing without any important obstacles.

Table 2: *Main strengths and issues of Katowice Airport according to stakeholders*

Katowice Airport strengths	Katowice Airport weaknesses
1. Location: - On global transit route - Near highly industrialized areas - Near densely populated area (11 ml inhabitants in catchment area), - Far from urban areas, low risk of future restrictions.	1. Unfavourable regulations regarding international trade - In terms of VAT in import, - Regulation practically preventing food import at the airport, - Low responsibility for decisions amongst customs duty officers.
2. Good quality and improving road infrastructure in southern Poland.	2. Monopoly in terms of fuel supply to the airport resulting in relatively high cost.
3. Very good weather conditions. Statistically only one non-flight day per year.	3. Low quality road infrastructure in some areas, especially in northern Poland.
3. Competitive prices of air cargo service operators at the airport.	4. Low correlation between GDP and air cargo growth.

Support agencies are not popular in Poland amongst entities specialised in air freight. According to the gathered opinions, the existing market agencies should act more effectively. Local authorities' support is mostly perceived to be lacking, such as increasing administrative process efficiency, support for airport development and reducing obstacles in access to new services and rationalization of customs clearance regulation. Furthermore, regarding expectations, deeper commitment in community decision making and greater support for companies implementing global standards were pointed out. Interviewees also expressed their policy recommendations. According to a Katowice airport representative, current tax regulations are most problematic and discouraging from developing international activity in the sector.

To sum up, the interviews indicated a significant development potential in Katowice airport, especially in comparison to other airports in Poland such as Warsaw or Gdansk, but also brought forward bottlenecks. The most notable strengths and weaknesses of Katowice airport are summarised in Table 2 below.

5. Conclusions

The current Eurozone crisis and the long-term EU economic and socio-political sustainability issues are still the most pressing topics for the future. The effect on air cargo will be substantial but difficult to predict exactly. The success of the Baltic Sea Region depends heavily on the continental and global economic climate. This paper lends support to optimism witnessed at stakeholders of Tallinn and Katowice airport, as the situation points to expansion. While in some respects Tallinn and Katowice airports are similar, in specific issues the situation is vastly different.

The growth of air cargo in Tallinn is expected, however, it is not going to change the airport dramatically. The most optimistic scenario for Tallinn would be to become involved in Asian flights, serving as an export hub with a catchment area extending across the Baltics, as well as handling some Asia-to-Europe cargo. Still, Tallinn will most probably not reach the level of Helsinki volumes, at least in the current long-term planning horizon of 20 years and remains in a noticeable distance. The main trend working against Tallinn airport in export cargo market in the long run is logistical integration with Europe with projects such as Rail Baltic (fast rail service to Germany, perhaps 10-year horizon) and a tunnel to Helsinki (perhaps 20-year horizon). When spokes become even stronger (as RFS has already leading market share), a secondary hub is mostly not needed.

Katowice Airport is characterised by the highly industrialised Silesia region. Whether the opportunities will be exploited depends highly on skilful airport management and, what is pivotal here, support of local authorities in terms of optimal legal solutions (amongst other, regarding VAT), as well as more intensive support of advanced technology development in the region. It is expected that proper implementations of these aspects will result in correlated growth of regional economy and airport tonnage, as well as taking care of some demand for air cargo which is currently satisfied by other nearby airports. A crucial success factor of Katowice is continuation of currently conducted infrastructure expansion on regional and airport level. However, the projects are based on European Structural Funds availability, which is not certain, especially in the cast of Eurozone crisis.

An optimistic scenario of Katowice Airport development forecasts the volume of 185 thousand tonnes in a 20-year horizon, with some elements of regional potential allowing for even higher volumes. Still, it is estimated that difficulties in master plan implementation can lead to only 25 of tonnes in 2030 – it is necessary to note that without European co-financing and active authority support the current situation is not going to change significantly.

The cases of Tallinn and Katowice show that regional airport management must consider global air cargo supply chains in order to enjoy long-term sustainable growth. In this context air cargo feeder services are playing an important role as in both cases RFS are dominating the scene and intermodalism is the key for successful supply chain solutions. In conclusion, there are three main differences between the outlooks of Katowice and Tallinn airport:

1. Tallinn airport export and import cargo is mostly determined by success or failure in passenger transport. Transit through Tallinn can only slightly be influenced by maintaining and improving the service quality. Katowice airport success depends mostly on economic growth in the catchment area and offering capacity whenever demand needs. Katowice is a cargo oriented airport and can be much more focused on serving local exporters. The potential of air cargo export in Silesia is much higher than in the Baltics.

2. Air cargo in Katowice has potentially less competition than in Tallinn. Tallinn is competing with Helsinki and Riga for passengers and airline attention and with a wider range of northern and eastern European airports for transit cargo. Katowice is mostly competing with road transport to offer more for exporters.

3. The future of Tallinn airport is dependent mostly on the market situation and available potential demand. There are no important legal or administrative barriers hindering the functioning of the airport in a significant way. However, Katowice airport, due to a number of impractical regulations, is not able to take advantage of already available potential resulting from its location and high level authority activity is needed to overcome the obstacles.

This is related to the main limitation of the interview approach to identify development actions. The case of Katowice revealed bottlenecks to overcome and needed actions, whereas Tallinn airport is much more affected by outside factors and is much less controllable.

References

Airbus. 2011. Cargo Global Market Forecast 2011–2030.
    http://www.airbus.com/company/market/forecast/cargo-aircraft-market-forecast/
    (05.05.2012)
Aircargonews.net. 2012. Cargo Heads Optimistic About Future.
    http://www.aircargonews.net/home/news/single-view/nachricht//cargo-heads-optimistic-about-future.html (02.05.2012)
Baum, H. 2005. The Impact of Airports on Economic Welfare. In Strategic Management in the Aviation Industry. Ashgate Publishing. 672 p.
Boeing. 2010. World Air Cargo Forecast 2010–2011.
    www.boeing.com/commercial/cargo/wacf.pdf (05.05.2012)
Central Statistical Office. 2010. Transport – Activity Results in 2010.
    http://www.stat.gov.pl/cps/rde/xbcr/gus/PUBL_tac_transport_activity_results_in_2010.pdf (07.05.2012)
Chiavi, R. 2005. Airfreight Development Supporting the Strategy of Global Logistics Companies. p489-516 in Strategic Management in the Aviation Industry. Ashgate Publishing. 672 p.
Civil Aviation Office. 2010. Statistics by Polish airports.
    http://www.ulc.gov.pl/index.php?option=com_content&task=view&id=324&Itemid=466 (07.05.2012).
Dewulf, W., Meersman, H., and Van de Voorde, E. 2011. From Carpet Sellers To Cargo Stars – A Typology Based on Management Strategies for Air Cargo Carriers. 4th National Urban Freight Conference METRANS2011.
Delfmann, W., Baum, H., Auerbach, S. and Albers, S. 2005. Moving Targets. Strategic Trends in the Aviation Sector. p1-15 in Strategic Management in the Aviation Industry. Ashgate Publishing. 672 p.
Doganis, R. 2006. The Airline Business. 2nd ed. Routledge. 311p.
EU Transport in Figures. Statistical Pocketbook. 2011.
    http://ec.europa.eu/transport/publications/statistics/pocketbook-2011_en.htm (02.05.2012)
Hellermann, R. 2006. Capacity Options for Revenue Management. Theory and Applications in the Air Cargo Industry. Springer-Verlag, Berlin Heidelberg. 216p.
Hertwig, P. and Rau, P. 2010. Risk Management in the Air Cargo Industry. Hamburg: Diplomica Verlag GmbH.
IATA. 2010. E-Freight factsheet. http://www.iata.org/whatwedo/cargo/efreight/Documents/e-freight-factsheet.pdf (06.05.2012).
ICAO International Civil Aviation Organization. 2011. Annual Report of the Council 2010.
Kasarda, J. and Green, J. 2004. Air Cargo – Engine For Economic Development. The International Air Cargo Association, Air cargo Forum, Bilbao 2004. 18p.

Katowice Airport. 2011. Annual Statistics
http://www.katowice-airport.com/en/airport/annual-statistics (02.05.2012).

Kleindorfer, P. and Visvikis, I. 2007. Integration of Financial and Physical Networks in Global Logistics. The Wharton School of University of Pennsylvania. Working paper. 25p.

Heusener, K. and Von Wichert, G. 2002. Profit Pressure in the Cargo Industry. The Wall Street Journal Europe, May 2002.

Kasilingam, R.G. 1997. Air Cargo Revenue Management – Characteristics and Complexities. European Journal of Operational Research. Vol. 96 Is 1, pp. 36–44.

Morrell, P.S. 2011. Moving Boxes By Air. The Economics of International Air Cargo. Ashgate Publishing Company, 353p.

OECD. 2002. Liberalization of Air Cargo Transport. Directorate of Scienc, Technology and Industry.

Otto, A. 2005. Reflecting the Prospects of an Air cargo Carrier. p451-472 in Strategic Management in the Aviation Industry. Ashgate Publishing. 672 p.

Peiser, P. 2003. Professional Real Estate Development. Dearborn Financial Publishing 2nd Ed. Unc., ULI, 414 p.

Riga International Airport. 2012. Statistics Report March 2012. http://www.riga-airport.com.

Schaecher, M. 2011. Air freight – The Future of the Industry. Raising the Awareness of Air Cargo. CNS Conference, Phoenix, May 2011.
http://www.cnsc.net/events/Documents/Air-Freight-The-Future-of-the-Industry-Michael-Schaecher.pdf (05.05.2012).

Senguttuvan, P.S. 2006. Air Cargo: Engine of Economic Growth and Development – A Case Study of Asian region. National Urban Freight Conference METRANS2006. 30p.

Tallinn Airport. 2011. Tallinn Airport Traffic Report
http://www.tallinnairport.ee/eng/associates/GeneralInfo/statisticsandsurveys/?articleID=1
355 (02.05.2011).

The International Logistics Quality Institute. 2003. The Air Cargo Quality Survey. Air Cargo World.

White Paper on Transport. Roadmap to a Single European Transport Area – Towards a Competitive and Resource-efficient Transport System. 2011.
http://ec.europa.eu/transport/strategies/2011_white_paper_en.htm (10.05.2012).

Transnational E-services for Efficient Oversize Logistics

Kristina Hunke[1]

Abstract

The implementation of the renewable energy Directive (2009/28/EC) of the European Commission and the resulting national renewable energy action plans of the member states opened up the market and trade of over-dimensional cargo. The transshipment of these oversize cargos causes comprehensive operations with a lot of bureaucracy as well as economic losses due to the need to build and reconstruct infrastructure and due to time consuming permission processes.

This paper will provide an analysis of selected national laws and regulations and will show differences and non-conformities but will also demonstrate similarities which can allow opportunities for perspective cooperation for international oversize transports. Furthermore, this paper will demonstrate different national e-services as well as a multinational solution resulting from a European funded project called OTIN (Oversize Transport Information Network).

Practical experiences from transport forwarders and industry clients substantiate the necessity of such coherent application services as the role of transnational oversize transports is an increasing share of the daily business.

JEL classification: R4, L9, O

Keywords: efficient logistics, e-services, transnational transport, Oversize Transport Information Network

1. Introduction

The implementation of the renewable energy Directive (COM 2009/28/EC) of the European Commission and the resulting national renewable energy action plans of the member states opened up the market and trade of renewable energy power plants and innovative power generating systems. New trade routes had to be found and demand for the exchange and transhipment of goods increased.

Demand for the usage of renewable energy power plants, especially in Eastern Europe, has increased enormously in the last years but, unfortunately, the industries of these countries are not yet ready to design and produce these innovative power generating systems for own demand. Therefore, large generators and windmills need to be shipped from Western Europe eastwards to the Baltic States. At the beginning such operations caused a lot of bureaucracy as well as

---

1 Wismar Business School / Molde University College, Philipp-Müller-Str. 14 Wismar Germany, E-mail: kristina.hunke@hs-wismar.de

losses of time and money because of the need to build and reconstruct parts of the roads and bridges along the way, long permission processes at administration level and the inexperienced personnel of transport operators.

The South Baltic Sea region, including Mecklenburg-Vorpommern in Germany, Southern Sweden, and Denmark is a very important export and transit market for these oversized transports to the Eastern countries due to its logistical location and connections to the new EU Member States. In addition to the increasing demand in regional oversized transports, worldwide project cargo (single segments of ships, power plants, machines, etc.) is becoming bigger and heavier with each year. According to the maritime transport forecast for 2025, prepared on behalf of the German Federal Ministry of Transport, Building and Urban Development (MV 2025), total goods handling in the four German ports included in the study: Rostock, Sassnitz/Mukran, Stralsund and Wismar, will more than double from just under 30 mln tonnes in 2004 to over 73 mln tonnes by 2025. The assumption is that the demand for handling oversized cargo will increase in this period correspondingly. Due to these facts, a new oversized transport strategy for the whole South Baltic Sea region, prepared within the EU project "Oversize Baltic", will gain high importance in future years. This includes the implementation of an innovative platform for e-solutions for application procedures. It is called Oversize Transport Information Network (OTIN). Furthermore, the infrastructure will be adjusted and improved as well as the safety of oversize transports. There are public benefits to outline, i.e. low congestions on roads and railways, lower emissions due to innovative transport routes and means, and consumer cost savings due to economical transport solutions.

2. Theoretical Framework

This section will give an introduction to the theoretical and legal background of the research topic. The oversize cargo will be defined and classified as well as various national legal regulations enforced in European countries will be analysed.

2.1 Definition of oversize transport

A look at the European transport statistics shows that oversize cargo is transported mostly by road. This means of transport is considered as the cheapest way and most flexible means of transportation even though road transport encounters difficulties arising from infrastructural and law limitations. New technological approaches and the globalization implies new technologies, like transport of the whole complete production line, so called "project cargo" where the whole compact production line or its part is being transported already assembled. After transportation either by road, rail, short sea shipping or inland shipping transport, readymade projects are installed in previously designated places accessible to the means of transport.

The choice of transport means and designated route is generally limited by the parameters of cargo. The transport availability of production and delivery places is crucial as well. Furthermore, some huge elements such as transformers, turbines generators are also being transported by all available means of transport. Construction of wind energy installations cannot be exercised without oversize transport, since most of the components of a wind turbine exceed standard dimensions. Road transport of oversize units (constructions, machinery) means considerable challenges. This is due to the on-going infrastructural expansion and renovations of roads, which might cause the necessity to deviate from the assumed route. Another barrier is connected to trees along the road, traffic lights and curve diameters of the road which hinder oversize movement.

Resuming from the different kinds of project cargo there exist no unique definition of oversize cargo. This is due to the multiplicity of forms which that kind of cargo has, including heavy lifts, over width, over height units and cargo which exceeds axle load. Oversized and abnormal transports are over-dimensioned vehicles, usually carrying the project cargo, or vehicles with heavy load of goods over 40 tonnes. German law regulations specify that an oversized transport is only allowed if the cargo is non-divisible (transport other than in one piece is impossible). However, next to the growing number of project cargo transports, the trend leans towards heavier cargo movements of goods with abnormal road trucks. A towing vehicle with trailer is allowed to have a maximum length of 18.75 m and a weight of 40 tonnes. There are initiatives and test cases for trucks with a length of 25.25 m and weight up to 60 tonnes. In other European countries, in Sweden for example, these trucks are already running. There are also special handling installations (terminals, factory sites, ports and docks) for oversize transport. It could be said that in all cases "oversize" determinants are:

1. cargo dimensions,
2. cargo weight,
3. available cargo space on the vehicle,
4. permissible pressure and stress on the loading surface,
5. permissible stress on surface of road and railways.

An additional important element is the shape of cargo, because its irregular geometry could negatively affect the static and dynamic stability of the vehicle. In every case handling, stowage and securing of such cargo must be done under the supervision of surveyors, proper calculations should be made prior to the transport, and necessary permits and certificates should be obtained (SBSR Oversize Strategy 2011).

As in all other European countries, oversize transport in Germany requires special permission from responsible transport authorities; mostly it is the official road authority of the respective Federal state. Today the permission process has been made easier, thanks to a one-stop-shop system for all oversize transports throughout Germany, called VEMAGS (Verfahrensmanagement für Großraum- und Schwertransporte). The operators are not bound to apply for permission at a specific authority (e.g. the starting point of the transport route or the location of the business) but can choose their preferred authority. Also, there are possibilities for a transport operator to apply for multiple permissions or long-term permission, which are bound to certain vehicle combinations or on fixed routes.

2.2 Legal basis for oversize transport

There exists an European Council Directive 96/53/EC, laying down the basis for the maximum authorised dimensions and the maximum authorised weights and relating parameters for certain road vehicles circulating in national and international traffic for abnormal road transports in Europe. However, the real implementation and application of these legal recommendations is left to the respective countries. Therefore the following chapter will show differences as well as similarities in the legal framework of the four analysed countries: Germany, Poland, Sweden and Lithuania.

There are a number of legal requirements concerning oversize transportation in Germany. Such transportations diverge from the norm of "Straßenverkehrs-Zulassungs-Ordnung (StVZO)." It is a regulation based on §6 "Straßen-verkehrsgesetz", enacted by the Ministry of Transport, Building and Regional Development. They cause immoderate using of roads and so they need a permission according to § 29 (3) StVO. The basis for this permission is an exception permit pursuant to § 70 StVZO. Depending on size and freight escort vehicles or police escort are required.

According to that, such transports are just allowed in specific periods. During holidays using of several motorways is principally not allowed. These periods are called „off-time". Oversize transports are allowed to proceed only between Monday and Friday 9 a.m. and 3 p.m. Nearly all transportations with a width above 3.2 meters have to be executed at night between 10 p.m. and 6 a.m.

The regulation in Poland is based on several national acts and laws. Oversize cargo transport is regulated by many acts of law issued by the Ministry. The most important ones are:

- Act of June 20th 1997 – Road traffic law (section II – Road traffic; chapter 5: Order and traffic safety on roads; chapter 4: Conditions for use of vehicles on the road, Art. 61 – 64, Dz. U. z 2003 r. No 58, poz. 515);
- Act of March 21th 1985, about public roads (Dz. U. z 2007 r. No 19, poz. 115);
- Act of September 6th 2001 about road transport (Dz. U. 2004 r. No 204 poz. 2088);
- Decree of the Minister of December 31st 2002 on vehicles technical conditions and range of their necessary equipment (Dz. U. z 2003 r. No 32, poz. 262 ze zm.)
- Decree of the Minister of December 16th 2004 on special conditions and permits issuing procedure for oversize vehicles transit (Dz. U. No 267, poz. 2660);
- Decree of the Infrastructural of July 26th 2004 about costs connected with transit route defining (Dz. U. No 170, poz. 1792);
- Decree of the Home Affairs and Administration of December 30th 2002, about road traffic control (Dz. U. z 2003 r. No 14, poz. 144 ze zm.);
- Decree of the Infrastructural Minister of April 26th 2004 about vehicles which make pilotage (Dz. U. No 110, poz. 1165).

Abundance of documents do not foster easiness and coherence of law applied to carriers, forwarders and institutions that operate oversize vehicle transport. Currently, there could be observed some effort to change and simplify the existing Road Traffic Law and other acts with the aim to reorganize existing legal order in the discussed area. The new act is being widely discussed and opened for public consultation.

The public road network in Sweden is divided into three weight classes: Weight Class 1 (BK1), Weight Class 2 (BK2) and Weight Class 3 (BK3). The highest weights are permitted on the BK1 road network, whose weight regulations apply on some 94% of the public road network. Abnormal transports within Sweden require an exemption (permit) from the traffic regulation (*trafikförordningen*, SFS 1998:1276). If the transport concerns only one municipality, the application must be sent to that municipality (the local authority). If the transport route concerns more than one municipality, the application must be sent to the Swedish Transport Administration (*Trafikverket*). Certain wide transports can be performed without a permit (the wide load does not exceed 3.1/3.5 m) if certain conditions are fulfilled (*Transportstyrelsen* VVFS 2005:102).

The maximum allowed vehicle dimensions, permissible axle(s) load, and the total weight allowed on Lithuanian roads have been set forth by Lithuanian Minister of Transport Decree 18-02-2002 No. 3-66 with the approval of the authorized maximum dimensions of vehicles, permitted axle(s) load, and total mass. Vehicles with heavy goods above the permissible weight and size are only allowed with track operator or an authorized authority permit. Oversize and heavy transport permits for use of national roads are granted by the State Road Transport Inspectorate under the Ministry of Transport, and permits for urban trips by track operator, i.e. a relative municipality of administrative unit. Heavy vehicle permit authorization and payment of public road taxes are regulated by the Minister of Transport Decree 20-04-2006 No. 3-150 on public road tax for heavy vehicles in the Republic of Lithuania Payment, Administration, Control and Licensing Procedure (Oversize Transport Handbook – Lithuania 2011).

3. Methodology

The objective of this research is to find a regional strategy for oversize transport in South Baltic Sea region and a design frame for a transnational e-service platform for permit issuing. The different kinds of oversize transport are observed, regarding the actual cargo as well as the possible transports in the future. The legal environment on the European level as well as on individual national level is analysed. Differences and similarities which will have an influence on the implementation of a transnational solution are shown. Finally, the businesses which benefit from an advanced oversize transport strategy and an implemented e-service are analysed and optimization procedures are provided.

In order to gather all necessary information for the development of this oversize strategy a number of different sources are used. First, secondary information is collected from the internet sources and publications from governmental institutions, private stakeholders and networks and initiatives. Due to the fact that secondary information was rarely and mostly limited to legal regulations and governmental guidelines, primary information was necessary to analyse the oversize transport topic. Therefore a few events connected to this topic were visited and individual meetings with experts from this field were conducted.

The literature about oversize transports is very rare even though some theoretical approaches for safety based analysis of heavy load transport (Wang et al. 2007; Yin et al. 2008) could be found in the literature. Furthermore, the density for juridical analysis of existing legislation is quite high (Kuehl and Lemmer 2009; Rebler 2004). However, this approach is very nationally oriented and does not imply to the aim of this research paper as it was only focused on implementation and providing interfaces between existing legal systems. To give recommendations for the change and adaptation of law regulations would be by far above the possible scope of this research.

Much information about the topic of transnational oversize transport was gained during the project duration of almost 3 years of the South Baltic Programme project "Oversize Baltic". The author was the responsible component leader for the strategic analysis of the national markets for oversize transport in all transport modes (road, rail, short sea shipping and inland waterways) for the four participating countries: Germany, Sweden, Poland and Lithuania. This includes also the profound investigation of the legal environment in these regions as well as the research about existing and planned transnational services in the European Union and smaller interregional initiatives. One official information point in the internet is the homepage of http://transportxxl.eu, which was created by an international project with European funds by several European countries. It provides a detailed overview about legislation and guidelines in the field of oversize road transports. However, it is still only limited to the participating regions and did not offer information about some of the national situations for the countries of interest in this research.

Additionally to the field research more primary information was collected from individual meetings with experts in the project "Oversize Baltic" and beyond. A number of visits of experts from the field of logistics and oversize transports helped to gain information about single case studies, individual challenges and successful solutions (cf. interview with André Lau Schwertransporte 2010). These meetings were held in Rostock and Wismar with international guests from the Baltic Sea States but also some cross-border visits were made to e.g. Klaipeda, Karlshamn, and Stettin. Additionally there were phone conferences with these experts during the research phase. A workshop organised by the Easyway project in March 2012 offered a possibility to present and introduce the transnational e-service OTIN (Oversize Transport Information Network) as a direct outcome of the "Oversize Baltic" project to the customers and industry representatives. During this workshop the accessibility and the customer-oriented approach was discussed. The result was positive as this is a very well developed tool which aims at improving the user-friendliness and the reduction of the bureaucratic burden for oversize transport permissions.

4. Results of the Research

By analysing and investigating the process of oversize transportation the basic procedure is to obtain permission for conducting transports with a special licence. Therefore, oversize transports must have a valid permit which has to be obtained from the responsible authority. For this purpose a request with addressor, receiver, measurements of loads, weights, vehicle registration number, axial distances and axle loads, number of wheels per axle and description of the route have to be conveyed. The responsible authority gives this request for consultation and waits for agreement and issues the permission. In Germany e.g. it is also common that oversize transport companies have a continuous permit for one year.

In the last years, some countries have tried to follow the European guidelines on electronic government and have implemented e-service solutions for the application of transport permissions. Since 2007 there is a new permission system for oversize transports in Germany. It includes all authorities of the 16 Federal States and is called VEMAGS (*Verfahrensmanagement für Großraum- und Schwertransporte*).

The VEMAGS-system is a tool which was developed to simplify and quicken the permission process of oversize transports all over Germany. It was initiated by the European Union aiming to provide a comprehensive system for oversize transport in the whole EU-region. Germany took the chance and established this VEMAGS-system even before the agreed deadline. VEMAGS replaces the earlier telefax-method, which had long waiting times and high transfer costs and was not economical anymore. The new system provides the whole process beginning with the application up to the approval and the actual transport on the road in real time. Important industries like construction industry and the energy sector asked strongly for such a new system. All stakeholders of the permission process for oversize transports in the Federal Republic of Germany benefit from the implementation of the VEMAGS-system. These stakeholders are applicants, permission authorities, administrations, road traffic authorities, responsible road enterprises and the police. The applicants can simply submit their application via the VEMAGS-system to the responsible permission authorities. They are supported by a route planning tool and a template system which stores their previous submitted data.

The VEMAGS-system covers the following aspects:

• structure of an operations management tool (internet instead of telefax/phone)
• communication platform and distribution of application data
• status tracking
• filing
• cooperation with existing systems (e.g. of the German military)
• training concept
• collection of data of bridges and buildings
• classified road nets including turns
• collection of routes with special requirements.

For using the VEMAGS-system only a simple internet access and a browser are necessary. The huge servers which keep the systems running are located in middle Germany and bundle and spread the relevant information to the responsible permission authorities in the federal states (German: *Länder*). There is no admission fee. The approval of the application according to the German legislation and guidelines is very complicated and comprehensive. The delivery of the approval is still possible via telefax, post or by personal pick up at the authority. If the applicant has the opportunity of a digital signature, which itself has some technical requirements, he can use it and gets the approval digitally as well. In Germany, the digital signature is the only way to circumvent the official signature with stamp of an authority.

The user who would like to submit an application for the transport of oversize cargo in Germany needs to register at the VEMAGS homepage. Some business data and formal information like name, address and so on are required. After the registration the user can fill in the application form (see attached paper version). The user must define the route he wants to travel, the information about his transport vehicle and of course the dimensions of his cargo (weight, height, length, etc.) and can also attach additional files. If everything is filled in he can submit the application. The VEMAGS-system automatically scans the application for mistakes or missing information. This application is now transferred in real time to the responsible authorities. The user can decide by his own to which authority he might submit the application. It can be the location of the business, the starting point of the travelled routes or any other authority in Germany. The application is now dealt by the permission authority. The permission authority which is responsible for the submitted application checks again if the application is complete and worth further approval. If so, the authority sends the application to the other authorities which are affected through the route of the transport. They have to decide whether the transport is possible on the suggested roads or whether there are some limitations. In this case the authority can suggest another route for the oversize transport and send this suggestion back to the responsible authority and further back to the applicant. As soon as all other involved authorities assign the approval of this transport the applicant gets his approval back and can start the transportation.

The safety concept is designed according to the BSI-Standard 100-2 and other relevant standards of the Federal Republic of Germany. In the process the following issues are considered: analysis of the structure of the application process, the required safety levels for different data defined in three levels (normal, high and very high) and categories (availability, confidentiality and integrity). According to these results, the demand for safety of the single components is assessed. These assessments must be also in accordance to the privacy data protection laws and the transport laws.

The most important motivation for the implementation of the VEMAGS-system was the enormous cost and time saving not only for the applicants but also for the permission authorities and road traffic authorities. Since the applicants already use the computer for the commercial correspondence and the editing of bookings and purchase orders it seems to be reasonable to use it also for the application for transport permissions. Earlier they had to fill in an application form manually and telefax or send it via post to the responsible permission authority. This step is redundant with VEMAGS. They can simply transfer the application via internet directly to the permission authority. The permission authority distributes the application further to other relevant authorities via internet. Through this digital correspondence the whole permission process can be shortened by half of the time. Earlier the process took about five working days and today the average process takes two or three days. Cost savings are next to the cuttings of personnel costs for the manual editing, the abolition of the mailing costs for telefax, phone or delivery by post.

In Sweden the application must be made to the local municipality or to the national transport authority. The application must contain information on the applicant, the desired transport route (including loading and delivery site), the vehicle or vehicle combination, type of load, the axle loads, the gross vehicle weight and the dimensions of the vehicle or vehicle combination including load. For heavy transports (with load) a consignor's affirmation must be attached to the application. The consignor's affirmation contains information on the consignor, dimensions and total weight of the load, and includes a statutory declaration on the accuracy of the data provided. For heavy transports or transports which exceed the maximum authorized lengths, vehicle registration documents must be included if the vehicles not are registered in Sweden.

The Swedish Transport Administration can make the following types of permits:

1. a specific permit for one transport on a certain route (valid for one month),
2. a specific permit for repeated transports on a certain route (valid for one month, or up to one year), or
3. a long-term permit (general permit) for a certain road network (valid for one year).

The period of validity of the permits and type of permits varies depending on the dimensions and weights. Every permit contains the conditions which are valid for the actual transport. When carrying out the transport, conditions for the marking of over-wide and overlong vehicles must be observed. These conditions also deal with the use of private escort vehicles and traffic directors. Furthermore, it is the driver's responsibility to assess whether the route is passable for this transport with respect to road construction sites and road clearance (height). If signs or other road equipment must be removed for the passage of the transport, permission must be requested from the respective owners. Sometimes escort may be required for the transport. In these cases licensed traffic directors must be contacted before the transport starts in order to make preparations. Sweden has had this system with private traffic directors since 2005. They have the legal right to direct, stop and give instructions to other road-users. Other road-user must obey a traffic director. In some cases the police may overtake an escort, but that is rare nowadays. The application procedure usually takes three workdays. However, a longer processing period is required if the permit can only be issued in connection with a police escort. Permits are normally valid for a one-month period. In the case of regularly repeated transports, permits can be issued with a validity period of up to one year. The application fee ranges from 600 to 1200 SEK (55 to 110 Euro), depending on the width, length and weight of the transport.

A new regulation was approved from 1st of October 2010, which allows exemptions from regulations of maximum width and length (TSFS-nr 2010:141, *Färd med bred odelbar last, and Färd med lång odelbar last*). The new regulation allows:

- transports with wide indivisible cargo up to 350 cm
- transports with a long vehicle (long indivisible cargo) up to 30 metre if certain specifications of the vehicle are fulfilled.

The combination of exceeding both width and length is not allowed. The conditions regarding route checking, signs on the vehicle etc. are the same as before. There is also an updated regulation concerning road assistance approved from 1st of October 2010 (TSFS-nr 2010:139, *Föreskrifter och allmänna råd om vägtransportledare*). In the new regulation some clarifications and some simplifications have been made.

Since 2011, in Sweden there is a new web-based system in operation. The system is called TRIX – Transport exemption management system for internal and external users. Until now the system only exists in a Swedish version; however, an English version is being planned. The system gives access to the entire application system and also offers simulation possibilities. The system has the following options:

- Simple application

- Advanced application
- Possibility to simulations

Frequent applicants will get authorisation after education as user of the entire system. The system gives the customer an overview of the conditions for their transport in respect to vehicles, routes, bridges and over restrictions. Benefits for the user are a better understanding for the permitting system, faster and more simplified process to get transport permission. Benefits for the permitting authority, the Swedish Transport Administration, are less phone calls and a more cost effective permitting system.

In Poland, General Directorate for National Roads and Motorways and Directors of Customs are responsible for issuing permits for carriers and forwarder transporting oversize cargo. The permits include:

- permit for single transit of oversize vehicle in appointed time (no longer than 7 days) and route, issued by the General Directorate for National Roads and Motorways,
- permit for single transit in appointed time (72 hours) for oversize vehicle crossing the Polish border, issued by the Customs Director, for vehicles satisfying minimum one of the following conditions:
  o height, total weight are normative,
  o total width does not exceed 3 m,
  o total length exceeds permissible value not more than 2 m,
  o axle loads exceed permissible value not more than 15%.

Carriers and forwarders contact the authority which is issuing the permit by telephone, fax or e-mail. Application is usually available on the website. Fulfilled and signed applications can be sent by fax or e-mail and original paper can be delivered afterwards. There is an application generator available on the internet website of the General Directorate for National Roads and Motorways, Central Department in Warsaw (www.gddkia.gov.pl), which is also available in German and English. Usually customers prefer to get the permit personally, because they are in a hurry, but there is a possibility to send it by post at the expense of the applicant.

An application to get a permit for oversize cargo transit has to include:

- name and address of the entrepreneur and the person acting on behalf of him,
- term and addresses of the beginning and end of transit, and in case transport starts or ends outside borders of the country – the place of border crossing,
- type of cargo and its total weight,

- unladen vehicle data: brand, registration number, weight, permissible cargo capacity, number of axles and number of wheels on every axle (in case of combined transport, this data is given separately for motor vehicle and trailer),
- dimensions and total weight of single vehicle/road train with and without cargo,
- wheel base and each axle load of laden vehicle,
- scheme of cargo stowing on the vehicle/trailer.

There are no corridors dedicated for oversize vehicles and every time the transit route is agreed upon with road directors of community, region, voivodship and divisions of GDDKiA. Transit route is appointed on the principle "the shortest way that fulfils the requirements on width, accessible load per axle/axles". Sometimes the shortest distance between two waypoints is to be elongated due to the obstructions on the shortest planned route. If detour is enforced, which is required regularly, three times longer distance has to be worked out. If road transport of one cargo unit is impossible, it is suggested to divide it or to change the mean of transport. Practically no refusal is observed, because applications are fulfilled after phone conference and customer knows beforehand whether the transport operation could be done. Frequently, preplanning of the route is needed so the carriers analyse the chances for the best passage. In some extreme cases, the additional expertise for permissible pressure on the road surface is to be done at the expense of an applicant.

According to the regulations, the maximum period for issuing the permit is 30 days, but practically the administration needs not more than two weeks. In some cases the permit is issued in two days. Issuance fee is established by a special computer program, which is used in the General Directorate for National Roads and Motorways. For a longer route and greater dimension excess the issuance fee is more expensive. Maximum price could be over 10.000 PLN.

In Lithuania, both permit provision and charges are established and framed by the Ministry of Transport and Communications of the Republic of Lithuania. The permits are issued by the State Road Transport Inspectorate under the Ministry of Transport and Communications.

The Inspectorate issues permits to drive on the state roads to vehicles (their combinations) the dimensions and (or) axle(s) weight and (or) vehicle weight with or without load exceeding the maximum authorized one. Loads can be carried by over-dimensional or heavy goods vehicles (their combinations) on the state roads paying the fee for the use of the state road and obtaining a permit. The permit can be issued only for carriage of an indivisible load and if such load may not be carried by other type of vehicle or there is no point to carry them by other types of vehicle. In order to obtain a permit to drive on the state roads for over-dimensioned and heavy goods vehicles (their combinations) the application should be submitted to the State Road Transport Inspectorate.

A permit shall be issued or refused on certain grounds within 5 working days from the date when the application has been received. In case of driving an over-dimensioned vehicle (their combination), when the vehicle (their combination) becomes dangerous to safe traffic, i.e. when the maximum authorized dimensions are exceeded more than: height – 50 cm, (or) width – 100 cm, and (or) length – 500 cm, and (or) a heavy goods vehicle (their combinations, when the authorized axle weight exceeds 8 tonnes, when the weight of a loaded vehicle (their combination) exceeds the authorized weight by two or more times, the permit shall be issued or refused on certain grounds within 20 days from the date when the application has been received.

Upon reception of the permit two different documents confirming payment of the state fees should be presented:

1. Which is for issue of the permit
2. Fee for use of the state roads. State fees must be paid when a decision to issue a permit is taken, in accordance with rates effective on the day of payment and before issuing the permit.

The fees for the permit and roads range depending on the width, length and weight of the transport, are calculated in every case individually.

The demonstration of these national application and permission issuing procedures show differences when it comes to transnational transports in the region. Every country requires valid permissions from the transport forwarder and the truck driver. In addition to obvious difficulties like language barriers, missing information about routes and roads, different tariff systems also invisible cultural differences might appear. Transport forwarders which would like to execute transport also abroad need to have profound knowledge about the foreign market, the infrastructure status and also business cultures of foreign partner companies. During the analysis of the different countries it turned out that business culture differs in regard to corruption, bride and inconsistency in tariff systems. Regional transport companies might have a very good working network with companies abroad which work in alliances for transnational transports. However, next to the "unofficial" cooperation when it comes to knowledge exchange for route planning, personnel exchange with local experience and agreements on return shipments, cooperation on the administration level was also requested.

For many, mainly small companies, is it a great effort to learn about the foreign legislation, legal requirements and permission procedures. The bureaucratic burden on these companies is tremendously high compared to their actual business, namely executing a transport with oversize cargo. Therefore, the European funded project "Oversize Baltic" aimed at introducing a platform for transnational permission application.

OTIN (http://otin.transportoversize.eu)

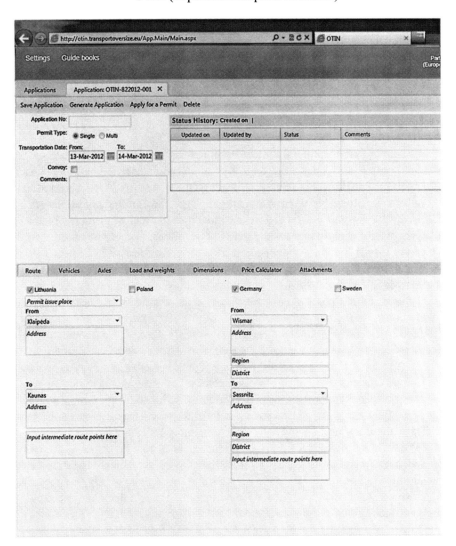

Fig. 1: Screenshot of OTIN application

Even though the one-stop-shop for oversize transport permissions was the first step, better cross-border legislation and regulations need to be implemented in order to harmonise the oversize transports in the South Baltic Sea Region. Further optimizations need to be found for the already limited capacities of the motorways and railways of the federal state. A further increase of individual public transport and the freight transports can be expected, which might lead to even higher maintenance costs (e.g. faster abrasion of the roads), more likely congestions both for passenger and freight transport, and less safety. This might have an influence on limitations for oversize transports with higher restrictions on safety, allowed transport times and permission fees.

5. Practical Implications

In order to be able to adjust the information network of oversize transports to the demanding business sector, this segment should be analysed. Transport clients are numerous, since not only local manufacturers use oversize transport in/ from/ to the regions, but the transit market is large. Two of the largest players in the oversize transport market are the maritime industry and wind energy sector.

There are many large-scale industrial locations, e.g. shipbuilding yards (Neptun Werft), offshore pipeline construction companies (EEW Special Pipe Constructions GmbH), construction companies for ships' engines (Mecklenburger Metallguss) and sites for maritime logistics in the region, which require over-dimensional transports and very heavy lifts. Furthermore, the Ministry of Agriculture, the Environment and Consumer Protection of Mecklenburg-Vorpommern expects a complete power supply through renewable energy sources by 2050. This leads to the assumption that demand for windmills will increase in the following decades. Not only there, however, but in other regions of Europe (Eastern Europe and the Baltic states) as well, establishing Germany as one of the most important locations for construction and export of windmills. In order to ensure a smooth transport chain for oversized cargo movements, specifically the East-West connections need to be more efficient.

Products transported regularly in the South Baltic region, not only internally but also as exports, are windmills and their parts. A standard housing of a windmill weighs around 70 tonnes, the new ones even more than 100 tonnes and the tower segments have a length of more than 22 m and a diameter of around 4 m. Considering that normal bridges across German roads have heights of 4.2 m and the tower segment lies on a trailer, it is the fact that there is almost no headroom left for the transport vehicle under the bridges. These make the transport of such a product challenging for the operator and the customers burdened with the costs for route planning, reconstructions and time investments in the end. All roads, curves, bridges and bottlenecks must be checked and approved even before such an operation starts.

The network for such transportations can be divided into different parameters, according to transport means and cargo classes. The usage of suitable transport means depends on the weight and dimensions of the oversized cargo. Some cargo does not fit on a road truck, some need to be transported to various locations where no other access than by road is possible.

In such cases where a high increase in oversized transports is expected, it might be efficient to build new connections, either road reconstructions or new railways (e.g. in the seaport hinterland in order to supply offshore wind parks). If such a need is confirmed, it may be reasonable to cluster oversize transport clients, since the conditions for a transport permit in Germany are the same for every business, regardless of the sector, company size or transport volume. However, there is no defined route functioning as a corridor so far, since oversized cargo transported in this region is treated more or less individually.

The South Baltic Sea region is not only a strategic location for new technological developments and construction, but also a very important transit market for oversized cargo. The main partners for the transit trade are Germany, the Scandinavian countries, Baltic States (with further connections to Russia), Poland, and neighbouring countries to the south. The increasing demand for oversized transports in the Baltic States and Russia will strengthen the South Baltic Sea region even more as a transit and export market.

The region has the logistical potential to fulfil the requirements of the transport strategy for oversized transports, which will only increase in the future. The main transport routes already exist and will be renewed and enlarged over the next years. Also, the seaports are assumed to be well prepared for oversize transports and are able to fulfil the positions as logistics centres in the oversize transport network.

6. Conclusions

The research results show that even though the one-stop-shop for oversized transport permissions was the first step, better cross-border legislation and regulations need to be implemented in order to harmonise the oversized transports in the South Baltic Sea Region. Further optimizations need to be found for the already limited capacities of the motorways and railways of the region. A further increase of individual public transport and freight transports can be expected, which might lead to even higher maintenance costs (e.g. faster abrasion of the roads), more likely congestions both for passenger and freight transport, and less safety. This might have an influence on limitations for oversize transports with higher restrictions on safety, allowed transport times and permission fees.

References

2025 Forecast for Transport Interdependencies across Germany, accessible http://www.bmvbs.de/cae/servlet/contentblob/43992/publicationFile/1131/2025-forecast-for-transport-interdependencies-across-germany-summary.pdf (21.05.2012)

BSI Standard 100-2 accessible https://www.bsi.bund.de/SharedDocs/Downloads/DE/BSI/Publikationen/ITGrundschutzstandards/standard_1002_pdf.pdf?__blob=publicationFile (31.01.2013)

COM (2009/28)EC. 2009. Directive 2009/28/EC of the European Parliament and of the Council of 23 April 2009 on the promotion of the use of energy from renewable sources and amending and subsequently repealing Directives 2001/77/EC and 2003/30/EC.

EEW Special Pipe Constructions GmbH accessible http://www.eewspc.com/de/ (31.01.2013).

Kuehl, T. and Lemmer, H. 2009. *Mehr Sicherheit fuer Grossraum- und Schwertransporte*, Polizei Verkehr + Technik, Vol. 54, pp. 176–7.

Lukauskas, V. 2011. *A Guide to Oversize and Heavy Transport through Klaipeda Port*, Klaipeda, accessible: http://www.transportoversize.eu/files/Main/strategy/Oversize%20Transport%20Guidebook%20-%20Lithuania.pdf (21.05.2012).

Mecklenburger Metallguss accessible http://www.mmgprop.de/index.php?id=1257 (31.01.2013).

Neptun Werft accessible http://www.neptun-werft.de (31.01.2013).

Rebler, A. 2004. *Das System von Ausnahmegenehmigungen und Erlaubnissen nach der StVO und StVZO, dargestellt am Beispiel der Grossraum- und Schwertransporte*, NVZ Neue Zeitschrift für Verkehrsrecht, Vol. 17, pp. 450–2.

SBSR Oversize Transport Strategy. 2011. Accessible http://www.transportoversize.eu/files/Main/strategy/SBSR%20Oversize%20Strategy%202011.pdf (21.05.2012).

Straßenverkehrsgesetz, accessible http://www.gesetze-im-internet.de/stvg/ (31.01.2013).

StVO, accessible http://www.gesetze-im-internet.de/bundesrecht/stvo/gesamt.pdf (31.01.2013).

StVZO, accessible http://www.gesetze-im-internet.de/stvzo_2012/BJNR067910012.html (31.01.2013).

Trafikförordning (1998:1276), accessible https://lagen.nu/1998:1276 (21.05.2012).

Transportstyrelsen (2005:102), accessible http://www.transportstyrelsen.se/Global/Regler/TSFS_svenska/TSFS%202010/TSFS%202010-143.pdf (21.05.2012).

VEMAGS. 2009. *VEMAGS Auswertung*, Hessisches Landesamt für Straßen- und Verkehrswesen.

Wang, W.; Lu C.; Li Y.; Zhang H. 2007. *Basic Economic Measures in Long-term Effective Mechanism for Administering Overload and Oversize of Motor Vehicles*. Journal of Highway and Transportation Research and Development. Vol. 06.

Yin X.; Wang Y.; Jia S. 2008. *Study on the Strategy of Managing Exceeding Limit and Overload Transportation Based on Transporter's Risk Preference.* Logistics Technology. Vol. 04.

Post-recession Values in Estonian Organisations

Eneken Titov[1], Karin Kuimet[1] and Mari Meel[2]

Abstract

Researchers have proved that sticking to core values is the key issue in an organisation's sustainability. Equally important is the persistence of core values, but also the ability of the leaders to make the employees follow these values. Nevertheless, all organizations have not realized the importance of organizational values and their role in ensuring the sustainability of the organization. The paper deals with the investigation of the values characterising post-recession (2009–2010) Estonian organisations and with the analysis whether these values support sustainability of the organisations.

The aim of our study was to find out whether the values characterising the Estonian organisations are in accordance with the values predicting the success and sustainability of an organisation. The research method used was qualitative method of data analysis. The paper enables to get information about alternations of organisational values under the conditions of economic crisis. As the main result the profiles of values due to the size and type of Estonian organisations were identified. One of the main results was that in all types of organisations the human-central values which support the organisational sustainability were in the focus.

JEL classification codes: L2, M1, D0

Key words: core values; economic crisis; organisational values, Estonia

1. Introduction

Nowadays organisations have the experiences from a whole economic cycle, its impacts and dangers (Arrak 2010), as well as how to connect the core values in the economic cycle to achieve success (Drucker, Peters, Waterman, Hultman etc). Generally, managers do not doubt the importance of corporate values. In the last decades new management theories have been developed (knowledge management, management by objectives, team-leadership etc) where an essential place is held by values. The most important approach is value-based management, which emphasises the prioritization of organisational values and connects these to other management activities. Several researchers have investigated the connections between organisational values, success and sustainability of organisations, confirming the link between innovativeness and success of an organisation (Merrill 2008) and also between cooperation and sustainability (Melé

---

1   Estonian Entrepreneurship University of Applied Sciences
2   Tallinn University of Technology

2012). An investigation of Estonian organisations has led to similar results (Übius et al. 2010; Virovere et al. 2011).

During an economic recession when most of any country's population falls to a lower level of Maslow's hierarchy of needs (with the primary problems being making a living and an increasing lack of jobs), many fundamentalist claims also rise in regard to managerial values: compared to developed societies, only legal obligations are met, while philanthropic and ethical obligations will be left waiting for better times. Based on the same logic, it can be assumed that company managers do not have constant moral certainties or values, but they shift and alter them according to the changes of economic conditions: during the good times they tend to behave according to virtues and humanist ideals – showing more care, respect, valuing the employees etc. On the other hand, during the recession employees are fired more easily and managers, especially when communicating with their employees, are stricter, more aggressive, and even autocratic. Only the values that are directly connected to the company's economic success and sustainability are taken into consideration.

Currently Estonian's general economic figures are improving and there are big expectations for economic growth and decrease of unemployment rate. The studies of the economic environment claim that the recovery of economic growth owes itself to an increase of productivity (Luikmel 2011), while export-oriented organisations fare especially well, due to both the swift economic recovery of major export partners and the elasticity of the labour force's wages, increasing Estonia's competitiveness (Eesti Konjunktuuriinstituut 2011). Estonia has exerted itself in the name of a recovering economic environment and the OECD Economic Survey 2011 brings forth Estonia's commendable activity during the financial crisis (OECD 2011). Nevertheless, the Estonian economy has still plenty of problems that also prevent the development of organisations. The Estonian Institute of Economic Research brings out inflation, unemployment and lack of demand, international competitiveness and qualified labour force as problems (Eesti Konjunktuuriinstituut 2011). Problems more specifically related to the entrepreneurial level, according to estimates by Professor Varblane, are a deficiency of ideas, a necessity to overview and alter current business models, the incapability of entrepreneurs to create intriguing, attractive businesses using their own ideas, a call for diversification of knowledge and the need to integrate or rope in younger generations with new technological proficiencies (Varblane, 2010). Becoming aware of the listed problems offers also the possibility to better the economy in general.

Based on the viewpoint that looking beyond the crisis, a successful business will want to develop strategic leadership capabilities with a strong foundation in ethics and values (Strack, Caye, Thurner, Haen 2009) the authors observed the effect of the economic crisis on Estonian organisations and the values those organisations represent.

The aim of the current study is to find out whether the values characterising the Estonian organisations are in accordance with the values predicting the success and sustainability of an organisation.

The respective research tasks are as follows:

- to find out the values that have been used by the management of Estonian organisations;
- to find out organisations' tactics to achieve sustainability in the period of recession;
- to compare the real values with the patterns of actual practice in the period of recession;
- to ascertain the differences between the real values of different economic sectors and between small and large organisations.

The economic crisis was an opportunity to connect the fundamentals of the theory of value and the behaviour of Estonian organisations, linking Estonian organisations' behaviour and values during the crisis. The paper gives a brief overview about the importance of organisational values and about their connections to the management activity, describes the collection methodology of empirical evidence about organisational values and specifies the real value models characterising the Estonian organisations, differentiating them based on the size and form of organisation.

2. Theoretical Framework: Importance of Organisational Values

Managers in global businesses can help their firms to be successful. An important aspect for the sustainability of an organisation is that the core values must support sustainability and the organisation's goals. All the visionary companies (companies that survived the economic crisis) had a powerful sense of identity and what they wanted to achieve (Collins and Porras 2002). Success is not provided by simple values, but core values. A value is defined as an enduring belief, a specific mode of conduct, which is preferable to other modes (Rokeach 1968). According to Fukuyama (2001), the sustainability of an organisation is directly linked to the question of core values – although we have shared values, they may not yet produce social capital if the values are wrong. Core values are the basic values that everyone in the organisation shares and truly believes in. Once they are embedded in the culture, core values help an organisation ride out difficult times (Evans 2005). In addition to right values (values that lead towards success and sustainability) in an organisation, another important facet is the stability and longevity of such values, since it takes time for values to firmly root themselves. Looking at the fast development of the Estonian economy and society, the style of leadership by Estonian leaders is largely not deriving from enduring values, but enduring leadership is considered to be important to secure sustainability. Enduring leadership is leadership that outlasts and transcends the individual – it has been shown by research to be a predictor of long-term success (Moon 2001). A common system of values and integration of such a system into the behaviour of the organisation gives the organisation an identity and a sense of belonging, which is an important factor in achieving the organisation's goals.

Researchers (Collins et al. 2003) prove that sticking to core values is the key issue in an organisation's sustainability. Wilson and Eilertsen (2010) ascertain that two thirds of managers were convinced that their actions during the crisis remained aligned with the values and visions of the organisation, despite the high pressure from the environment (Wilson et al. 2010). Collins (2003) shows that not all managers let their moral values be shaken by the outside environment. Especially in times of recession, only the companies that did not cross the line beyond their core values managed to survive (Collins et al. 2003).

With reference to Corporate Ethical Values, Hyman (1990) contends that a positive perception of the values and beliefs of the top management by employees will lead to higher performance outcomes. Bergeron (2007) concludes that individuals perceiving high congruity between an organisation's ethical values and their own will feel more motivated. Schwepker (2001) suggests that congruity between the values of an employee and their organisation will positively influence the employee's performance (Sharma et al. 2009). Values can serve as a great unifying force, providing that both corporate and individual values are reasonably congruent binding people together as they move toward the achievement of organisational objectives. Alternatively, dissonant and conflicting values are generators of stress and friction, which undermine managerial leadership. A key metric of good management, then, is whether clear and consistent values have permeated the organisation (Klenke 2005). Deal and Kennedy (1982) associate employees' satisfaction and persistent organisational values, emphasising the managers' job in shaping and enhancing values.

The statement of having the right purposes and values is considered to be important in organisations, but also the leaders' ability to make employees follow those values (Haslam et al. 2010; Whitmire 2005) and to be a model in following those values (Klenke 2005). Alas and Tuulik emphasise the importance of managers in strengthening the values and believe that common values can be attained through improved training and improved management practices, and also by having the right leaders for the job (Alas et al. 2004). Employee orientation as a leader's first value is also emphasised (Jensen 2011) to gain a customer's support and profit in a longer run.

Dealing with values at a difficult time gives a more meaningful result. The literature has examined that links exist between the results and values of an organisation and that periods of crisis affect the results of organisations. Changes in the general environment elicit a need to overview previous values and management activities. It is vital to concentrate on finding the right values and deciding on a plan of action that supports organisational success. Actually, according to Maslow's hierarchy, self-realisation and commitment would enable an organisation to cope with changes while remaining innovative and sustainable (Wilson et al. 2010).

Wang (2009) recommends connecting concrete objectives and values: human resource management performance is associated with partner orientation and harmony; growth potential might be related with global orientation, entrepreneurship, and honesty. Boxx, Odom and Dunn (1991) used Peters and Waterman's seven values of excellence, stated in 1982 (superior quality and service, innovation, importance of people as individuals, importance of details of execution, communication, profit orientation, and goal accomplishment) and analysed their correlation to work satisfaction. According to Maslow's theory, during a time of crisis, concentrating on primary values would be advisable and important

Summing up the theory, there is no doubt that the organisational values play an important role in successful organisational performance and sustainability. Long-term adherence to the organisational values and their connection with the management activities seem to be as important as any other organisational characteristic. Researchers do not quite agree on what the specific values of the organization should be, but in generalised level the basic ethical values and human-oriented value groups are broadly emphasised.

3. Research Design

This research can be classified as a critical discourse analysis (detailed description in Laherand 2008, or Fairclough 2002). In a similar way, we use reports compiled by the students of a management institution for specialised practice. Hirsijärvi (2005) suggests that a data gathering method based on documents, mostly along with other data gathering methods, can be used as an independent method (Flick 2006). In order to determine the effect of the economy on organisations and their values, the authors analysed data derived from 68 reports by management students in practical positions in different organisations. The specialised practices took place in the timeframe of December 2010 till February 2011. The reports are formatted according to a previously formed structure that includes a chapter handling the effect of the economy on an organisation. The compulsory structure also comprised of a chapter handling the strategy, mission, vision and values of an organisation. To ensure validity and reliability of our investigation we used Creswell's (2003) proposed researcher triangulation, which means using different observers to discover or minimise mistakes that come from the researcher's person. Two researchers read independently each report and noted down the values carried by the description. Next, the discovered values were analysed. Values agreed upon were added to the database. Where different values appeared, our third researcher read the report too. If her opinion was the same as either of the two others, those values were added to the database; if not, values were not added.

Since 16 descriptions of organisations did not include, or did not clarify, the values of the organisation, the final selection consists of 68 organisations that related themselves to 187 values. The values were grouped and a common denominator was found for essentially the same ones (e.g. communication skill, communicativeness, communication etc. were grouped as the value "communication"). Further analysis was based on the list of values that consists of the value groups.

By size, the surveyed organisations were divided as small (23), medium sized organisations (25) and large organisations, which accounted for 20 of the total number of organisations, by field: public sector organisations (16), manufacturing organisations (11) and organisations relating to service (41).

4. Results

The activities of organisations in the years 2009–2010 were most affected by the decreasing demand for products and services and decrease of the income basis (mentioned in 32 instances). Lowering of the expenses was achieved in 19 cases by decreasing staff expenses, also by lay-offs or minimising working hours (mentioned in 14 instances). In response to changes in economic circumstances, some organizations were able to create new markets and new services (mentioned in 10 instances). In five instances, structural changes were carried out in order to manage changes. Four of the studied organisations were not affected by the economic crisis and one organisation even gained better opportunities for development.

The most frequently appearing values in the organisations under research were competency and cooperation. By rate of occurrence, values such as development, fairness and friendliness followed.

Comparing the represented values by the field of organisation, it became apparent that manufacturing organisations held quality and fairness in high regard. Organisations providing services mentioned competency and cooperation the most. In organisations in the public sector, two values – friendliness and competency – were dominant. As important for organisations in the public sector, by rate of occurrence, were social responsibility, ethics, motivation, cooperation and development (Fig. 1).

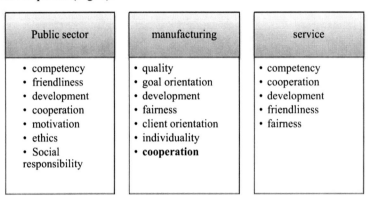

Fig. 1: The most frequent values by field of organisation. Source: compiled by the authors

The results of the public sector differ from the results of manufacturing and services sector on the basis of two values: neither manufacturing nor service sector organisations pointed out such values as ethics and social responsibility. Only manufacturing organisations valued the goal orientation. At the same time, manufacturing organisations attached high importance to quality and client orientation (those values were mentioned also in service organisations, but only on a few occasions), according to our results – in the public sector cases those values were not mentioned.

As a result of this study, it is possible to claim that smaller organisations value cooperation, fairness and quality. Medium sized organisations were dominated by the value of development and cooperation also, while large organisations concentrated on friendliness, followed by cooperation (Fig. 2).

Based on the size of organisation, the values differed less, only two differences can be brought out – only large-sized organisations regarded helpfulness as essential and quite surprisingly, large organisations did not mention the significance of quality at all.

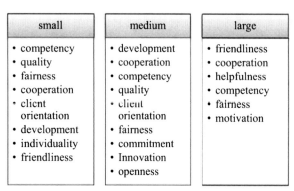

Fig. 2:   The occurrence of values by size of organisation (under 50 – small, 51–250 –
           medium, and over 250 – large organisation). Source: compiled by the authors.

The results of this study support the stance that in the case of value-based
leadership in reality all organisations are value-driven (Fitzgerald et al. 2004)
and also the opinion of Marie J. Kane (2009), who has also described how core
values affect performance. Comparing the behaviour of the organisations under
study during the recession and juxtaposing them with the values they represent,
it is clear that the organisations that attempted to develop new services or expand into new markets in a tough economic climate were most fond of competency, quality, speed, entrepreneurship, courage, orientation towards family, orientation towards development and achieving goals. Somewhat paradoxically, for
the organisations that mostly utilised cutting of expenses, and lay-offs to adapt
to a new economic environment, the apparently popular values were friendliness, cooperation, motivation, support, family orientation, fairness and trust.

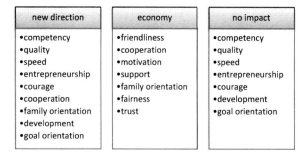

Fig. 3:   The most frequent values according to organisations' behaviour during the
           crisis. Source: compiled by the authors

These organisations whose economic indicators were only slightly touched by the crisis pursued such values as competency, quality, speed, entrepreneurship, courage, development and goal orientation (Fig 3). The common feature for the organisations, which in the years of decline had no need for the policy of strict saving, was sharing such values as competency, quality, speed etc. At the same time, for the organisations, which had to maintain the policy of saving the most frequent values were friendliness, cooperation, motivation, support etc – that is the employee-centred values.

5. Discussion and Conclusions

In this paper we researched post-recession management values. We started out with the idea that in difficult economic conditions less attention is paid to the ethical values, and economy-based values will take their places. At the same time, several earlier researches made us doubt that. They stated that those companies whose core values and mission remained constant in long-term plans, survived any crises better. The research confirms the importance of ethical values such as fairness, friendliness, cooperation, motivation, supportiveness, family-orientation, benevolence, trust, understanding and honesty, as important for securing sustainability. According to that, the previous opinion is proved right, meaning that in hard times economic concerns prevail over ethical and philanthropic.

The results of the study conclude that the organisations are more intent on finding new solutions instead of cutting costs to overcome the crisis. At the same time it points out that organisations' intent on opening up to new markets or developing their services in a time of crisis were dominated by values hinting to entrepreneurial tendencies. The results also indicate that the organisations which managed the recession the best respected entrepreneurial values like professionalism, quality, speed, entrepreneurship, proactivity, courage, orientation towards development and achieving goals. Those results can be compared to a study undertaken in Japanese organisations, claiming that value orientation of entrepreneurship might possibly contribute to innovative activities and new value creation in the future, and therefore, affect the long-term performance (Wang 2009). The difference between the studies lies in the fact that the Estonian organisations, in a time of economic crisis, were more intent on optimising costs and activities associated with it, rather than developing the organisations, so values directed towards entrepreneurship were not as prevalently present. The authors believe that the lack of entrepreneurial values might also derive from our historical background since the socialist economic climate of the Soviet Union did not support entrepreneurship and proactivity, and inclination towards such values might have even brought along sanctions.

The explicit model of organisational culture and effectiveness, which is based on four cultural traits of effective organisations, says that effective organisations empower people, organise around teams, and develop human capability (Denison and Mishra 1998; Denison et al. 2002). In our research the results were the opposite – for the organisations which were forced to severely cut the expenses the main object of the cut was the employee-centred values. Such results could be caused by the common concept of the traditional behaviour in economic crises – saving at any price – so the managers are forced to give up the core values that are common for times of well being. Other researches (Katzenbach 1993; Spreitzer 1995) bring out that employees at all levels feel that they have input into decisions that will affect their work and they see a direct connection to the goals of the organisation – our results confirmed this statement – goal orientation seems to be one of the most important values and supports the organisation's sustainability in the times of crisis.

A value which many authors have emphasised as ensuring sustainability is client orientation – adaptable organisations are driven by their customers; they take risks and learn from their mistakes, and have capability and experience at creating change (Nadler 1998; Senge 1990). So also based on our investigation, the client orientation was one of the most frequent value, although the frequency of its occurrence was not high enough for estimating its influence on the behaviour of organisations in the crisis. Moorman points out that the most important value is fairness and it should even be one of the core values of the organisations (Moorman et al. 1993). Fairness was the most prevalent value in organisations dealing with manufacture and in organisations that were rather small. Comparing our results to Hultman's important values (Hultman et al. 2002), fairness can be mentioned again.

The comparison of values and activities in Estonian organisations, which deal with the managing of the financial crisis, showed that differences between managing to deal with the crisis and expressed values of organisations did exist. The values based on humanity were more popular in Estonian organisations during the period of crisis – values such as fairness, cooperation, friendliness, motivation, support, family-orientation, honesty, trust and understanding. In a central position is survival rather than competition, but still more successful managing is related to values such as competency, professionalism, quality, speed, entrepreneurship, courage, orientation towards development and achieving goals.

In conclusion, it can be said that since sustainability in a society depends on the sustainability of organisations, and studies confirm that values play a vital role in successful managing, then paying attention to the given topic and applying values as instruments to better leadership is inarguably important and worth disserting. It can also be concluded that the Estonian organisations' behaviour and change of values during the crisis are similar to the general principles of the theory of value. Nevertheless, according to the possibility to interpret the results in many ways and emphasising the context of Estonia, our research added new aspects for further investigation. Also, the correlation between the change of the organisational values and the major redundancies in the organisation could be an important research goal.

6. Limitations and Future Research

As always, a qualitative research leaves room for assumptions. Finding and grouping the values is subjective and largely dependent on researchers, but hopefully the consensus analysis we used helped reduce the subjectivity. Research of organisational values based only on some of the reports is clearly not sufficient for making generalizations on all trends in organisational practices. To get applied results a research in management practices of organisations would be necessary and to get better results and verify the results another research on effective management practices and management objectives in organisations will be necessary. To learn about organisation's actual micro climate and system of relations the research should be continued using conflict as a tool for measuring ethics at workplace and on the basis of that, work out methods for organisations for adopting higher values.

In the future, a similar study should be conducted in order to find out whether a change in the economy results in discernible changes in the core values of organisations.

References

Alas, R. and Tuulik, K. 2004. Ethical Values and Commitment in Estonia companies// EBS Review. Vol. 19.

Arrak, A. 2010. Quo vadis, kriisijärgne majandusteadus? Postimees. March 4, 2010.

Bergeron, D. M. 2007. The Potential Paradox of Organizational Citizenship Behavior: Good Citizens at What Cost? // The Academy of Management Review. Vol. 32, No. 4.

Boxx, W. R., Odom, R. Y., & Dunn, M. G. 1991. Organizational values and value congruency and their impact on satisfaction, commitment, and cohesion: An empirical examination within the public sector. Public Personnel Management, 20, pp. 195–206.

Collins, J. and Porras, J. 2002. Heast suurepäraseks (Good to Great). Tallinn: OÜ Väike Vanker.

Collins, J. 2003. Loodud kestma (Built to last: Successful Habits of Visionary Companies). Tallinn: OÜ Väike Vanker.

Creswell, J. W. 2003. Research Design: qualitative, quantitative, and mixed methods approach (2nd ed.). Thousand Oaks, California: Sage Publications.

Deal, T. E. and Kennedy, A. A. 1982. Corporate Cultures: The Rites and Rituals of Corporate Life. Harmondsworth: Penguin Books.

Denison, D. R. and Mishra, A. K. 1998. Does organizational culture have an impact on quality? A study of culture and quality in 92 manufacturing organizations. Acad. Management Convertion, San Diego, CA (August).

Denison, D. R., Cho, H. J., Young J. L. 2002. Diagnosing organizational cultures: Validating a model and method. Working paper, International Institute for Management Development, Lausanne, Switzerland.

Drucker, P. F. 1972. Concept of the corporation. New York: John Day Co.

Drucker, P. F. 2000. Juhtimise väljakutsed 21. Sajandiks (Management Challenges for the 21st Century). Tallinn: Pegasus.

Eesti Konjunktuuriinstituut. Konjunktuur No. 1, 176. Internet access: http://www.ki.ee/wordpress/wp-content/uploads/2011/04/Konjunktuur_nr_1_2011_176_esitlus1.pdf [Accessed May 3, 2011]

Evans, B. 2005. Best way to improve your performance: improve how you impart core values // Handbook of Business Strategy. Vol. 6, No 1.

Fairclough, N. 2001. Language and power (2nd ed.). Harlow: Longman.

Fitzgerald, G. A. and Desjardins, N. M. 2004. Organizational Values and Their Relation to Organizational Performance Outcomes // Atlantic Journal of Communication. Vol. 12, No. 3.

Flick, U. 2006. An introduction to qualitative research. London: Sage.

Fukuyama, F. 2001. Suur vapustus: inimloomus ja ühiskondliku korra taastamine (The Great Disruption). Tallinn: Kirjastus kirjastus Tänapäev.

Haslam, S. A., Reicher, S. D., Platow, M. J. 2010. The new psychology of leadership: Identity, influence and power// London & New York: Psychology Press.

Hirsjärvi, S., Remes, P., & Sajavaara, P. 2005. Uuri ja kirjuta. Tallinn: Medicina.

Hyman, M. R. 1990. Ethical Codes are not Enough // Business Horizons. Vol. 33, No. 2.

Hultman, K. and Gellerman, B. 2002. Balancing Individual and Organizational Values: Walking the Tightrope to Success // San Francisco, CA: Jossey-Bass/Pfeiffer.

Jensen, J. 2011. Presentation at the 2011 North European Exchange Meeting, Norway, May 5–6.

Kane, M. J. 2009. CEO's Speak On Leadership – Authenticity // The CEO Refresher, 24.05.2009.

Katzenbach, R. 1993. The Wisdom of Teams: Creating the High Performance Organization. Harvard Business School Press, Boston, MA.

Klenke, K. 2005. Corporate values as multi-level, multi-domain antecedents of leader behaviors // International Journal of Manpower. Vol. 26, No. 1.

Laherand, M. L. 2008. Kvalitatiivne uurimisviis (Qualitative research). Tallinn: OÜ Infotrükk.

Luikmel, P. 2011. Eesti majandusest pärast krooni. Paper presented PARE's Conference, Tallinn, November 1.

Melé, D. 2012. Management Ethics: Placing Ethics at the Core of Good Management. PalgraveMacmillan, London.

Merrill, P. 2008. Creating an Innovation Process and Innovative Culture. ASQ Quality Press, Wisconsin, Milwaukee.

Moon, H. 2001. The two faces of conscientiousness: Duty and achievement striving within escalation decision dilemmas // Journal of Applied Psychology. Vol. 86.

Moorman, R. H., Niehoff, B. P., Organ, D. W. 1993. Treating Employees Fairly and Organizational Citizenship Behavior: Sorting the Effects of Jobs Satisfaction, Organizational Commitment, and Procedural Justice // Employee Responsibilities and Rights Journal. Vol. 6, No. 3.

Nadler, D. 1998. Champions of Change: How CEOs and Their Companies Are Mastering the Skills of Radical Change. Jossey-Bass, San Francisco, CA.

OECD Economic Surveys: Estonia 2011. 2011. OECD, p 124.

Peters, T. and Waterman, R. 1982. In search of excellence: Lessons from American's best-run companies. New York: Warner Books.

Rokeach, M. 1968. Beliefs, Attitudes and Values: A Theory of Organization and Change. San Francisco, CA: Josey-Bass.

Schwepker, C. H. 2001. Ethical Climate's Relationship to Job Satisfaction. Organizational Commitment and Turnover Intention in the Salesforce // Journal of Business Research. Vol. 54, No.1.

Senge, P. 1990. The Fifth Discipline: The Art and Practice of the Learning Organization. Doubleday/Currency, New York.

Sharma, D., Borna, S., Stearns J. M. 2009. An Investigation of the Effects of Corporate Ethical Values on Employee Commitment and Performance: Examining the Moderating Role of Perceived Fairness // Journal of Business Ethics. Vol. 89.

Spreitzer, G. 1995. Psychological empowerment in the workplace: dimensions, measurement, and validation. Acad. Management J., 38 1442–1465.

Strack, R., Caye, J-M., Thurner, R., Haen, P. 2009. Creating peoples advantage in time of crisis. The Boston Consulting Group.

Übius, Ü. and Alas. R. 2010. The Innovation Climate – Predictor for Corporate Social Responsibility, EBS Review, No 27, pp. 70–87.

Varblane, U. 2010. Eesti teel majanduskriisist välja. Internet access: http://www.tallinn.ee/est/g7636s50597 [Accessed April 14, 2011].

Virovere, A., Titov, E. and Meel, M. 2011. Change of Management Values in Estonian Business Life in 2007–2009. Chinese Business Review. 10(11).

Wang, Y. 2009. Examination on Philosophy-Based Management of Contemporary Japanese Corporations: Philosophy, Value Orientation and Performance // Journal of Business Ethics. Vol. 85, No. 1.

Whitmire, K. 2005. Leading through shared values // Leader to Leader. Vol. 37.

Wilson, J. W. and Eilertsen, S. 2010. How did strategic planning help during the economic crisis? // Strategy & Leadership. Vol. 38, No.2

Propagated and Real Values in Estonian Organisations according to Conflict Management Analysis

Anu Virovere[1], Eneken Titov[2], Karin Kuimet[2] and Mari Meel[1]

Abstract

The main indicator of continuous organisational success is sustainability, whereas sustainability of an organisation is directly connected to the shared values of it. The authors suggest three groups of organisational values: described, propagated and shared or real values. Most talk in organisations is about propagated values, but an important question is whether the propagated and real values of an organisation match. Otherwise the culture and the actions of the organisation are not in harmony with each other. The main aim of the paper is to demonstrate the differences between propagated and real values in Estonian organisations. The authors point out the possibility to use conflict analyses for estimating which are the real (shared) values of an organisation. The methods of case study (case analyses) and critical discourse analyses are used for the investigation.

In the ideal case, propagated and real values ought to coincide, but the results of the research demonstrate that while propagated values in Estonian organisations are on higher levels of value systems, then the real values are usually placed on the lower level. One of the results of the study is that Estonian managers know and speak about values that are important for remaining/becoming sustainable, but in real life they do not follow these values. The results of the research confirm the need for a change in this field.

JEL classification codes: L2, M1, D0

Key words: Values, organisational values, described values, propagated values, real (shared) values; value systems, conflict management.

1. Introduction

The command-and-control approach to management has become less and less viable in recent years. Globalisation, new technologies and changes in how companies create value and interact with customers have sharply reduced the efficacy of a purely directive, top-down model of leadership (Groysberg and Slind 2012). Still the old managerial methods and paradigms are hard to disappear and in reality the development of value-centred way of thinking is slow. Lencioni (2012) said that there are two parts to the equation of organisational success, being smart and being healthy. According to Lencioni (2012), on the smart side of the equation there are the elements of strategy, marketing, finance and technology. On the healthy side of the equation are minimal politics, mini-

---

1   Tallinn University of Technology
2   Estonian Entrepreneurship University of Applied Sciences

mal confusion, high productivity and low turnover. Business leaders mostly focus on the smart side of the equation, and just do not pay much attention to the healthy side (Lencioni 2012). At the same time, no common understanding of the definition of "good management," which also considers the principles of "being healthy," is present. Melé says that an essential part of "good management" is ethics and considering the manager's action and its dynamism, that is, the effects of such action and the subsequent consequences for future actions" (Melé, 2012a). In order to lead the organisation to success with a smaller amount of rules, policies and with greater flexibility more attention should be paid to the organisational values.

The authors suggest three groups of organisational values: described (which exist only formally), propagated (which managers regard to be right) and shared or real values (which are factually used in managerial practices). Described values are the least option for an organisation to deal with values. Usually it only means naming the values. Propagated values are the values that managers regard to be right; real values are those that the managers actually use in their managerial practice, decision-making and conflict management.

One important guideline for developing good management is given in the literature about organisational values. In general it carries two approaches – philosophical and anecdotal – and in both cases managing values has been tied to the success of the organisation (Buchko 2007). The companies that are classified as high performers are assumed to have a strong value-driven culture and their core values guide the decisions and actions of organisational members (Ofori and Sokro 2010). And again the most important part in value management lies among the managers. For example, Collins presents a five-level managerial classification (Collins 2000, 2011) where the highest, fifth level is characterised by the following: they share core values, they don't need to be tightly managed, they understand that they do not have a job – they have responsibilities and they do what they say and they will do it 100 percent of the time.

An organisation's value system reflects the patterns of conflict and compatibility among values, not the relative importance among values. Hocker and Wilmont (1995) defined a conflict emphasising the independence of parties involved: a conflict is a communication process between two individuals who are dependent on each other and both sense mutually discrepant goals and intrusion into reaching their goals (Likert 1976). "The strategies and principles used by a society and all its organisations for dealing with disagreements and conflict reflect the basic values and philosophy of the society" (Likert 1976).

Often in organisations the values are described and an effort made to propagate them to the employees and integrate in everyday actions. A more complex question remains how to evaluate if the desired values have imprinted themselves in the organisation. One way of evaluating if values have been imprinted is through conflict management practices. The analysis of conflict management demonstrates which the real values in an organisation are.

Previous conflict researches in Estonia (Virovere and Rihma 2008) and abroad (Harigopal 1995) have presented the most common causes of conflicts due to organisational issues (limited resources and their distribution, interdependency, differences in goals and in viewpoints, managerial mistakes, unclear status and communication problems). While analysing conflicts it is important to determine whether the conflict is solved or unsolved and then we discover which values have been used during the conflict solving and decision making process. In addition to the main characteristics of conflict three important aspects can also be brought out: conflict is always related to relationships, there are several parties in a conflict and there is a problem or main question that has caused the conflict (Virovere and Rihma 2008).

The main aim of the paper is to demonstrate the differences between propagated and real values in Estonian organisations. Until now there have been many investigations about organisational values, and on the other hand, also investigations about conflict management. But there is a gap in connecting of these two phenomena. The authors of the present paper proceed from the hypothesis that the real (shared) values of an organisation reveal themselves in the behaviour and decisions of the managers and in how they manage conflicts. Therefore through investigation of the conflict cases we can find out which are the real values in the organisations. For testifying the hypotheses we at first focus on the investigation of the cases of conflict management in Estonian organisations to find out which are the real values the managers proceed from. As follows, we analyse the values the Estonian managers propagate: these are the values they consider to be right. By comparing these two groups we can find out how essential the gap between real and propagated values in our organisations is. We believe that such an investigation makes it possible to create development systems for the organisations to minimize the gap between propagated and real values and to harmonize the management of organisations.

2. Theoretical Framework

2.1. Conflict as a research tool for revealing organisation's general status and values

A comprehensive review of the conflict literature yielded this consensus definition: conflict is a process in which one party perceives that its interests are being opposed or negatively affected by another party (Wall and Callister 1995). Deutsch (1973, 1980) proposed that individual values affect everyone's expectations, interactions and outcomes as they deal with conflict. Conflict as a research tool is a very informative phenomenon for revealing an organisation's general status. A conflict is the result of a closer spatial distance between two actors or firms, leading to a contact stimulus and a reciprocal stimulus, which is perceived as a threat for the respective security or identity (Cappellin 2011).

Usually people do not believe that conflict might be a good thing. According to Lencioni (2012), arguing and discussing issues (solving a conflict) tend to form stronger and healthier teams. The conflict management is a major function of every organisation, including business firms and governmental agencies (Likert 1976). Conflict solving style is directly linked to the microclimate of an organisation (Volkema and Bergman 1995).

Conflicts are a way of confronting reality and create new solutions through problems and conflict is necessary for true involvement, empowerment and democracy. Through debating different perspectives, people voice their concerns and create solutions responsive to several points of view. Conflict provides an opportunity to form and express our needs, opinions and positions (de Dreu and de Vliert 1997). A well-managed conflict is an investment for the future. People trust each other more, feel more powerful and efficient, and believe their joint efforts will pay off. Feeling more able and united, people are more prepared to contribute to their groups and organisations. Success in turn further strengthens relationships and individuality (Tjosvold 1997). The consequences of a positive conflict – strong relationships, productivity and individuality – have to be managed (de Dreu & de Vliert 1997). Through conflict management we can find out what is the organisation's culture, values and microclimate. Inappropriately managed conflicts at the organisational and individual level have resulted in dysfunctional consequences for both, while effectively managed conflicts have contributed to mutual survival, growth and well-being (Harigopal 1995). The essential elements of each conflict and methods of resolving them reveal a lot about organisational culture, workplace relations end ethics.

The conflict study carried out in EBS (Estonian Business School) shows that many conflicts in Estonian organisations have been left unsolved or have been solved by using power over the employees and they have often left the company (Virovere and Liigand 2002). As we want to evaluate organisations at the level of competitiveness, ethics and success originated from theories of intellectual capital (Roos et al. 1997), internal marketing (Ballantine and Christopher 1995) and business ethics (Chryssides and Kaler 1996), the success and goal achievement of an organisation depend on how the people inside the organisation are treated. Conflict management strategies show vividly how employees are treated in the organisation and thereby it is possible to demonstrate the values that the organisation exploits. Values and value-driven leadership have received a lot of attention in the last decade. Companies are defining their values in the same way as individuals are seeking theirs (Sydänmaanlakka 2007).

The appearance of a certain type conflicts in an organisation depends on people's beliefs and values. While solving the conflicts managers' real values become essential. Constructive conflicts are connected to organisation's development. Failure tolerance and giving the employee an opportunity to learn from mistakes has been found to be a building block of organisational innovativeness (Jaakson et al. 2011). Also constructive conflict handling and free expression of opinions is positively related to innovation (Leavy 2005, Bhates and Khasawneh 2005, Dobny 2008).

In the case of constructive conflicts it can be seen that while solving the conflict all parties' interests, needs and values have been taken into consideration. Sydänmaanlakka introduces the principles of ethical leadership, which provide a foundation for the development of sound ethical leadership. According to these principles, ethical leaders respect others, serve others, are just, honest and build a community. To be an ethical leader, we must be sensitive to the needs of others, treat others in the ways that are just and care for others (Sydänmaanlakka 2003). In Mele's opinion the willingness of managers to serve others with a sense of selflessness, and even self-sacrifice is important. This requires concern for other people, helping them to achieve worthy objectives (Melé 2012a).

Conflicts are an important source for a new solution and they should not be suppressed, even though they are emotionally difficult. Bringing conflicts upfront assumes trust and trust is also at the core of employee participation (Bhates and Khasawneh 2005).

2.2. Values in organisations

The word "values" is used frequently but it is difficult to define it unanimously. The concept of organisational values has no single and widely accepted definition (Ofori and Sokro 2010). Values can be observed at different levels (individual, organisational and group values), they can be differentiated by the degree and place of exposure (Schein 2004, Gini 2004, Lencioni 2012), scope (Rokeach 1973) and other characteristics. Even more complexity to value research is added by using words "principles", "beliefs" etc as synonyms to "values" (Ofori and Sokro 2010, O'Reilly 1989, Debrah and Quick 2006). The confusion continues until an agreement about common instruments and concepts will been reached (Connor and Becker (1994). Extensions such as exposed values, shared values, core values, stated values etc are also widely used while describing the organisational values.

Although there is a lot of confusion using the concept of values a common understanding has been reached in some aspects – the values cannot be seen or heard and can only be observed in how they manifest themselves through attitudes, preferences, decision making, and other behaviour. If values are not passed on, they cease to exist; values have to be kept constant (Schein 2004, Rokeach 1973, Edvardsson et al. 2006).

Different values that are hierarchically bound create a value system. There are several value systems, the best known of them probably are the Schumacher's model of organisation as a value system, Melé's model of five levels of human quality, and Beck's and Cowan's eight-value system. A value system is frequently understood as the ordering and prioritisation of a set of values (principles, standards or qualities considered worthwhile or desirable) that an actor or a society of actors holds. However, the values that a group or an actor holds may fall into several different categories since the concept of values is multifaceted (Abreu and Camarinha-Matos 2008). Every employee brings into the organisation his/her own values. These values give the organisation its „face", which develops when individual value systems coincide sufficiently and have a common understanding to smooth the difference. Usually, in this way a small number of interrelated shared values develop instead of one particular value. These values form the organisation's value system. None of these value systems is internally better or worse than any other.

The existing distribution of values/ systems is not uniquely related to the level of awareness within the organisation's values. According to previous studies and results, for this research, organisational values are divided into three groups – described, propagated and shared (real) values (figure 1) – that are mutually hierarchically bound. Described values are the least option for an organisation to deal with values. Usually it only means naming the values without concentrating on their propagation to the employees or implementing them in everyday practices. Propagated values are the second level where trying to communicate described values to the employees or using them in everyday actions are present. The third and highest level of values is shared values. In that case describing values and propagating them to the employees has been successful – values are used in real work and decision-making processes. In every organisation only those values are accepted that are exploited by management.

It is possible and necessary to manage organisational values and strong culture and inner agreement on the values guarantee the success of the organisation (Martin and Frost, 1999). An important role in managing values lies on the management of the organisation because values are a means of influencing be-

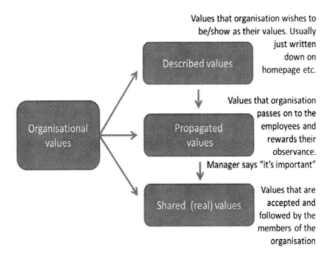

Fig. 1: Simplified hierarchy of organisational values. Source: compiled by the authors

haviours without the need to resort to formal structures, systems, strategies, or control mechanisms (Viinamäki 2012). Leaders should create a clear definition of organisational sustainability values, which is consistently communicated and reinforced throughout the organisation. It is also the tasks of managers to guarantee that the values are in harmony with each other (Driscoll and Hoffmann 2000) and also with the organisation's mission, vision and strategy (Jaakson 2010). Variance in values is one of the sources of conflicts. Value congruence exists when there is no conflict between the various elements in a value system. Value congruence predictably produces positive outcomes and affect that will result when an individual's values are congruent with those of other persons or entities (e.g. a supervisor or an organisation) (Klenke 2005).

In the context of value systems it can not be said that the value is good or bad, it is very difficult to give an estimation of whether the values of the organisation are useful or not. In this study the Mele's Value System is used to compare the described and real values of the organisations. From the very beginning organisations and their managers have been focusing on people to improve the efficiency, trying to achieve goals using minimal resources, "treating" employees as values for their "selves", and achieving the effectiveness and sustainability – these are the phenomena that accompany the first value (Melé 2012b, Schumacher 1973). Melé divides organisations into five groups according to the attitude towards people in them. In management, five levels of human quality in dealing with people can be distinguished: (1) mistreatment, (2) indifference toward people, (3) respectful treatment, (4) concern for people's interests, and (5) favouring mutual esteem and cooperation (Melé 2012a). Each level is character-ised by certain values following of which characterises the quality of manage-ment.

Mistreatment of people is the lowest level of human quality in dealing with people. All of these behaviours violate basic human rights and are, therefore, blatant injustice, contrary to the respect due to human dignity and to the Golden Rule (Melé 2012a). When people are mistreated in an organisation their motiva-tion to work declines essentially and therefore also the organisation's sustaina-bility sinks. Also many ethical conflicts occur at that level. The analysis of con-flicts in Estonian companies showed that among ethical rights the employees' right to participation and right to job satisfaction were violated most frequently (Virovere et al. 2002).

On the second level of treatment there is no external mistreatment, but peo-ple do not receive any encouragement, emotional support, consideration or recognition. People are used for achieving economic goals, maybe employing some psychological technique to obtain more profitability from them, but with-out any consideration beyond this utilitarian goal. Many conflicts and discontent of employees may occur at this level (Mele 2012a).

The third level is characterised by justice – give to each what is due, includ-ing respect and the promotion of human rights. From the management point of view, this level lacks shared vision and common shared values. Frequent con-flicts also occur at this level, however, caused rather by lack of mutual under-standing (Mele 2012a). The study of conflicts in different companies in Estonia has showed that both managers and employees lack emotional competence based on emotional intelligence (Virovere et al. 2002).

The fourth level expresses acting toward people not only with recognition and respect, but also showing concern for their interests and compassion for their problems (Melé 2012a). The level describes wide-spread understanding of excellent management; however, although attention is given to the employees in such organisation, social responsibility is not sufficiently prioritised. However, while taking care of each employee's well-being and interests, one must not for-get the common goals and sustainability of the organisation.

On the fifth level of human quality concern is not limited to justice and care, but to pro-actively promoting a high consideration of the person and concern for personal development, mutual esteem among people, and a willingness for co-operation and service toward the common good. This level corresponds to the Values-Based View of Strategy in O'Reilly's (2000) approach, meaning that the ability to execute a strategy depends on an organisation's ability to attract and retain great people and, more important, to use their knowledge, wisdom, and insights. At this level a willingness of cooperation and service toward the common good are revealed. Merrill (2008) argues that collective knowledge is fundamental for innovation. A new product portfolio must include a number of long-term and potentially major innovations in order for an organisation to have a healthy future.

3. Research Design

To discover the propagated values we used papers published in a leading Estonian managerial magazine „Director" (year 2011). To detect the real values we used cases of conflict management. Conflict management refers to how members of the organisation deal with the conflict situation.

Based on the results of a study by Enterprise Estonia (EAS) and professional practice reports (EAS 2011, Titov, Kuimet and Meel (forthcoming)) it can be seen that so-called higher values are not used by Estonian organisations. The higher values are values which are described in the top of the value hierarchies (systems). The main aim of the paper was to demonstrate the differences between propagated and real values in Estonian organisations according to Mele's values system (hierarchy). To investigate either of these value groups we had to use different research methods. To discover the real values we chose conflict analysis as the research tool, because conflict is very informative – in the conflict resolution process the appearing behaviours and strategies demonstrate the values and principles present in the organisation and that allows us to see the status of the organisation in general. The basis for gathering data included student papers that described real conflict situations in specific organisations. The choice was made from analyses of conflict situations written in 2011. The students had to describe a conflict that took place in a specific organisation, analyse the cause, type and resolution (or unsettlement) of the conflict. The sample constituted of 39 TUT (Tallinn University of Technology) and 21 EBS (Estonian Business School) student papers. While analysing the cases we paid attention to the issue of resolution of the conflict. We anticipated that successful resolution of conflicts necessitates behaviours and solutions that are connected to so-called higher values like mutual esteem and cooperation, concern for people, respectful treatment and indifference toward people. Altogether 60 conflict descriptions were analysed. According to the size of organisations that were the basis for the conflict descriptions, the sample divided into three groups – small enterprises (24), medium sized enterprises (9) and large enterprises (27). In 15 organisations horizontal and in 45 organisations vertical conflicts took place. To reduce the subjectivity at least two members of our research group read each conflict analysis. Based on the conflict we discovered the values that caused the conflict and also those values that were used in resolving or not resolving the conflict.

For discovering the propagated values we used critical discourse analysis that is frequently used for qualitative studies (look, e.g. Laherand 2008 or Fairclough 2001 or Lauristin 2000): we used above-mentioned magazine papers as the documents for our study. To ensure validity and reliability of the investigation, similarly to real values finding process, we used researcher triangulation proposed by Creswell (2003): two of us read independently each paper and wrote down the values that the paper carried. Next the discovered values were analysed. Values in the paper that we agreed upon us were added to the database. If different values appeared, the third of us read the paper by oneself. If her opinion was the same as either of the others, those values were added to the database; if not, the values were deleted. In 2011, there were 21 papers that revealed no clear values. The values added in the database were analysed and similar ones were gathered together. If necessary, the same papers were re-read to make sure that similarly named values would represent values with the same meaning. One hundred and fifty four papers in 2011 issues were read and 514 values were written down. The values were then grouped and a common denominator was found for essentially the same values (e.g. communication skill, communicativeness, communication etc were grouped as one value: communication).

After ascertaining the real and propagated values, it was determined on which Melé's level (mutual esteem and cooperation, concern for people, respectful treatment, indifference toward people, mistreatment) those values were positioned. Melé has used 10 principles in the areas of human rights, labour, the environment and anti-corruption (principles of the UN Global Compact) (Melé 2012a) while describing his levels. To guarantee better compliance the authors of this paper used the same principal descriptions while placing the values on Melé's levels.

4. Results

Depending on the type of conflict, two types appeared most frequently – conflicts due to communication mistakes and due to goal differences. In spite of the dominant economic environment only one limited resource conflict appeared among 60 analysed conflicts. No direct connection was found between the type of the conflict and the value level defined by values used in solving the conflict – irrespective of the conflict type different values were used in solving the conflict. No connection was found between the size of the organisation under research (where the conflict took place) and the value level either.

Figure 2 presents the number of propagated values and real values on Melé's value system levels. While the propagated values rather represent higher levels of Melé's classification, then reality is more focused on lower level values. Still, extremes have not been met in either case – propagated values cannot be found on the lowest level (level 1 that is described by mistreatment) and based on the real values, organisations have not reached the highest level (level 5 that is described by mutual esteem and cooperation). On the opposite side the other extremes have been met – in the case of real values unfortunately the lowest level i.e. mistreatment has appeared frequently and in the case of propagated values enough values can be pointed out that show the highest level i.e. mutual esteem and cooperation. As Melé's system describes growth towards ethics, then based on that we can say that the managers of Estonian organisations know which the right values are but they have not been accepted/imprinted in the organisations.

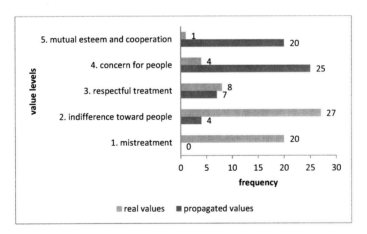

Fig. 2:   *The propagated and real values according to Melé's value system. Source: compiled by the authors.*

Table 1 shows which values have been used to describe the levels of Melé in both studies. Although Melé does not use values while describing the value system levels the results of the current study enable to show each level by describing the specific values. Although the goal of the propagated and real values research was not to find specific values that comply with Melé's certain levels, a preliminary list of values still has been developed due to the methods of research (to find values that describe certain situations). According to the goal of this research it can be seen that while the number of values that describe different levels is totally different among the propagated and real values (except 3rd level), then values that were used to describe one or another level partly overlap. For example, in both studies values like cooperation, valuing the values (meaning that the presence and acceptance of both individual and organisational values by everyone is important) were used to describe the 4th level. In the case of the 3rd level "honesty" has the same meaning but also "goal-orientation" and "shared goals" refer to similar values.

Table 1.   The examples of propagated and real values detected, which describe the Melé's value system. Source: compiled by the authors

Levels of Melé's values	propagated values	real values
5. mutual esteem and cooperation	innovation and creativity, flexibility, commitment, courage, teamwork, passion	support, trust
4. concern for people	social responsibility, valuing the values, trust, motivation, openness, cooperation, entrepreneurship	valuing the values, good microclimate, cooperation, friendliness, helpfulness
3. respectful treatment	honesty, communication, goal-orientation	competency, honesty, quality, environment, shared goals
2. indifference toward people	analysing skills, no learning, lack of client orientation, efficiency, routine	lack of cooperation, no shared values, client-conflicts, employee as a resource, no common goals, demotivation, profit-orientation, irresponsibility
1. mistreatment		immorality, not-valuing the employees, hurrying, domination, fear, power, bribery

In the case of each conflict we determined if it was a vertical or horizontal conflict. We expected that a vertical conflict would be directly linked to management thereby demonstrating management quality. Out of 60 conflict cases 43 were vertical conflicts. This clearly demonstrates shortcomings in the quality of management.

5. Discussion and Conclusions

The changed nature of the business environment has involved the rising importance of people as creators and thinkers. From the point of view of organisations it becomes more important to create an environment that supports teamwork, innovation and development of collective knowledge. Our investigation points out the difference between propagated and real values in Estonian organisations: it lies mostly in the fact that while people-centred values are being propagated, then based on real values it can be said that employees are being treated as a resource and the person who does the work is not valued. The same problem has been raised in several previous Estonian management studies. For example, the 2011 Estonian management field research claims that management principles and values are not in harmony with the values of a sustainable organisation, management is authoritarian and employees are not being involved (EAS 2011). This is confirmed also by a study by Zernand-Vilson and Elenurm (2010) arguing that management practices, such as focusing on employee individuality and personality or self-directed work teams do not appear as growing directions. The Estonian Development Fund's report about the Current Status of Competitiveness of Estonian Economy (Varblane et al. 2008) points out that the business models in use do not develop fast enough, new markets are not pursued and management is quite conservative. Vadi and Türk (2009) in their 2007 Estonian managers' survey show that the leaders of Estonian organisations often lack managerial competencies and they cannot value or manage innovation.

While studying the propagated values it was clearly seen that teamwork as a value was considered important. But in the conflict analysis the same results did not appear. Based on the conflicts researched we can say that common interest among the group, department and even the organisation is often missing. Also, an understanding of everyone's necessary input to reaching the final goal is missing. The results of the research show that teamwork that is highly valued as a propagated value appears significantly less often as a real value. The explanation can be that teamwork is possible in organisations that are (according to Melé's theory) developed into 4th or 5th level. Thus, Estonian organisations have a huge growth area in the field of managerial practices and also value based management. That has also been confirmed by previous studies (EAS 2011, Übius and Alas, 2010, Zernand-Vilson and Elenurm 2010). While "cooperation" appeared very often in the propagated values, another possible problem may be that although organisations often declare teamwork as their strength it is not the case in reality – teamwork only applies to work and projects which are done physically at the same time and in the same location but essentially no teamwork or cooperation criteria (interest towards work, synergy, harmony in work process) are met. As a positive result of the study it can be brought out that only a few cases out of all cases analysed were placed on Melé's first level. That means that Estonian organisations are hopefully overcoming the entrepreneurial problems of developing country – manipulation, knowingly bending and not complying with the law (i.e. violation of laws).

It is also a logical result that propagated values are more ethical in essence than the real ones. That shows accordingly that Estonian managers in general know what important values are. It also may point to a possible problem that managers have learned to give „correct" answers and retain a proper outlook but in reality these values are not being used. It has to be taken into account that implementing of the values can take years and as changes in raising and training Estonian managers are only recent the results can appear after many years. Conflict is a good tool for researching real and accepted behaviour because the results present the reality.

Based on the results of the research it can be said that in the case of the organisations under investigation we are not dealing with good management organisations according to Melé's value system levels. While good management is a prerequisite for creating a sustainable organisation we can say that in the year 2011 the real values in Estonian organisations do not support the wish of sustainable organisations and sustainable economy. First and foremost, too little attention is being paid to creation of positive and strong organisational culture; management lacks people-centred values in leading people.

In the ideal case, propagated and real values ought to coincide, but the results of our research demonstrate that while propagated values are on higher levels of Melé's value system i.e. 4th and 5th level then real values are usually placed on the 2nd level of Mele's system. Values reflect management and management quality in an organisation directly. Thereby the results of the studies described in this paper support Maaja Vadi and Kulno Türk's notion made after researching Estonian organisations in 2007 that the managers of Estonian organisations lack managerial skills (Vadi and Türk 2009).

Since in the conflict analysis the biggest number of organisations are placed on the 2nd of Melé's value system and in the case of propagated values Estonian organisations are placed on the 4th and 5th level we can say that managers of Estonian companies lack the skills to behave in accordance with propagated values and do not include propagated values in everyday management practices.

What we can conclude from our investigation is that Estonian managers know and speak about values that are important for remaining sustainable, but in real life they do not follow these values. The results of our research confirm the need for a change in this field.

As it was shown in the theoretical overview there have been many investigations about organisational values, as well as investigations about conflict management. But there was a gap in connecting these two phenomena which our research aimed to fill. Therefore for the first time, by investigating the conflict cases the real values in the organisations were found. We believe that using a conflict as a tool justified itself. Based on the knowledge gained from this research it would be possible to create training programmes for managers and use the knowledge for developing business and management study programmes.

6. Limitations and Future Research

The authors are aware that the propagated values identified on the basis of the journal articles do not show their utilisation in Estonian organisations, but express rather the trends propagated by management. Although the papers also contained case descriptions, they often show the situation better than it actually is. Data for this research come from the papers that express the desired reality rather than the real situation. We also understand that regardless of the fact that at least two members of the research group analysed each case study, some subjectivity may be present in the evaluations. That is due to the analysers' life experience, knowledge and personal values. Finding and grouping of the values is inevitably subjective and largely dependent on experts, but hopefully the consensus analysis helped to reduce the subjectivity.

Another possible problem in analysing the propagated values is that the articles which the analysis was based on may not be sufficiently representative for management styles since editors of the journal and authors selected the journal articles. At the same time, the topics and content of the articles were decided also by managers' expectations, experiences and needs, and global management trends. Because of the large amount of articles, this in turn increases the likelihood that the research results reveal the actual trend.

Also the gathered conflicts may not be representative enough and the choice of conflict to be described naturally depends on the describer. To minimise that problem the describers were beforehand thoroughly instructed on the principles of choosing and describing conflicts. Another problem with gathering conflicts lies in the situation where the describer describes the conflict from his/her point of view. But as there are always several parties involved in a conflict the personal values and notions of the describer can influence the outcome. We omitted from the analysis of the research results some negative values with the minimal rate of occurrence compared to positive values (in general, occurred once only). Based on the principle that although negative values occurred in the articles, the content of the article clearly inclined the reader to admit that neither the manager nor organisation would benefit from using this value, therefore that negative value is not listed among the propagated values.

So further we could look for reasons why propagated and real values differ so much. In further research it would be interesting also to find out how values are managed in organisations if conscious organisational culture development is practiced; also to investigate how much Estonian managers know about the benefits and need of values management and what could be the reasons why certain values are propagated but not followed in reality.

References

Abreu, A. and Camarinha-Matos, L. M. 2008. On the role of value systems to promote the sustainability of collaborative environments. International Journal of Production Research, 46(5), pp. 1207–1229.

Ballantine, D., Cristopher, M. and Payne, A. 1995. Improving the Quality of Service Marketing: Service (Re) Design is the Critical Link, Journal Marketing Management 2, pp. 7–24.

Bhates, R. and Khasawneh, S. 2005. Organizational earning culture, learning transfer climate and perceived innovation in Jordanian organizations. International Journal of Training & Development, 9(2), pp. 96-109.

Buchko, A. 2007. The effect of leadership on values-based management. Leadership & Organization Development Journal, 28(1), pp. 36–50.

Cappellin, R. 2011. The Governance of Conflicts and Partnerships in Knowledge and Innovation Networks, in Manas Chatterji, Darvesh Gopal, Savita Singh (eds.) *Governance, Development and Conflict (Contributions to Conflict Management, Peace Economics and Development)*. Emerald Group Publishing Limited, 18, pp. 31–70.

Chryssides, G. D., and Kaler, J. H. 1996. Essentials of Business Ethics. London, McGraw-Hill.

Creswell, J. W. 2003. Research Design: qualitative, quantitative, and mixed methods approach (2nd ed.). Thousand Oaks, California: Sage Publications.

Collins, J. 2011. Great by Choice: Uncertainty, Chaos, and Luck – Why Some Thrive Despite Them All. Harper Business.

Connor, P. and Becker, B. 1994. Personal values and management: What do we know and why don't we know more? Journal of Management Inquiry, 3(1). pp. 67–73.

Debrah, L. N. and Quick, J. C. 2006. Organisational Behaviour: Foundations, Realities and Challenges, (5th Edition). South-Western: Thomson.

De Dreu, C. and De Vliert, E. 1997. Using Conflict in Organizations. Sage Publications, London, 229 p.

Dobny, C. B. 2008. Measuring innovation culture in organizations. European Journal of Innovation Management, 11(4), pp. 539–59.

Driscoll, D. M. and Hoffman W. M. 2000. Ethics Matters, How to Implement Values-Driven Management. Massachusetts: Center for Business Ethics, Bentley College, Waltham.

Edvardsson, B., Enquist, B. and Hay, M. 2006. Values-based service brands: narratives from IKEA. Managing Service Quality, 16(3), pp. 230–246.

Enterprise of Estonia. 2011. Eesti juhtimisvaldkonna uuring. EAS, Tallinn.

Fairclough, N. 2001. Language and power (2nd ed.). Harlow: Longman.

Gini, A. (2004). Moral leadership and business ethics. In J. B. Ciulla (Ed.), Ethics, the heart of leadership (pp. 23-43). Praeger.

Groysberg, B., Slind, M. (2012) Leadership Is a Conversation, Harward Business Review.

Harigopal, K. (1995). Conflict Management. Oxford: IBH Publishing Co. 189 p.

Hocker, J. L., Wilmont, W.W. (1995). Interpersonal Conflict (4th ed.) Madison: Brown&Benchmark.

Jaakson, K. (2010). Management by values: are some values better than others?, Journal of Management Development, 29(9), 795–806

Jaakson, K., Tamm, D. and Hämmal, G. (2011). Organisational innovativeness in Estonian biotechnology organisations. Baltic Journal of Management, 6(2), 205–226.

Klenke, K. (2005). Corporate values as multi-level, multi-domain antecedents of leader behaviours. International Journal of Manpower, 26(1), 50–66.

Laherand, M. L. (2008). Kvalitatiivne uurimisviis (Qualitative research). Tallinn: OÜ Infotrükk.

Lauristin, M. (2000). Kas see ongi siis nüüd see Eesti aeg? Muutuste diskursus Eesti ajakirjanduses. In M. Lauristin (ed), Kõnelev ja kõneldav inimene: Eesti erinevate eluvaldkondade diskursus (pp. 63-84). TPU, Tallinn.

Leavy, B. (2005). A leader's guide to creating an innovation culture. Strategy & Leadership. 33(4), 38-45.

Lencioni, P. M. (2012). The Advantage: Why Organizational Health Trumps Everything Else In Business. Jossey-Bass, 241 p.

Likert, R., Likert, J.G. (1976). New Ways of Managing Conflict. USA: McGraw Hill, 375 p.

Martin, J., Frost, P. (1999). The organizational culture war games: A struggle for intellectual dominance. In S. R.Clegg, & C. Hardy (Eds.), Studying Organization: Theory and method. (pp. 345-367). London: Sage.

Melé, D. (2012a). Management Ethics. Placing Ethics at the Core of Good Management. Palgrave Macmillan, IESE Business School. 182 p.

Melé, D. (2012b). The Firm as a "Community of Persons": A Pillar of Humanistic Business Ethos. Journal of Business Ethics. 106(1), 89-101.

Merrill, P. (2008). Creating an Innovation Process and Innovative Culture. ASQ Quality Press, Wisconsin, Milwaukee.

Ofori, D. F., Sokro, E. (2010). Examining the Impact of Organisational Values on Corporate Performance in Selected Ghanaian, Global Management Journal, 52-67.

O'Reilly, C. A., Chatman, J. (1996). Culture as social control: Corporations, Cults, and Commitment. Research in Organizational Behavior, 18, 157-200.

O'Reilly, C. A., Pfeffer, J. (2000). Hidden Value: How Great Companies Achieve Extraordinary Results With Ordinary People. Harvard Business Press.

O'Reilly, C. A. (1989). Corporations, Culture, and Commitment," Californian Management Review, 31, 9-23.

Rokeach, M. (1973). The nature of values. New York: Free Press.

Roos, J., Roos, G., Dragonetti, N.C., Edvinsson, L. (1997). Intellectual Capital: Navigating in the New Business Landscape. Macmillan: London.

Schein, E. H. (2004). Organizational Culture and Leadership. 3rd Ed. San Francisco: Jossey-Bass Publishers.

Schumacher, E. F. (1973). Small Is Beautiful. NY, Harper.

Sydänmaanlakka, P. (2007). Intelligent Self-Leadership. Perspectives on Personal Growth. Pertec, Espoo. 359 p.

Sydänmaanlakka, P. (2003). Intelligent leadership and leadership competencies. Developing a leadership framework for intelligent organizations. Helsinki University of Technology. Dissertation for the degree of Doctor of Philosophy to be presented with due permission of the Department of Industrial Management. 179 p.

Titov, E., Kuimet, K., Meel, M. (2012). Post-Recession Values in Estonian Organizations. Business Development in Baltic Sea Region. (82 - 94). Berlin: Peter Lang Verlag [in press]

Tjosvold, D. (1997). Conflict within Independence: Its Value for Productivity and Individuality. K.W. Carsten, C. de Dreu, E. de Vliert (eds). SAGE Publications, London. 23-37.

Übius, Ü., Alas. R. (2010) The Innovation Climate – Predictor for Corporate Social Responsibility, EBS Review. 27, 70-87.

Vadi, M., Türk, K. (2009). Behaviour patterns in Estonian enterprises from the perspective of the Value chain. Baltic Journal of Management. 4(1), 34–50.

Varblane, U., Eamets, R., Haldma, T., Kaldaru, H., Masso, J., Mets, T., Paas, T., Reiljan, J., Sepp, J., Türk, K., Ukrainski, K., Vadi, M., Vissak, T. (2008). The Estonian Economy Current Status of Competitiveness and Future Outlooks. Short version of the report. Estonian Development Fund, Tallinn.

Viinamäki, O-P. (2012). Why Leaders Fail in Introducing Values-Based Leadership? An Elaboration of Feasible Steps, Challenges, and Suggestions for Practitioners. International Journal of Business and Management. 7(9).

Virovere, A., Liigand, J. (2002). Conflict as a Way of Executing Power, Stability and Dynamics of Power- JAREP/SABE. Conference Proceedings.

Virovere, A., Rihma, M. (2008). Ethics Auditing and Conflict Analysis as Management Tools, Working Papers in Economics, 26. School of Economics and Businesss Adm.

Volkema, R., Bergmann, T. (1995). Conflict styles as Indicators of Behavioral Patterns in Interpersonal Conflicts. Journal of Social Psychology. 135(1), 5-16.

Wall, J.A., Callister, R. (1995). Conflict and Its Management. Journal of Management. Journal of Management, 3, 517.

Zernand-Vilson, M. and Elenurm, T. (2010). Differences in implementing management and organization development directions between domestic and foreign companies in Estonia. Baltic Journal of Management. 5(1), 82–99.

Improving Non-profit Organizations' Capability through Open Architecture Model

Anu Leppiman,[1] Iivi Riivits-Arkonsuo[2] and Kristel Kaljund[3]

Abstract

This empirical paper investigates the mechanisms through which the civil society can develop dynamic capability. The paper offers a new perspective to developing the capability of an organization through acquiring a sense of achievement. Efficiency improvement takes place through collective learning and doing things together; as a result both activities and behaviour change. Our research focuses on analysing family camps as products, as environments of learning, experiencing and offering social support. The results of the analysis, based on empirical data collected in a long-term ethnographic and participatory action research carried out in several stages, will be presented through an open architecture model. The model, consisting of functionality, communality and experiences, is adaptable to changing economic conditions thanks to its customizability, changeability and open design. We argue that if civil society actors used the conception of learning through acquiring a sense of achievement, their capability to balance the interests of business sector and public power would improve. The dynamic capability perspective is a new one in academic discourses discussing the civil society actors.

JEL classification codes: M1, L3, D2

Keywords: dynamic capability, experiential learning, experiential product, sense of achievement, non-profit organizations, open architecture model

1. Introduction

Business and other organizations, as well as people working in them act in a constantly changing environment. Business organizations operating in a rapidly changing environment need competitive advantages. One of the presuppositions of successfully managing life is developing capability to find the competitive advantages.

Dynamic capability (DC) is a conception that academic literature mostly addresses in the context and on a sample of large international business organizations (Teece et al. 1997; Winter 2002; Teece 2007; Wang and Ahmed 2007;

---

1 Tallinn University of Technology, Akadeemia tee 3, Tallinn 12618, Estonia, Phone: +3726203975, e-mail: Anu.Leppiman@.ttu.ee

2 Tallinn University of Technology, Akadeemia tee 3, Tallinn 12618, Estonia, Phone: +3726203972 , e-mail: Iivi.Riivits@ttu.ee

3 Tallinn University of Technology, Akadeemia tee 3, Tallinn 12618, Estonia, Phone: + 3725042465, e-mail: kristel.kaljund@googlemail.com

Ambrosini et al. 2009). The constantly changing business environment, techno-logical changes and strong competition create the need for relocation and inno-vation of resources. Wang and Ahmed (2007) define dynamic capabilities as a business organization's behavioural orientation to integrate, reconfigure, renew and recreate constantly its resources and capabilities in response to the changing environment in order to attain and sustain competitive advantages. Dynamic ca-pabilities involve adaption and change since they build, integrate and reconfig-ure other resources and capabilities (Helfat and Peteraf 2003).

Teece et al. (1997) have pointed out that unlike other assets, distinctive competences and capabilities must usually be created as they cannot be bought. In this sense, competences and capabilities are positioned aside other non-tradable 'soft' assets like values, culture and organizational experience. The de-velopment of such assets is a long-term process. Business organizations may develop their dynamic capabilities from their unique starting points and through their unique paths. The ability to create a set of distinctive capabilities that ena-ble it to stand out in the competition is the key to the survival and success of a business organization (Wang and Ahmed 2007). A significant agent in the crea-tion and development of dynamic capabilities is learning.

Like other organizations, institutions of the civil society can also be seen as learning and changing organizations that can be encompassed with the concep-tion of DC. To the authors' knowledge civil society actors have not been ana-lysed using the DC concept so far, so the dynamic capability perspective is a new one in academic discourses discussing the civil society actors.

Habermas (1998) defines civil society as 'composed of those more or less spontaneously emergent associations, organizations, and movements that, at-tuned to how societal problems resonate in the private life spheres, distil and transmit such reactions in amplified form to the public sphere.' These organiza-tions aim at a general profit in their activities, thinking of the public, of the whole society. In spite of the fact that voluntary organizations, associations and movements that form the civil society are non-profit, they are as well affected by the changing social and economic conditions and the competition is hard for them as well.

There is an important difference though: while business organizations see themselves as 'winners', assuming to be successful, civil society actors tend to be passive. It is the post-soviet discourse of 'winners' and 'losers' (Lauristin 2004) still prevalent in Estonia and elsewhere in Eastern Europe, whereby the stereotype of 'winners' includes traits related to consumer society values charac-teristic of higher social classes presupposing a high income, that dooms the suc-cess of the civil society actors, condemns them to passivity. Passivity, though, excludes DC. Since civil society actors are seen as 'losers' both by the society as well as by themselves (Kaljund and Peterson 2007), they are forced into a marginal – while business organizations dare to adopt measures and conceptions, to be innovative, the civil society actors do not. Yet, the rules of the market apply no less to them as to business organizations.

The present paper assumes that the civil society actors just like business organizations perform under continuously changing social conditions and must improve their efficiency, their capability to function. The latter takes place through collective learning and doing things together. Thus the vicious circle of learned helplessness, internalised self-disrespect (Rommelspacher 1995) created by social stereotypes, by being labelled as 'losers', can be broken, i.e. the feeling that different market rules apply to business compared to non-profit organizations – something that often becomes a self-fulfilling prophecy, can be broken.

The aim of this paper is to describe and analyse family camps as products, as environments of learning, experiencing and offering social support, and to examine elements through which the model of a family camp that offers a sense of achievement and social support could be developed. Family camps as a product of the experiential learning environment were designed by the civil society actors.

In the following sections, we review the conceptions of the capability of organisations and individuals; present the model of experiential learning through acquiring a sense of achievement; and the experience pyramid model. Next, we show how an open architecture model was constituted in the course of a long-term ethnographic and participatory action research carried out in several phases. A content analysis of the empirical data collected in the family camps was carried out and the results interpreted. The open model consists of three basic categories: communality, functionality and experiences. Our research enabled us to add a fourth category to the model: the camp-based experiential family work as a welfare product. An advantage of the model is its customizability, changeability and openness. We suggest that since the model has open architecture, it can be used to develop the capability of different organizations.

2. Theoretical Considerations

While analysing the capability of an organization we use a resource-based view (RBV). According to the RBV, all assets, capabilities, organizational processes, attributes, information, knowledge etc. controlled by a business organization are the organization's resources that enable it to conceive of and implement strategies that improve its efficiency and effectiveness. Thus, the essence of the RBV lies in the emphasis of resources and capabilities as the genesis of competitive advantage. Resources are heterogeneously distributed across competing business organizations (Wang and Ahmed 2007).

The RBV, though, offers no explanation to why some companies react faster to changes in the environment than others (Teece and Pisano 1994). Therefore we base our research on the idea of three types of capital (fig. 1) that together form the capability of organizations and individuals alike. It was Pierre Bourdieu (1985) who first spoke of the three types of capital. The idea was used in the empirical part of the paper as input.

The assets and finances of a business organization form its economic capital. It can be managed rationally, which makes that kind of capital relatively easy to calculate and predict (Pruulmann-Vengerfeldt 2004). An organization rents or buys human capital depending on the skills, abilities, knowledge, experience and behavioural culture of the individuals (Coleman 1990; Edvinsson 2004). Social capital is not that simple to define or, respectively, to measure.

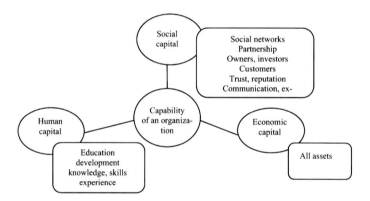

Fig. 1: *Capability of an organization. Source: Leppiman, 2010*

Bourdieu described social capital as "the aggregate of the actual or potential resources which are linked to possession of a durable network of more or less institutionalized relationships of mutual acquaintance and recognition" (Bourdieu 1985).

In organizational context, social capital is a capital of notability and trust that helps to attract important clients and is based on mutual acquaintance and recognition (Bourdieu ibid.). Putnam uses James Coleman's definition of social capital: "the norms, the social networks, and the relationships between adults and children that are of value to the child's growing up" (Coleman 1990), saying that social capital includes informal sociability, social trust, community volunteerism, engagement in public affairs, and community organizational life; it is a community-based trust (Putnam 2000). Social capital refers to traits of social organization like social networks and trust that can raise the effectiveness of a society through joint activity. Thus, social capital creates resources for common benefit.

Coleman (1990) sees in social capital an activity-based resource for both individuals and organizations existing in obligations, expectations and social norms. It is a network capital in resources that we become through communicating, trust, and belonging to a group resp. organization (Leppiman 2010). According to the capability lifecycles conception, social capital and social ties as a resource are important in the founding stage of the capability lifecycle since people belonging to the group bring those along, as Helfat and Peteraf (2003) put it.

Social support is defined (Cobb 1976) as information leading the subject to believe that he or she is loved, esteemed, and belongs to a network of mutual obligation. It is an interpersonal transaction involving four types of support: emotional (liking, empathy), material, i.e. instrumental aid (goods or services), information (about the environment) and appraisal (information relevant to self-evolution) (Caplan 1974; Thoits 1982; House 1981; Cohen and Syme 1985; Morgan 1990; Rautiainen and Keskinen 1999; Leppiman 2004, 2006, 2010).

The starting point for obtaining and offering social support is the existence of social relationships and a social network. The social network that offers support refers to being in touch with those with whom the individual interacts always or temporally, and it involves those types of support that can be given or received through interaction (Cohen and Syme 1985; Dunkel-Schetter and Bennett 1990; Leppiman 2010).

The mechanism of improving capabilities is similar for organizations and individuals. Individual capabilities alike depend on economic, human and social capital (see fig. 1). The economic capital is formed by the material assets, the income and the aid the individual gets. The human resource is constituted by the individual him- or herself with his/her skills, abilities, knowledge, and communication culture. Social capital manifests itself in his/her social networks – the working place (while communicating within the organization), the family or the circle of friends etc. The capability of the individual depends not only on his/her education and skills but also on his/her health, marital status, existence of children, possibilities of further education, existence and quality of a job and a communication network, existence of material resources and the social support that one can obtain when needed. Also families draw their capabilities from the aforementioned three types of capital.

The capabilities of both an organization and an individual are vulnerable – endangered by the possibilities of bankruptcies taking place, jobs being lost, social capital being deficit etc. Thus, both organizations and individuals are confronted with the necessity to balance their capabilities and work on their efficiency. In the organizational context it means that people have to motivate themselves, create a work environment that enables both development and learning. In the individual context it means creating a new learning environment where things are done in a different way, i.e. the person obtains a sense of achievement through everyday experiences (Leppiman 2010). Thanks to learning both activity and behaviour change. We suggest that the sense of achievement enables exactly that.

Ambrosini et al. (2009) emphasise that learning is considered a dynamic capability itself. Learning has been identified as a process by which repetition and experimentation enable tasks to be performed better and faster. In the context of a business organization, learning has several key traits involving organizational as well as individual skills. While individual skills are of relevance, their value depends on the employment, in particular in organizational settings. Learning processes are social and collective (Teece et al. 1997). Important collective learning takes place when individuals express their principles and beliefs. Organizational competence improves as members of an organization become more aware of the overall performance implications of their actions (Zollo and Winter 2002).

In our paper we concentrate on experiential learning, i.e. on learning through acquiring a sense of achievement. Hall's (1988) model is based on the psychological success cycle. Figure 2 shows the closed cycle of the sense of achievement. If an organization or an individual is being challenged, he or she has to make an effort. If the goal has been reached, the self-esteem improves: the individual experiences a sense of achievement. Both an individual as well as an organization develop a new identity. The motivation to accept even bigger challenges and to use the resources in order to succeed improves as well. Though, the model has two constrictions: first, an improved quality requires an external impulse, and second, challenges in a closed cycle are a one-time-experience that do not reproduce themselves thus limiting the possibilities for learning.

If we assume that new social resources are formed through experiences, the possibility to change and the possibility that new challenges occur is the most important trait of an experiential learning environment and an experiential product. The change does not have to be major; for example, one can adopt a new attitude towards life or a competence necessary in life thanks to an advanced training or a company trip.

While discussing experience economy, Pine and Gilmore (1999) as well as Pine and Korn (2011) define experiences as memorable events. According to them, experience economy is the next economic cycle, the economy following the agrarian economy, the industrial economy, and the most recent service economy.

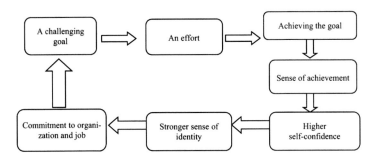

Fig. 2:   Cycle of the sense of achievement; Source: Hall, 1988

In this paper, we define experience as an economic offering and a meaningful relationship, communication between a business organization, a service, and customers who perceive and experience meaningfully.

Experiences are positive irritants that enable a new experience that launches changes thanks to learning. The experiences of self-overcoming, coping and succeeding gained through social experiences can direct the activities and behaviour of both organizations and individuals. Through affection cognition is adopted about personal capabilities as well as a conation to change one's life (Leppiman 2010). Deriving from aforesaid, we argue that in business today experience innovation is necessary. Experience economy is understood as a new, more open type of economy that includes changed production and consumption. Offering innovative products and services and fulfilling promises given to markets at the same time presupposes new attitudes and customization in product development (Riivits-Arkonsuo and Leppiman 2013). Progression of economic value and competitiveness is achieved through experience economy. When the added value of a product or service increases, the expected profit from the provision of such also increases – that makes the experiential product and providing an experience especially interesting from the perspective of a business organization. At the same time customer's needs and degree of customization gain importance (Pine and Gilmore 1999, 2011; Pine and Korn 2011).

The Lapland Centre of Expertise for the Experience Industry (LCEEI) defines experience as a strong, multisensory, memorable and individual experience
(Tarssanen and Kylänen 2007), following the experience pyramid model that
sees "experience [as] a multisensoral, positive and comprehensive emotional
experience that can lead to personal change" (Ibid.). By influencing the elements
of experience, i.e. "individuality, authenticity, story, multi-sensory perception,
contrast and interaction it is possible to offer guest and customer something
memorable and unique" (Ibid.).

The experience pyramid model in figure 3 represents an ideal product that
takes into account all the elements at all levels of a meaningful experience. In
the context of the present paper the product stands for service design.

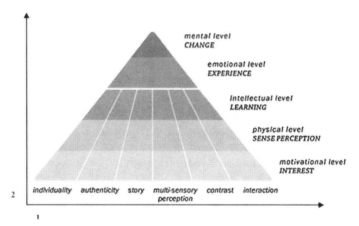

Fig. 3:   *The experience pyramid; Source: Tarssanen and Kylanen, 2007*

Elements of meaningful experiences (the horizontal axes 1) are the following: individuality refers to uniqueness, i.e. the same or similar product is not
available elsewhere. Authenticity refers to the credibility of the product, determined by the customer himself. Story is closely connected to the authenticity of
a product: it is important to bind the various elements of the product into a coherent story in order to make the experience coherent and catching; a credible
and authentic story adds social significance and content to the product, giving
the customer a good reason to experience it. Multi-sensory perception refers to
the fact that all sensory perceptions are carefully designed to strengthen the chosen theme, as well as to support immersion. The customer experience may suffer
if there are too many or annoying sensory perceptions. Contrast means difference from the perspective of the customer. The product should be different with
respect to the customer's everyday life. Interaction means successful communi-

cation between the service provider and/or other customers, as well as between the product and its producers.

The vertical axis (2) of the experience pyramid model illustrates how the customer experience is constructed from interest to the actual experience and to the conscious processing of it, which again leads to a meaningful experience and mental change. The customer interest is awakened on the motivational level. In the cycle of acquiring a sense of achievement the motivational level is a challenge, the goal that needs to be achieved. The next, physical level means creating an environment for learning. For that a place is needed where people gather, and people who learn and who teach, even if it means life-long learning. The intellectual level means learning, thinking, applying knowledge and forming opinions. A good product provides the customer with a learning experience, a possibility to learn something new, to develop and gain new knowledge, either consciously or unconsciously. The meaningful experience is actually experienced on the emotional level. Since it is hard to predict and control individual emotional reactions, it is quite likely that the customer will have a positive emotional experience if all basic elements for a meaningful experience have been well taken into account on motivational, physical and intellectual levels. On the mental level a positive and powerful emotional experience may lead to an experience of personal change, resulting in rather permanent changes in person's physical state, state of mind, or lifestyle.

On individual level learning through acquiring a sense of achievement means a professional change, a change in identifying him- or herself with the organization and with the job, thus, improving the satisfaction with work. The person is ready to accept new goals and achieve them. In organizational context the change means that the organization is more coherent and competent. New resources in social and human capital improve also economic success, i.e. economic capital. Since these three types of capital act in concurrence, the capability of the organization to accept new challenges, to set new goals and achieve them improves. Without an acquired sense of achievement no such change will take place. Only business organizations that can and want to change all three types of capital, i.e. their capability, survive in the competition. If we talk about civil society actors, though, we see much more passivity and noncommittal behaviour. We argue that if civil society actors would use the model of learning through acquiring a sense of achievement their capability to balance the interests of the business sector and public power in the society would improve.

3. Methodology

The subject of our ethnographic research (Atkinson 1990; Hammersley 1991, Leppiman 2010, Moisander and Valtonen 2011) containing elements of participatory action research (Dick 1993, Leppiman 2010) is a family camp as an experiential product. The purpose of the study is to describe and analyse family camps as a novel environment for experiences and social support.

Ethnographic research aimed at producing the knowledge while participatory action research enabled to design the family service model. Action research is in general used in development studies as means of creating novel solutions, models, and possibilities for change (Argyris and Schön 1978; French and Bell 1990; Dick 1993; Heikkinen 2001; Leppiman 2010). Characteristic of the method are researcher's active participation in the activities and intervention, creating new knowledge together with the target group, collecting data from various sources, the long-term nature of the research (Engeström 1995; Denscombe 2000; Isokorpi 2003; Veijola 2004; Leppiman 2010), and unifying activity and research (Roberts 1997). Participatory action research is in its essence a qualitative process of added knowledge (Dick 1999; Leppiman 2010).

One of the authors of the present paper participated in the family camps during a prolonged period of twelve years; the participation included both planning and coordinating of the activities of the camp as well as research activities (Leppiman 2010). The empirical data used in this paper were collected in this period of time. The study started in 1999 and was motivated by the need to support the families with children that struggle for their livelihood. The study took place in the context of the international family work project 'Weekdays'. The research team put together with the aim to carry out research as well as to design a service for the target group, the families, consisted of the academic teaching staff and students from four countries, Estonia, Finland, Germany and Russia. The general aim of the research project was to design for supporting the target group, the families, an innovative model of social service (in other words, a product) based on the idea of networking activities. The pilot project of the research, a family camp, took place in 1999. The idea behind it was to strengthen the DC of the family as an organization via learning and communicating with other families, as well as via promoting understanding as well as respect for the own singularity thanks to intercultural communication and joint activities. The research project included week-long intensive family camps (1999–2001), joint learning seminars with the participants of the family camps and researchers who took part in the ethnographic study (2002–2007), and analysing the activities as well as developing the family camp model (2007–2010).

102 family members and 48 volunteers participated in five family camps. The material was collected in interviews (n=79), focus groups (n=36), surveys (n=43), and documents of participatory observation (n=41). The collected material was analysed using qualitative content analysis (Mayring 2000). The research question has guided the decisions concerning the analysis. It has been a systematic and at the same time flexible and continuous process. In 2001, the research material that had been produced in the family camps was gathered and decisions were made. Since the method of analysis chosen for the present study is theory-centred, it was necessary to study and constitute the theoretical references, before the interpretation process could start. Thinking of the product development, not only the research data but also theories play an important role in the research. Qualitative analysis consists of simplifying observations, compressing material and grouping it in order to produce and interpret the findings (Alasuutari 1993, 2001; Eskola and Suoranta 1998, Törrönen 2002; Mason 2007; Gibbs 2009). Thus, in the first phase of the analysis the research material was categorised, coded, segmented and compressed to make it readable; at the same time the interviews were transcribed. At first general categories of functionality were created emanating from theories, followed by typologies of needs, and finally analytical meaningful categories of functionality emerged. The latter were placed into the family camp's model of the social process.

In the next phase of the analysis, topics indicating the situation of the families, social support and DC were formed. The answers to the questionnaires were included in the analysis, highlighting again topics like the DC of the families or social support. The category 'functionality' that emerged in the first phase of the analysis became more apparent and the material produced in interviews brought out topics related to the DC, interaction as well as communality and experientality.

A contextual answer (Geertz 1988; Leppiman 2010) to the research question forms in the third phase of the research, i.e. when researchers start with the writing process and thus produce interpretations and new definitions. The fourth phase of the analysis can be called the clarifying phase. In the present study, in this phase the interpretations crystallised as the phenomena of communality, functionality and experiences, and slowly the logic and strategy of the new product – camp-based family work model (see figure 4) developed. Definitions emerged from interpretations with the help of the results of the analysis, theoretical considerations (House 1981; Pine and Gilmore 1999, 2011) as well as the experience pyramid model designed by the LCEEI (Tarssanen and Kylänen 2007, 2009). The analysis of the results was carried out based on the elements of meaningful experiences (the horizontal axes (1)) and the customer experience (the vertical axes (2)) from the LCEEI experience pyramid model (see figure 3).

The co-authors of the paper joined the process as DC analysts-researchers, bringing along their own theoretical considerations and interpretation capacity that resulted in new viewing angles.

4. Results

The situationally related activities in the family camp are based on authentic communication dynamics expressed by the activity, by the new meanings and insights that are created in communication situations, and by changes in the environment of activity and in everyday life. The product development of the family camp where the material was collected, was based on the theoretical research model of the LCEEI (Tarssanen and Kylänen 2007; Pine and Tarssanen 2008) since the latter enables to estimate the experientality of the family camp as a product.

We analyse the family camp as a product, as an environment of learning, experiencing and offering social support, teaching among other things how to produce experiences. There are many ways to define a *product*. A product can be physical, tangible, but it can also refer to a service. The result of the production process can be an object, a service or information satisfying the needs of consumers. Thus, the product of family work can be a playground, an event for resting or entertainment of the families, a family camp, a book, a computer game or a family housing. The product of family work can also be an idea, a model or a system facilitating establishing livelihoods – it can be something entirely innovative. The purpose of creating a product is to offer the clients experiences.

Thus we define a product as a tool for a procedure, for instance offering a family service. When talking about the family work, the concept 'welfare product' is used. Such products are analysed considering the needs, principles and expectations of the clients. Clients are included in creating the products of family work, i.e. in the process of 'product development'. The welfare product is created together or it is customised so that the client experiences the product as a possibility to solve a problem (Leppiman 2010).

Looking at the family camp service through the experience pyramid, embracing both the theoretical background as well as the empirical material, i.e. seeing the family camp service as an experiential product, we identified that it met all six criteria of an experiential service. First, a family camp is always individual and different since no camp is ever the same as another that occurs in another place or at another time. Every family camp is custom-made, deriving from the needs and expectations of the families attending the camp and the knowledge, skills, experiences, attitudes and principles of the people working at the camp. Second, every family camp is authentic for two reasons: there is no such thing as universal naturalness, each client determines the authenticity him- or herself, and the authenticity alias naturalness of an experiential product has to do with trust. Thus, the family camp as a product is authentic if the family experiences it as trustworthy and natural. Third, there is always a story involved: it is related to the authenticity of the family product and lends the product and the experience a social meaning. In today's experience society the stories have various meanings, thus also in a family camp. The stories enable to offer the parents a possibility to create stories themselves as well as understand themselves better thanks to other people's stories. In order to include all senses, a family camp has to be planned in a balanced and attractive manner. The activities of a family camp can be experienced with different senses: by seeing, hearing, touching, through colours, sounds, tastes. Fifth, the contrastivity of the situation compared to the everyday: the activities in the camp and the situation enable personal testing in communication, sports, arts as well as everyday routines. That is a novel and surprising situation for the families compared to their everyday. Sixth, while talking about family work probably the most important criterion to meet is communication. Communication creates a feeling of belonging to a community, experiencing something together, being a family, a team. Being together, doing things together, communicating – these are the most important traits of a family camp, thus the everyday family camp model meets the criteria of an experiential product. Producing experiences implies to creating experiential possibilities and/or environment, and therewith products that offer the clients and organizations a sense of achievement and to improve efficiency through that (Tarssanen and Kylänen 2007). Service products in general need to appeal to emotions and offer new, meaningful experiences (Kylänen 2012).

As a result of the qualitative content analysis (Mayring 2000) of the data, three important categories emerged: communality, functionality and experiences. These form the open architecture model alias the product. The idea behind designing a family camp is to produce an innovative environment and a social experience through a product of communal and experiential activities in the camp. Participating in a family camp can take the family to changes both in their minds and in everyday activities. In short, the study revealed rich possibilities for family services. Different variables influence family work and the way family camps are organised since families' needs are different. There is no single model to describe family work. Figure 4 presents the open architecture model consisting of the three above-mentioned categories that were identified as most important while interpreting the results of the content analysis (Leppiman, 2010). The model can be customised and changed according to the needs of the target group.

Camp-based experiential family work as a welfare product has been included in the model as a product emerging from the present empirical research. It
can be replaced by any other experiential product designed for another organization, including motivation, physical environment to implement the model, learning, a sense of achievement and changes in efficiency. The advantage of the
model is its customizability, changeability and openness. Based on the open architecture model, products and services can be worked out and designed for different organizations, to answer the needs of both business and non-profit organizations.

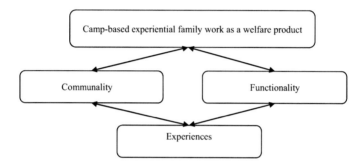

Fig. 6:   *The open architecture model of developing an experiential product; Source:*
            Leppiman 2010

The study presented in this paper emphasises the numerous possibilities of
the camp-based experiential family work. Family work and the design and content of family camps are influenced by several variables since needs of families
are different. As it was said, family work cannot be described using only one
model (Pulkkinen and Launonen 2005).

All the five family camps that served as basis of the present study were carried out according to the needs and wishes of the respective participants, the
goal of the project and the resources of the people involved. The everyday family work model that was worked out based on the study relies on the life situation
of families. Emanating from that, the elements of the camp-based experiential
family work are functionality, communality and experiences. The aim of the
ethnographic study of family camps was to work out new, innovative forms of
family work. The study focused on the social experience (Leppiman 2010).

5. Discussion

As a result of the research the term *everyday experiences* emerged (Leppiman 2010) describing little things of the everyday that are important for people and that they learn to see in a new way and that lead to changes. In an organization, which can be seen as a DC to re-evaluate existing resources or use them in an innovative way according to the changing needs of the organization.

The research shows that voluntary work based on strong motivation, economic calculations and readiness to accept challenges are suited to serve as elements of the camp-based experiential family work as a product. The product is put into practice as an intensive experiential family camp centring on the competency, participation and personal willingness to contribute to the work. The society profits from the camp-based family work as an experiential product as material support and helplessness decrease (Leppiman and Puustinen-Niemelä 2006; Leppiman 2010).

The civil society actors would use the model of learning through acquiring a sense of achievement and thus their capability to balance the interests of the business sector and public power in the society would improve. Thus the post-soviet specialty, a vicious cycle – through social labelling of 'winners' and 'losers', where the civil society actors are seen as the 'losers' (a label they have internalised) – of learned helplessness in the competition in spite of the everyday life that demands competing, demands success – can be broken: first, by creating an innovative product, second, by daring to enter the market since through acquiring a sense of achievement the self-esteem has improved.

The development of the third sector, as the civil society is often called in reference to the public sector, started in Estonia at the beginning of the 1990s (Lagerspetz, Rikmann, Ruutsoo 2007). Volunteer associations that are non-profit in their intentions were actively established then. The need for the active establishment of civil society organizations came from economic and social changes taking place in the Estonian transition society. For example, there were 103 non-profit organizations dealing with rights and needs of children registered in Estonia in 1999 as the preventive intervention methods related to families and welfare were studied the first time (Leppiman 2010). After the re-establishment of the Republic of Estonia in 1991, the society started shifting towards an information, knowledge and experience society, based on a market economy. Unfortunately lots of families did not adapt to the major social changes and were no more able to manage their lives (Leppiman, ibid.). Presently there are over 200 non-profit organizations dealing with producing and offering family services in Estonia. It shows that the need for services that help clients manage a crisis has not diminished but increased, especially if we think of the actual depression: obviously, there is a correlation between the economic crisis and families' struggle for livelihoods. In the years of economic growth the living standard in Estonia improved considerably. In 2008, the situation changed, the economic growth was replaced by the depression which brought along a downfall of the welfare of the families and what's worse, unemployment. That meant a growing danger of poverty for the more vulnerable social classes. The elderly people were affected less by the depression as their income is fixed. Poverty endangers first of all unemployed working-age people, especially singles and single parents.

The central social problem in this context is the conflict between the expectations, demands on establishing livelihoods and social skills of the families, on the one hand, and the possibilities offered by the Estonian society, on the other hand. The society expects the families to act as independent subjects, at the same time not being able to supply the endangered families sufficiently with social support. Guaranteeing the latter presupposes strengthening of the natural support mechanisms of the society as well as developing innovative forms of social support (Leppiman ibid.).

Because of the fast changes taking place in the society in general as well as in economy, the challenge while designing products and services lies in the dynamic nature of the latter. Thus it is important to design products and services that are easy to change, i.e. they must have open design architecture. The camp-based experiential family work as a welfare product as well as an innovative definition that was designed as a result of our research, has open architecture and can thus be altered according to needs in no time (Leppiman ibid.). Open design architecture is one of the strategies for practice. We believe that the emerging practice of service design is complex and dynamic, and demands, among other things, interdisciplinary teamwork, prototyping as a vehicle for dialogue, open design architecture; and involves negotiations between functional and emotional benefits (see also Moritz 2005; Leppiman 2010; Lockwood 2010; Park 2010; Saco and Goncalves 2010; Leppiman et al. 2012).

Summarising the aforesaid, we come up with the following conclusions: first, the capabilities of both an organization and an individual are vulnerable. Both of them are confronted with the necessity to balance capabilities and work on efficiency. The mechanism of improving capabilities is similar for organizations and individuals. Thanks to experiential learning through acquiring a sense of achievement both activity and behaviour change. Both an individual and an organization develop a new identity. Even more: the motivation to accept even bigger challenges and to use the resources in order to succeed improves as well.

Second, new resources in social and human capital improve also economic success, i.e. economic capital. Through experiences new social resources are formed. Experiences are positive irritants that enable a new experience that launches changes thanks to learning. The experiences of self-overcoming, coping and succeeding gained through social experiences can direct the activities and behaviour of organizations as well as individuals. Today, in the field of business experience innovation is necessary.

Third, the civil society actors can often be described as passive and noncommitted in their behaviour in Estonia today. We argue that if the civil society would use the model of learning through acquiring a sense of achievement, their capability to balance the interests of the business sector and the public power in the society would improve.

Fourth, based on the open architecture model, experiential products and services can be worked out and designed for different organizations, to answer the needs of both business and non-profit organizations. The model consists of functionality, communality and experiences. It is customizable, changeable and open, and thus adaptable to changing economic conditions.

We know that the open architecture model functions in a non-profit organization. In the future the challenge is to analyse whether the model is applicable to different organizations, in order to create something new via sense of achievement, communality and functionality – be it working out a new product, designing a new service or carrying out a project.

References

Alasuutari, P. 1993. Laadullinen tutkimus.Vastapaino. Tampere.

Alasuutari, P. 2001. Johdatus yhteiskuntatutkimukseen. Hanki ja Jää. Gaudeamus. Yliopistopaino. Helsinki.

Ambrosini, V., Bowman, C. and Collier, N. 2009. Dynamic Capabilities: An Exploration of How Firms Renew their Resource Base. British Journal of Management. Vol.20, pp. S9–S24.

Argyris, C. and Schön, D. 1978. Organizational Learning. Addison Wesley. Reading.

Atkinson, P., Coffey, A., Delamont, S., Lofland, J. and Lofland, L. 2001. Handbook of Ethnography. Sage Publications Ltd. London.

Bourdieu, P. 1985. Distinction: A Social Critique of the Judgement of   Taste.Cambridge (Mass.): Harvard University Press.

Caplan, G. 1974. Support Systems and Community Mental Health: Lectures on Concept Development. New York: Behavioural Publications.

Cobb, S. 1976. Social Support as a moderator of Life Stress. Psychosomatic Medicine 38, pp. 300–314.

Cohen, S. and Syme, S. L. 1985. Social Support and Health. Academic Press. USA.

Coleman, J. 1990 Foundations of Social Theory. Mass. Harvard University Press. Cambridge.

Denscombe, M. 2000. The good Research Guide for small – Scale Social Research projects. Open University Press. Maidenhead. PA.

Dick, B. 1993. You want to do an Action Research Thesis? A Guide on how to conduct and report Action Research. http://www.scu.edu.au/schools/sawd/arr/arth/arthesis.html

Dunkel-Schetter, C. and Bennett, T. L. 1990. Differentiating the Cognitive and Behavioral aspects of Social Support. In: Social Support: An interactional view. Sarason, Barbara R. & Sarason, Irwin G. & Pierce, Gregory R. (Eds.): Whiley & Sons. New York, pp. 267–296.

Edvinsson, L. 2004. The Intellectual Capital of Nations. Handbook on Knowledge Management 1, Knowledge matters, pp.153–163.

Engeström, Y. 1995. Kehittävä työntutkimus: perusteita, tuloksia ja haasteita. Hallinnon kehittämiskeskus. Helsinki.

Eskola, J. and Suoranta, J. 1998. Johdatus laadulliseen tutkimukseen. Vastapaino. Tampere.

French, W.L. and Bell, C.H. 1990 Organization Development. Behavioural Science Interventions for Organizational Development. Prentice Hall. New Jersey.

Geertz, C. 1988. Works and Lives: the Anthropologist as Author. Polity Press. Cambridge.

Gibbs, G. 2009. Analyzing Qualitative Data. The SAGE Qualitative Research Kit. London: SAGE.

Habermas, J. 1998. Between Facts and Norms, Cambridge: Polity Press.

Hall, D. T. 1988. Career development in organisations. Jossey-Bass. San Francisco.

Hammersley, M. 1991 and 1998. Reading Ethnographic Research: A Critical Guide. Addison Wesley Longman. London & New York.

Heikkinen, H. 2001. Toimintatutkimus, tarinat ja opettajaksi tulemisen taito: Narratiivisen identiteettityön kehittäminen opettajankoulutuksessa toimintatutkimuksen avulla. Väitöskirja. Jyväskylä yliopisto. Jyväskylä.

Helfat, C.E. and Peteraf, M.A. 2003. The Dynamic Resource-based View: Capability lifecycles. Strategical Management Journal. 24, pp. 997–2010.

House, J. S. 1981. Work Stress and Social Support. Addison-Wesley. Reading, MA.

Isokorppi, T. 2003. Tunneälytaitojen ja yhteisöllisyyden oppiminen reflektoinnin ja ryhmäprosessin avulla. Tampereen yliopisto & Hämeen AMK. Akateeminen väitöskirja. Saarijärven Offset Oy. Saarijärvi.

Kaljund, K. and Peterson, A.-L. 2007. Avalikkuse eeldustest Eestis: kodanikualgatusega seotud stereotüpiseerivad pildid meediasuhtluses. Algatus, osalus ja organisatsioonid: uurimusi Eesti kodanikuühiskonnast. Tallinn, pp. 86–106.

Kaljund, K. and Peterson, A.-L. 2012. The 4th Task and the 4th Power: Newly Formed Civil Society Actors Captured by the Estonian Post-Socialist Mass Media? Forthcoming.

Kylänen, M.2012. Service Design Meets Hospitality Industry. Service Design Magazine. Lahti University of Applied Sciences, series C, part 107, p.35.

Lagerspetz, M., Ruutsoo, R. and Rikmann, E. 2007. Sissejuhatus: kaks aastakümmet kodanikualgatust, poolteist aastakümmet kodanikualgatuse uurimist Eestis. Algatus, osalus, organisatsioonid: uurimusi Eesti kodanikuühiskonnast, ed. E. Rikmann. Tallinn, pp. 7–21.

Lauristin, M. 2004. Eesti ühiskonna kihistumine. Eesti elavik 21. sajandi algul: ülevaade uurimuse Mina. Maailm. Meedia tulemustest, Tartu, pp. 251–285.

Leppiman, A. 2004.Tööturule kogemuse kaudu õppides. In V Sotsiaalteaduste aastakonverents. Inimkapital ja sotsiaalne kapital globaliseeruvas maailmas. Estonian Social Science ONLINE: www.psych.ut.ee/esta/online/ Tartu Ülikool. Tartu.

Leppiman, A. 2006. Oppimaan opettaminen – oppimisen iloa ja hämmennystä. In: Lehtonen, H. Oppijan kasvun tukeminen. Tampereen yliopisto. Opettajankoulutuslaitos. Hämeenlinna, pp. 93–106.

Leppiman, A. and Puustinen-Niemelä, S. 2006. Joy of learning in project work: Sustaining the learner and the teacher. In: Pipere, Anita (Eds.): Education and Sustainable Development: First Steps Toward Changes Volume 1, Baltic and Black Sea Circle Consortium Institute of Sustainable Education Daugavpils University, Saule, Daugavpils, pp.101–118.

Leppiman, A. 2010. Arjen elämyksiä – Leiri- ja elämyspohjainen Arkipäivät-perhepalvelu sosiaalisen kokemuksen tuottajana/ Everyday Experiences: Camp- and Experience-Based Weekdays Family Service as a Producer of Social Experience, Rovaniemi: Lapland University Press.

Leppiman, A., Laitinen, M. and Pohjola, A. 2012. Service Design: Consumer Behavior in Social Work. Forthcoming.

Lockwood, Thomas (Ed.) 2010. Design Thinking. Integrating Innovation, Customer Experience, and Brand Value. New York: Allworth Press.

Mason, J. 2007. Qualitative researching. London: Sage Publications.

Mayring, P. 2000. Qualitative Content Analysis, Qualitative Methods in Various Disciplines I: Psychology, 1 (2) June, Forum: Qualitative Social Research Socialforschung (http://www.qualitative-research.net/index.php/fqs/article/view/ 1089/2385).

Moisander. J. and Valtonen, A. 2011. Interpretive Marketing Research: Using Ethnography in Strategic Market Development In: Marketing Management A Cultural Perspective London: Routledge.

Morgan, D. L. 1990. Combining the Strengths of Social Support, and Personal Relationships. In: Duck, Steve & Cohen, Roxane (Eds.): Personal Relationships and Social Support. Sage. London, pp. 190–215.

Moritz, S. 2005. Service Design: Practical Access to an Evolving Field. (MA Thesis: Köln International School of Design). http://stefan-moritz.com/welcome/Service_Design.html (15.10.2012)

Park, M. 2010. Design overview: Contextual Perspectives. In: Kathryn Best (Ed.) The Fundamentals of Design Management. AVA Publishing SA, pp. 66–67.

Saco, Roberto M., and Goncalves, Alexis P. 2010. Service Design: An Appraisal. In: Thomas Lockwood (Ed.) Design Thinking. Integrating Innovation, Customer Experience, and Brand Value. New York: Allworth Press.

Pine, J. B. II and Gilmore, J. 1999/2011. The Experience Economy, Cambridge, MA: Harvard Business School Press.

Pine, J. B. II and Tarssanen, S. 2008. A Deep Dive into the Experience Economy, Workbook, Strategic Horizon LLP and LCEEI, Rovaniemi.

Pine, J. B. II and Korn, K.C. 2011. Infinite Possibility: Creating Customer Value on the Digital Frontier. Berrett-Koehler Publishers, Inc.

Pruulmann-Vengerfeldt, P. 2004. Kultuuriline, sotsiaalne ja majanduslik kapital: Eesti inimeste ressursid erinevateseluvaldkondades. Eesti elavik 21. sajandi algul: ülevaade uurimuse Mina. Maailm. Meedia tulemustest. Studia Societatis et Communicationis I. Tartu, pp. 217–230.

Pulkkinen, L. and Launonen, L. 2005. Eheytetty koulupäivä: Lapsilähtöinen näkökulma koulupäivän uudistamiseen. Edita Prima Oy. Helsinki.

Putnam, R. D. 2000. Bowling Alone: The Collapse and Revival of American Community. New York: Simon and Schuster.

Putnam, R. D. 2002. Community-based social capital and educational performance. New Haven: Yale University Press.

Rautiainen, V. and Keskinen, S. 1999. Sosiaalinen tuki päiväkotihenkilöstön voimavarana. In: Keskinen, Soili & Virtanen, Nana (Eds.): Päiväkoti työyhteisönä. Helsingin yliopiston Lahden Tutkimus- ja Koulutuskeskus. Tammer-Paino Oy. Tampere.

Riivits-Arkonsuo, I. and Leppiman, A. 2013. Consumer online word-of-mouth – analysis through an experience pyramid model. Forthcoming.

Roberts, Gerard M. 1997. Action Researching: My practice as a facilitator of Experiential Learning with Pastoralist Farmers in Central West Queensland. http://www.scu.edu.au/schools/gcm/ar/art/t-groberts00.html. (13.11.2012)

Rommelspacher, B. 1995. Dominanzkultur: Texte zu Fremdheit und Macht. Orlanda Frauenverlag, Berlin.

Schulze, G. 1992. Die Erlebnisgesellschaft. Kultursoziologie der Gegenwart. Campus   Verlag. Fulda.

Tarssanen, S. and Kylänen, M. 2007. A Theoretical Model for Producing Experiences – A Touristic Perspective, in Kylänen, M. (Eds.), Articles on Experiences 2, Lapland Centre of Expertise for the Experience Industry, Rovaniemi: Lapland University Press, pp. 134–154.

Tarssanen, S. and Kylänen, M. (2009). Handbook for experience stagers. In Tarssanen, S. 5th ed. Lapland Center of Expertise for the Experience Industry, Rovaniemi: OY Sevenprint Ltd.

Teece, D. J. 2007. Explicating dynamic capabilities: the nature and microfoundations of (sustainable) enterprise performance. Strategic Management Journal, 28, pp. 1319–1350.

Teece, D.J., Pisano, P. and Shuen, A. 1997. Dynamic Capabilities and Strategic Management. Strategic Management Journal. Vol. 18, No7, pp. 509–533.

Teece, D. and Pisano, G. 1994. The dynamic capabilities of firms: an introduction. Industrial and Corporate Change, 3(3), pp. 537–556.

Thoits, P. A. 1985. Social Support and Psychological Well-being: Theoretical possibilities. In Sarason, I. G.and Sarason, B. R. Social Support: Theory, Research and Applications. Martinus Nijhoff publishers. Dordrecht, Netherlands, pp. 51–72.

Törrönen, J. 2002. Tieteellisen tekstin rakenne. Tieteellinen kirjoitaminen. Vastapaino. Tampere, pp. 29–49.

Veijola, A. 2004: Matkalla moniammatilliseen perhetyön: lasten kuntoutuksen kehittäminen toimintatutkimuksen avulla. Oulun yliopisto. Oulu.

Wang, C.L. and Ahmed, P.K. 2007. Dynamic capabilities: A review and research agenda. International Journal of Management Reviews. Volume 9, Issue 1, pp. 31–51.

Zollo, M. and Winter, S.G. 2002. Deliberate Learning and the Evolution of Dynamic Capabilities. Organization Science. Vol.13, No 3, pp. 339–351.

Europe's Goal for Better Workplaces: Development of the Legislation for Occupational Exposure to the Electromagnetic Fields

Tarmo Koppel[1] and Ülo Kristjuhan[1]

Abstract

This paper tackles the development of the new European Union's occupational electromagnetic fields (EMF) directive. The directive was called for to answer the European workers' need for protection from emerging health risks, such as electromagnetic fields. The aim of the study was to determine the readiness of the stakeholders to adopt this new occupational health and safety legislation. The strengths and weaknesses of the directive are analysed based on the study conducted amongst the stakeholders of the new directive. The authors asked from scientists, legislators, employees, work inspectorate employees and medical personnel their expectations and possible problems with the new directive. As a result, several shortcomings were pointed out, but weighted differently by different parties. The researchers see that the new directive does not encompass all the biological effects of the electromagnetic fields. The workers share the opinion of the researchers, but are also worried about the long-term effects the directive does not cover. The employers are most concerned with the administrative and financial burden. The doctors and work inspectors feel that they are not trained to identify and deal with the EMF related health effects. The authors also discuss the economic impact of the directive and find the most affected to be small and medium-sized enterprises.

JEL classification codes: H5, Q5

Keywords: EU directive, electromagnetic fields, occupational exposure, national legislation, policy development

1. Introduction

Annually 5,500 workers lose their lives in the EU as a result of work accidents, additionally 159,000 die from work-related illnesses (European Agency for Safety and Health at Work – EASHW 2012c). A large number of these consequences could have been prevented if proper occupational health and safety measures had been implemented and workplace risks properly managed. The financial loss from badly managed occupational health and safety (OHS) does not only reflect in the costs of work accidents and cure and care of occupational illness but much more. The European Agency for Safety and Health at Work sets a formula for calculating total financial loss or gain from occupational

---

1   Tallinn University of Technology, Ehitajate tee 5, Tallinn Estonia,
     E-mail: tarmo.koppel@ttu.ee

health and safety management that includes (EASHW 2002): work related absenteeism; excessive personnel turnover due to poor working conditions; administrative overhead; legal costs, fines, indemnities; damaged equipment and materials; investigation costs; effects on insurance premium; lost production (reduced output); orders lost; rework, repairs, rejections related to OHS; warranties related to OHS; more work due to safety procedures; lost attractiveness to potential customers; worse position on the labour market, less attractive to new personnel. Therefore one could easily see the vast influence of a badly managed occupational health and safety system on company's financial outcome.

This paper tackles the occupational health and safety legislation from one aspect only – the electromagnetic fields (EMFs). The EMFs have been classified as a new and emerging risk factor. The developments in technology during the last 15 years have only recently introduced the European worker to greater amounts of electromagnetic fields than ever before in history. The unprecedented levels of EMFs have raised concern amongst the European workforce so that the European leaders have decided to address it by developing new legislation. The importance of occupational health and safety (OHS) has also become a matter of priority in the legislation issued by the European Union (EU). The urge to develop occupational health and safety in the EU can largely be attributed to political will induced by the European workers' values towards their health. Also, a known proverb „good ergonomics is good economics" says it best: the more healthy and comfortable the workplace, the more productive the worker is. Although making workplaces safe and ergonomic may require substantial investments, in turn it reflects in the increased revenues of the company. The latter principle might just be a driving force for the European leaders – as the European economy has entered into the recession, new solutions are required to ensure the region's competitiveness in the global scale.

Europe is facing a challenge from new environmental exposures such as high frequency (HF) electromagnetic fields, used widely nowadays in telecommunications, mobile communications, data transfer etc. Utilization of switching circuits has also increased exposure to intermediate frequencies. This has raised a concern amongst general population in regard to the safety of the workplaces. European leaders have addressed the concern by starting the development of new legislation. This paper addresses the new occupational electromagnetic fields directive – the role it will have among the stakeholders. The full name of the law is: the directive of the European Parliament and of the Council on the minimum health and safety requirements regarding the exposure of workers to the risks arising from physical agents (electromagnetic fields).

The European Parliament passed the directive on 29th of April 2004, just two days before welcoming ten new member states to the EU. One could argue whether hurrying with the directive was reasonable, as the directive is still not in force. The 2004 version of the directive implemented the ICNIRP (International Commission on Non-Ionizing Radiation Protection) 1998 guidelines. In 2008, the decision was made to delay the enforcement of the directive as member states were not ready and a call was made to revise the directive according to new scientific knowledge. Since in 2011 the European Commission issued a draft for the new directive replacing the 2004 version, member states have worked to develop a compromise for the new version, which, when ready, is to be finally approved by the European Parliament.

In countries where legislative attention has been paid to electromagnetic fields exposure, one of the three systems has been adopted: 1) IEEE (Institute of Electrical and Electronics Engineers), 2) ICNIRP and 3) Eastern Europe (former Soviet Union system) (Muc 2001). The first two are not so much different, but the last one has roots in soviet research that came into different conclusions from western counterparts with stricter safety limits in regard to health effects. The European Union has based its directive on ICNIRP (western) guidelines, as it is more comprehensive compared to the others and is mainly a European based organization. Most of the countries that use ICNIRP guidelines use IC-NIRP 1998 Guidelines (ICNIRP 1998). In 2010, ICNIRP issued new guidelines for the frequencies from 1 Hz to 100 kHz, which supersede ICNIRP 1998 guidelines in ICNIRP's own eyes (ICNIRP 2010). ICNIRP's guidelines differentiate effects from central nervous system (CNS) and peripheral nervous system (PNS). In rough comparison, CNS is considered human head and PNS the body. ICNIRP provides different limits for PNS and CNS (ICNIRP 2010). Besides basic restrictions ICNIRP guidelines also provide reference levels. Reference levels are introduced as a vast majority of the workplaces do not exceed the basic restrictions. Therefore a more simple approach is applicable with reference level without the need for specialised and costly EMF measurements to determine the compliance with basic restrictions. The reference levels are also for both CNS and PNS effects.

IEEE does not distinguish between exposures to general population and workers whereas ICNIRP does. IEEE has still two sets of limits: for public and for controlled environments (Swanson 2011). In authors' opinion it is necessary to separate general population and occupational exposure as when indeed safe limits are exceeded in some instances, the economy should not need to suffer from such restrictions. Indeed, some workplaces do require above the average exposure to electromagnetic fields, as otherwise it would be impossible to provide the society/economy with the important services such as distribution of electricity or arc welding in metal workings. As seen from the example of chemical agents' regulations in EU, the workplaces do get safer in regard to chemicals, but actually, many of such workplaces are moved out of Europe, like South-East Asia where OHS legislation is easier in regard to these workplace factors. Reasons for moving workplaces are many, operational costs being one of the most considered ones, where OHS costs do play a role.

As ICNIRP and IEEE are non-governmental organizations their guidelines only offer advice and are not mandatory. Their guidelines are not issued as ready-made solutions for protecting people against harms from EMFs. According to ICNIRP, their guidelines are based on scientifically sound evidence to mark the EMFs strengths that produce scientifically established adverse health effects.

Taking into account the rapid development and widespread use of mobile communications and data transfer technology in the past years, the issue of safety and health from electromagnetic fields has heated debates not only amongst scientists. Recent developments in Europe have stressed the relevance of considering the electromagnetic fields as a potential environmental risk factor. Such top-level attention towards a specific environmental health factor, though most rapidly increasing one, has also gained much attention all over the world. The recent steps include a report from the committee of the Council of Europe (not to be mistaken with the Council of the European Union) in May 2011 saying that the technologies have "potentially harmful" effects on humans, and immediate action is required to protect the children (PACE – Parliamentary Assembly of the Council of Europe 2011). The report calls for actions to protect humans and the environment from the high-frequency electromagnetic fields (PACE 2011).

In May 2011, the World Health Organization's group of experts at the International Agency for Research on Cancer raised the danger level classification of radiofrequency electromagnetic fields to "possibly carcinogenic" (group 2B) for humans (IARC 2011).

The European Parliament's resolution 2008/2211(INI) on health concerns associated with electromagnetic fields points out the rapid increase of man-made electromagnetic fields due to the implementation of new technology (Wi-Fi, WiMAX, Bluetooth, DECT) and their possible adverse health effects on humans (EP – European Parliament 2009).

Indeed, the EU directive's legislators have taken the precautionary principle as a cornerstone of the directive. The European Commission considers the precautionary principle as: "where preliminary objective scientific evaluation indicates that there are reasonable grounds for concern that the potentially dangerous effects on the environment, human, animal or plant health" (EC – European Commission 2000). By the Commission's approach the precautionary principle is accompanied by the structured approach to the analysis of risk, comprising risk assessment, risk management, risk communication (EC 2000). All of these three steps are also paid attention to in the framework of the EMF directive.

This paper serves the reader by providing an analysis for the affected parties (stakeholders) of the coming directive. The reader will get an understanding of the process that has been going on for more than ten years and which will have an influence on the entire EU workforce. This paper will also cover the economic aspects of the directive from the point of view of the European companies. The general goal of this paper is to determine how well prepared different sectors of economy are in regard to implementing the new occupational EMF directive. Also it is discussed if such legislation is at all needed and what the possible problems associated with it are.

2. Method

The data used to analyse the readiness of the stakeholders for the new directive were collected by questioning the parties affected. The interviewees were selected to cover the range of stakeholders affected by the new EMF directive (fig. 1).

The method of this study included 1) reviewing the literature concerning the occupational EMFs directive and 2) obtaining relevant points of view by different stakeholders by means of questioning.

The questionings conducted were seeking answers to the following questions:

- what is the level of knowledge on EMFs,
- are there persons appointed to deal with the EMF issues in that establishment,
- what type of discussions have taken place in regard to the EMFs,
- what problems have arisen in regard to the EMFs at the workplaces.

To get a better overview from a specific sector and not only a reflection to the issue from one company, mainly a trade union chairman or an appointed representative was selected to be questioned. The questionings included one-on-one interviews, one-on-one interviews by telephone or teleconference, group interviews and written interviews.

The answers to the above mentioned questions allowed the authors to determine the readiness of the stakeholders to implement or to submit to the new rules set by the coming directive. Also, the questionings revealed the attitudes and the motivations of the stakeholders towards the directive.

2.1 The stakeholders

The stakeholders involved and/or affected by the new EMF directive have each a different role to play that must be taken into account in the final document. The following conceptual model was used as a basis for the analysis in this study. Let's take a look at the type of impact each group has from the new directive (Fig. 1).

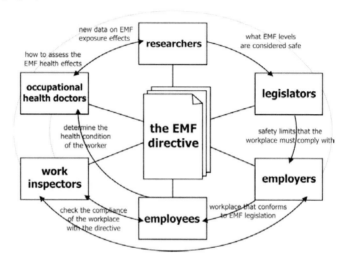

Fig. 1:   *Stakeholders of the occupational EMF directive and their interaction. Source:*
author's drawing

The **researchers'** role is to provide the scientific body of knowledge. The research on health effects caused by EMFs is the basis for drawing up the safety limits. As the findings of one research must be confirmed by others, the scientific process is time consuming. Therefore we still do not have a full overview of what direct and indirect effects can be related to electromagnetic fields' exposure. This makes the issue of electromagnetic fields and the possible danger from them a controversial subject with a wide range of opinions and recommendations. Nevertheless scientists offer the legislators the most up to date knowledge on what levels of EMFs are considered safe and what are not.

The **legislators** answer the general public's (voters) demand for protection from environmental risk factors. A worker today needs to retain his/her workability tomorrow. Otherwise not only the worker suffers but also national budget from many of similar case workers. The legislators carry a leading role in designing the directive and involving all the other stakeholders. The EU member states' national legislations are based on the EU directive and must have no contradictions to it. The idea behind the EU directive is to give the member states a basic framework for occupational EMF regulation and let the states do their own modifications, based on their needs, given that they do not contradict (are looser) than those stated in the directive. So, the directive might be considered as a compromise between 27 member states, a common agreement, and a starting point from where to develop their own national legislation. The legislators use consultations from scientists, employers and employees' representatives to draw up the legislative acts that are to regulate the EMF level in workplaces.

The **employers'** role is to see that the workplaces meet the requirements stated in the national legislation. The requirements' central part is the safety limits; but also other issues must be taken into account, such as how to do the EMF risk assessment, manage and communicate the risks associated with the EMFs. In the directive's development process the employers' organizations report to the legislators what limits are reasonable and what limits are unrealistic to achieve, considering the existing electro-technical infrastructure. These reports will also result in some exceptions granted by the directive.

The **employees** are unable themselves to determine whether electromagnetic fields at their workplaces represent any danger to their health. They must rely on legislative safety limits and trust their health to employers' hands. The workers are represented by trade unions. Trade unions collect the reports from their members regarding the suspected EMF related health effects. Trade union representatives forward their concerns and opinions to the legislators to be considered in forming the safety limits. But also researchers are involved with the employees whilst conducting studies on occupational exposure to the EMFs.

Governmental agencies supervising the exposure to EMFs at workplaces such as work inspection authorities do regular inspections to workplaces and advise employers on how to comply with the directive. After the implementation of the directive, the work inspectorate is to play an important role in sharing know-how, as the matter of electromagnetic-fields is one of the most complicated ones from all work environment stressors. Unlike other stressors, a human being is not capable of seeing, hearing, smelling or feeling the EMFs. Only in case of overexposure a person may start to develop symptoms, but then it is too late. Therefore sharing good knowledge on how to manage EMFs at workplaces is an important task on behalf of the occupational health and safety authorities.

Doctors, especially occupational health specialists are responsible for supervising the health of the workers and detecting and confirming possible EMF related problems. The challenge of doctors in this conceptual diagram (figure 1) is to adequately connect the worker's health symptoms to EMFs exposure – a task that the doctors are not yet prepared to do. Case studies and research done by medical professionals is also providing the basis for future improvements of the legislation (EU directive). In the authors opinion physicians have a great role to play in this matter, as many of the EMF caused ailments are mistakenly diagnosed as a stress from other various reasons. The reason for this is that the medical personnel are not trained to diagnose symptoms from EMF overexposure and most of them have little knowledge regarding the EMFs.

2. Results

3.1. Legislation

Inevitably there are some occupations that carry a high exposition to the electromagnetic fields and there are those that have minimal exposition. The authors provide an overview of the most EMF affected occupations in table 1. The list does not pretend to present all the occupations that have a significant EMF exposure on workers body, but to provide most typical ones to give the reader an idea both of the occupation and of the EMF exposure characteristics. As the exposure to the electromagnetic fields comes from the electrical equipment surrounding the worker, such high levels as these professions may come into contact with may also be experienced by other workers due to faulty, outdated or incorrectly used equipment or settings. Therefore the most significant way the workers can diminish their exposure to the electromagnetic fields is to obtain a good level of knowledge on 1) what are the sources of the EMFs, 2) how are the EMFs propagated and 3) by which mechanisms the EMFs affect human's physical or mental health.

Table 1: Typical occupations with greater exposure to the electromagnetic fields

Sector of economy /society	Typical occupations	Typical frequencies of EMF sources
mobile communications	cell phone mast, uplink antennas technicians, transmitter station operators (near amplifier station or antenna)	GSM, 3G, 4G etc. at UHF 806-2690MHz
broadcasting	TV and radio transmitter station technicians	AM radio mainly at 520-1610kHz FM radio 76-108MHz TV VHF channels at 174-230MHz, TV UHF channels at 470-862MHz
transportation	streetcar, trolley bus, locomotive, metro operators, technicians	DC (0Hz); AC 16,7Hz; AC 50Hz

electrical industry	linesmen, power station operators, stationary engineers, electrical technicians	SLF power frequency at 50Hz; DC (0Hz) and LF 20-100kHz at low voltage systems
metal-workings	welders arc welders	ELF an SLF at 20-400Hz; VLF and LF at 10-100kHz; pulsing nature according to discharges
medical sector	MRI (magnetic resonance imaging) operators and technicians	DC (0Hz); SLF and ULF at 100-1000Hz; HF and VHF at 10-100MHz
military, boarder guard, air traffic	radar post operators, technicians, mobile transmitter station operators	from HF at 3MHz to EHF at 40 GHz
various sectors	radiofrequency sealers' operators industrial heaters' operators thermoelectric equipment workers	1-100MHz HF and VHF

Abbreviations: ELF (Extremely Low Frequency), SLF (Super Low Frequency), ULF (Ultra Low Frequency), VLF (Very Low Frequency), LF (Low Frequency; "longwave"), HF (High Frequency; "shortwave"), VHF (Very High Frequency), UHF (Ultra High Frequency), EHF (Extremely High Frequency).
Sources: Authors; Muc 2001; Keevil et a. 2005; Luck 2008; Miller et al. 1997, Stuchly 1980

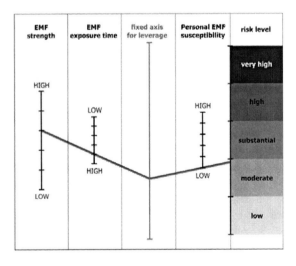

Fig. 2:   EMF exposure determinants. Example: person with low susceptibility to EMFs works at a workplace with higher than average electromagnetic field strength but spends a little time in the vicinity of those EMF sources – this person's occupational EMF exposure risk level is assessed as moderate. Source: Koppel

As presented in Fig. 2, the authors have derived the conceptual relations between EMF exposure and EMF strength to produce EMF risk level, based on the semi-quantitative risk analysis calculation based on 3 dimensions. The nomogram as presented in Figure 2 represents an interactive risk measurement method that would calculate the overall risk score based on the three dimensions. The importance of the nomogram (Fig. 2) is to give the reader an understanding of three crucial factors affecting EMF risk level of the worker: 1) EMF strength, 2) EMF exposure time, and 3) personal susceptibility to EMFs. However, the occupational EMF directive under study in this paper considers only one of these dimensions (EMF strength) to determine whether the workplace is safe or not. In authors' opinion safety level cannot be reliably assessed based only on the EMF strength. The strength of the electromagnetic fields is nevertheless the most important factor of the exposure risk assessment, but dismissing other two factors that are known to have a role in reflecting the EMFs effect on worker's well-being, makes the directive less reliable. The weakness of using only one dimension (EMF strength) in the directive is known to the legislators and therefore a corresponding remark is added to the text. However, worker's representatives have expressed the desire to see the directive not only to cover acute, short-term effects from the EMFs, but also long-term effects. Still, the legislators are unable to accompany long-term effects into the directive as the scientific body of knowledge is scarce in regard to the long-term effects. Therefore the directive was seen as a necessity to address the European workers' concern regarding the EMFs, but doing so only accompanying short-term effects. In authors' opinion a directive that addresses some of the concerns of the electroclimate of the workplaces is still better than none. Still, one must take into account what kind of adverse effects the directive is meant to protect the workers from – short-term acute effects, as otherwise the workers may have an impression that the directive protects them from all the adverse effects from the EMFs.

Another type of misconception that the directive may inexperienced reader to give is the claimed protection from all known adverse health effects from the electromagnetic fields (EP&EC 2004). As already explained, short-term effects are only covered dismissing the effects from long-term EMF exposure. Long-term effects are not included as it is yet quite unclear what effects, under which circumstances occur under long-term exposure. Therefore a claim cannot be made for the directive to cover all known adverse health effects and to provide workers with high level of safety.

Secondly, the directive is based on the ICNIRP (International Commission on Non-Ionizing Radiation Protection) guidelines, which only consider some of the adverse effects: mainly thermal effect, stimulation of peripheral and central nervous system (ICNIRP 1998, ICNIRP 2010). Other adverse health effects reported by the scientific research have been dismissed by ICNIRP as not yet confirmed. Therefore, in the authors' opinion, in the atmosphere of many new potential adverse health effects that have been associated with the electromagnetic fields but that have not yet found recognition by the international guidelines, it is not sound to claim the directive to provide a high level of protection as indeed a high level of uncertainty remains in the scientific community in regard to those effects.

The Bioinitiative Report issued by the international group of scientists, public health and public policy experts was a kind of a meta-summary, aimed to pointing out non-thermal health effects from the EMFs that have been taken into account neither in ICNIRP guidelines, IEEE nor EU directive (Bioinitiative 2007). The assessment of the Bioinitiative experts was that existing EMF public safety limits are inadequate (Bioinitiative 2007). The Bioinitiative group offers an explanation why the non-thermal effects have been disregarded by the legislation: as exposure limits are developed by scientists and engineers belonging to professional societies that have traditionally developed recommendations, the process has little input from other stakeholders outside professional engineering and related commercial interests (Bioinitiative 2007). The division amongst the scientists can also be referred to as 1) thermal effects proponents and 2) non-thermal effects proponents. Exposure limits at high frequency are currently based on the presumption that tissue heating or induction of electric currents in the body are the only things to concern when exposed to EMFs (Bioinitiative 2007). The non-thermal proponents acknowledge that tissue heating, even for a short period is harmful and need to be protected against, but disagree on dismissing non-thermal effects from the legislation and guidelines.

Shortly after the Bioinitiative Report, the European Environment Agency compared electromagnetic fields to other environmental hazards like smoking and lead in petrol to stress the need for precautionary and preventive measures (EEA – European Environment Agency 2007).

Another topic for discussion is the cognitive effects from the electromagnetic fields' exposure. These are not considered as adverse health effects by the directive, however, the authors argue that if a worker is unable to perform his/her task with a customary efficiency due to the scrambled brainwaves or another neurological condition, then the effect from EMFs does indeed affect the person's workability. In addition, the economic outcome of the entire workgroup exposed to such electromagnetic radiation is also affected, resulting in overall decrease in company's revenues.

The question of cognitive effects can be especially raised in regard to occupations requiring high attention where the person is performing a high responsibility job. Such cognitive effects – changes in brainwaves (measured by EEG –

electroencephalogram) – are found to be caused by common microwaves used by most mobile communication devices such as mobile phones (Hinrikus et al. 2005). Now, when the employer, workplace hygienist, worker representative or any other person reads the EU directive that promises him/her a high level of protection against all known health effects, the person is unlikely to suspect any other danger, like afore-discussed cognitive effect. What most specialists who deal with the directive are probably not qualified to conclude is that the cognitive effects are not considered as adverse health effects. The authors agree that cognitive affects might not represent danger to person's physical health, but the question still remains – to what extent the performance of the person is affected in regard to the occupational safety.

3.2. Stakeholders' responses

A total of 21 persons from various sectors of the economy/society in Estonia and Finland were interviewed. The authors present the results of the questionings per each stakeholder in table 2. The MRI and military sector are pointed out separately under the employers section, as the new EMF directive deals with these sectors particularly in regard to derogations.

Table 2:   Main findings of the study/interviews

Sector of economy/society	Strengths	Weaknesses, problems (in implementing)
Legislators	There is national legislation for both public and occupational exposure. National EMF standards on methodology are available, complemented by European standards. European legislation is implemented without major obstacles.	Postponement of the directive has resulted in gaps in national legislation in regard to some frequencies (Estonia).
Employers	Most workplaces with higher EMF exposure have EMF risks already under control, even without the directive.	Additional administrative burden. Possible new investments in workplaces and installations required that would most affect SMEs. Training of workers required. Shortage of measurement service providers.
MRI workers	There are already specific MRI safe practice standards that are being followed; yearly MRI safety trainings; aim of the medical staff is to provide patients the best available MRI service	Possible limitations on work procedures of how the MRI is used. Additional training required for MRI operators.

Military	The military personnel are already using a corresponding NATO standard (STANAG 2345) to manage EMF related health risks.	Some of the military operations may not comply with the EU directive and in order to grant the sustainability of such operations, derogations are called for.
Employees	As workers health is in line, they welcome the new directive and see that it is followed by the employers. EMF related discussions in trade unions have taken place. Some trade unions have designated persons dealing with the EMFs. Some companies have also work environment trustees being aware of the issue.	Some are afraid that the directive will not provide a sufficient level of protection as health problems arise within the assumed safety limits. Concern is raised in regard to the long-term effects that the directive will not cover.
Work inspectorate	Readiness to respond to the new directive as it is approved.	Work inspectors have a limited know-how on EMFs – additional schooling required. Scarce full-range measurement service providers.
Occupational health doctors	When information regarding the health mechanisms of EMF exposure is provided by the scientists, physicians are the best qualified professionals for assessing the entire package of EMF related ailments and effects.	No methodology to assess human exposure to the EMFs (except exposure to high intensity radiofrequency fields that cause burns). A comprehensive training of workplace hygienists and physicians is required.
Researchers	Sufficient body of knowledge in regard to adverse health effects from thermal mechanism and peripheral and central nervous system stimulation.	Limited knowledge on long-term effects and exposure from low frequency EMFs. Division amongst the scientists – thermal-effects proponents and non-thermal effects proponents – disagreements.

In the following sections the data obtained from the questionings are discussed further stakeholder by stakeholder.

3.2.1 Legislators

National legislators follow and participate actively in the development of the new EU directive. Also they acknowledge the lack of sufficient measurement services as a hindrance to the enforcement of the directive.

Both the national and European legislators see the need to consider the needs of both the workers and the employers. Especially considering the economic decline of the European economies, the legislators see the need for the directive not to exhaust European companies. One of the principles is also not to create an excessive administrative burden. Also, taking into account that amongst the global economies the European economy is in a risk of becoming a periphery, following the global leaders in economic growth and innovation (USA, Japan and China) – the prospect of that is not pleasurable for European nations. This has set the legislators to follow the principles that 1) the new EMF directive should not restrict the competitiveness of the companies, but, at the same time, 2) would grant workers a safe working environment. In the authors' opinion these two principles are in contradiction, as on a company level, every euro and hour spent to deal with the compliance issues is a non-business cost with no economic benefit to the company. The only exception would be if indeed EMFs were affecting workers' workability in a way that decreased their productiveness. Analysis of the national exposure limits of Europe show that most of the countries are satisfied with the ICNIRP guidelines and have implemented them one-on-one to national legislation. Exceptions are Switzerland, Italy and Sweden, which have used precautionary principle in establishing stricter exposure limits.

3.2.2 Employers

The implementation of the directive will produce additional obligations to the companies. A new set of procedural rules and operational guides are probably to be formulated, followed by the implementation and training. One of the main nuisances as seen by the companies is the additional administrative burden. But also additional investments may become unavoidable if the current equipment does not comply with the directive and therefore needs replacement.

The general vision is that the legislation should not make everyday operations of the companies too rough, as many of the companies, especially SMEs (small and medium-sized enterprises) operate with older equipment. Therefore a sudden legislative move could illegalise such business operations, forcing the companies to acquire new technologies, investment in which could become unbearable. As the lack of funds for investing into new equipment determines whether the company can continue or must stop its business operations, it could drive these companies into bankruptcy, especially considering that the economic crisis that exhausted the economy is not yet quite over. Larger companies will likely manage successfully with such changes, but SMEs are to carry the heavy financial burden if, for example, the main production line needs to be replaced. Therefore companies would rather prefer voluntary safety limits or legislation with high tolerance on behalf of the occupational health and safety authorities.

Regarding the acknowledgment of the EMF safety issues, these are more discussed in companies where workers come more often into contact with the electric power and telecommunications: power utilities, transportation, telecommunications (TV, mobile phone network operators). These companies also inform them having a designated person dealing with the matter when problems should arise. For example, mobile phone network operator reports of best practice instructions that are followed by the workers to reduce the exposure to EMFs (such as avoiding the direct radiation from working antenna).

3.2.3 MRI sector

The MRI technicians and doctors see no need for the directive to encompass MRI personnel and workplaces as MRI workstations have already been managed under the appropriate MRI standards (issued by IEC – International Electrotechnical Commission) that are to ensure the health and safety both of the operators and of the patients. In addition, annual trainings of best practices take place to teach the personnel how to reduce EMF exposure around MRI devices. Therefore there is a strong desire to be excluded from the directive or granted derogation. The MRI personnel emphasise the need to provide the patients with MRI services as best as technically possible, as the information obtained from such imaging plays a crucial role in diagnosing health conditions and assigning treatments. The MRI personnel see the benefit from such imaging services greatly outweighing the possible health effects they have from MRI devices. As we noted, the MRI devices have been around for 20–30 years and people who have been operating them for so long show no adverse health effects, neither short-term nor long-term. Therefore the possibility that the new EU directive might even to some extent limit their use of the MRI equipment, resulting in a decreased quality of service, was not welcomed.

Although most of the working positions in the vicinity of the MRI magnet do not contradict the EU directive, still the problem is seen when the MRI technician needs to lean into the bore to check how the patient is doing or to calm the anxious patient. The MRI personnel see the EMF directive to prohibit some of the needed activities, therefore definitely calling for derogation.

3.2.4 Military

As some of the EU member states are not part of the NATO and most are, there are different standards to deal with the EMF related health risks in armed forces. Like MRI services are considered irreplaceable by any other services, so are some of the operations of the armed forces that use high level electromagnetic fields. An example is a radar station guarding the sea or air, on which technicians and operators may have to conduct works under high exposure conditions. Also a radio operator in forest carrying a high-output transceiver may be exposed to higher levels of EMFs. Such operations are considered vital and a prospect of them being limited by the directive is not welcomed and is seen unreasonable. The armed forces see the need for derogation under the occupational EMF directive as the EMF health risks are already covered with the corresponding NATO STANAG standard 2345. Also, it is pointed out that the military occupation is different from the civilian occupations in its nature and therefore workplaces in armed forces should be treated differently. Such and some other military workplaces may indeed expose people to higher levels of EMFs.

3.2.5 Workers

Several trade union representatives were questioned in the course of the study. As trade unions differ in regard to the occupations they encompass, so do the typical EMF levels these occupations are exposed to. For example, persons working with the radiofrequency sealers, mobile communication antenna towers or on the radar facilities have many factors of greater exposure than others. Also the same type of occupational exposure may have a different effect on different people, especially considering people with special needs. In the authors' opinion there is a need to broaden and clarify the concept of workers with special needs under the EU occupational EMF directive.

In the scientific communities the term "electrohypersensitivity" (EHS) is replaced recently with "environmental sensitivity contributed to the electromagnetic fields" or similar. A reason for that is, as many of the studies conducted on persons claim, symptoms induced by the electromagnetic fields in their environment were found to have little or no association with these symptoms and the EMFs. This led the scientists to conclude that the problem of electrohypersensitivity is more of a psychological in nature than biological. However, some scientists are convinced that the failure to identify the causal link between the EMFs and electrohypersensitivity symptoms is due to the lack of proper research methodology to study this phenomenon. Indeed, in Sweden the research on electrohypersensitivity has taken another pace compared to other Europe, so that EHS is officially recognised as a disability and considered under the UN resolution 48/96 (UN 1993).

Worker representatives from such companies which have more applications on electric power (such as power utilities and transportation) reported that discussions have taken place among workers and within trade unions regarding occupational exposure to EMFs. The trade unions also reported having a designated person to deal with the EMF exposure issues. Companies using a lot of electrical power also have work environment trustees acquainted with the topic. Workers from the public transport sector also pointed out worsened health conditions after the braking energy accumulators (which were placed above their heads) were installed. Similar reports were given by bus drivers regarding the LCD information panels installed behind their head. Workers from several companies have complained about possibly EMF related ailments, but the issue has not reached anywhere, as according to the employers, all working conditions satisfy the safety limits. The workers still suspect EMFs as a cause for the ailments, but are unable to take the matter further due to the lack of scientific support in the investigations.

3.2.6 Work inspectorate

How well the national safety limits are enforced in European countries is unclear as no such study is available, just because they are legally obligatory doesn't mean they are followed by the letter or implemented at all. The authors' interviews revealed that the level of knowledge regarding the enforcement, measurement, risk assessment of EMFs is varying. Companies which have dealt with the EMF issue are more of an exception than a rule.

Work inspectors have limited or no knowledge about the EMFs. Training programs are required to educate the work inspector on the issues of: EMF measurement, EMF caused health effects, EMF overexposure prevention. The work inspectors are seen to fulfil the role of inspection but also supervising and guiding the employers in dealing with the EMF risk factors.

3.2.7 Occupational health doctors

The directive will provide the physicians with an unprecedented task to assess the EMF exposure effects. Currently there are no special training programs that teach medical personnel to diagnose EMF related health problems.

Representatives of the medical sector in some member states already have addressed the issue of the EMFs as a new emerging health risk. The Austrian Medical Association has recently issued a guideline for diagnosing and treating EMF-related health problems and illnesses (AMA 2012). The document achieved a consensus in the meeting of environmental medicine officers of the Regional Medical Association and the Austrian Medical Association. The position of the association is that a sharp rise in unspecified health problems has taken place, often associated with the stress (AMA 2012). The association stresses the need for differential diagnoses to encompass electromagnetic fields, which is considered challenging due to the nature of EMF exposure. For that purpose a guideline was issued to aid the physicians, the core part of which is the patient questionnaire (AMA 2012).

In the authors' opinion the task of the doctors is the most difficult one since there is a lack of medical methodology in determining the health problems associated with the EMFs. This is greatly due to the mechanism how the electromagnetic fields attack person's health: as the immune system fails under the constant bombardment of EMFs (chronic exposure), different symptoms will start to develop. The current medical science is only able to establish causal relationships between high frequency (microwaves) high level overexposure and the resulted health symptoms, but not medium or low intensity exposure and definitely not medium and low frequency exposure. In regard to the latter two cases, the doctors can only guess the health symptoms' connection to EMFs based on the available scientific research where studies have found a correlation between certain EMF exposure and typical symptoms caused by them. As the EMFs weaken the body's immune system, which from some point forward is unable to deal with the environmental agent attacking it, the symptoms could be various, depending on the person's predisposition to certain ailments. In the view of that, the environmental agent causing the illness might not only be the EMFs but also chemical agents or other environmental stressors that now have a greater effect on the person as the immune system fails keeping the body healthy. Again, there is no data available on how to assess combined exposure from multiple stress agents (EMFs and toxic chemicals together).

3.2.8 Researchers

The topic of human health affecting electromagnetic fields affecting requires the scientists to be knowledgeable in many fields of science. Having a good knowledge only in physics or medicine will be insufficient as the comprehensive understanding of the overall picture remains uncovered, which in turn may lead the scientists to wrong conclusions. In the authors' opinion the following fields must me encompassed to successfully deal with the occupational EMFs: physics, electrotechnics, physiology, biology, psychology and more specified sciences such as bioeletromagnetism, ergonomics etc.

There is a division among the scientists: 1) some see the current safety limits to be inadequate to protect the population against adverse health effects, 2) others are satisfied with the limits and see no proof to think otherwise, and then there are 3) those who wish for more studies to reach a conclusion. The claim from the first fraction is that the second group disregards the results of the studies that prove the non-thermal adverse health effects from the EMFs.

The authors' judgment is there are indeed a number of studies that indicate other effects besides those covered by the directive. But the authors also like to point out that the directive has also set limits on itself, by covering only short-term, acute effects. The lack of a sufficient amount of scientific studies in the ELF (extremely low frequency), EMFs and long-term exposure is not under debate, as all parties agree on the need to invest time and money in such studies.

Most of the scientists agree that the scientific knowledge on EMFs is limited. There is a need to conduct more research to determine 1) the effects of low frequency EMF exposure and 2) long-term EMF exposure at relatively low levels. Another field of investigation is the personal susceptibility of the human – whether and to what extent the characteristics such as age, height, weight, previous health conditions (such as allergies) etc. play a role in developing adverse health effects from EMF exposure. Some research already shows that some of these characteristics may indeed have an importance. If this is confirmed by the future studies it will significantly broaden the directive's approach to people with special needs. Then attention to these workers must also be paid in the EMF risk assessment, management and communication. For example, persons carrying large metal implants in their body should avoid working in high level electromagnetic field workplaces as the metal inside their body starts to collect the electric or magnetic fields and convert it to heat and/or electrical current inside the body.

It was expected for the stakeholders to have different views about and expectations for the new directive. The role of the legislator is to consider all of them, as best as possible, and to produce a compromise. Therefore the directive, being a compromise document, cannot completely satisfy any of the parties.

4. Conclusions and Discussion

The results of this study concluded that the implementation of the occupational EMF directive will inevitably encounter obstacles, lack of resources in the SMEs being one of the most crucial ones in the authors' opinion. Besides technical capabilities in implementing the directive attention must also be paid to cooperation, training and providing know-how. To aid the SMEs in this matter a special support program should be prepared by the government, otherwise a situation may follow where the directive is implemented *de jure* but not *de facto* by the SMEs.

The European study on worker representation and consultation on health and safety found that worker representation in developing safe methods of work was more present in larger organizations, in the public sector, organizations with older workers and in workplaces where health and safety, and the views of workers were seen as a priority (EASHW 2012). The primary finding of that study was that involvement of workers indeed plays a significant role in ensuring that new occupational health and safety policies and action plans are successfully implemented in practice. The same study conducted two years earlier came into similar results (EASHW 2010). Probably the reader is not surprised about such findings, as they are in line with the previous studies, where a connection between worker representation and good practice was identified. The results from the improvements in occupational health and safety are likely to be better when worker representatives are involved in various ways, such as quality circles, collective agreements and also trade unions. The effective implementation of the EMF directive in all the sectors of the economy is crucial for obtaining the level of safety targeted by the policy makers. Therefore cooperation between the stakeholders, covered by this study, should be the priority of the government policies and programmes should be started already a few years before the directive is enforced. One might expect the new EMF guidelines be better implemented in construction, mining, health and social work industries, as occupational health and safety arrangements are already the best in these branches compared to others, as shown by the analysis of data of the European Survey of Enterprises on New and Emerging Risks (EASHW 2012b). Also, as reported by the same study, smaller establishments have fewer occupational health and safety measures in contrast to larger ones. The implementation of new EMF OHS measures becomes critical in companies with less than 100 workers, as the study reports in such establishments the number of such measures to decrease at much faster rate in relation to the establishment size. This confirms the need for a special learning program targeted to small and medium-sized companies (SMEs) when the new EMF directive gets enforced.

The key factor in getting the new OHS rules implemented is the use of worker representatives. Additional OHS tasks, besides their regular work, will require them to work extra hours. Therefore the European Trade Union Confederation has taken the issue as a priority, to see that the worker representatives get the support they need not only from the employers, but also workers and trade unions (EASHW 2012c).

In the authors' assessment there is also a shortage of specialised EMF risk management methods that would help the employers implement the directive. Such detailed risk management methods are necessary as general knowledge on the EMFs is scarce and therefore the improvised risk management using classical risk management tools may not give the results intended by the policy makers. One of the ideas, as proposed by the authors in figure 2, is to better encompass worker's personal susceptibility to the EMF's risk assessment. Next to the EMF dosage, as determined by the EMF strength and exposure time, personal characteristics may play a significant role in the development of adverse health effects. This would allow better consideration of the needs of persons in risk groups, such as pregnant women, people wearing medical implants and other endangered groups yet to be determined.

The scientific body of research has well established acute effects from electromagnetic fields' exposure, but there are uncertainties regarding the long-term effects because of the limited number of such studies. Therefore the precautionary approach, as discussed earlier, is justified. A conclusion made by the World Health Organization recommends not to strengthen the safety limits to arbitrary levels in the name of precaution as such levels my get to be expensive to follow and the effect is questionable (WHO 2007). The authors see that more effort should be made by the EU and the member states to endorse voluntary safe practice procedures that would minimise the EMFs at workplaces, setting them well below the legal limits. In this way 1) the precautionary principle is followed, 2) workers are provided with a high level of protection; 3) the excess administrative burden to the employers is avoided and 4) no need to establish stricter legal limits, which would require a lengthy process.

The authors see room for improvement in the directive's coverage of other health effects. Instead of promising European workers protection against all known adverse health effects from the EMFs, which is an arguable statement in the framework of the directive itself, as the directive only covers acute health effects, the directive should reflect a compromise approach. The employers and workers should be made aware of the various EMF related health issues and also acknowledge that in order to get the work done, exposure to some levels of EMFs is inevitable. So, even when there are disagreements among the scientists in regard to the indirect and long-term health effects, the stakeholders are made aware of the health effects under discussion. It should be left for the workers to decide whether they see the risk worthy or not. A bonus pay has been suggested to compensate the work under high levels of EMFs. Such higher salaries are also practiced, for example, in aviation, where flight crews are exposed to significantly higher doses of cosmic ionizing radiation than on the ground.

Implementing of the directive based on a limited number of health effects might lead the European workforce to believe that they are protected against all health effects. This in turn might open the European workers to unintended occupational EMF exposure and consequently undermine the authority of the European legislators when new data from additional health effects not covered by the directive is discovered.

It is clear that today's society will not give up the use of electrical power. Therefore the authors would prefer to see a compromise approach, with the emphasis on educating the workforce and employers following the voluntary safe practice procedures.

The choice of whether to make the EU EMF safety limits legally non-binding or binding was indeed under consideration for many years. However, the majority of the stakeholders preferred a binding directive (legally obligatory).

As the modern society is based on the utilization of electric power, it operates all the corners of today's public and business activities. Any hindrance to the use of electrical power may have a significant effect on the business operations and result in financial loss. Therefore, limitations to the use of electrical power, by limiting the use EMF-generating equipment, must be scientifically sound. Fortunately a wide range of measures can be implemented to diminish the propagation of electromagnetic fields from electrical appliances, some of these measures are effective and not expensive, but some require significant investments, having a definite effect on the company's financial outcome. It is clear that any large investment which is not directed to improving the productivity or any other enhancement of the business operations is a burden for the companies and may have an effect on its competitiveness in the market.

The limitations of the current study include a limited number of the respondents, which might not give a perfect general view of their stakeholder group. Also, as the study was based on qualitative data, the analysis might have missed or overestimated some of the issues due to the sample size.

The authors see that future research in this issue is justified. After the implementation of the directive, the studies should address the following questions: 1) did the directive help to improve the work conditions, 2) what was the financial and administrative burden for the companies and to what extent did it affect their competitiveness. 3) what kind of problems did the occupational doctors and work inspectors meet.

References

AMA – Austrian Medical Association, 2012, Guideline of the Austrian Medical Association for the diagnosis and treatment of EMF-related health problems and illnesses (EMF syndrome).

Bioinitiative report: A Rationale for a Biologically-based Public Exposure Standard for Electromagnetic Fields (ELF and RF), 2007, Organizing Committee: Blackman, C., Blank, M., Kundi, M., Sage, C.

EC – European Commission, Health and Consumer Protection Directorate-General, 2000, Commission adopts Communication on Precautionary Principle, [http://ec.europa.eu/dgs/health_consumer/library/press/press38_en.print.html]

EASHW – European Agency for Safety and Health at Work, 2012, Worker representation and consultation on health and safety: An analysis of the findings of the European Survey of Enterprises on New and Emerging Risks (ESENER), [http://osha.europa.eu/en/publications/reports/esener_workersinvolvement/view?utm_sou rce=oshmail&utm_medium=email&utm_campaign=oshmail-120]

EASHW – European Agency for Safety and Health at Work, 2012(b), Management of occupational safety and health: Analysis of data from the European Survey of Enterprises on New and Emerging Risks (ESENER), [http://osha.europa.eu/en/publications/reports/management-of-occupational-safety-and-health-analysis-of-data-from-the-esener/view]

EASHW – European Agency for Safety and Health at Work, 2010, European Survey of Enterprises on New and Emerging Risks (ESENER) – Managing safety and health at work, [http://osha.europa.eu/en/publications/reports/esener1_osh_management]

EASHW – European Agency for Safety and Health at Work, 2012(c), Worker participation in occupational safety and health – a practical guide.

EASHW – European Agency for Safety and Health at Work, 2002, Economic appraisal of preventing work accidents at company level, Factsheet 28.

EFHRAN – European Health Risk Assessment Network on Electromagnetic Fields Exposure, 2010, Risk analysis of human exposure to electromagnetic fields.

EEA – European Environment Agency, 2007, Radiation risk from everyday devices assessed, [http://www.eea.europa.eu/highlights/radiation-risk-from-everyday-devices-assessed]

EP – The European Parliament resolution of 2 April 2009 on health concerns associated with electromagnetic fields [http://www.europarl.europa.eu/sides/getDoc.do?type=TA&reference=P6-TA-2009-0216&language=EN&ring=A6-2009-0089]

EP&EC – The European Parliament and the Council, 2004. DIRECTIVE 2004/40/EC of the European Parliament and of the Council of 29 April 2004 on the minimum health and safety requirements regarding the exposure of workers to the risks arising from physical agents (electromagnetic fields) (18th individual Directive within the meaning of Article 16(1) of Directive 89/391/EEC), Official Journal of the European Union L 159 of 30 April 2004.

Hinrikus, H., Bachmann, M., Tomson, R., Lass, J. 2005, Non-Thermal Effect of Microwave Radiation on Human Brain, The Environmentalist, 25, pp. 187–194.

IARC – International Agency for Research on Cancer, 2011, IARC Classifies radiofrequency electromagnetic fields as possibly carcinogenic to humans, Press release No 2008, 31 May 2011, [http://www.iarc.fr/en/media-centre/pr/2011/pdfs/pr208_E.pdf]

ICNIRP – International Commission on Non-Ionizing Radiation Protection, 1998, Guidelines for limiting exposure to time-varying electric, magnetic, and electromagnetic fields (up to 300GHz), ICNIRP Guidelines, Health Physics Society.

ICNIRP – International Commission on Non-Ionizing Radiation Protection, 2010, Guidelines for limiting exposure to time-varying electric, magnetic, and electromagnetic fields (1 Hz to 100 kHz), ICNIRP Guidelines, Health Physics 99(6), pp. 818–836.

Keevil, S.F., Gedroyc, W., Gowland, P., Hill, D.L.G., Leach, M.O., Ludman, C.N., McLeish, K., Mcrobbie, D.W., Razavi, R.S., Young, I.R. 2005, Electromagnetic field exposure limitation and the future of MRI, British Journal of Radiology, No 78, 973, [http://bjr.birjournals.org/content/78/935/973.full]

Luck, J. 2008, What's your frequency – the role of adjustable output frequency in GTAW, Practical Welding Today – A publication of the Fabricators & Manufacturers Association, International, Jan. 1st 2008, [http://www.thefabricator.com/article/arcwelding/whats-your-frequency]

Miller, R.D., Neuberger, J.S., Gerald, K B 1997, Brain Cancer and Leukemia and Exposure to Power-Frequency (50- to 60-Hz) Electric and Magnetic Fields, Epidemiologic Reviews, Vol. 19, No 2, The Johns Hopkins University School of Hygiene and Public Health.

Muc, A. M. 2001, Electromagnetic Fields Associated with Transportation Systems, Radiation Health and Safety Consulting.

PACE Parliamentary Assembly of the Council of Europe, Resolution 1815, 2011: The potential dangers of electromagnetic fields and their effect on the environment. Text adopted by the Standing Committee, acting on behalf of the Assembly, on 27 May 2011 [http://www.assembly.coe.int/Mainf.asp?link=/Documents/AdoptedText/ta11/ERES1815 .htm]

Stuchly, M.A., Repacholi, M.H., Lecuyer, D., Mann, R. 1980, Radiation Survey of Dielectric (RF) Heaters in Canada, Journal of Microwave Power, 15(2).

Swanson, 2011, Power-frequency EMF exposure standards applicable in Europe and elsewhere, Revision 5e May 2011 [http://www.emfs.info/NR/rdonlyres/96AD1550-AEFE-4832-9405-8F9A119363DA/0/standardscompilationv5emay2011.pdf]

UN – United Nations, The Standard Rules on the Equalization of Opportunities for Persons with Disabilities, Adopted by the United Nations General Assembly, forty-eighth session, resolution 48/96, annex, of 20 December 1993 [http://www.un.org/esa/socdev/enable/dissre00.htm]

WHO – World Health Organization, 2007, Extremely Low Frequency Fields Environmental Health Criteria Monograph No. 238 [http://www.who.int/peh-emf/publications/elf_ehc/en/index.html]

Organizational Culture as Predictor of Innovation Climate

Ruth Alas[1], Ülle Übius[1] and Mary Ann Gaal[2]

Abstract

This paper analyses how organizational culture predicts innovation climate in Asian and East-European countries. The survey was conducted in Chinese, Japanese, Russian, Slovakian and Czech electric-electronic machine, retail store, and machine-building enterprises. The total number of respondents was 5119. The results of linear regression analysis show that in Japan and China three organizational culture types – clan, market, and adhocracy – predicted innovation climate. In Slovakia and Czech Republic two organizational culture types – market and adhocracy – predicted innovation climate, while in Russia only adhocracy culture type predicted innovation climate. Differences between their national cultures may explain these results.

Keywords: innovation climate; organizational culture; Asia; Eastern Europe

JEL classification: M1, O3

1. Introduction

As more and more enterprises seek new markets and compete in existing ones, the ability to innovate, both internally and externally, adds a significant competitive advantage to enterprises. Our research looks to see whether organizational culture predicts innovation climate and further, how that may be influenced by national culture. We use Cameron and Quinn's (1999) competing values model to describe the organizational climate. According to previous studies, culture is the lens through which a leader's vision is manifested and helps build the climate necessary for organizations to become innovative (James, Choi, Ko, McNeil, Minton, Wright and Kim 2007). According to Yukl (2002), specific leadership behaviours may influence innovation through compliance as part of the organizational culture. Research has shown that certain organizational cultures are more conducive to innovation and creating an innovation climate (Çakar and Ertürk 2010; Tellis, Prabhu and Chandy 2009). Global competition requires enterprises to be market driven, innovate, and adaptable. As enterprises expand to various areas in the world the ability to create an organization that will innovate becomes a competitive advantage. As such, it is important to investigate how and if national culture plays a role in understanding the organizational culture and its influence on innovation climate.

---

1   Estonian Business School, Estonia
2   Franklin Pierce University, USA

Therefore, this research studies 5 countries; Japan, China, Czech Republic, Slovakia, and Russia, which have been sparingly researched to date, to analyse the connection between organizational culture, innovation climate, and national culture. The research question is: How does organizational culture predict innovation climate? Despite the enormous amount of theoretical writing about the connections between organizational culture and innovation climate, there are relatively few empirical studies about the connections between four organizational culture types – clan, adhocracy, market, and hierarchy according to Cameron and Quinn (1999), and innovation climate in Asian and East-European countries.

We start with the theoretical framework for organizational culture types and innovation climate. The national culture of each country is discussed using Hofstede's (2001) cultural dimensions. This is followed by analysis and discussion of the results and our conclusions. This study will add to the body of research that has tested Cameron and Quinn's model as it pertains to innovation climate, as well as discuss any connections these have to a nation's culture.

2. Theoretical Foundation

2.1 Organizational Culture

According to Schein (1992), organisational culture represents the values, assumptions, expectations, collective memories in an organization. Schein (1992) states that organisational culture is the pattern of basic assumptions that a group has invented, discovered, or developed in order to learn to cope with problems of external adaptation and integral integration. He states that organizational culture is a pattern of shared basic assumptions that has worked well enough to be considered valid and, therefore, to be taught to new members as the correct way to perceive, think, and feel in relation to those problems. According to Trice and Beyer (1993), organisational culture is a collective response to uncertainty and chaos.

Cameron and Quinn (1999) have created an organizational culture framework. According to their framework, culture defines the core values, assumptions, interpretations, and approaches that characterise an organization. The competing values framework uses a four quadrant model to describe organizational cultures. The horizontal axis compares the emphasis an organization places on employees or internal concerns versus placing more concern with its external constituents. The vertical axis compares an organization's disposition towards change and flexibility versus maintaining stability and control. The framework is based on four dominant culture types – clan, adhocracy, market, and hierarchy. The Clan cultural type is dominated by collaboration, participation and open communication values. The Adhocracy cultural type is dominated by innovation, creativity, and transformation as values. The Market cultural type is dominated by a sense of competition, dominance, and driven by goals as its values. The Hierarchy cultural type consists of values such as consistency, efficiency, and control. Most organizations develop a dominant cultural style. More than 80 per cent of the several thousand organizations they have studied are characterised by one or more of the culture type identified by the framework. Those that do not have a dominant culture type either tend to be unclear about their culture or they emphasise nearly equally the four different cultural types. Kwan and Walker (2004) validated the competing values framework as a tool which can be used to differentiate the organizational cultures. The competing values model has been used extensively for describing organizational cultures.

2.2 Innovation Climate

The basic foundation for innovation theory is derived from Joseph Schumpeter's idea that creative destruction occurs when innovation makes old ideas and technologies obsolete and therefore, causes the creation of new economic structures (Schumpeter 1911). Many recent studies have researched connections between innovation and individual values, attitudes, and behaviour. Torokoff (2010) states that positive emotional climate is important in managing the innovation process. Sedziuviene and Veinhardt (2010) state innovativeness as the ability and continuous readiness to re-organise and initiate changes, which in turn creates value in an organization in competitive markets.

According to Damanpour and Schneider (2006), the climate for innovation is a direct result of top managers' personal and positional characteristics. Many authors (Van de Ven 1986; Unsworth and Parker 2003) have found that individual innovation helps to attain organizational success. Employees' innovative behaviour depends largely on their interaction with others in the workplace (Zhou and Shalley 2003; Anderson, Dreu and Nijstad 2004). Support and encouragement are predicted to influence actual innovation in the organization (Mumford and Gustafson 1988; Martins and Terblanche 2003). In the current study the innovation climate is defined as the degree of support and encouragement an organization provides its employees to take initiative and explore innovative approaches. The assessment tool has been derived from the research by Ekvall, Arvonen and Wladenstrom-Lindblad (1983).

2.3 National Culture

Hofstede's (2001) work on cultural dimensions has been used extensively in research to explain the similarities and differences of countries. While Hofstede's original study (1980) only included 50 countries his subsequent study (2001) included Asian countries. However, the Czech Republic and Slovakia were not included. The cultural scores are located in Table 1. The Czech Republic and Slovakia scores were taken from Kolman, Noordhaven, Hofstede, and Dienes's (2003) study that compares Eastern and Central European countries' cultural dimensions. While Hofstede's research is controversial, recent research on the constructs compared to other available dimensions maintains that Hofstede's dimensions are valid (Magnusson, Wilson, Zdravkovic, Zhou and Westjohn 2008).

Table 1:   Cultural Dimensions Scores

	Power Distance	Uncertainty Avoidance	Individualism	Masculinity	Long-term orientation
China	75	35	10	50	98
Japan	50	92	40	89	75
Russia	95	90	50	40	10
Czech Rep	78	81	68	81	28
Slovakia	86	57	40	127	52

Of the five countries Japan ranks the lowest in Power Distance while Russia is the highest. China ranks the lowest in Individualism making it a highly Collectivist society, Japan and Slovakia are the two highest in Individualism. Japan and Czech Republic score the highest in Uncertainty Avoidance, while China is the lowest in Uncertainty Avoidance. Russia's score is the lowest in Long-term Orientation, making it quite short-term oriented. China is the highest Long-term Oriented society. Slovakia is the highest Masculinity scoring society while Russia is the lowest scoring of the five countries. Previous research has analysed the influence national culture has on organizational culture (Lin 2009) and its influence on innovation (Allred and Swan 2004; Jones and Davis 2000). These ties will be discussed further.

2.3 Organizational Culture, Innovation Climate, and National Culture

According to Sarros, Cooper, and Santora, (2008) organizational climate can be regarded as the expression of underlying cultural practices that arise in response to contingencies in the organization's internal and external environment. This view confirms the "climate-for" innovation approach as a valid accompaniment to studies of organizational culture (Ostroff, Kinicki and Tamkins 2003). Glisson and James (2002) stated that climate and culture should be studied simultaneously.

Kimberly (1981) stated that centralised decision making enhances an organization's ability to implement innovations, particularly in a more stable environment. However, in a dynamic environment this may not hold. According to Amabile, Conti, Coon, Lazenby, and Herron (1996), organizational encouragement encompasses the following aspects: encouragement of risk taking and idea generation, supportive evaluation of ideas, collaborative idea flow, and participative management and decision making. According to Kanter (1983), organizational structures and cultures that provide support and do not punish have great influence on creativity and innovation. More recently, research by Tellis, Prabhu, and Chandy (2009) found that 6 organizational practices or values were significant in the promotion of innovation, willingness to cannibalise, future market orientation, risk tolerance, product champions, and incentives. They suggest that internal corporate culture is an important driver of radical innovation.

National culture also seems to have influence on innovation within organizations. Lin (2009) suggested that low power distance has a positive effect on innovation because of the role of decentralization in decision making. Decentralization has a flatter hierarchy expectation, and has more equality in the power structure. All of this leads to greater trust which is needed to foster a successful innovative climate. Lin (2009) also proposed that a lower uncertainty avoidance score would more likely lead to more positive innovation since ambiguity is tolerated more as opposed to a high uncertainty avoidance score. According to Hofstede (2001), a high uncertainty avoidance score suggests the society is more resistant to change and is more risk averse. In a study by Dwyer, Mesak, and Tsu (2005) results showed that a more collectivist index positively affected innovation due to the promotion of team cooperation and communication. Highly individualistic societies are more "me" societies, according to Hofstede (2001) and therefore, make collaboration and innovation within an organization more difficult. Lin's (2009) findings were that a high uncertainty avoidance score negatively affected innovation, while long-term orientation scores positively affected innovation. Allred and Swan (2004) also found that a Confucian dynamic, long-term orientation was more favourable in an organization for innovation.

Van Muijen and Koopman (1994) suggested that a low power distance index and low uncertainty avoidance index would lead to an adhocracy organizational type; it would be more innovative, fluid and organic. If the power distance index and uncertainty index are high it would be a hierarchy organizational type and the innovation would be low due to the bureaucracy, standardization and written procedures.

With these previous studies as our basis we would posit that the countries with similar national culture scores for power distance, individualism, and long-term orientation and uncertainty avoidance have similar results in the organizational context. We do not specifically discuss masculinity because there has not been significant data for supporting a particular position. Based on the relevant literature suggesting the type of culture, both national and organizational that will promote innovative climate the following hypotheses are proposed:

Hypothesis 1. *Clan organizational culture type will lead to innovation cli mate within an organization.*

Hypothesis 2. *Market organizational culture type will lead to innovation climate within an organization.*

Hypothesis 3. *Adhocracy organizational culture type will lead to innovation climate within an organization.*

Hypothesis 4. *Hierarchy organizational culture type will not lead to innova tion climate within an organization.*

Hypothesis 5. *China and Japan will respond similarly to clan, market, adhocracy, and hierarchy cultural types.*

Hypothesis 6. *Czech Republic, Russia, and Slovakia will respond similarly to clan, market, adhocracy, and hierarchy cultural types.*

Hypothesis 7. *Response to the four organizational culture types – clan, mar ket, hierarchy and adhocracy will predict innovation climate differently in China and Japan than Czech Republic, Russia, and Slovakia.*

3. Methodology

3.1 Assessment tools

The research task was to identify connections between the innovation climate and organisational culture types on the basis of hypotheses that were developed in the theoretical framework. The authors used questionnaires worked out by the Denki Ringo research group in Japan for measuring the organisational culture types. The questionnaire was translated from English into Chinese, Japanese, Russian, Slovakian and Czech.

Innovation climate scale. The authors developed an innovation climate scale based on the Innovation Climate Questionnaire introduced by Ekvall, Arvonen, and Wladerstrom-Linblad (1983). Items to measure the innovation climate were selected. A five-point scale was used. The internal consistency, or Cronbach Alpha coefficient was 0.70. The final version of the questionnaire for measuring innovation climate consisted of 14 items. Six innovation climate facets – commitment, positive realationship, shared view, freedom, idea-support and risk-taking – were measured. Ekvall et al.'s (1983) innovation climate questionnaire (ICQ) incorporates thirteen scales: commitment, freedom, idea-support, positive relationships, dynamism, playfulness, idea-proliferation, stress, risk-taking, idea-time, shared view, pay recognition and work recognition.

Organizational culture scale. The scales for measuring organizational culture were developed by the author on the basis of a measure developed by the Denki Ringo research group (Ishikawa, Mako and Warhurst 2006) and Cameron and Quinn (1999). The author developed the scales for measuring four types of organisation culture – clan, market, hierarchy and adhocracy. By using a varimax rotation, factor analysis and reliability tests, 19 items of organisation culture were obtained, and the final version consists of 19 items, which form four subscales – clan with 5 items, market with 4 items, hierarchy with 5 items and adhocracy with 5 items. The internal consistency or Cronbach Alpha coefficient is .92 for the clan culture type, .90 for the market culture type, .87 for the hierarchy culture type and .91 for the adhocracy culture type.

3.2 Sample

The survey was conducted among Chinese, Japanese, Russian, Slovakian and Czech electric-electronic machine, retail store and machine-building enterprises. The total number of respondents was 5119. There were 1150 respondents from Chinese enterprises, 1570 from Japanese enterprises, 605 from Slovakian enterprises, 1110 from Czech enterprises and 684 respondents from Russian enterprises. The companies were selected in a non-random manner. The organisation registers do not have a correct basis for random sampling. Only a fraction of the registered enterprises are active in China, Japan, Russia, Slovakia and the Czech Republic. The authors obtained the file with Japanese, Chinese, Slovakian, Czech and Russian respondents' answers from the Japanese co-partner of the Denki Ringo (Ishikawa et. Al, 2006) research group in order to conduct comparative analyses of the data. The authors conducted the linear regression analysis, which enabled them to find statistically relevant connections between organizational culture and innovation climate.

4. Results

4.1 Four Organisational Culture Types

The analysis was completed on the mean and standard deviation of each country and their respondents for the organizational culture types.

The Hierarchy Culture. Table 2 shows respondents' opinions about their organization as a hierarchy culture type. Respondents rated highly the statements: organisation must have strict hierarchy (m=4.25, sd=1.32) and one needs to control spending of resources strictly, or total disorder will happen (m=4.06, sd=0.90). Respondents rated low the statements: we have informal norms and rules which are to be followed by everyone (m=3.21, sd=1.77) and rules of the company must not be disobeyed even if employee thinks that he acts in favour of the company (m=3.34, sd=1.84).

Table 2:   The Hierarchy Culture

Items	M	SD
1 – we have informal norms and rules which are to be followed by everyone	3.21	1.77
2 – rules of the company must not be disobeyed even if employee thinks that he acts in favour of company	3.34	1.84
3 – instructions and regulations are needed to govern every process of work	3.55	1.82
4 – organisation must have strict hierarchy	4.25	1.32
5 – one needs to control spending of resources strictly, or total disorder will happen	4.06	0.90
Total	3.68	1.57

The Market Culture. Table 3 shows respondents' opinions about their organization as a market culture type. Respondents rated highly the statement: it is very important to feel market changes to react contemporarily (m=4.23, sd=0.85). Respondents rated low the statement: during conflict everybody tries to solve it quickly and mutually profitable (m=3.35, sd=1.06).

Table 3:   The Market Culture

Items	M	SD
1 – customers' interests are never ignored in decision making of organization	3.50	1.16
2 – we constantly improve our methods of work to gain advantages over rivals	3.61	1.07
3 – during conflict everybody tries to solve it quickly and mutually profitable	3.35	1.06
4 – it is very important to feel market changes to react contemporarily	4.23	0.85
Total	3.67	1.04

The Clan Culture. Table 4 shows respondents' opinions about their organization as clan culture type. Respondents rated highly the statements: in group everyone must put maximum effort to achieve common goal (m=4.12, sd=0.88) and reward for success must go to department, because everyone put an effort (m=4.12, sd=0.96). Respondents rated low the statements: agreement is easily achieved even concerning hard problems in organization (m=3.11, sd=1.04).

Table 4:   The Clan Culture

Items	M	SD
1 – agreement is easily achieved even concerning hard problems in organization	3.11	1.04
2 – competition between colleagues usually brings more harm than use	3.29	1.11
3 – it is not accepted to talk about people behind their back	3.33	1.23
4 – in group everyone must put maximum effort to achieve common goal	4.12	0.88
5 – reward for success must go to department, because everyone put an effort	4.12	0.96
Total	3.59	1.12

The Adhocracy Culture. Table 5 shows respondents' opinions about their organization as adhocracy culture type. Respondents rated highly the statements: new ideas must be applied immediately otherwise they become old and obsolete (m=3.85, sd=0.94) and most competent representative of group must make decisions even if formally he is not a leader of the group (m=3.56, sd=1.10). Respondents rated low the statements: workers of any division have equal perspectives (m=3.07, sd=1.19) and projects are coordinated easily through all functional units (m=3.11, sd=1.03).

Table 5:   The Adhocracy Culture

Items	M	SD
1 – workers of any division have equal perspectives	3.07	1.19
2 – information is available for everyone. One can get any needed information	3.20	1.16
3 – projects are coordinated easily through all functional units	3.11	1.03
4 – new ideas must be applied immediately otherwise they become old and obsolete	3.85	0.94
5 – most competent representative of group must make decisions even if formally he is not a leader of the group	3.56	1.10
Total	3.35	1.14

ANOVA analysis was completed to test for significant variance of the means between countries. Table 6 presents the mean and standard deviation for each organizational culture type by country. All of the culture types were statistically different between countries.

Table 6:   Organisational Culture Types

		Hierarchy	Market	Clan	Adhocracy
China N=1150	M	3.79	3.84	3.66	3.83
	SD	1.03	1.01	1.06	1.04
Japan N=1570	M	3.21	3.28	3.02	3.04
	SD	0.87	0.84	0.83	0.83
Russian N=684	M	3.33	3.60	3.42	3.34
	SD	1.03	0.94	1.13	1.05
Czech N=1110	M	3.70	3.27	3.46	3.25
	SD	1.05	1.08	1.07	1.07
Slovakia N=605	M	3.85	3.51	3.64	3.23
	SD	1.05	1.02	1.08	1.09

$p < 0.05$

4.2 Innovation climate

There are some similarities and also differences concerning the opinions of the respondents in different countries about the innovation climate. ANOVA analysis showed statistically significant differences between country scores. Table 7 shows the opinions of the respondents about the innovation climate at their organization by question. The statements were rated high in Chinese (m=3.56, sd=1.05) enterprises and low in Japanese enterprises (m=3.01, sd=0.93).

Since the ANOVA results varied significantly between country scores we continued with our analysis to evaluate how organizational culture predicts innovation climate. In the linear regression analysis organizational culture was taken as an independent variable and innovation climate as a dependent variable. We calculated a standardized regression coefficient Beta. It enabled us to predict how strongly the four types of organizational culture predict innovation climate. Analysis was applied separately to four organizational culture types. Analysis to measure connections between organizational culture types and innovation climate was also applied separately for five countries.

Table 7:   *The innovation climate in China, Japan, the Czech Republic and Slovakia*

		1	2	3	4	5	6	7	8	9	10	11	12	13	14	SUM
China N=1150	M	3.94	4.45	2.82	2.82	3.20	2.76	3.30	3.87	3.61	3.04	3.80	3.83	4.14	4.24	3.56
	SD	0.88	0.92	0.45	1.28	0.94	1.21	1.24	1.12	1.18	1.33	1.09	1.10	1.01	0.91	1.05
Japan N=1570	M	2.94	3.53	2.63	2.67	2.81	3.03	3.02	2.75	3.07	3.09	3.20	2.54	3.19	3.59	3.01
	SD	0.88	1.09	0.55	0.91	0.88	0.90	0.81	0.82	0.83	0.98	0.90	0.84	2.70	0.83	0.93
Czech N=1110	M	3.33	4.23	2.60	3.01	3.03	3.10	3.32	3.00	3.45	2.83	3.29	2.98	3.41	4.03	3.26
	SD	1.01	1.00	0.60	1.16	1.16	1.10	1.06	1.14	1.19	1.29	3.36	1.18	1.15	1.03	1.24
Slovakia N=605	M	2.50	4.06	2.73	3.02	2.98	2.81	2.84	2.75	3.29	2.86	3.15	3.07	3.91	4.31	3.16
	SD	1.01	1.05	0.51	1.03	0.96	1.16	1.10	1.17	1.21	1.36	1.18	1.22	1.20	1.01	1.08

$p < 0.05$

Notes: 1 – How do you think are you estimated properly at your work, 2 – What do you feel toward the firm you are working, 3 – Have you attended courses or seminars organized by the firm inside or outside in the last five years, 4 – The rules of the firm are occasionally disobeyed when an employee thinks it would favour the firm, 5 – Our organisation relies more on horizontal control and coordination rather than strict hierarchy, 6 – Most capable persons commit in decisions to solve an urgent problem, 7 – Fresh creative ideas are actualized on time, 8 – Current vision creates stimuli for workers, 9 – Company realises a clear mission that gives meaning and sense to work, 10 – If the department is short of hands, the department's head may hire temporary workers himself, 11 – Our organisation cares even about temporarily hired workers, 12 – We can all clearly imagine the future of our organisation, 13 – Failure is considered as a stimulus to learning and development, 14 – All the employees should be aware of the important role of their firm in society.

Results in Table 8 indicate that in China ($R^2=.085$, $F(4.999)=24.314$, $p<0.01$) and Japan ($R^2=.257$, $F(4.1421)=124.36$, $p<0.01$) three organizational culture types – clan, market and adhocracy – predict innovation climate. In Slovakia ($R^2=.247$, $F(4.523)=44.278$, $p<0.01$) and Czech ($R^2=.004$, $F(4.1104)=2.3816$, $p<0.01$) two organizational culture types – market and adhocracy – predict innovation climate. In Russia, one organizational culture type – adhocracy ($R^2=.201$, $F(4.679)=44.209$, $p<0.01$) – predicts innovation climate. Hierarchy culture type did not predict innovation climate in any of the countries studied while adhocracy culture type predicted innovation climate in all five countries.

Hypothesis 1, 2, and 3 proposed that clan, market and adhocracy culture types will lead to innovation climate within organizations. The results of the regression analysis supported these hypotheses – clan, market and adhocracy culture types predict innovation climate. However, these do not all predict innovation climate in all countries investigated.

Table 8:   Regression Analysis (standardised regression coefficient Beta)

	B	Beta	T	Sig.		B	Beta	T	Sig.
Clan					**Hierarchy**				
China	.122	.167	5.526	**.000***	China	-.000	-.046	-1.526	.127
Japan	.280	.118	4.391	**.000***	Japan	.013	.006	.284	.776
Russia	.128	.084	1.518	.129	Russia	.007	.066	1.481	.138
Slovakia	-.135	-.057	-1.249	.212	Slovakia	.125	.058	1.301	.193
Czech	-.170	.057	-1.147	.251	Czech	-.170	.051	-1.105	.269
Market					**Adhocracy**				
China	.089	.138	4.530	**.000***	China	.095	.162	5.295	**.000***
Japan	.292	.098	3.834	**.000***	Japan	.844	.396	15.288	**.000***
Russia	.085	.063	1.279	.201	Russia	.419	.294	5.163	**. 000***
Slovakia	.809	.268	5.688	**.000***	Slovakia	.649	.306	6.685	**.000***
Czech	.165	.064	1.651	**.001***	Czech	.345	.123	2.480	**.001***

Notes: * p<0.01

Hypothesis 4 proposed that hierarchy organizational culture type will not lead to innovative climate within an organization. Based on the results, the hypothesis was supported. This cultural type was not significant for any of the countries investigated.

Hypothesis 5 proposed that China and Japan will respond similarly to clan, market, adhocracy, and hierarchy cultural types. This hypothesis was supported. Clan, market, and adhocracy predicted innovation climate in both Japan and China and the hierarchy culture type did not predict innovation climate.

Hypothesis 6 proposed that the Czech Republic, Russia, and Slovakia will respond similarly to clan, market, adhocracy, and hierarchy cultural types. This hypothesis was partly supported. The adhocracy culture type predicted innovation climate in three investigated Eastern European countries – Czech Republic, Slovakia and Russia while hierarchy and clan culture types did not predict innovation climate. Market culture type predicted innovation climate in Czech Republic and Slovakia but did not predict innovation climate in Russia.

Hypothesis 7 proposed that the response to the four organizational culture types – clan, market, hierarchy and adhocracy – will predict innovation climate differently in China and Japan than in the Czech Republic, Russia, and Slovakia. This hypothesis was partly supported. There were differences but also similarities between the Asian and Eastern European countries. Clan culture type predicted innovation climate only in Asian countries – Japan and China. On the other hand, adhocracy predicted innovation climate equally in all five Asian and Eastern European countries. Hierarchy culture type did not predict innovation climate again equally in all five investigated Asian and Eastern European countries.

5. Conclusions

The results indicate that in Asian countries three organizational culture types – clan, market and adhocracy – predict innovation climate. In Eastern European countries, Slovakia and Czech, two organizational culture types – market and adhocracy – predict innovation climate and in Russia one organizational culture type – adhocracy – predicts innovation climate. Hierarchy culture type does not predict innovation climate at all.

The national culture where the organization is operating influences the connection between organizational culture and innovation climate. Teamwork, employee involvement programs, corporate commitment to employee, participation, loyalty and traditions are highly valued in clan culture type organizations, which is common to organizations in Asian countries and therefore this culture type has also impact on the innovation climate in Asian countries. However, it seems that the organizational culture has stronger influence than the national culture. This could be due to the specific industry and the need to remain competitive. The internal culture becomes more of an island that can promote and influence different values than the national culture in its employees.

According to Naranjo-Valencia, Sanz-Valle, and Jiménez-Jiménez (2011), organizational culture is a clear determinant of innovation strategy. They state that adhocracy cultures foster innovation strategies while hierarchical cultures promote imitation cultures. Naranjo-Valencia et al. (2010) stated that organizational culture is considered to be one of the key elements in both enhancing and inhibiting innovation. Adhocracy cultures could enhance the development of new products or services, hierarchical cultures inhibit product innovation.

Adhocracy culture type has been considered as one very important organizational culture type in contemporary organizations, which is strongly related to innovations. The results of the current study support the idea adhocracy predicts innovation climate in Asian and Eastern European countries and therefore it is not influenced by the national culture where an organization operates.

The main characteristics of hierarchy culture type are rules, specialization, meritocracy, hierarchy, separate ownership, impersonality and accountability, which have been considered as impediments for innovation. The results of the current study support that hierarchy does not predict innovation climate in Asian and Eastern European countries and therefore the lack of connection is not influenced by national culture. Since many of the countries studied have a high power distance index and high uncertainty avoidance index we would have expected a hierarchy culture type to be significant.

Our findings are consistent with the following studies. According to James et al. (2007), culture is the lens through which leader vision is manifested and helps build the climate necessary for organizations to become innovative. As the environment changes and in turn demands organizations to change and adapt to new conditions, innovations are the vehicle to introduce change into outputs, structure and processes and factors at different levels – individual, organizational and environmental (Fariborz, 1991). It is interesting to note that for the organizations in Russia only the adhocracy organizational type was significant. This may be still due to their national culture; successful organizations must realign themselves to be competitive in the global market. The underpinnings for clan and market organizational types are not in significant existence.

Implications for managers from this study are the following: innovation climate is a complex entity and three organizational culture types from four predict innovation climate. Therefore, it should be taken into account when leaders create an innovative climate in an organization. But as results are somewhat different in Asia and Eastern Europe, the cultural environment where the organization is operating should still be taken into account. Findings are more important for expatriate managers operating in subsidiaries located in studied countries. Schein (1992) stated that leadership is mainly the creation, the management, and the destruction and reconstruction of culture. Leaders must evaluate how well the culture performs and when it needs to be changed. Evaluating and improving organizational culture and determining when major cultural transformations are necessary are very important to the success of the organization. Management of differentiated cultures and creation of synergies across these cultures is a very important leadership challenge. Effective culture management is very important in order to assure that organizational changes succeed. Collins and Porras (1994) found that companies with long-term success had a strong set of timeless core values that did not prevent organizational change over time.

Future study going deeper into the relationship between the national cultural dimensions and organizational types is needed. Also, this study aggregated the different industries surveyed therefore it would be advantageous to research whether industry is a moderator in the influence of national culture, or organizational culture and innovation.

References

Amabile, T.M., Conti, R., Coon, H., Lazenby, J. and Herron, M. (1996) Assessing the work environment for creativity. *Academy of Management Journal* 39(5), pp. 1154–1185.

Anderson, N.R., de Dreu, C.K.W. and Nijstad, B.A. (2004) The routinization of innovation research: A constructively critical review of the state-of-the-science. *Journal of Organisational Behaviour* 25(2), pp. 147–174.

Cakar, N. D. and Erturk, A. (2010) Comparing innovation capability of small and medium-sized enterprises: Examining the effects of organizational culture and empowerment. *Journal of Small Business Management.* 48(3). pp. 325–359.

Cameron, K.S. and Quinn, R.E. (1999) *Diagnosing and Changing Organizational Culture: Based on the Competing Values Framework.* Reading, MA: Addison-Wesley.

Collins, J.C. and Porras, J.I. (1994) *Built to Last: Successful Habits of Visionary Companies.* New York: Harper Business.

Damanpour, F. and Schneider, M. (2006) Phases of the adoption of innovation in organizations: effects of environment, organization and top managers. *British Journal of Management* 17, pp. 215–236.

Dwyer, S., Mesak, H., and Hsu, M. (2005) An exploratory examination of the influence of national culture on cross-national product diffusion. *Journal of International Marketing,* 13(2), pp.1–28.

Ekvall, G., Arvonen, J. and Waldenstrom-Lindblad, I. (1983) Creative Organizational Climate: Construction and Validation of a Measuring Instrument. Stockholm: The Swedish Council for Management and Organizational Behavior. Report no. 2.

Fariborz, D. (1991) Organizational innovation: A meta-analysis of effects of determinants and moderators. *Academy of Management Journal* 34(3), pp. 555–590.

Glisson, C. and James, L.R. (2002) The cross-level effects of culture and climate in human service teams. *Journal of Organizational Behavior* 23, pp. 767–794.

Hofstede, G. (1980) *Culture's Consequences.* London: Sage.

Hofstede. G. (2001) *Culture's Consequences.* London: Sage.

Ishikawa, A., Mako, C. and Warhurst, C. (2006) *Work and Employee Representation: Workers, Firms and Unions.* Tokyo: Chuo University Press.

James, L.R., Choi, C.C., Ko, C-H. E., McNeil, P.K., Minton, M.K., Wright, M.A., and Kim, K. (2007) Organizational and psychological climate: A review of theory and research. *European Journal of Work and Organizational Psychology* 17(1), pp. 5–32.

Kanter, R.M. (1983) *The Change Masters: Innovation for Productivity in the American Corporation.* New York: Simon and Schuster.

Kimberly, J.R. (1981) Managerial innovation. In: P.C. Nystromand and W.H. Starbuck (eds.) *Handbook of Organizational Design.* Oxford, England: Oxford University Press, pp. 84–104.

Kolman, L., Noorderhave, N. G., Hofstede, G., Dienes, E. (2003) Cross-cultural differences in Central Europe. *Journal of Managerial Psychology, 18*(1), pp. 76–88.

Kwan, P. and Walker, A. (2004) Validating the competing values model as a representation of organizational culture through inter-institutional comparisons. *Organizational Analysis, 12* (1), pp. 21–37

Lin, L., (2009) Effects of national culture on process management and technological innovation. *Total Quality Management, 20*(12), pp. 1287–1301.

Magnusson, P., Wilson, R. T., Zdravkovic, S., Zhou, X., and Westjohn, S. A. (2008) Breaking through the cultural clutter, *International Marketing Review, 25*(2), pp. 183–201.

Martins, E.C. and Terblanche, F. (2003) Building organizational culture that stimulates creativity and innovation. *European Journal of Innovation Management* 6(1), pp. 64–74.

Mumford, M.D. and Gustafson, S.B. (1988) Creativity syndrome: integration, application, and innovation. *Psychological Bulletin* 103, pp. 27–43.

Mumford, M.D. and Licuanan, B. (2004) Leading for innovation: conclusions, issues and directions, *Leadership Quarterly* 15(1), pp. 163–171.

van Muijen, J. J. and Koopman, P. L. (1994) The influence of national culture on organizational culture: A comparative study between 10 countries, *European Work and Organizational Psychologist, 4* (4), pp. 367–380.

Naranjo-Valencia, J.C., Jiménez-Jiménez, D. and Sanz-Valle, R. (2011) Innovation or imitation? The role of organizational culture. *Management Decision* 49(1), pp. 55–72.

Naranjo-Valencia, J.C., Sanz-Valle, R. and Jiménez-Jiménez, D. (2010) Organizational culture as determinant of product innovation. *European Journal of Innovation Management* 13(4), pp. 466–480.

Ostroff, C., Kinicki, A.J. and Tamkins, M.M. (2003) Organizational culture and climate. In: I.B. Weiner, W.C. Borman, D.R. Ilgen and R.J. Klimoski (eds.) *Handbook of Psychology.* Hoboken, NJ: John Wiley, pp. 565–594.

Sarros, J.C., Cooper, B.K. and Santora, J.C. (2008) Building a climate for innovation through transformational leadership and organizational culture. *Journal of Leadership and Organizational Studies* 15(2), pp. 145–158.

Schein, E.H. (1992) *Organizational Culture and Leadership.* Jossey Bass Publishers.

Schumpeter, J.A. (1911) *Theorie der Wirtschaftlichen Entwicklung.* Leipzig: Duncker and Humblot.

Sedziuviene, N. and Vveinhardt, J. (2010) Competitiveness and innovations: role of knowledge management at a knowledge organization. *Engineering Economics* 21(5), pp. 525–536.

Tellis, G. J., Prabhu, J. C. and Chandy, R. K. (2009) Radical innovation across nations: The preeminence of corporate culture. *Journal of Marketing, 7*, pp. 3–23.

Torokoff, M. (2010) Analysis of directing the innovation process and its relation to middle level manager's work: The case of Estonian enterprises. *Engineering Economics* 21(4), *pp.* 435–445.

Trice, H. and Beyer, J. (1993) *The Cultures of Work Organizations.* Englewood Cliffs, NJ: Prentice Hall.

Unsworth, K. and Parker, S. (2003) Proactivity and innovation: Promoting a new workforce for the new workplace. In: D. Holman, T. Wall, C. Clegg, P. Sparrow and A. Howard (eds.) *The New Workplace: A Guide to the Human Impact of Modern Working Practices.* Chichester: Wiley, pp. 175–196.

Van de Ven, A.H. (1986) Central problems in the management of innovation. *Management Science* 32(5), pp. 590–607.

Yukl, G. (2002) *Leadership in Organizations.* New Jersey: Prentice Hall.

Zhou, J. and Shalley, C. (2003) Research on employee creativity: A critical review and proposal for future research directions. In: J.J. Martocchio and G.R. Ferris (eds.) *Research in Personnel and Human Resource Management.* Oxford, England: Elsevier, pp. 165–217.

Strategic Management and Organisational Culture of Family Business in Estonia

Maret Kirsipuu[1], Juhan Teder[2] and Urve Venesaar[3]

Abstract

Family business traditions in Estonia were broken in connection with the incorporation of Estonia into the Soviet Union and the accompanying implementation of the socialist economic model. In 1991, after Estonia regained independence, private entrepreneurship started to grow fast; among other things, entrepreneurs started to restore previous farm places and many, especially in rural regions, set up a family business. Twenty years later family entrepreneurship is more advanced in rural areas and family entrepreneurship has a substantial role in the Estonian economy.

Management and organisational culture of family businesses have been studied in traditional stable market economies but less in former socialist countries. This research seeks to identify the family entrepreneurs' considerations and motives that pushed them to decide in favour of family business, to point out special features in family business management and organisational culture, as well as to map the similarities and differences in family businesses, their social and cultural aspects. The novelty of the research consists in that it is the first extensive research on Estonian family businesses and the data obtained can be used as input data in future research.

Based on data collected in the years 2006–2011 and using qualitative and quantitative methods of analysis (databases, questionnaires, interviews, cluster analysis, multidimensional scaling) the authors demonstrated that the dynamic development of a family business and continuing valuation of organisational culture is ensured in the first generation and give family businesses a competitive advantage in development of entrepreneurship in Estonia.

Keywords: family business, family entrepreneur, strategic management, organisational culture

JEL Classification Codes: M10; M13; M19

Acknowledgements

Publication of this paper is granted by the Doctoral School of Economics and Innovation established under the auspices of the European Social Fund.

---

1   E-mail: *Maret.Kirsipuu@sisekaitse.ee*
2   Tallinn University of Technology, Akadeemia tee 3, 12618 Tallinn, e-mail: *Juhan.Teder@ttu.ee*
3   Tallinn University of Technology, Akadeemia tee 3, 12618 Tallinn, e-mail: *Urve.Venesaar@ttu.ee*

1.   Introduction

Family entrepreneurship/entrepreneur is defined in different ways where the control of the entity, participation in management and the desire for continuity are usually the main factors used to define family business (Casillas, Acedo & Moreno 2007, p. 18). Still, there is less consensus regarding which of these factors are strictly necessary in order to classify family business. In this paper the authors define family business as an undertaking where family of the undertaker is participating in the business, family members are the spouse, children, parents, sisters-brothers, aunts-uncles and their spouses. It is of no significance whether the conjugal relations are official or not, only cohabiting counts.

Family firms dominate in the economies of all developed countries, playing an important role in the economic systems of these countries (Casillas, Acedo & Moreno 2007, p. 23). Research on family entrepreneurship has been mostly conducted in traditional stable market economies where self-employed people or sole proprietors have always been appreciated. For example, a family entrepreneurship research conducted among 601 family businesses from eight countries (Argentina, USA, Egypt, Serbia, Kosovo, France, Croatia and Kuwait) reached a conclusion that 60% of the output is produced by family firms, which divided as follows on the basis of legal form: 47% sole proprietors, 20% private limited companies and the rest were other companies. 43% were first generation businesses, only 19% were third generation businesses. Family businesses are unsustainable because of the management problems, especially insufficient knowledge about management (Lussier et al. 2012).

Research papers on family entrepreneurship in former socialist countries are scarce and only a few individual family business related issues have been addressed. Researchers have analysed single areas and provided recommendations for investigating the same areas of family businesses operating in different areas of activity in different countries. First of all, they have recommended to study dynamics of family business development (Leenders 2001); family businesses' organisational culture (Bhalla et al. 2006); factors that were the reasons for starting family business in a particular country (Wadhwa et al. 2009); relationships between family property and management (Shea 2006); presence of strategic management (Finich 2005), differences in family business composition (Ferguson 2011).

Family business traditions in Estonia were broken in connection with the incorporation of Estonia into the Soviet Union and the accompanying implementation of the socialist economic model. In 1991, after Estonia regained independence, private entrepreneurship started to grow fast, among other things entrepreneurs started to restore previous farm places and many people, especially in rural regions, set up a family business. On the basis of the research conducted in Estonia it is possible to say that twenty years later family entrepreneurship is more advanced in rural areas and family entrepreneurship is playing an important role in the economy (Kirsipuu 2012). According to the studies conducted by Praxis Centre for Policy Studies among small and medium-sized businesses, 66% of the Estonian entrepreneurs identified themselves as family businesses (Kaarna et al. 2012).

Enterprising people in Estonia have set up family businesses mainly in the sphere of services, agriculture, tourism or manufacturing (Põllumajandusministeeriumi... 2009). Over time, agricultural family business has been an important area of activity and source of income for Estonian people. Estonia is one of the best provided countries in the European Union with farmland: 0.64 ha per capita (the same indicator in Germany – 0.21 ha and in France 0.43 ha) (Põllumajandusministeeriumi... 2009). A negative tendency is that the number of people employed with agriculture and forestry in Estonia has been decreasing from year to year, and the number of rural population is also decreasing. Rural regions can be made more attractive by diversifying business activities, including fast growth of tourist farms. Tourist farms offer active recreation, opportunities to take part in everyday activities of the family business and so-called „put hands into the soil". For example, 20% of the beef cattle breeding family businesses have a tourist farm as a secondary activity, where tourists can spend time on beef cattle pastures, feed or drive cattle from one paddock to another (Kirsipuu 2009).

The problem is that there is no comprehensive picture of family entrepreneurship in Estonia and the role of family entrepreneurs in society is not comprehended. There is no awareness of the special nature of management, strategy and organisational culture of family businesses.

The aim of the current research is to identify the main features of strategic management and organisational culture in Estonian family businesses. The research questions are:

1. Who and why have started family business in Estonia?
2. What are the differences and similarities between different groups of family businesses?
3. What factors limit the growth of family businesses?
4. Is the first generation dynamic development ensured only when employees are family members?
5. What are the specific features of organizational culture (incl. values) in family businesses?

6. What is the practice of strategic management in family businesses in Estonia?

The novelty of the research consists in that it is the first extensive research on Estonian family businesses and the data obtained can be used as input data in future research. Research into strategic management and organisational culture of family business issues and the related problems and finding ways for solving them can contribute to the achievement of the target of the Estonian entrepreneurship policy to value regional, local and sustainable development (Estonian Enterprise... 2009).

The paper is divided conditionally into three parts: the first part provides an overview of the theoretical sources of the research topic and describes the significance of family businesses in Estonian economy. The second part gives an overview of the research process and methods of research, and suitability of the methods. In the third part the results are analysed and the findings are presented. Finally, the paper is concluded.

2. Theoretical Framework: Strategic Management and Organisational Culture of Family Businesses

A strategy represents a set of main ways and principles of action for the achievement of long-term objectives, serving as the basis of managing an business development. Strategic plans help businesses make rearrangements, fulfil tasks and expand products and services, as well as increase business's market position and competitiveness (Leimann et al. 2003). When family business entrepreneurs are aware of the need for strategic management they are more competitive (Huybrechts et al. 2011).

Strategic management in family business is focused on activity and attends to what and when to do, and in which way specific activities should be carried out; a family business strategy is to be planned in detail; all stages have a specific content and have to be carried out consistently. The organisational culture of family businesses is focused on human relations; their aim is continuous development and training of the family and non-family workforce; confidential relations are dominant in family businesses; everybody cares for each other, they are helpful and communicate also outside the work environment. Factors contributing to the development of family businesses are a well-advised management of the family business, a fixed strategy and strong organisational culture. For making changes in the strategy both family business management and structure need to change, and as a result, often especially the roles of managers change. It is often the case that plans are made but they do not want to change the existing management strategy and this becomes an obstacle to new developments. Every family business must consider their abilities and take such strategic decisions that are suitable just for them (Kirsipuu 2004, 2009).

New strategies help family businesses to make rearrangements, carry out tasks and expand products and services, as well as improve family business's market position and competitiveness. Businesses have a risk to stagnate, especially when the same managers manage them for a long time, which in family businesses is typical. To avoid that, enterprises must stay open to changes. One cannot provide unambiguous guidelines to family businesses – what works well with one may not work with the other. So as to update the existing strategy, family businesses are recommended to consistently carry out the strategies, comply with the terms and objectives and be open to changes, especially those arising from the economic environment. Organisational culture is of great significance in the implementation of a management strategy (Leimann et al. 2003). Previous research has brought out that continuing valuation of family business organisational culture is greater in those family businesses where the management comprises family members; reacting to changes is faster in those family businesses where the management is not family members (Khaemasunun 2004). It is hard to find an optimal balance (Khaemasunun 2004).

Sustainable organisational culture in family businesses is ensured by motivation and willpower, and if these are missing, activity will be terminated during the first five years of operation (Halttunen 2004). Organisational culture in family businesses must be developed; owners of family businesses are constructive, they have fixed ideas that influence the organisation's behaviour, which in turn influences the economic performance (Conant 2007). One of the major reasons for survival under competition of those family businesses which have operated for a long time and which have a strong organisational culture is that they are flexible in their management strategy and have an ability to change rapidly and in a creative way, and develop according to the economic environment (Zahra et al. 2008). Strong and stable organisational culture will provide for family businesses a competitive advantage, since employees, both family members and outsiders, have the same value judgements, which ensure the best results for the achievement of goals (Voordecker et al. 2007; Conant 2007). In those family businesses which have a strong and stable organisational culture, family members are able to plan free time better and keep the family and work apart. They can also involve all of the family business team in the off-duty relations; all employees of the family business feel as one family and enjoy the off-duty time spent together (Rautamäki 2007). Organisational culture in family businesses differs from that of non-family businesses due to the strong family traditions and historical background of the family business (Chami 1997).

The manager's role is most important in the development of the organisational culture in a family business. The manager's value judgements influence the organisational culture. The manager's focus on the task of organisational culture is revealed in the clients' satisfaction, long-term competitive advantages, ethical convictions, concern for the consequences, moral responsibility and power motivation. Manager's focus on the relationship of organisational culture is revealed only in the ethical convictions, concern for the consequences, moral responsibility and power motivation (Alas 2002).

The organisational culture of family businesses must observe and take account of changes in various processes in the society, go with them in order to ensure success to the family business (Littunen 2001). A specific feature of the organisational culture of family businesses is that employees in the first generation businesses are only family members and starting from the second generation workforce is hired outside; family members usually remain to work along with the non-family workforce in order to ensure a dynamic development of the organisation of family business (Nedlin 2003).

Those family businesses which attach great importance to the principles of the learning organisation educate themselves and have training and entrepreneurship activity related, have a stronger organisational culture, since learning gives value added to the family business and helps the family business establish social networks (Juutilainen 2005). Organisational culture contributes to collaboration between employees of the family business, which in turn is not limited only to collaboration within the family business but involves also cooperation between family businesses. The initiative group of the creators of the cooperation network comprises mainly family businesses which have a strong and stable organisational culture; networks help create knowledge and values in family businesses, participation in them will ensure cooperation capacity for family businesses and will increase growth of competitiveness within the networks (Niemela 2003). Of great significance in cooperation between family businesses is the cultural compatibility of different nations; in most of the countries owning a family business is regarded as a competitive advantage, whereas specialists of family businesses act similarly regardless of the different national culture; and they rather reckon with family traditions (Brice 2005).

Family relations, collaboration, motivation, commitment, capability will enable family businesses to continuously improve the organisational culture (Chirico 2006). By improving the organisational culture they increase cooperation between family members and ensure transfer of a successful organisational culture from generation to generation (Ibid.). Organisational culture will give family businesses a competitive advantage since employees, both family members and outsiders have the same value judgements, which ensure the best results for the achievement of goals (Voordecker et al. 2007; Conant 2007). Those family businesses which take account of changes in the society are capable of creating a strong organisational culture (Eddleston 2008). Building of an organisational culture of a family business must focus attention on social capital and types of organisation, which is the type of human relations, open system, performance targeted and internal processes (Pearson et al. 2008; Chrisman et al. 2008) and it has been found that strong social networks encourage joint activity, which contributes to reinforcement of the organisational culture in the family business.

Organisational culture has three levels which differ from one another by the rate of awareness: observable culture, which consists of the physical layout of work spaces (e.g. furniture, work equipment), dress codes and communication style; shared and accepted values, which are values accepted in the organisation and which in turn may be a very important source of motivation for the members (e.g. loyalty, accuracy, helping each other, fair remuneration) and collective understanding and beliefs (Vadi 2001). The types of culture are power culture, which often occurs in small businesses; is characterised by centralised power, informal communication and trust; role culture, characterised by bureaucracy and formality; task culture, which is characteristic of organisations with a matrix structure, where power is in the point of intersection of power lines; and person culture, where individuals are superior to the organisation; it is important that people decide to come together since they consider joint action mutually useful (Brooks 2008). Such an organisation where the entrepreneur who established the organisation him/herself is trying to manage and take responsibility for everything is called a sun-shaped organisation; in that organisation assignments, orders and rights are given one at a time and the subordinates may enjoy the „fatherly sunshine"; with the capable entrepreneur such an organisation may prove to be efficient (Üksvärav 1992).

An important family business management and organisational culture theory background for this research is the statement that in the first generation dynamic development and continuing valuation of organisational culture of a family business is ensured only when workforce are family members, which causes in comparison with non-family businesses a difference in management and organisational culture (Nedlin 2003; Khaemasunun 2004; Miller et al. 2007).

3. Data, Method of Research and Analysis

3.1. Study Design

The research was based on Kluge's (2000) four-step empirically grounded grouping model and the methodological research principles developed by Wahl (2011) where the general principles are established and the sequence of research composition stages decided, at the same time enabling combining of different methods, which in turn increases the reliability of the results.

The research is based on family business entrepreneurs' decisions and feelings; grouping data on the basis of personality traits, opinions and feelings it is possible to identify the value judgements, which help to determine the strategic behaviour since value orientations differ from each other by type of motivational goal that represents the value (Schwartz 1992), while different value groups have different relationships with strategic behaviour (Chuah 2010).

Abduction as a scientific method is used in the research. It is based on explaining the primary assumptions that definitely need to be tested later (Peirce 1931). Abduction is the only logical operation that introduces new ideas and determines the assumption using deduction and regularities so as the assumption in turn would explain the deduction (Wahl 2011).

Interviews are cognitive and express the views of interviewees about a certain subject (Thietart et al. 1999). The interviewee may not always provide information impartially (Researching... 2000). The interview method was chosen because it enables to personally communicate with the interviewee and ask supplementary questions later. Notwithstanding that interview has a cognitive approach, the results may be expressed also factually in numbers, which in turn proves that strength of the researcher's argument has great significance in research (White 2000).

In this research different groups were formed based on entrepreneur (gender, education, age); composition of family business (spouse, children, kins, members outside family); organisational type of family business (human relations, openness, performance orientation, inner processes); type of organisational culture (person, task, role, power culture); organisational level (observable, shared values and understandings); business management (strategic plan, objectives, competitive advantage); economic activity (principal and secondary field of activity, area and region of activity); legal form (sole proprietorship, private limited company, public limited company, other: general and limited partnership, commercial association).

In the next stage, the questionnaires and interviews were coded, the results were grouped and empirical regularities were analysed.

Then the relationships in management and organisational culture were analysed and the feature space groups were formed on the basis of similarities, which contain a certain number of sub-groups, for every feature its own. The feature space groups were formed with the help of data and prior theoretical knowledge.

The last stage of the research comprised analysis of the regularities characterising the groups and the results. Mathematical processing methods were used for analysing the regularities, for every feature a median and standard deviation were calculated; additionally the results were summed, the arithmetic mean was found and the percentage shares of certain features were calculated.

3.2. Data Collection and Sample

Based on the research problem and research tasks the most widespread method in social sciences was chosen for gathering input data for the research: questionnaire and interview. The data collection was carried out in the period 2006–2011. The database gathering started in 2008. First, data were collected and then, in 2011, systematic coding of data began. Originally the database was formed of family businesses and principal questions. When interview transcripts and questionnaires were coded, groups and sub-groups were added to the database. At the beginning of the research, not random sample but a specific sample was used, which was formed of beef cattle breeders doing performance testing in 2006 and sport horse breeders in 2008, those who had registered their horses in the sport horse database. Data were received from the database *Liisu* of the Estonian Animal Recording Centre and from the database of horses (Liisu… 2007; Hobuste… 2008). A random sample was generated using the principle of systematic random sampling that was applied since 2009. For every county a hypothetical list of family businesses in alphabetical order was drafted; the sample was formed starting from a hypothetical family business with a random number in the list and advancing by a predetermined step. The same principle was used for generating the interview samples. The random sample size was 10% of the businesses in the respective rural region. Input data for the sample were received from the Agricultural Registers and Information Board's (PRIA) register of farm animals, from the holding register (PRIA…. 2009). The 2010 random sample was selected from among the businesses registered in Estonia; the authors removed from the sample those businesses which had registered their holdings in PRIA's animal register and those whose legal address was in Tallinn. Input data for the sample were received from on-line information system of the Commercial Register accessible for registered users in the Ministry of Justice's Centre of Registers and Information Systems (Äriregistri… 2010).

A total of 2035 hypothetical family entrepreneurs were questioned in writing in the years 2007–2011 to find out whether they regarded themselves as family businesses or not. Questionnaires were sent to 1500 respondents who regarded themselves as family entrepreneurs, verifying that 1188 of the respondents can be regarded as family businesses; with more than one thousand interviews were conducted, and with 76 of the latter in-depth interviews were carried out. The questionnaires were sent mostly by e-mail; those who had no e-mail address available in the database were called and they answered by phone, and those who had neither an e-mail address nor phone number in the database the questionnaires were sent by post. 1690 (83%) responded. The authors received back 1320 completed questionnaires, i.e. 88%.

Questionnaires were sent to all enterprises selected in this way, with those who responded the author conducted interviews, including in-depth interviews. An abductive coding of questionnaire and interview transcripts was performed in the computer programme (excel); data of the completed questionnaires were recorded; data processing was anonymous.

The results of the questionnaires and interviews were presented by aggregating the following data: family business areas and composition of the family business; family business strategy, management and organisational culture; problems for family entrepreneurs. The gathered and coded data were entered into the database, which contains also family business codes, feature space groups and subgroups, median and module for every feature, standard deviation, sum, maximum, minimum, arithmetic mean, percentage share of features. The database contains data on 1212 family businesses from different regions across Estonia. Since family business statistics is missing in Estonia the total sample population might be the number of enterprises in the statistical profile of Statistics Estonia, which at the end of 2011 was 103,833; the sample size is 1.2% of the total population of enterprises. If to take that family businesses account for approximately 66% of the total number of enterprises (Kaarna et al. 2012), then 1.8% of them are in the sample. The names and contact details of entrepreneurs and businesses are known, but the promise has been given to keep them anonymous and disclose only the names of those entrepreneurs and businesses who gave their permission.

3.3. Data Analysis

For data analysis qualitative and quantitative methods of analysis are used (databases, questionnaires, interviews, cluster analysis, nonmetric multidimensional scaling). Data were gathered with both questionnaires and interviews; the qualitative data were coded and aggregated; graphs were made on the basis of data where structured data relationships are revealed. All groups were coded and an analysis was conducted to identify the differences and similarities and to choose the groups with the results reflecting the objective of this research. Open-ended questions with the purpose to enable to answer freely, based on personal convictions and understandings, were not coded, but the information was aggregated, assorted and processed, and presented graphically. Computer based data analysis was used for processing the answers: first a database was generated in excel tables and then the database was processed with a freeware data analysis package PAlaeontological Statistics, hereinafter PAST (Hammer et al. 2001), version 2.00.

To find the structure of data a hierarchical cluster analysis was used first, which enabled to form groups on the basis of features. So as the outcome were correct the data had to be aggregated so that one group or cluster contained similar data. A feature space had to be found for every feature with a t-dot (Sneath et al. 1973), in this paper the t-dot is family business. An advantage of cluster analysis is repeatability and objectivity; the method does not have one and only solution; the results have to be interpreted according to the theory chosen (Wahl 2011). A separate cluster was formed for every object in the cluster analysis; then the closest clusters were merged so that by the end of processing there was an optimal amount of clusters. Cluster analysis was conducted in the data processing package PAST.

Different algorithms and similarity measures were used in data analysis, in order to choose the most similar from the solutions. On the basis of different algorithms dendrograms were generated, which provide an overview of the outcomes of analysis. The quality of the hierarchical structure of the dendrogram can be measured with the help of correlation coefficient: the closer the coefficient value to one, the higher the dendrogram quality and reliability of data (Hammer et al. 2001).

The data processing programme PAST enables to group the results on the basis of businesses as well as features. Irrespective of the principle of grouping, mathematical results are the same (Sneath et al. 1973). Using Ward's method for PAST cluster analysis appropriate feature spaces can be selected; the results were the smoothest using Hamming (Fig. 1) and Kulczynski's (Fig. 2) similarity measures.

The hierarchically clustered dendrogram enables to reduce clusters on the basis of similarity and using the distances between the clusters to define groups of family businesses. The correlation coefficient of the outcome is the highest if to apply the average algorithm joining in Morisita (Coph. Corr. = 0.9994) and Horn (Coph. Corr. = 0.9944) similarity measure. With the smoothest structure is the dendrogram of hierarchically clustered family businesses on the basis of

Kulczynski similarity measure with Ward's method (Fig. 2). The correlation co-efficient (Coph. Corr. = 0.3563) is remarkably smaller than one; the dendrogram still enables to determine the number of clusters. Evaluating the relative distance of clusters in the family business dendrogram, we can determine the number of clusters used in the analysis, which is described by an unrooted dendrogram in the neighbour joining clustering (Fig. 3) where five different groups of family businesses are formed. Neighbour joining clustering is considered an alternative method to hierarchical cluster analysis (Hammer et al. 2001).

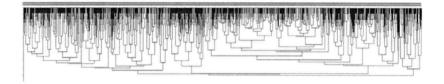

Fig. 1:   Dendrogram of hierarchically clustered family businesses using Ward's method on the basis of Hamming's similarity measure, R mode, Coph. Corr.: 0.3563 (PAST ver. 2.00; calculation on the basis of data collected)

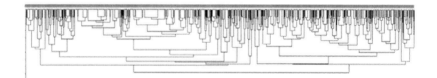

Fig. 2:   Dendrogram of hierarchically clustered family businesses on the basis of Kulczynski's similarity measure using Ward's method, R mode, Coph. Corr.: 0.3563 (PAST ver. 2.00; calculation on the basis of data collected)

Distances between the groups of family businesses (Fig. 3) are different based on when family business was started: in the period from 1991 to 2009, five groups of family businesses were formed on the basis of similar attributes, where in turn subgroups were formed on the basis of activity area and in the area of activity at the level of organisational culture types.

Fig. 3:   *Unrooted dendrogram from neighbour joining cluster analysis, Euclidean similarity measure (PAST ver. 2.00; calculation based on data collected)*

To find differences and similarities in the results of data analysis, data of visualising statistical information were scaled by nonmetric scaling in the data processing programme PAST, choosing different similarity measures. Scaling in the PAST enables to choose different similarity measures: Gower, Euclidean, Correlation, Rho, Dice, Jaccard, Kulczynski, Ochiai, Simpson, Bray-Curtis, Cosine, Morisita, Raup-Crick, Horn, Hamming, Chord, Manhattan, Jukes-Cantor, Kimura (Hammer *et al.* 2001). In the scaling the features have to be positioned using the algorithm based on the selection as dots in a two (2D) or three-dimensional (3D) feature space; the features can also be positioned in the family business space. Figures can be illustrated with dots, labels as well as graphs. Graphs allow describing relationships between family businesses that can be compared with the dendrogram obtained in hierarchical cluster analysis.

The quality of the outcome is assessed with the help of indicators such as stress and sample determination coefficient, which can be found on figure; the more precise the figure, the more evenly the dots are positioned on the line; the lower the stress value, the better the result; the stress value depends on the procedure and data analysed: the value 0.0 is perfect, value higher than 0.4 not any more (Malhotra 2007). The value of determination coefficient should be as high as possible: value 1.0 is perfect, value higher than 0.6 is significant still (Malhotra 2007).

Data processing programme PAST was used for the distribution into feature groups; as a result of scaling the feature groups were divided into five on the basis of when family businesses were started: 1991–1995; 1996–2000, 2001–2003; 2004–2006; 2007–2009. Result scaling in a three-dimensional feature space characterises the positioning of groups better than Hamming listing; t-dots (family business) positioned on a straight line (Fig. 4) and in a common feature space (Fig. 5) show that the feature groups have been divided in the best possible way (stress 0.1257). In the division on the basis of other features, the stress value of all other listings was higher than 0.4, hence the feature groups chosen are of good quality.

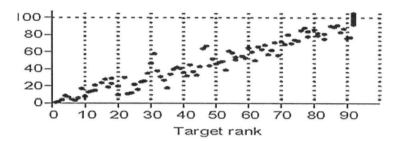

Fig. 4:   *Family business feature spaces t-dots positioned, Hamming similarity measure*
            3D, stress 0.1257 (PAST ver. 2.00; calculation on the basis of data gathered)

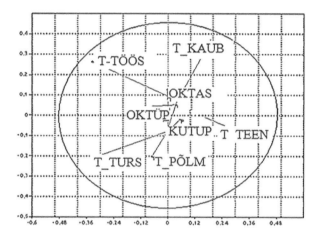

Fig. 5:   *Family business features in spaces, Hamming similarity measure 3D, stress*
            0.1257 (PAST ver. 2.00; calculation on the basis of data gathered)

Multi-dimensional scaling enables to analyse groups of features formed in
the neighbour joining clustering. The feature groups in turn are divided on the
basis of importance of the objective (turnover, profit and increase in market
share; improvement of quality and financial status; increase in technological
level) and competitive advantage (workers' skills, competence; product/service
quality; best servicing; managerial skills and experiences; low operating costs;
business flexibility) into two feature spaces, demonstrating a strong correlation
between the feature spaces; the determination coefficient value is higher than
0.8. Reliability of the relationships is assessed with the value of the determination coefficient, significant values are between 0.6...1.

Source data are from the statistics (Statistics Estonia; Ministry of Justice; Estonian Animal Recording Centre; Estonian Agricultural Registers and Information Board); the questionnaire surveys and interviews with family business entrepreneurs were carried out by Maret Kirsipuu in 2006–2011.

4. Results

4.1. Analysing Feature Groups of Family Businesses

Inside a feature space relationships can be identified; for example, family businesses which are oriented to improving their financial status attach importance to members' skills and competences; those wishing to increase turnover regard quality of products/services as a competitive advantage; those for whom the priority is introduction of new products regard customer service level as the main competitive advantage.

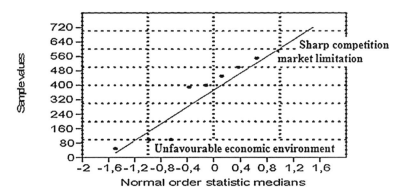

Fig. 6:   Factors that limit family business growth, division of probability (PAST ver. 2.00; calculation based on data collected)

Factors that limit the growth of business (Fig. 6) are thought to be sharp competition, unfavourable economic environment, insufficient investment capital, missing export skills, unsuitable technology, shortage of skilled labour, difficulties in cash flow management, unsuitable workspace, high labour costs and market limitation. Absence of factors that limit the growth of business in Fig. 6 would have been described by a straight line; distance of factors from the straight line describes the weight of the factor: the closer the factor to the straight line, the smaller the limiting effect on the business growth. Fig. 6 demonstrates that only one factor (market limitation) has a small limiting effect; the biggest effect is exerted by sharp competition and unfavourable economic environment, including product quotas and purchaser's agreed prices.

In a common feature space it is possible to describe the feature groups on the basis of organisational culture level (OKTAS), type of organisation (OK-TÜP) and type of culture (KUTUP) (Fig. 7); dominating in the feature space among the organisational culture levels (shared values, shared understandings, observability) are shared values, 73.8%; among the types of culture (person, task, role, power culture) person culture, 57.6%, and from among the types of organisation (orientation to human relations, openness, performance, inner processes) human relations orientation with 53.9%. In the feature space, power culture (9.2%) and organisational type oriented to inner processes (6.9%) can be distinguished.

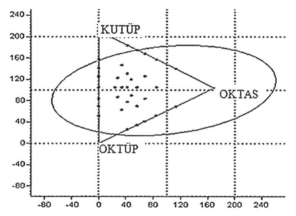

Fig. 7:   *Relationships in family business organisational culture in feature spaces, based on entries (PAST ver. 2.00; calculated on the basis of data)*

92.3% of the family businesses surveyed have built a sun-shaped organisation where the entrepreneur him/herself manages everything and is responsible for everything. 7.7% of the family businesses consider themselves as sharing responsibility. Family businesses which have expanded activity to different regions have lost control over the management of the family business (28.4%). In order to regain control over the management they need to make changes both in the management of the family business and in the organisational culture.

The interviewees can feel a strong organisational culture and are satisfied with it; 92.3% of the family business members are of the opinion that the organisational culture is transparent and management is appropriate and equitable. Family entrepreneurs are of the opinion that the organisational culture is focused on human relations, most important in a family business is to appreciate values. A strong organisational culture in family businesses helps avoid power conflicts, which tend to occur when there is no uniform organisational culture or the existing one is inadequate; disputes arise regarding who will set rules, laws and customs. On the basis of the type of culture, 57.6% of the family businesses regard themselves as focused on person culture, 53.9% believe that they have a human relations type of organisational culture. With a non-existent organisational culture, the usual situation when a business is being founded, there are more conflicts in both family and business relations as well as between generations. The clearer the organisational culture in a family business, the fewer the tensions and conflicts.

The need to change the organisational culture substantially was perceived by family entrepreneurs who had started the family business in the early 1990s; they have realised that the organisational culture they had established „had influences from the occupation period and had grown outdated". Introduction of changes to the organisational culture was, although they understood the need for changes, an extremely painful and time-consuming process. At the same time, such family businesses where an educated family member who had worked elsewhere in the meanwhile returned, could make changes to the organisational culture less painfully and faster, since they „still trust one of your own rather than a stranger". It is believed important that only family members are in the management of family business, since this would ensure instant mutual understanding: „you needn't end a sentence, the other already knows", „material welfare for the family is provided". They find that when the family business expands it is increasingly difficult to discriminate between work and family, which in turn leads them drawing apart from each other and will raise family business interests higher than personal interests; there is no more free time. Conflicts arise, which may lead to collapse of the family. A solution is found in appreciation of values.

On the basis of legal form, the most numerous in agriculture (T_PÕLM), tourism (T_TURS) and services (T_TEEN) are sole proprietors, in trade (T_KAUB) private limited companies and in industry (T_TÖÖS) commercial associations (Fig. 8). The graph on Figure 8 depicts the distribution of legal form and field of activity; most of the sole proprietors are concentrated into the feature space; grouped outside the feature space T_KAUB are private limited companies and in the feature space T_TÖÖS commercial associations. The feature space contains mostly sole proprietors (66.9%).

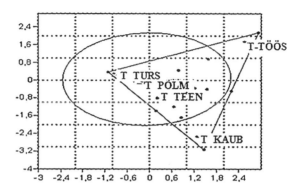

Fig. 8:   *Relationship graph of family business' legal form on the basis of feature groups*
            (PAST ver. 2.00; calculations made on the basis of data)

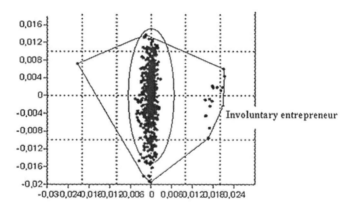

Fig. 9:   *Relationship graph of family businesses' area of activity on the basis of feature*
            groups (PAST ver. 2.00; calculations made on the basis of data)

Family businesses form a whole, where involuntary entrepreneurs and those
who have a secondary activity in addition to the principal activity can be distinguished (Fig. 9). Involuntary entrepreneur (whom employer has constrained to
register as a legally independent service provider) has secondary education and
those who had a secondary activity had higher education (Fig. 9). The core on
the graph in Fig. 9 contains businesses operating only in the principal activity;
around them is a smaller circle of businesses which also have a secondary activity and a wider circle of involuntary entrepreneurs.

A family business is based on shared values, person culture and human relations, which all together form an integrated whole (Fig. 10) where values, beliefs, moral, traditions, habits, skills obtained, inborn skills, knowledge, rights are intertwined.

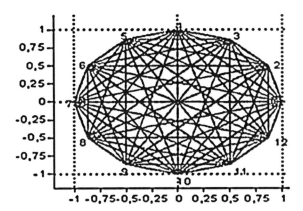

Fig. 10:   Family businesses' value in organisational culture, unitary associations graph gk; relationships between types of culture and organisation, PCA Xcatter diagram (PAST ver. 2.00; calculation made on the basis of data collected)

Family businesses operating in industry are oriented to inner processes, observable level of organisation and power culture; similar by type of culture and organisation (Fig. 11) are trade, service and tourist businesses; in agriculture the role culture and performance orientation are more important. In the common feature space of feature groups a group of entrepreneurs less than thirty years of age with no children can be clearly distinguished from the homogeneous central group of family entrepreneurs.

Most of the family businesses surveyed have built a sun-shaped organisation and they can feel that the organisational culture is focused on human relations; most important in a family business is to appreciate values. Family business is based on shared values, human relations and organisational culture, which all together form an integrated whole.

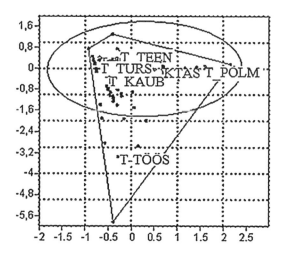

Fig. 11:   *Family businesses similar by type in organisational culture, unitary associations*
           graph gk; relationships between types of culture and organisation, PCA Xcatter
           diagram (PAST ver. 2.00; calculation made on the basis of data collected)

4.2. Main Characteristics of Family Businesses

The qualitative data gathered with questionnaires and interviews were coded and aggregated. Mind maps were made on the basis of the data, where the structured data relationships are revealed.

49% of the family businesses are operating in the principal activity only; however, all family entrepreneurs are of the opinion that business activity should be expanded, but they say „they lack initiative", „let children come and do"; „I would do but have no time to go to training courses". Secondary activities are essential and offer additional opportunities, and are „necessary to diversify risk". Although they are interested in business growth, 71.5% of the entrepreneurs thought in the year of survey that the firm would continue with a stable volume, 19.7% expected a decline and 8.8% a fast growth.

Women accounted for 40.2% of those who had started a family business. In the period of data collection, the average age of entrepreneurs was 38.6 years; the youngest was 21 and the oldest 66 years of age. 25% of the entrepreneurs have been in family business on average 15 years (the first started in 1991), 75% six years (latest start-up year 2009). 31.7% of the family entrepreneurs have higher education, 26.4% secondary education, 20.6% specialised secondary,

20.3% basic education. Family businesses' regions of operation are divided into fourteen; from fifteen counties of Estonia Hiiumaa and Saaremaa are merged and Tallinn is merged with Harjumaa. The most analysed family businesses are in Läänemaa (34.1%), Hiiumaa and Saaremaa (13.9%), the least in Raplamaa (3.2%) and Ida-Virumaa (3.0%). On the basis of area of activity, businesses were divided as follows: agriculture (40.7%); tourism (21.5%); services (19.6%); trade (9.2%) and manufacturing (9.1%).

Strategic plans formulated in writing are few (26%, as many have a vision and mission formulated in writing); most of the strategic plans have been formulated in entrepreneur's mind (65.2%), the others have none whatsoever. Lack of strategic plan in writing is induced by that in 93.7% of the cases owners and executive managers are the same. 72% of the family businesses have a fixed planning system, 58% of them have been able to adhere to the planning system without deviation, and of great significance has been cooperatives' assistance to selling products.

Family entrepreneurs in the sample have studied different specialties, for example, agronomy, zoology, animal breeding, tailor, food technology, electrician work, bookkeeping, design, pedagogy, bookbinding, journalism, metalworking, veterinary, medicine, art, dramaturgy, etc. Family business founders were 60% men and 40% women. It means that the start-up initiative came in 60% of the cases from men, who then invited their wives and then children and relatives. In 99% of the cases the spouse was involved first, then children and only after that other relatives. When starting the business the entrepreneurs were 21 to 66 years old. 55% of the family entrepreneurs had been operating for more than 10 years, 45% less than 10 years.

Those family business entrepreneurs who have been in family business longer than ten years are nearly all legally married; those who have been in family business less than ten years have preferred cohabitation. The question why their marriage has not been officially registered was answered „I see no need", „registration won't make the bond stronger", „We prefer to be free", „When children go to school, then we shall register". Nearly all family business entrepreneurs who started family business after Estonia regained independence had children already and their average age at the start-up moment was 45 years. Those family business entrepreneurs who have started the business in near past rather have no children yet; they wish to lay a solid material groundwork for the family and only then start planning offspring; however, some people found just after children were born that they have to set up their family business.

The family composition has been variable in the business start-up phase; they have started with two to six of them, hence starting of a family business does not depend on the size of family, but the needs, ambitions and enterprising spirit of the family.

Most of the family business entrepreneurs (66.9%) have registered their family business as a sole proprietorship, 30.7% as a private limited company and the others (2.4%) have founded a commercial association, public limited company, limited or general partnership. Public limited companies were founded on the basis of previous collective or state farm ancillary businesses or entities. 90% of the family farmers are sole proprietors, because the business can be registered with the farm name and one's own and family business's money need not be kept separately. Some family entrepreneurs who have transformed into private limited company consider it a mistake since the family business funds cannot be used for family needs; others who have changed the legal form are content that they could transform from sole proprietorship into private limited company without additional taxation, since they believe their liability is now limited to the equity of the private limited company. Those who started a family business immediately after Estonia regained independence choose public limited company for the legal form; however, when the minimum share capital requirement increased, the business was re-registered as a private limited company. Sometimes several forms of entrepreneurship are used in parallel.

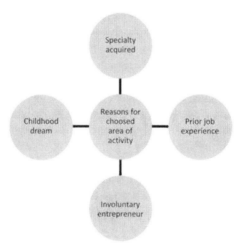

Fig. 13:   Mind map on reasons for choosing the area of activity (compiled by the authors)

Family businesses are operating in nearly all areas of activity, 49% are operating in only one area of activity; most have chosen a secondary activity to spread risk. The choice of family business's area of activity (Fig. 13) depends on various reasons: specialty obtained; past work experience in the same area; fulfilment of a childhood dream; interest in handicraft; employer urged; various reasons such as „was inherited with the farm"; „more vegetables and fruits than the family could consume".

Fig. 14:   *Mind map on the reasons for setting up a family business (compiled by the authors)*

A family business has nearly always been its founder focused; the operation location for 70% of the family businesses is home; only 30% are operating away from home. Family businesses have different households: there are businesses which actually lack a household since they provide services in client's place; some have only one building, however, farms have land (1...500 ha), forest (1...60 ha) and animal breeding buildings (cattle-shed, stables, storehouses, grain dryers etc). The answers to the question what was the reason for starting the family business were different (Fig. 14). For example, they wished to be their own master, feel freedom, use the skills they had acquired previously, provide welfare for their family members, preferred certain lifestyle and green thinking, had to start a business to earn living.

The reasons for setting up a family business have changed over years. New family business entrepreneurs are thinking more of environment saving and do not attach so much importance to being their own master. They now wish more to create something that will go over to future generations; green thinking is more widespread than previously, for example, organic production is expanding.

Family businesses' organisational culture is focused on human relations; members of family businesses listed the values by order of importance as follows: relationships between people; good inner climate; unity; cooperativeness; teamwork; positive work environment (Fig. 15).

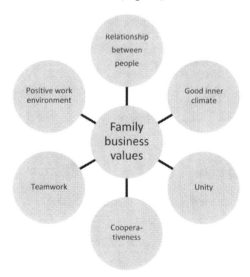

Fig. 15:   Mind map of family business values (compiled by the authors)

72.7% of the family business entrepreneurs believe that organisational culture in their family business facilitates achievement of the objectives and the family business culture is continually the same in all locations of activity. They are convinced that organisational culture is focused on human relations, they are satisfied with the existing organisational culture, priority for them is the appreciation of values. Problems are caused by that family business entrepreneur cannot stay away from the management process and is constantly interfering.

The question what is special in the organisational culture of your family business was answered, for example, „All family members are treated equally", „We are one family", „All members have equal leisure opportunities", „We have definite rules that are unambiguously for everybody to obey", „We have the best inner climate", „We have quarterly social events and Christmas presents for all employees and their children", „We are characterised by cooperativeness", „We are all friendly in one pot". Family businesses with strong organisational culture have good relationships with business partners, clients and local authorities. They speak well of cooperation and substitute service, participating themselves in local activities or operation of local businesses, being, for example, chairman of the nursing home or chairman of the municipality council.

The core of the family business organisational culture (Fig. 16) as an integral whole is the values the family business members count on and what the family business wants to show outside; these values regulate the behaviour of employees, operating processes and help achieve the family business objectives.

Fig. 16:   *Mind map on the organisational culture in a family business (compiled by the authors)*

The mind map contains the best and most desirable features. In real life a family business organisational culture with perfect features does not exist, certain supplements are added rather, caused either by the composition of features or by area of activity.

The research results enabled to compare family businesses' specific features to other research where non-family businesses were addressed (Wahl 2011) and clear differences were identified.

1. Family entrepreneurs are convinced that most important is to satisfy the family needs and continue family business traditions; they wished expansion not as much as to provide welfare to their family. At the same time, non-family entrepreneurs believe that the main mission of companies is to maximise profit, be more successful than the competitors, create new values, improve people's life quality.

2. Family entrepreneurs consider it important that family members (spouse, children, kin) could be employed with the family business. On the other hand, company owners underline the social role as employer and tax payer.

3. Family entrepreneurs manage their business themselves, write strategic plans and design family business culture. The collective will of owners of

non-family businesses may be expressed as ownership strategy, which may not always coincide with the company strategy.

4. In the first generation family businesses the manager is mostly owner and hence no conflicts occur in management and in working out strategic plans. Non-family entrepreneurs are of the opinion that owner getting a clear idea of him/herself will ensure adequate behaviour and an intense discussion between parties will help avoid conflicts.

5. Family entrepreneurs attach importance to human relations in a family business and are mostly oriented to person culture. More important for non-family entrepreneurs is income from being owner (including capital growth); they find that power is achieved on the basis of personal authority followed by identification (charisma, pattern, knowledge), rewarding (money, praise, attention), power obtained on the basis of formal ownership right and compulsion (money, punishment, dismissal).

6. Family entrepreneurs hope that the business will last and what they have done will pass on to the next generation. Non-family businesses at the same time are ready to sell their shares or some of them.

7. Family entrepreneurs find that in an ideal case 100% of the family business is in family ownership, but definitely more than 50%. Non-family entrepreneur finds often that a 10 to 50% ownership in a company is sufficient.

5. Conclusions

The authors analysed family entrepreneurs, family businesses, their social and cultural aspects using different methods of analysis to identify the characteristics of strategic management and organizational culture in family businesses. This is the first so extensive research on family business entrepreneurs in Estonia; information collected from more than thousand family businesses has been analysed. The results can be considered reliable. Abduction that was chosen as the scientific method proved the best and enabled different groupings with the help of which the authors could create different mind maps. The methods of research enabled to reach a new solution, create new relationships and identify differences and similarities in different feature groups. The relationships identified in the analysis have been described and presented in charts; their theoretical background has been addressed in the paper, hence it is not only a descriptive paper but an explanatory one.

Family entrepreneurship has been growing substantially in recent decades, above all in rural areas. In terms of legal form, the most widely used is sole proprietorship as the simplest form of entrepreneurship. Before starting a family business a future family entrepreneur needs to be sure the family members want to participate in the family business, since the success of a family business depends on how strong the mutual relations between the family members are. All family members must be interested in the business to be successful and exert every effort for that. When there are strong and stable family relations between members of the family, they are more likely to achieve success; however, they still have to be able to set definite limits from the very beginning to reconcile between work and home. Most of the failures have been due to that they could not set priorities and do not take into consideration that the family business may take all the free time at the beginning; at the same time, they do not believe that family members are not able to perform all works for what they lack skills and they don't hire workforce outside the family. Strategic management in family businesses is often informal. 65% of the family businesses interviewed by the authors had a strategic plan only in their mind, partly because owners and managers are the same. At the same time, this approach may not be good when the business expands and new investors are included among the owners. The significance of strategic management may also increase in the course of generation change. In Estonia family businesses are being passed on to the next generation, which is a long process and requires a balanced preparation. In the first stage a business is managed only by the head of family; then he/she starts training him/herself and then the successors, simultaneously he/she has to develop the family business. The appropriate transfer of management is one of the preconditions of family businesses' longevity. At the same time, it improves the continuity when business's long-term development directions have been discussed and fixed rather than in the mind of one person.

Family businesses also have weaknesses. Due to their small size they are more vulnerable; their reserves are small or nearly non-existent for surviving the periods of crisis. Risk is increased by dependence on one area of activity only. One possibility for family businesses is to cooperate, not only with cooperative societies but with other family businesses and local authorities.

In the changing situation many family businesses need to revise their strategies, which is a precondition for surviving. This is very hard to comprehend by older generation entrepreneurs who „are used to follow a beaten path". For further development of business activity one needs in addition to the skills one already has, also various other skills: knowledge of market, business administration, strategy development, client management, teamwork, stress resistance etc. Start-up entrepreneurs are in a better situation, they are more eager to learn and open-minded, they want to acquire knowledge for what they seize every opportunity: they are members in cooperative societies, use advisory services and search for contacts with family entrepreneurs in the same area of activity.

Although many family entrepreneurs are initially active only in one area of activity, they are often of the opinion that one cannot achieve success in a single area of activity. To spread risks they have taken up secondary activities, for example, hiking trails, restoration of antiquities, beauty services, growing plants, woodworking, ecological products, growing herbs, folk medicine, etc. Such diversification of risks is possible only when family members have many skills, and they all want to work together in the family business to provide welfare for themselves and future generations.

The research allows drawing a conclusion that the wish to work together in one or several areas of activity for a long time and grow into a family business with long traditions and a well-established family business culture, is dominating among family entrepreneurs. In recent years they have started to pay more attention to responsible entrepreneurship, development of organic farming, saving of the nature environment.

This is in harmony with the Estonian entrepreneurship policy objectives and the Estonian rural life development plan. Based on the latter, local resource based non-agricultural production, rural tourism, handicraft and services related entrepreneurship are preferred for raising the life quality of rural areas. First of all, diversification of smaller agricultural businesses' activity with other non-agricultural rural entrepreneurship is encouraged (Estonian Rural... 2009). The following measures can be recommended for the achievement of these objectives: organise entrepreneurship training courses for family entrepreneurs; organise continuing specialised training courses; organise training courses for transferring management to successors; promote cooperation and social activities in rural areas; more than so far propagate family entrepreneurship; provide free of charge advice for finding supplementary finances; streamline cooperation between local authorities and family entrepreneurs and pay greater attention in university curricula to family entrepreneurship.

This research demonstrated that the difference between family and non-family businesses in the first generation does not depend on whether employees are family members or not. Hence it can be argued that the dynamic development of a family business and continuing valuation of organisational culture will be ensured in the first generation, irrespective of the employees. The family businesses analysed in this research had on average 8.2 employees, only half of them family members. Hence, in this respect the authors cannot agree with the viewpoints expressed by Nedlin (2003), Khaemasunun (2004) and Miller et al. (2007); whereas they can agree with that strategic management of family businesses and valuation of organisational culture ensure dynamic development of the family business and that family businesses are capable of existing successfully until the generation change. This research clearly underlined that planned management and valuation of organisational culture are competitive advantages. The differences between family businesses and non-family businesses have been compared to the outcomes of Wahl's (2011) ownership typology and clear differences were found in the results.

Family businesses' differences are caused by long traditions and by orientation to different values. The gist of a family business's organisational culture as a whole is the values the family business members have to reckon with and what the family business wants to show outside; these values regulate the behaviour of employees, family business performance processes and help achieve objectives of the family business. Arising from values, the organisational culture is focused on human relations; their objective is to continuously develop and train the family and non-family employees. Confidential relations are dominating in family businesses; everybody takes care of each other, they are helpful and communicate also outside the work environment. A stable culture is supported by strong traditions where all employees of the family business are involved; so-called „extended family" evolves.

Investigation of family businesses is a sensitive subject. When interpreting the results one has to take into consideration that personal questions are sensitive and that answers to them may not be "sheer truth" and often dependent on the respondent's state of mind. Moreover, the history of family entrepreneurship in Estonia is short and therefore this research probably does not open all aspects of this type of entrepreneurship, including generation change related issues. It is definitely necessary to conduct in the future a more focused research, based on some specific area.

Future research on family business and family entrepreneurs might be connected to the existing ones, even if to test the validity of the existing method of research and expand the results available. New methods of research should be definitely applied, from among which one of the newest and most interesting one is text digging, which is not limited only to text but sound, video, as well as voice are included (Liiv 2010).

The fact that this is the first so large research in former socialist countries is an important implication not only for family businesses but for the wider economy and society and has been designed as an example with the other former socialist market economies. The next task is to inform wider public about the research results; knowledge about family businesses' specific features will be useful not only for family entrepreneurs themselves, but also, for example, for local government authorities. Knowing and understanding the relationships in family businesses, the family entrepreneurs would be able to pass on to the next generations the specific organisational culture and values of the family business.

References

Alas, R. 2002. Muudatuste juhtimine ja õppiv organisatsioon. Kirjastus Külim.

Bhalla, A.; Henderson, S.; Watkins, D. 2006. A Multiparadigmatic Perspective of Strategy: A Case Study of an Ethnic Family Firm. International Small Business Journal, Vol. 24, No. 5.

Brice, W. D. 2005. The cultural basis of management strategy professional vs family business management in three countries. University of Hawai'i at Manoa, 157 pages; AAT 3198349.

Brooks, I. 2008. Organisatsioonikäitumine. Tallinn: Kirjastus Tänapäev.

Casillas, J.C., Acedo, F.J., Moreno, A.M. 2007. International Entrepreneurship in Family Businesses. Edward Elgar.

Chami, R. 1997. What's Different About Family Businesses? Social Science Research Network, id 38041. [WWW] http://papers.ssrn.com/sol3/papers.cfm?abstract_id=38041 (14.02.2012).

Chuah, S.-H. 2010. Do Human Values Explain Economic Behavior? An Experimental Study. Nottingham University Business School Research Paper No. 2010-01. [Online] SSRN (05.06.2012).

Chirico, F. 2006. The creation, sharing and transfer process of knowledge in family firms. Evidence from comparative case studies. In Family Firms as Arenas for Trans-Generational. Value Creation: A Qualitative and Compulational Approach. No. 24/2006, University of Jyväskylä School of Business und Economics, pp. 14–36.

Chrisman, J. J.; Chua, J. H.; Kellermanns, F. W.; Matherne III, C. F.; Debicki, B. J. 2008. Management Journals as Venues for Publication of Family Business Research. Entrepreneurship: Theory & Practice, Publisher Blackwell Publishing Limited: Sep 2008, Vol. 32 Issue 5, pp. 927–934.

Conant, D. 2007. Exploring leadership style, organizational culture, and financial performance in family firms. Gonzaga University, 232 pages; AAT 3287355.

Eddleston, K.A. 2008. Commentary: The Prequel to Family Firm Culture and Stewardship: The Leadership Perspective of the Founder. Entrepreneurship: Theory & Practice, Publisher Blackwell Publishing Limited: Nov 2008, Vol. 32 Issue 6, pp.1055–1061.

Estonian Enterprise Policy 2007–2013. Ministry of Economic Affairs and Communications. [WWW.] http://www.mkm.ee/failid/Estonian_Enterprise_Policy_2007_2013.pdf (01.12.2008; 01.08.2009).

Ferguson, K. E. 2011. Non-Family Employee's Identification with Family: The Moderating Effect of Culture in Family Firms. SSRN, Working Paper 11th Annual IFERA Conference: Intelligence and Courage for the Development of Family Business, 2011, id 1908154 (15.02.2012).

Finich, N. 2005. Identifying and addressing the causes of conflict in family business. SSRN Online, id 717262 (16.02.2012).

Halttunen, J. 2004. Teollisten perheyritysten kasvudynamiikan systeemiteoreettinen tarkastelu. Jyvaskylan Yliopisto, 302 pages; AAT C820640.

Hammer, Ü., Harper, D. A. T., & Ryan, P. D. 2001. PAST: Paleontological Statistics Software Package for Education and Data Analysis. Palaeontologia Electronica, 4(1), 9. [WWW] http://palaeo-electronica.org/2001_1/past/issue1_01.htm (01.05.2012).

Hobuste andmebaas. Jõudluskontrolli Keskus. [WWW] http://www.jkkeskus.ee/htr/ accessible in intranet (18.06.2008).

Huybrechts, J.; Voordeckers, W.; Lybaert, N.; Vandemaele, S. 2011. The distinctiveness of family firm intangibles: a review and suggestions for future research. Journal of Management & Organization, Vol. 17, No. 2, pp. 268–287.

Juutilainen, S. A. 2005. Pienen matkailuyrityksen yrittajan taival: Oppiminen yrittajyysprosessissa. Lappeenrannan Teknillinen Korkeakoulu, 191 pages; AAT C823223.

Kaarna, R.; Masso, M.; Rell, M. 2012. Väikese ja keskmise suurusega ettevõtete arengusuundumused. Tallinn: Poliitikauuringute Keskus Praxis.

Khaemasunun, K. 2004. Three essays on the profitability, risk, and viability of family firms in a developing economy. West Virginia University, 87 pages, AAT 3159343.

Kirsipuu, M. 2004. Füüsilisest isikust ettevõtjate roll majanduses ja nende tegevuse reguleerimine. Master's Thesis. Tallinn University of Technology.

Kirsipuu, M. 2009. Strategic management in family enterprises: the case of beef animal breeders in Estonia CD IV rahvusvaheline konverents "Juhtimisteooria ja -praktika: sünergia organisatsioonides" 3–4 April 2009, Tartu.

Kirsipuu, M. 2012. Sustainability of Rural Family Enterprises. BMW Berliner Wissenschafts-Verlag GmbH, Mattimar OÜ, 2012, pp. 83–104

Kluge, S. 2000. Empirisch begründete Typenbildung in der qualitativen Sozialforschung. Forum Qualitative Sozialforschung / Forum: Qualitative Social Research, 1(1), Art. 14. [WWW] http://nbn-resolving.de/urn:nbn:de:0114-fqs0001145 (01.04.2012).

Leenders, M.A.A.M.; Waarts, E. 2001. Competitiveness of family businesses: Distinguishing family orientation and business orientation. SSRN Online. Id 370909 (14.02.2012).

Leimann, J.; Skärvad, P.-H.; Teder, J. 2003. Strateegiline juhtimine. Tallinn: Kirjastus Külim.

Liisu JKK lihaveiste programm. Jõudluskontrolli Keskus. [WWW] http://www.jkkeskus.ee/liisu/?owner_id=&module=HerdList. Accessible in intranet (01.10.2007).

Liiv, I. 2010. Seriation and matrix reordering methods: An historical overview. Statistical Analysis and Data Mining, 3(2), pp. 70–91.

Littunen, H. 2001. The birth and success on new firms in a changing environment. Jyvaskylan Yliopisto, 261 pages: AATC809225.

Lussier, R.; Sonfield, M. 2012. An eight-country comparative analysis of "micro" versus "small" family business. 1 Small Business Institute. National Conference Proceedings. Vol. 36, No. 1.

Malhotra, N. K. 2007. Marketing Research: An Applied Orientation, 5th Edition. New Jersey: Pearson Prentice Hall.

Miller, D., Breton-Miller, I., Scholnick, B. 2007. Stewardship vs Stagnation: An Empirical Comparison of small Family and Non-Family Businesses. Journal of Management Studies.

Nedlin, M. B. 2003. Unified Blended Family Business(c): A new perspective for the 21st century understanding relationships in family businesses. Nova Southeastern University, 271 pages; AAT 3090289.

Niemela, T. 2003. Inter-firm co-operation: A processual empirical study on networking family firms. Jyvaskylan Yliopisto, 199 pages, AATC 816839.

Pearson, A. W; Carr, J. C.; Shaw, J. C. 2008. Toward a Theory of Familiness: A Social Capital Perspective. Entrepreneurship: Theory & Practice, Publisher Blackwell Publishing Limited Nov 2008, Vol. 32 Issue 6, pp. 949–969.

Peirce, C. S. 1931. The Collected Papers Vol. V: Pragmatism and Pramaticism. [WWW] http://www.textlog.de/peirce_pragmatism.html (01.04.2012).

PRIA Loomade register, ehitiste otsing. Põllumajanduse Registrite ja Informatsiooni Amet. [WWW] http://neptuun.pria.ee/lr/faces/lr/lr.jsp. Accessible in intranet (01.08.2009).

Põllumajandusministeeriumi valitsemisala arengukava 2009–2012. Põllumajandusministeerium [WWW] http://www.agri.ee/public/juurkataloog/ARENDUSTEGEVUS/VAU_2009_2012_28_0_08.pdf (11.01.2009).

Rautamäki, H. 2007. Psykologinen omistajuus ja työnilo perheyrittäjyydessä. Jyväskylän yliopisto. Yrittäjyyden tutkimus XXIII taloustutkijoiden kesäseminaarissa, 160, pp. 37–47.

Researching and Writing Dissertations in Bussiness and Management, Riley, M., Wood, R. C., Clark, M. A., Wilkie, E., Szivas, E. 2000. Croatia, 280 pp.

Schwartz, S. H. 1992. Universals in the Content and Structure of Values: Theoretical Advances and Empirical Tests in 20 Countries. In M. Zanna (Ed.), Advances in Experimental Social Psychology, 25, pp. 1–65. New York: Academic Press. [Online] ScienceDirect (11.04.2008).

Shea, H. 2006. Review article Family Firms: Controversies over Corporate Governance, Performance, and Management. SSRN Online andmebaas. Id. 934025 (14.02.2012).

Sneath, P. H. A.; Sokal, R. R. 1973. Numerical Taxonomy: The principles and practice of numerical classification. San Francisco: W. H. Freeman and Company.

Zahra, S. A., Hayton, J. C., Neubaum, D. O., Dibrell, C., Craig, J. 2008. Culture of Family Commitment and Strategic Flexibility: The Moderating Effect of Stewardship. Entrepreneurship: Theory & Practice, Publisher Blackwell Publishing Limited, 32, (6), pp. 1035–1054.

Thietart et al. 1999. Doing Management research, London, 425 pp.

Voordeckers, W., Gils, A., Van den Heuvel, J. 2007. Board Composition in Small and Medium-Sized Family Firms. Journal of Small Business Management, 45, (1), pp. 137–156.

Wadhwa, V.; Aggarwal, R.; Holly. K. Z.; Salkever, A. 2009. The Anatomy of an Entrepreneur: Family Background and Motivation. Social Science Research Network, id 1431263 [WWW] http://papers.ssrn.com/sol3/papers.cfm?abstract_id=1431263 (14.02.2012).

Wahl, M. F. 2011. Kapitaliühingute lõppomanike alusväärtuste ja tahte uurimine ning omanikkonna tüpoloogia konstrueerimine. Tallinna Tehnikaülikooli Kirjastus, 186 pp.

White, B. 2000. Dissertation Skills for Business and Management Students, London, 168 pp.

Äriregistri teabesüsteem. Justiitsministeeriumi Registrite ja Infosüsteemide Keskus. [WWW] https://ariregister.rik.ee/login.py. For registered users (01.08.2010).

Üksvärav, R. 1992. Organisatsioon ja juhtimine. Tallinn: Kirjastus Valgus

Tough Competition and Burnt-out Employees: Why Internal Customer Orientation Could be the Answer

Andreas von Schubert[1]

Abstract

There are many leadership theories that can provide quite helpful guidance for managers in their daily work with their group of direct reports. However, they implicitly assume relatively stable market conditions. It is therefore not surprising that even experienced leaders reach their limits with directive leadership, given the ever more complex, more international and increasingly dynamic structures in today's companies. New approaches to leadership are therefore needed, which take into account those organisational developments.

The leadership concept of internal customer orientation transfers the key factors of customer excellence to the internal organisation. The philosophy is quite simple: internal customer orientation is leadership, which not only carries the customer wishes through the organisation, but which regards the employees themselves as customers. Due to the fact that every employee is internal customer to at least one, mostly several other employees, and that he himself in turn is internal "supplier" to again other employees, everyone's own self-interest ensures active and focused cooperation in this system of internal suppliers and customers.

Directive leadership is henceforth only needed in exceptional cases, because customer satisfaction is assured out of the employees' self-interested considerations.

JEL classification: M1, M5

Keywords: leadership, competition, burnt-out employees, customer orientation, performance

1. Introduction

The basic philosophy of economic leadership is that the outcome of leadership activities must always be worthwhile for every person involved. Worthwhile means that everybody is able to attain his personal goals: the leader as well as his subordinates and, of course, the company and its customers. Leadership is economic, if it not only allows for the legitimately economic behaviour[2] of all persons involved, but also even supports this behaviour actively and integrates it

---

1   Wismar University of Applied Sciences, Wismar Business School, P.O. Box 1210, 23952 Wismar, Germany, e-mail: andreas.vonschubert@hs-wismar.de

2   Definition of "economic behaviour" – to strive for realisation of personal goals and thus for maximisation of self-interest as rationally as possible, given the limitedness of information which are required to make a sound decision. Depending on personal preferences, the intended benefit can lie in materialistic things, or in non-material benefits, such as praise. But it could also lie in the possibility to realise certain intended behaviour. In this respect even altruism can be economic behaviour.

into the company's economic considerations. That the goals of different parties, particularly the company and its employees, can be quite conflictual is self-evident. But that is exactly why the principles of economic leadership are so important. The task is to realise the goals of all stakeholders (company, customers, colleagues, subordinates) as efficiently as possible by adapting the leadership approach accordingly.

Economic leadership means to thoroughly match the leadership behaviour with the situation, and to be flexible enough to react to varying leadership demands quickly. In the ever more complex and internationally interlinked structures of today's companies this is a challenging task and requires in-depth knowledge of as many different leadership theories as possible. And it requires the ability to apply them correctly as the situation demands. Economic leadership thus means to accept the activity of leading as a fully-fledged profession, which has to be acquired as thoroughly and comprehensively as any other profession (such as financial expert, engineer, or medical doctor), even though managers with leadership duties used to be technical experts in one of those fields: once promoted to a leadership position, they are no longer technical experts. Their new profession is: manager, manager with leadership duties. Their subordinates are technical experts.

The term "economic leadership" is chosen deliberately. It illustrates that the way in which the leadership tasks are carried out has a significant impact on the economic success of the company. In addition, it helps to recall that the level of professionalism of leadership behaviour has a significant effect on subordinates' abilities for own economic behaviour. And finally it reveals that the effectiveness of leadership with respect to corporate goals, as well as its efficiency in day-to-day business depends on how comprehensively a manager masters his set of leadership tools.

Taking into account that managers all over have to deal with highly interlinked structures and that the people they lead quite often have no sense of loyalty to their employer (Geissler and Sattelberger 2003, p. 41; Schubert 2008), it is not sufficient anymore to acquire the profession of leading only "on the job". Just like nobody would visit a doctor, employ a lawyer or an architect who pursues the profession without proper professional education, holding a leadership position without comprehensive knowledge of as many leadership theories as possible is negligent and neither for the subordinates nor for the company advantageous.

The principle of economic leadership is not a new leadership theory. It is the request or maybe even demand to professionally and comprehensively prepare for all possible leadership situations by reviewing all relevant, or at least the major leadership theories. Which leadership situations one has to prepare for is determined by the company's strategic challenges on the market.

However, having a closer look at the traditional leadership theories, their limitations in accomplishing leadership tasks in complex, internationalised company structures become quite apparent. And the question arises if the traditional approaches to hierarchical and more or less directive leadership are suitable to meet these challenges adequately. Not quite surprisingly, the answer is no. But the problem is even more fundamental. Because even though the traditional theories of unilateral-directive leadership are important for the professional realisation of leadership relationships between two persons, they are almost damaging, if it comes to the accomplishment of more complex leadership tasks in the already mentioned increasingly dynamic and internationalised company structures. The latter tasks frequently overstrain managers who are used to act within the traditional thinking patterns of directive leadership. This becomes particularly apparent for instance in the phenomenon of "downward mobbing", which accounts for 57% of all cases of mobbing in Europe and for even 81% in the United States (Vandekerckhove and Commers 2003, p. 42). According to Vandekerckhove and Commers (2003), the reason for this kind of mobbing or "bossing" is an inadequate reaction of managers, who are unable to cope with the implications of the highly dynamic global competition on their own daily business.

A way out of this dilemma of both importance and harmfulness of traditional leadership theories is to avoid the conventional unilateral leadership approaches and to replace them by the same mechanisms that made the company successful on its markets: customer orientation, internal customer orientation between the different work groups in the company.

Internal customer orientation allows the company to reduce organisational friction losses from inadequately directive leadership in complex and highly volatile structures to a minimum. And at the same time it provides the opportunity to disburden managers from the permanent challenge to solve conflicts, calm somebody down, and to keep off rough waters from at least their own team – like a harbour wall. Leadership through internal customer orientation means to develop organisational structures that are largely self-directing, because cooperating is worthwhile for all parties involved.

The self-directing effects of internal customer orientation, however, cannot replace directive leadership entirely. At least in the case of interpersonal or personality-related problems, direct and hierarchically executed leadership can still necessary and efficient. Therefore it is still mandatory to study traditional leadership theories thoroughly.

2. Traditional Leadership Theories: Not for Complex Situations

Over the past decades a whole range of quite enlightening and meaningful leadership theories have been developed. However, because they examine leadership activities from very different points of view, they often arrive at quite different conclusions. For this reason it is so important to know as many different leadership theories as possible and to apply one or the other as the situation and the leadership problem demand.[3]

2.1. Giving Orientation: Relevant Leadership Dimensions

By the late 1950s the so called Ohio State Leadership Studies (Fleishman 1955; Stogdill and Coons 1957; Weissenberg & Kavanagh 1972, p. 119) and comparable studies at the University of Michigan (Kahn and Katz 1972, p. 119) were among the first in modern leadership research to investigate the question of how to resolve the conflict between productivity goals of the company and socio-psychological needs of the employees (Weissenberg and Kavanagh 1972, p. 119). Until then, the success of leadership was mainly explained by certain personality traits of the respective leader. However, the question which personality traits in particular would be mandatory could not be settled. Not least, because even though leaders would behave quite differently, they could still be equally successful – entirely independent of personality and attitudes. For this reason different leadership behaviours were empirically researched in the course of the Ohio and Michigan Studies. The outcomes of the study were two still generally accepted basic dimensions of effective leadership behaviour: concern for people ("consideration") and task orientation ("structure") (Weissenberg and Kavanagh 1972; Skinner 1969; Fleishman and Simmons 1970).

There is of course no universally valid answer to the question how much consideration on the one hand and how much task orientation on the other hand would produce the best results. It always depends on the kind of people one has to deal with, and on the type of tasks that shall be accomplished. And because there is indeed no easy answer, managers are often in search for checklists and simple to use tools that would tell them what to do: "Monday Morning, 9 o'clock". Or they try to acquire leadership knowledge by reading biographies of famous managers, and attend seminars in which they shall learn adequate leadership behaviour by working with horses or dolphins or which animals ever.

Leadership however is one of the few tasks which cannot be learned just by comparing to others and also not by practicing certain techniques like in sports.

---

3   For a deeper review of leadership theories and their chronological development comp. "The Social Scientific Study of Leadership: Quo Vadis?" by House and Aditya (1997)

The most important prerequisite for effective leadership is to get to know one-self and to develop a very personal leadership style. A style that is appropriate because it fits to oneself, to the person who shall be leading and to the situation. And which thus makes the manager come alive, of course, on the basis of sound leadership knowledge on leadership, and way beyond checklists.

2.2. Developing One's Own Style: the Managerial Grid

The Managerial Grid by Blake and Mouton can help to develop a personal leadership style. Unlike other leadership theories, the Managerial Grid does not advise certain possibly adequate leadership behaviour. It rather helps managers to review their personal attitudes towards important leadership tasks.

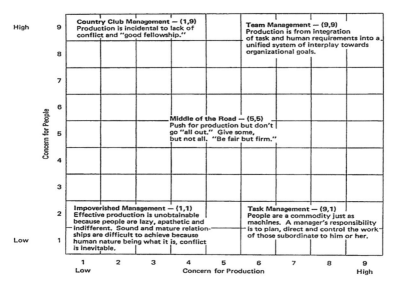

Fig. 7:   Managerial Grid by Blake and Mouton (Blake and Mouton 1975, p. 31)

Blake and Mouton, who developed the Managerial Grid (comp. Figure 1), do not regard the two leadership dimensions (consideration / structure) as two separate types of behaviour which would have to be applied in varying degrees, depending on the situation. Their emphasis is rather on the leader's attitudes towards the leadership tasks. And because attitudes are always determined by both dimensions at the same time, they called their model Managerial *Grid* (Blake and Mouton 1982b, p. 22). Becoming aware of the duality of these dimensions is an important first step in the process of getting to know oneself as a leader. A manager, for example, who primarily wishes to accomplish tasks precisely to standards, probably puts more emphasis on task orientation. But if the same manager would be more concerned about the well-being of his people, and would not in good conscience assign tasks to his people that would collide with their personal goals, then consideration is obviously more important to him than structure. Keeping this in mind, one can check whether one's own "natural" leadership style reflects both leadership dimensions well enough or not, and further develop it, if necessary.

2.3. Responding to the Abilities of Subordinates: Life Cycle Theory

With their Life Cycle Theory Hersey and Blanchard also refer to the two leadership dimensions: "concern for people" and "task orientation". However, their primary focus is not on determining personal attitudes that could be adequate for certain leadership tasks. They are more concerned with adequate behaviour, which of course cannot be determined in general, but must be adapted to the situation a manager and his subordinates have to deal with. For this purpose they introduce a third important criterion for the adequateness of a leadership style – the task related level of maturity, which is defined as: "level of achievement-motivation, willingness and ability to take responsibility, and task relevant education and experience of an individual or a group. While age may affect maturity level, it is not directly related to the type of maturity focused on by Life Cycle Theory. The theory is concerned with psychological age, not chronological age." (Hersey and Blanchard 1974, p. 28).

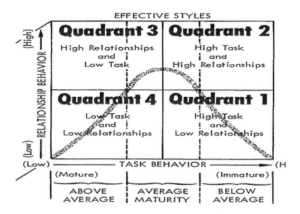

Fig. 8:   *Hersey and Blanchard's Life Cycle Theory (Hersey and Blanchard 1974, p. 29)*

The intention of the Life Cycle Theory is to determine the level of task related abilities and competencies of an employee, and to actively develop them further. One thing however is important: the goal can only be to support the person in accomplishing the given tasks more efficiently and effectively. It must never have a parenting character, as human personality and dignity is always inviolable and line managers or other superiors in companies are neither qualified nor entitled to exert influence on personality traits. Relevant in the Life Cycle Model therefore is only the job-related level of maturity and not personal maturity of whatever kind.

Hersey and Blanchard suggest to roughly dividing the task related level of maturity into three parts: average, below average and above average. In the case of below average level of maturity authoritarian leadership can be absolutely reasonable. In this context "authoritarian" means nothing more than mainly task-oriented leadership under temporary negligence of the employee's personal motives. This leadership style is advisable e.g. when dealing with young professionals or even in the case of experienced seniors who are new in their current job. In these cases high relationship behaviour is not that necessary because these people are highly intrinsically motivated, otherwise they would not have applied for the job in the first place. This leadership dimension becomes more important in later stages.

In the course of time the employee will be more and more able to cope with the demands of the job. His task related level of maturity increases and task-oriented leadership therefore becomes less and less important. This development relieves the superior, who should invest the spared time in more people-oriented leadership activities. Because with growing experience in the current task, the employee will more and more question the relevance of his duties for his personal goals. At this point it becomes important to be concerned with and well informed about the personal goals of the employee, because motivation and intrinsic willingness to perform are of vital importance for successful accomplishment of the tasks. In case of conflict of goals it might even be advisable to adapt the business tasks to better match the personal goals. These issues typically arise at an average level of task-related maturity, for which reason a leadership style according to quadrant 2 or 3 (comp. Figure 2) is most effective in this case.

Once the employee really knows "his stuff" and personal goals are more or less in line with the company's objectives, the superior can reduce his operational leadership activities to a minimum. Neither task related nor people related leadership is necessary any longer. The superior can delegate tasks or even entire projects without having to control the process of task execution. Probably not every employee will move on to this phase. Because he is lacking above average competencies, or because he just does not want to take the responsibility. On the other hand, if somebody who is mature enough to cope with delegated tasks would be task-oriented, then the result would inevitably be demotivation. Simply because the manager's (well-meant) advice expresses a lack of confidence in the subordinates' competencies. From the manager's point of view, therefore, delegation is ideal, because it reduces workload in his operational daily business. The Life Cycle Theory shows that correctly applied leadership knowledge can satisfy both – the employee with his legitimate personal goals, and the superior in his continuous strive for operational efficiency and effectiveness.

It is interesting that both theories, the Managerial Grid and the Life Cycle Theory, refer to the same basis – the two leadership dimensions "concern for people" and "task orientation". And still they come to entirely different conclusions. With respect to their Managerial Grid, Blake and Mouton pose the rhetorically meant question: "Should we teach managers to change their behaviour to fit situations or to change situations by bringing them in line with sound principles of leadership?" (Blake and Mouton 1982a, p. 39), Blake and Mouton are probably right that managers' behaviour cannot be fundamentally changed. For this reason their appeal to rethink one's own attitudes is so important. The Managerial Grid deserves the credit, having initiated this. On the other hand, personal leadership style and behaviour must of course be adapted to the situation. Insofar Blake and Mouton's severe criticism (comp. Blake and Mouton 1982a) of the principles of situative leadership, like for instance proposed by the Life Cycle Model, is not altogether understandable. The common denominator of both approaches is the appeal to managers, to deliberately think about their attitudes and behaviour and, on the basis of this increased awareness, to choose an appropriate leadership style conscientiously and on the basis of sound knowledge.

2.4. Fairness to All Employees: Exchange Theory

The Leader-Member-Exchange (LMC) Theory sees the leadership problem from a totally different angle. It is not so much concerned with the individual employee's goals and competencies, but rather with the manager's conduct, namely with regard to the level of fairness from the manager to his people. The LMX Theory is based upon the phenomenon that leaders often behave quite differently towards different subordinates – independently of the subordinates' competencies, abilities and motivation.

The LMX Theory also asks managers to be aware of the consequences of their behaviour. If they actually mean what their subordinates figure they wanted, it does not matter. Important for successful leadership is only the effect of the managers' activities on their subordinates. Studies show, for example, that the subordinates whose relationship with the superior is not so good are under the impression that they have to compensate for the bad relationship by even better performance if they want to be involved in important decisions (Scandura, Graen et al. 1986, p. 207). Subordinates constantly monitor their boss and try to find out how likely it is that they will be able to realise their personal goals under the given circumstances.

The LMX Theory points out that employees who are valued by their superior get much more attention from him than others. The superiors spend more time with them, share information more freely with them and are altogether more open with them than with subordinates they for some reason dislike. It is quite plausible that employees who have more information and who have more opportunities to interact with their boss will tend to come to better results than those who get only minimal and mainly formal attention. Of course, they do not achieve better results because they were higher qualified and more competent, but solely because their superior has for some reason put them into his personal "in-group". Likewise the other employees who have to get along with only a minimum of contact with their superior because for some reason, which even the boss himself often is not aware of, they ended up in his personal "out group", are not necessarily less competent. Due to the limited contact, they just have to get along with much less information when preparing decisions, and thus run a much greater risk of taking wrong decisions. As "members" of their boss' out-group they are forced to establish networks outside their own work groups. In the end the superior is not able to ensure the accomplishment of his department's goals and, even worse, has no clue why this happens, just because he is not aware of the LMX Theory.

The Leader-Member-Exchange Theory strongly suggests managers to always deliberate about whether they really treat all their people with equal measure, or whether they accidentally have established personal in- and out-groups. It is in their vital self-interest, as Wilson, Sin, et al. (2010) point out in an interesting study.

2.5. Implementing Changes: Transformational Leadership

But what happens if corporate goals all of a sudden change fundamentally? If, for example, changes in the competitive environment require a fundamental reorientation of the entire company. Chances are that at least temporarily the goals of the employees do not fit to the company's new direction anymore. And this will result in significant uncertainty of the employees about the implications of the company's re-orientation on their own goals. Stress and at least temporary resistance is then a quite common and definitely comprehensible human reaction, even if the line managers should have led professionally until then and had not build up in- and out-groups among their people.

Particularly in times of significant uncertainty companies tend to rely on the principle of transformational leadership. According to Yukl (1999), the most extensively researched version of transformational leadership is the one by Bernhard Bass: "Transformational leaders, however, raise the consciousness of followers about the importance of outcomes and how to reach those outcomes by going beyond their own self-interests" (Bass 1997, p. 21).

Transformationally led companies manage to get top performance from their people by approaching them emotionally and urging them to identify themselves with the company. The resulting performance is however quite often performance at a level that, according Bass (1997), exceeds the level of performance the employees originally were prepared to deliver. And in many cases it also goes beyond the people's abilities. Identification appeals to a human being's altruism, thus to his or her readiness to support others even against one's own interests. This personality trait is eminently important for society. But the trait is misused if people are continuously urged to work more than contractually agreed – in absence of any immediate physical need, but purely for self-interested purposes of a private enterprise.

Of course, every human being is willing to exceed his or her personal limits temporarily in order to help other human beings or organisations. But if the exception becomes the norm, then there is a significant danger that the individual's personal resources won't be sufficient for the new norm. However, for moral reasons the person in question can hardly withdraw "help", because he or she has not been asked for help transactionally[4] as the company's business partner, but emotionally as a human being and member of the "corporate society". The outcome can very easily be permanent personal overload, with all physical and psychological implications. Harrison (1987) comes to the same conclusion. Under the heading "The Darker Side of the Achievement Orientation" he notes: "In their single-minded pursuit of noble goals and an absorbing task, people lose their sense of balance and perspective; the end can come to justify the means. The group or organization exploits its environment, and its members – to the detriment of their health and quality of life – willingly exploit themselves in the service of the organization's purpose" (Harrison 1987, p. 12). Transformational leadership can very well be necessary in the short term. However, it should then be converted to transactional leadership as soon as possible. Because on the long

---

4   For a deeper review of leadership theories and their chronological development comp.
     "The Social Scientific Study of Leadership: Quo Vadis?" by House and Aditya (1997)

run transformational leadership is unfair and therefore not a suitable means of leadership.

So far a brief overview of classic leadership theories was provided. Of course there are also interesting findings concerning the intercultural challenges in dealing with colliding group identities (Chrobot-Mason, Ruderman et al. 2007). And the question of coping with the challenges top executives face, which Hambrick, Finkelstein, et al. (2005) researched, is interesting as well. But even without going into too much detail there, it becomes apparent that despite all the differences not only in direction of thought, but also in derived recommendations, each leadership theory presents important advice what to consider when dealing with people inside a corporate hierarchy – and that it is important to memorise the different leadership approaches in order to be able to pull one or the other out of the personal toolbox, depending on the actual leadership problem. Because in the end leadership has the same effect on the performance of a company as any other key success factor – the more comprehensive the leadership knowledge of managers on all hierarchical levels and the more professional leadership tasks are thus carried out in the company, the bigger and more difficult to copy is the competitive advantage.

Unfortunately, when recapitulating the above discussed leadership theories, it also becomes apparent that none of the classic leadership theories gives suitable advice how to master the challenges of the highly dynamic, internationally linked and very complex cooperation processes in today's companies. A conclusion that is also supported by the already mentioned study on "downward workplace mobbing" by Vandekerckhove and Commers (2003), and which can further be drawn from the work of Ancona and Backman (2010) on *"distributed leadership"*: "Leaders face shrinking revenues, increasingly competitive markets, and a race to develop new products. Leaders have been woefully inadequate at solving these problems." The system-immanent problem of excessive demands from (line-) managers can only be solved by establishing an organisation in which operational, direct leadership is no longer needed, because employees work on company goals out of self-interest. Of course they only do so if it is worthwhile for them. And worthwhile it is from the employees' point of view if they realise their personal goals and wishes not despite but because they work on fulfilling the objectives of the company.

3. Economic Leadership through Internal Customer Orientation

Companies must make profit. Customers must profit. And so do employees.

Customers are human beings whose wishes and goals one should always try to fulfil, so that they are repeatedly willing to "hand over" their money. Employees are human beings whose wishes and goals one should try to fulfil, so that they are ongoingly willing to provide labour. The former is self-evident, the latter in many cases is not, but nevertheless a prerequisite for customer satisfaction. Needed is therefore what one could call "customer-oriented leadership". Leadership that's purpose is not only to carry the customer wish through the organisation, but that regards the employees themselves as customers of the company and thus makes sure that the employees have an intrinsic interest in putting all their capabilities into serving the customers of the company. Within the work-sharing value-added processes of a company this works without any difficulties, because every employee is always internal customer of at least one, usually several colleagues, and himself in turn internal supplier to again other colleagues. Everybody involved has a legitimate self-interest to get actively involved in this system of internal suppliers and customers and directive leadership is thus only necessary to set the general direction.

The resources which are released through less cross-hierarchical leadership can be reinvested otherwise and in a more sensible way. And exactly this is the goal of internal customer orientation: an organisation which manages itself efficiently and effectively, without individual overwork and unintentional demotivation – for the best interest of all members of the organisation. A prerequisite however is to know the main functional and personal goals of all parties involved.

3.1. Disseminating Information – Identifying Interests

In the leadership concept of internal customer orientation managers are basically nothing more than a market place for information whose primary task is to disseminate information purposefully. But why do human beings have to do this? Wouldn't it be much more sensible to organise the company so that all information that is necessary for the operational fulfilment of tasks, for the balancing of different interests and for securing voluntary performance, could be disseminated without active involvement of any individual?

Internal customer orientation is most likely to manage itself if the interests of all parties involved can be aligned without involvement of any additional layer of management. However, with one restriction: experience shows that it does not work if to store all supposedly relevant information in a so-called knowledge database, which then can be accessed by everybody. Because the fundamental problem is not an eventually missing piece of information or a lack of accessibility, but the correct interpretation of available information and the question what a certain piece of information means for an individual and his personal interests. What is needed therefore is a procedure for matching different interests and for resolving conflicts of interests within a workgroup, a procedure that a work group is able to manage itself without involving additional hierarchies.

Aligning of interests starts with getting to know them. Goals of customers are regularly assessed through various methods of market research and are therefore usually quite well known to the company. The question however is whether the goals of the customer are only principally known to the company as such and stored away in various databases, or whether actually every single individual in every single department is aware of them. Quite often, unfortunately, the latter is not the case. Particularly upper management usually has only very seldom direct customer contact, because due to their various strategic tasks they have literally no time to catch up on the goals and wishes of the customers, which they could do by, for example, accompanying their people on trips to the customer every once in a while.

Managers can compensate for this deficit by asking their subordinates for their customer perception. But due to their own extreme work load particularly in top management, they have literally no time to do so and thus rely on their own past experience, which however does not necessarily reflect today's business. Hambrick, Finkelstein et al. (2005) reviewed several studies and came to the not very reassuring conclusion for many companies that "Executives who face high job demands will economize in their strategic decision making by relying on their experiences to search for and interpret information, as well as to select among options. They will be drawn to what has worked for them before, what they find familiar or comfortable, and what fits their cognitive schema. Accordingly, decisions made by executives who are under significant job demands will closely reflect their backgrounds – their functional backgrounds, educational experiences, and age and tenure – as well as their psychological dispositions" (Hambrick, Finkelstein et al. 2005, p. 478). Available information is thus not sufficiently evaluated in the course of decision-making processes. It is often replaced by assumed and not sufficiently questioned experience of life. In addition, particularly upper management and notably senior executives often are virtually cut off from most information flows, because subordinates do not dare to correct their potentially wrong assumptions. As a result, the real customer goals and management assumptions about them may differ fundamentally. The challenge thus is to educate upper management as gently as possible about what their customers really want.

The problem of a certain mismatch between actual customer goals and management perception about them does however not exist only in the relationship with the customers of the company, but also to at least the same extent in the internal customer relationships. How often does one department assume to know exactly what the neighbouring department needs – and until when? And how seldom do they really ask the next department down the line if these assumptions are correct? If however one would actually interview the "customer-colleagues" about their real objectives, then it quite often becomes apparent that the own procedures would have to be changed fundamentally in order to be able to synchronise them with the demands of the next department down the line. It might be safer not to ask in the first place. And that inevitably leads to the next escalation step: to proof oneself that interviewing is not necessary anyway, as one knows precisely what the neighbouring department needs already. What follows are the well-known conflicts between departments which are responsible for inefficient cooperation and which seem to require direct leadership.

On the other hand, it is senseless to put human beings with their unfounded perceptions on the hot spot. For this will not lead to cooperation, but rather to more denial. A portfolio-analysis of customer goals can help there to compare factual customer goals with management perception about these goals, without having to expose individuals with their probably not altogether correct assumptions.

The first step in this method is to assess the goals of the customers – through market research in the case of external customers, and through interviews done by intermediaries (e.g. from the HR department) in case of internal customers. Thereafter the departments are directly asked what they think their external/internal customers need. Important though is to always ask several persons and to only use anonymised averages for the analysis, so that single individuals are not exposed in front of the group. This reduces resistance and increases the willingness to actually listen to what customers really want. The advantage of this method is that subsequently the goals of the customers are not only known in principle, but that every single person is verifiably aware of them. Friction losses from ignorance are thus impossible.

A remaining challenge is that customer relationships inside a company are not as distinct as between the company as such and their external customers. This is due to the fact that each department always has several internal customers and by oneself is internal supplier to several other departments. In addition, each department can be customer and supplier to the same neighbouring department in the course of time.

Internal customer relations are thus more complex than external ones. And if it comes to problems of cooperation in the internal value chain, then it is quite often not always apparent what the cause is and whose fault it is. In such a situation however it is impossible for managers to solve the problem by means of disciplinary authority – no matter how much leadership knowledge and experience he might have. Because the people involved will take advantage of the complexity of the multifaceted interactions between the different work groups and of course blame others for the problem. Everybody is concerned with his own backyard. In this situation, in which all traditional methods of directive leadership must fail, the manager is bound to rely on the self-monitoring abilities of the group and can at best support them with analytical tools, such as value stream analysis.

3.2. Enabling Self-Monitoring

One of the fundamental tasks of line managers when applying internal customer orientation is to link the interests of their own people with those of other groups. They coordinate tasks and processes of their own department with those of others and thus avoid friction losses along the value chain. They are not concerned with the subsequent operational execution of the tasks and processes. That is the sole responsibility of their subordinate professionals. In the case of upper management and senior executives this applies accordingly to a higher strategic level.

Of course, at some point of time the question arises how many layers of management are needed for the operative execution of tasks to monitor itself without any noteworthy intervention by management. Internal customer orientation will indeed reduce the amount of management layers significantly. Because all the tasks of managers that so far have been accepted as self-evident and which in real life mainly have to do with conflict management, fall away. If customer oriented processes can monitor and steer themselves, why then monitoring and (directive) leading by (upper) management?

One thing however must be mentioned – as the concept of internal customer orientation can steer itself it can also fail through itself. As hierarchical pressure is for a good reason not applied, internal customer orientation as a management tool is dependent on voluntariness and thus on trust between the different protagonists. Because even if one partner would actually serve his internal customers as well as possible, he still has to rely on his colleagues to do the same for him. It is however difficult to have the necessary amount of trust in others if the relationship between colleagues and departments is affected by long lasting conflicts and "battles". Of course, each department has probably a "good" reason not to trust the other department. But in the end they rather work in parallel than together, and quite often even against each other.

Experience shows that asking for mutual understanding cannot solve this problem, because quite often they all look back on a long history of trust and unfulfilled expectations. It is therefore senseless to call on the colleagues for trust. However, everybody should be clear about the advantages of trusting in others – it reduces the complexity of one's own future, because to trust in someone means to exclude certain future incidents from further consideration (Luhmann 2009). We are confident, for example, that the person we trust in will not do something that could be harmful to us. Trusting in someone therefore means to be vulnerable, because we are not prepared for incidents we do not expect to happen. To a certain extent we thus put ourselves into other people's hands. The advantage however of trusting in others is that it saves us plenty of time, because we only have to take very few of the theoretically possible future moves of others into consideration. In this respect trusting in other people can even be worthwhile economically. But how do you ensure that proven trust is not misused? Malik advises: „Trust everybody as much as you can – and in doing so go as far as you can, until the very limits. (...) (a) However, make certain that you will always find out when your trust is betrayed; (b) make further certain that your subordinates and colleagues know that you would find out; (c) make furthermore certain that each abuse of trust will have severe and inevitable consequences; (d) and finally make certain that your people unmistakably take notice of that, too" (Malik 2004, pp.149–150). [5]

But to trust and at the same time to make certain that trust is not misused is a contradiction in itself, because trusting implies a possible violation in case of an abuse of trust. Trying to exclude all vulnerability a priori means not even try to trust in others, but to control them. How imperceptly and subtly ever – this is control and not trust. Control however always comes across demotivating and is hardly realisable in non-hierarchical relationships anyway.

On the other hand, having to rely on colleagues is only necessary in the very beginning of the implementation phase of internal customer orientation. In this phase trust is important, because everyone has to start treating the colleagues as internal customers simultaneously and cannot wait for their work results and for proofs of their attitudes and conduct. Lacking trust in the implementation phase of internal customer orientation is a problem. It could eventually and in the worst case be replaced by direction and control. That wouldn't be too much of a problem, because trust in colleagues' activities will be replaced by verifiable reliability very soon, anyway. Direction and control would be just acceptable in this exceptional case, as it serves everybody's objectives and would only temporarily be applied.

On the other hand, lacking trust and pattern like "I know that you cannot be trusted" is always a sign of fundamental problems in a business relationship and must always be actively worked on, independently of the type of leadership concept to be implemented.

---

5   English translation by the author

3.3. Reliability even without Trust

Problems of cooperation, such as lacking trust, can have three different causes: goals that do not match, differing information, and one-sided scopes of action.[6] The latter can result from differences of power as well as from one-sided informational advantages (Personal antipathies shall not be considered here.)

In each of the three cases, the basic cause of problems is the ability of individuals or groups to act against the interest of the business partner. Goals that do not match, for instance, only become a problem if one of the business partners takes advantage of the differences at the expense of his partner. Similarly differing information and one-sided scopes of action are not problematic as such, but only in combination with the will and power to not only utilise the differences, but to exploit them at others' expense.

The real problem however is that such negative conduct cannot be prevented. Even in private enterprises everyone is basically free to act at one's own discretion. And even in the case of clearly predetermined activities and only very limited scope of decision, the actual behaviour can hardly be controlled. Firstly, because every kind of supervising control binds management capacity and thus causes (unnecessary) transaction costs. And secondly, because control always demotivates.

The only option is to appeal to each individual to not outrival others. That is bad news to companies that are used to organise tasks by means of precisely defined objectives. But there is no alternative if the business relationship is to be kept in the narrow corridor of mutually motivated cooperation.

Appealing to others only makes sense if there is a certain amount of sense of responsibility on behalf of the respective business partner. On the other hand, it is not advisable to entirely rely on the partner's sense of responsibility. And even a psychological contract, which every once in a while is brought into play from Human Resources people, will not be able to guarantee the necessary amount of reliability of interdepartmental cooperativeness. Because a psychological contract is nothing else than an "idiosyncratic set of reciprocal expectations held by employees concerning their obligations (i.e. what they will do for the employer) and their entitlements (i.e. what they expect to receive in return)" (McLean Parks, Kidder et al. 1998, p. 698), which of course applies to expectations between colleagues as well. A psychological contract is thus not precise enough to provide a reliable basis for interdepartmental cooperation. It does not go beyond the level of "whether or not the employee feels that 'the deal' has been honoured or violated" (ibid.), and "the subjectively perceived high predictability of adequate behaviour of the contractual partner" (Marr and Fliaster 2003, p. 178).

---

6 for motivational problems in business relationships comp. Jost 2008, p. 484 ff.

And that is not enough given what is at stake – the company's success on the one side and the feasibility of personal goals (in life) on the other side.

If one can only appeal to others, then it must by no means be worthwhile for them to act against the person's interests. In practice, a customer purchases a product, because the selling company has warranted certain product characteristics. Even if other pieces from the same production line would have been tested and approved by an independent institute, then still the customer cannot verify the quality of the product in question himself and has to count on that his product is of the same quality; for example, that it is not made of hazardous materials. He will only be able to verify this after having purchased the product and even then not always.

Companies do not appeal to customers to please trust them. They issue warrantees to convince the customers that the product does comply with the standards and promises. In some industry branches competitors meanwhile try to outrival each other with ever-longer warrantee periods, because they know that to call on customers to trust in them is a rather weak argument. Warranty periods have a much greater effect than appeals, because in case of product defects it is not the customer but the supplying company who has to bear the damage. This way it is made sure that trusting in a supplier is worth it, and that disregarding comprehensible customer expectations does not pay off.

In the relationship with external customers issuing of warranties is a practical solution, particularly in connection with independently executed product tests. But what could warranty bonds look like, by means of which trust in internal suppliers and sense of responsibility towards internal customers shall be established?

3.4. Performance and Results – "Guaranteed"

Malik's controlling trust is no option. The most effective kind of warranty within the company is consequence, consequence of action with the partner's goals in mind, and irrespective of one's own goals. Because to issue warranties means to avert damage from the customer and to take it upon oneself. However, in this connection it is important to define the term "warranty": Warranties are only convincing for the partner if the damage in case of noncompliance with the warranted product attributes is economically significant for the person who is responsible for the damage. Behaviour is not consequent if the warranty indeed helps out the partner, but does not really do any harm to oneself. Only, if noncompliance actually leads to own damage, the appeal to be trusted is effective. Because only the combination of preventing damage to others – in their own definition of damage[7] – and taking the damage upon oneself in return generates the necessary amount of consequence in the relationship with customers. In-house it provides for consistent and reliable good conduct between the employee and the employer and even between colleagues and departments.

However, it is a bit more complicated to implement this internally than in the relationship with external customers. Because the usually low exit costs of external customers provide credibility to their threat to change to another supplier. Exit costs of employees are much higher, as they cannot test a new employer without resigning from the current job. That makes internal warranty agreements much more complicated, but at the same time all the more important. Because nothing is worse than demotivated employees whose unwillingness to perform cannot be proven, and who at the same time are not ready to leave the company.

The most important prerequisite for the functioning of a company – internal "cooperation warranty" is to make it independent of psychological contracts, as those remain on the level of appeals and subjective interpretations. In addition, the cooperation warranty should be generally accepted, independently of the attitude of individual managers towards it, because the level of personal leadership excellence usually varies quite a bit. The mutual proof of readiness to cooperate works best if it is based on a number of small incidents which the partners regard as being in line with their personal interests. This method has already proven its potential, even in highly critical phases of fundamental business transformations. Basically it is "planning for and creating short-term wins" (Kotter 2007, p. 99, and Kotter and Cohen 2002, p. 125 ff.).

While psychological contracts focus on emotional factors, such as feelings and attitudes, cooperation warranties are only based on calculative commitment. Under the assumption that every employee already has a set of clearly defined personal goals in mind, even before he enters the company (Schubert 2011), calculative commitment is not only easier to establish but also more sustainable. Calculative commitment works as follows:

- I receive something that is interesting for me. You receive something that is interesting for you.
- I will only receive something from you that is interesting for me if you regard the necessary effort on your part as investment and not only as cost factor (Schubert 2007, p. 147 ff.)

---

7   Only what one regards as damage is damage. If other people regard something as a damage which however one would not view as damage, then actually no damage occurred – independently of the other people's interpretation of the term 'damage'.

- If I receive something from you that is interesting for me, then I can follow that you do not question my position here altogether. Otherwise you would not have invested in the cooperative relationship with me.

The latter is a mutual and recurring proof that one needs each other. This kind of calculus applies to every form of cooperative relationship in a company: between colleagues and also across hierarchies. Because colleagues only invest in cooperative relationships with others if they plan to work together for a longer period of time. Otherwise they would try to get around the respective person and exclude him or her from further cooperation. Superiors invest into the relationship with their subordinates only if they expect positive results from them over a longer period of time. Otherwise they would try to get rid of the person.

A proof of being needed as an employee is the more stable and effective, the more persons ratified it. If two people would recurrently reconfirm each other how irreplaceable any of them was, then this is only of limited relevance. Because, whether or not they would treat other internal customers with the same amount of respect and helpfulness cannot be concluded from this. However, if several people would invest into the cooperative relationship with one particular person, then this is a proof of the importance others attach to this person's contributions. A proof that can safeguard his position in the company and that will also protect him against caprice and "downward workplace mobbing".

Goal-relevant contributions and achievements give evidence of a person's value for the company. If several internal customers associate a particular achievement with the same person, then this increases the reliability of the statements. This is beneficial to the company, because it receives reliable information about the true value-added of individual employees. And the respective employee also benefits, because it enables him to assess the chances that the company will keep him. This of course has no meaning in times of mass layoffs, or if social criteria for redundancy must be applied. But provided that decision has to be made about a particular individual, then standardised evaluations from several persons, be it superiors or colleagues, are highly valuable and a good basis for taking decisions.

Such feedback which is based on concrete performance along the value chain and which furthermore can be collected in a formalised way is an important prerequisite for a fair and objective assessment of a person's contribution. And it allows colleagues of a particular employee to assess the real level of his internal customer orientation. Did a few people consider his work results satisfactory, many others however rather negatively then there is quite probably some room for improvement in the way he deals with internal customers. Of course sub-optimal work results can have many reasons, but *force majeure*

would certainly be taken into account at least by most of the colleagues and superiors who judge the outcome of his work. The assessment of someone's work
results by as many people in the company as possible is therefore an unmistaka-
ble sign of his internal customer orientation and at the same time a safeguard for
him against caprice. The following assessment criteria would be suitable:

- Performance as a ratio of:
  o work results in per cent of the internal customers' demands
  o work results in per cent of the maximum possible according to own es-
    timation and to the internal customers' estimation
- Number of assessing persons.

The ratio of demand and maximum possible allows for an objectified estimation of the actual performance profile and thus allows for a comparison of
performance profiles of different employees in different functions, independent
of their specific work targets. The performance ratio is of course only meaningful if the number of assessing persons does not fall below a certain limit. The
result of the assessment can be displayed in a simple grid with the axes representing the two assessment criteria.

And to conclude, a quick word to the often heard objection against the
concept of internal customer orientation that, opposite to most external customers, internal customers would have no real alternative to cooperating with the
internal suppliers – if cooperation would only work under the threat of imminent
nothingness, then there would be a whole range of problems that have to be re-
solved independent of a particular system of internal cooperation. In any other
case, internal customer orientation is a practical means to successfully overcome
the limitation of directive leadership in complex and dynamic company structures.

References

Ancona, Deborah and Backman, Elaine. 2010. Distributed Leadership, in: Leadership
Excellence, Vol. 27, No. 1, Executive Excellence Publishing, pp. 11–12.
Bass, Bernard M. 1997. Personal Selling And Transactional/ Transformational Leadership, in:
Journal of Personal Selling & Sales Management, Vol. 17, No. 3, M.E. Sharpe, pp.
19–28.
Blake, Robert R. and Mouton, Jane Srygley. 1975. An Overview of the Grid, in: Training &
Development Journal, Vol. 29, No. 5, American Society for Training & Development,
pp. 29–37.

Blake, Robert R. and Mouton, Jane Srygley. 1982a. How to Choose A Leadership Style, in: Training & Development Journal, Vol. 36, No. 2, American Society for Training & Development, pp. 38–47.

Blake, Robert R. and Mouton, Jane Srygley. 1982b. A Comparative Analysis of Situationalism and 9,9 Management by Principle, in: Organizational Dynamics, Vol. 10, No. 4, Elsevier Science Publishing, pp. 20–43.

Chrobot-Mason, Donna, Ruderman, Marian N., et al. 2007. Illuminating a cross-cultural leadership challenge: when identity groups collide, in: International Journal of Human Resource Management, Vol. 18, No. 11, Routledge, pp. 2011–2036.

Fleishman, Edwin A. 1955. Leadership and supervision in industry; an evaluation of a supervisory training program, 1. ed., Ohio State University, Columbus, Ohio.

Fleishman, Edwin A. and Simmons, J. 1970. Relationship between leadership patterns and effectiveness ratings among Israeli foremen, in: Personnel Psychology, Vol. 23, No. 2, Wiley-Blackwell, pp. 169–172.

Geissler, Harald and Sattelberger, Thomas. 2003. Management wertvoller Beziehungen: wie Unternehmen und ihre Businesspartner gewinnen, 1. ed., Gabler, Wiesbaden.

Hambrick, Donald C., Finkelstein, Sydney, et al. 2005. Executive job demands: new insights for explaining strategic decisions and leader behaviors, in: Academy of Management Review, Vol. 30, No. 3, Academy of Management, pp. 472–491.

Harrison, Roger. 1987. Harnessing Personal Energy: How Companies Can Inspire Employees, in: Organizational Dynamics, Vol. 16, No. 2, Elsevier Science Publishing, pp. 5–20.

Hersey, Paul and Blanchard, Kenneth H. 1974. So You Want To Know Your Leadership Style?, in: Training & Development Journal, Vol. 28, No. 2, American Society for Training & Development, pp. 22–37.

House, Robert J. and Aditya, Ram N. 1997. The Social Scientific Study of Leadership: Quo Vadis?, in: Journal of Management, Vol. 23, No. 3, Sage Publications, Ltd., pp. 409–473.

Jost, Peter-Jürgen. 2008. Organisation und Motivation: eine ökonomisch-psychologische Einführung, 2. ed., Gabler, Wiesbaden.

Kahn, Robert L. and Katz, Daniel. 1953. Leadership practices in relation to productivity and morale, in: Cartwright, DorwinZander, Alvin Frederick (Ed.). Group dynamics, research and theory, 1. ed., Peterson Row, Evanston, Illinois.

Kotter, John P. 2007. Leading Change, in: Harvard Business Review, Vol. 85, No. 1, Harvard Business School Publishing, pp. 96–103.

Kotter, John P. and Cohen, Dan S. 2002. The heart of change: real-life stories of how people change their organizations, 1. ed., Harvard Business School Press, Boston.

Luhmann, Niklas. 2009. Vertrauen: ein Mechanismus der Reduktion sozialer Komplexität, 4th ed., Lucius & Lucius, Stuttgart.

Malik, Fredmund. 2004. Führen, Leisten, Leben: wirksames Management für eine neue Zeit, 16th ed., DVA, Stuttgart.

Marr, Rainer and Fliaster, Alexander. 2003. Jenseits der "Ich AG": der neue psychologische Vertrag der Führungskräfte in deutschen Unternehmen, 1st ed., Hampp Verlag, Munich.

McLean Parks, Judi; Kidder, Deborah L., et al. 1998. Fitting square pegs into round holes: mapping the domain of contingent work arrangements onto the psychological contract, in: Journal of Organizational Behavior, Vol. 19, No. 1, John Wiley & Sons, Inc., pp. 697–730.

Scandura, Terri A.; Graen, George B., et al. 1986. When Managers Decide Not to Decide Autocratically: An Investigation of Leader-Member Exchange and Decision Influence, Academy of Management Best Papers Proceedings, Academy of Management, Briarcliff Manor, NY.

Schubert, Andreas von. 2007. Loyalität im Unternehmen: Nachhaltigkeit durch mitarbeiterorientierte Unternehmensführung, 1. ed., Peter Lang Verlag, Frankfurt.

Schubert, Andreas von (2008): "Aus Opportunismus loyal", in: Personalwirtschaft: Magazin für Human Resources, vol. 35, no. 4, Luchterhand, Wolters Kluwer, pp. 53-55.

Schubert, Andreas von. 2011. What is Worthwhile: Self-Interest, Altruism and Social Interaction in Private Enterprises, Department of Social Sciences, University of Eastern Finland, Kuopio, date of presentation: 31 March 2011.

Skinner, Elizabeth W. 1969. Relationships between leadership behavior patterns and organizational-situational variables, in: Personnel Psychology, Vol. 22, No. 4, Wiley-Blackwell, pp. 489–494.

Stogdill, Ralph Melvin; Coons, Alvin E. 1957. Leader behavior: its description and measurement, 1st ed., Ohio State University, College of Administration, Science Bureau of Business Research, Columbus, Ohio.

Vandekerckhove, Wim and Commers, M. S. Ronald. 2003. Downward Workplace Mobbing: A Sign of the Times?, in: Journal of Business Ethics, Vol. 45, No. 1, Springer Netherlands,p p. 41–50.

Weissenberg, Peter and Kavanagh, Michael J. 1972. The independence of initiating structure and consideration: a review of the evidence, in: Personnel Psychology, Vol. 25, No. 1, Wiley-Blackwell, pp. 119–130.

Wilson, Kelly Schwind; Sin, Hock-Peng, et al. 2010. What about the leader in leader-member exchange? The impact of resource exchanges and substitutability on the leader, in: Academy of Management Review, Vol. 35, No. 3, Academy of Management, pp. 358–372.

Yukl, Gary. 1999. An evaluation of conceptual weaknesses in transformational and charismatic leadership theories, in: Leadership Quarterly, Vol. 10, No. 2, Elsevier Science Publishing, pp. 285–305.

Critical Success Factors of Lean Thinking Implementation Process: Example of Estonian Manufacturing Companies

Aleksandr Miina[1], Maksim Saat[1] and Ene Kolbre[1]

Abstract

The process of lean thinking implementation is a difficult and resource consuming activity. Many companies which have started the process to become lean have failed and never achieved the targets they promoted in the start. This aspect of lean philosophy has been weakly covered in lean literature and as a result companies are still missing a clear path to become lean.

This study proposes a lean implementation process for the manufacturing companies and seeks for the critical success factors of lean implementation process based on the example of Estonian manufacturers. The data are gathered from semi-structured interviews, observations, field notes and company documents and then analysed and assessed. The assessment is based on lean thinking criteria with respective determinants.

The results of the research prove the proposed lean implementation process model and bring out that construction of a company's own production system in the form of lean house is critical in terms of success of the whole lean journey.

JEL classification codes: O32

Keyword: lean thinking, lean house, implementation process, Estonia.

1. Introduction

Lean thinking principles give an opportunity for the companies to increase efficiency and productivity and thus are in the circle of interest for them (Trombly 2002; Trott 2008). Lean thinking (hereinafter just lean) is defined as the systematic elimination of waste (Santos et al. 2006). Ohno (1988) saw lean thinking as a time line where a company must look to from the moment the customer gives it an order to the point when the company collects the cash. Additionally, Womack et al. (1990) define lean thinking as shortening lead time by eliminating waste in each step of a manufacturing process that in turn leads to best quality and lowest cost, while improving safety and morale. And finally, Liker (2004) writes that company must see the value from customer perspective, remove all unnecessary activities and then make the process better and better, producing as much as customer wants, no more or less.

---

1   Tallinn School of Economics and Business Administration, Akadeemia tee 3, 12618 Tallinn, Estonia

By waste lean the authors understand everything that does not contribute to the final product or service value and value is regarded from the customer's point of view. The lean concept brings 7 basic types of waste (Womack et al. 1990; Liker 2004; Santos et al. 2006; Voss 2007): overproduction, excess stock, excess transportation, excess motion, over processing, waiting and defects. Customer value is all activities during the manufacturing of products which are paid for by the customer (Womack et al. 1990). To define value, company should know what the customer wants from that process (Liker 2004). "Value is a capability provided to the customer at the right time at an appropriate price, as defined in each case by customer" (Womack and Jones 1996).

Though lean seemed to work very well in Toyota factories, companies outside of Toyota were not able to achieve the same results. Lean was developed in Toyota and thus is natural for Toyota. Other companies had to find their personal way to implement those ideas in a successful manner and it turned out to be very complicated. Since then the lean topic was studied very widely and different aspects of lean implementation were investigated, though still there is no standard framework or roadmap of successful lean implementation (Pepper and Spedding 2010; Repenning and Sterman 2001; Hogg 1993). Despite this unclear aspect of lean implementation, this concept is regarded as the method for processes, efficiency, productivity and quality improvement (Voss 2007).

Based on the above, the main problem of lean implementation could be formulated as follows: the standard framework for successful lean implementation has not been studied sufficiently and as a result manufacturing companies either are not starting lean initiative or fail to implement it successfully. There are a lot of studies (Teresko 2002; Bhasin 2011; Olexa 2002a, b; Bateman 2002; Moore 2001; Voss 2007; Liker 2004) trying again and again to rethink what is lean; there are also studies which point out which tools of lean to focus on during the implementation and how to implement those tools, but still there is a deficiency of step-by-step process descriptions for the lean implementation. Additionally, other researchers (Achanga et al. 2006; Oprime et al. 2011; Bhasin and Burcher 2006; Sohal and Eggleston 1994) point out that there are some critical aspects which influence the lean implementation process the most – factors which could secure sustainable and continuous lean implementation in manufacturing companies and assure them constant and fast growth in productivity.

A potential solution to that problem would be a standard process model of lean implementation where companies could see step-by-step instruction for the implementation of lean thinking principles. The model would also bring out critical factors for the success of the lean initiative. Critical success factors are certain steps in the process which defines the overall success of lean implementation initiative. The failure of a critical success factor brings the fail of the whole process.

According to the present statistics, the productivity and value added situation per employee compared to the European Union countries is weak in Estonia. Based on the above, the authors decided to investigate the situation of the lean concept in Estonia – how widely known it is and how widely used amongst manufacturing companies. The first attempt was made in the year 2006. It turned out that the adoption of lean management paradigms in Estonia was weak at that time.

The authors propose that in order to solve these two problems a successful and continuous implementation of lean thinking ideas and principles in Estonian manufacturing companies should be accomplished. The lean thinking implementation process would be successful if a clear step-by step path of that is present and critical success factors are indicated.

The objective and the main aim of the current research is to develop the lean thinking implementation process model, which could be adapted in manufacturing companies in order to secure the desired results of lean implementation.

The main contributions of the current paper to the theory are: first, the development of the model of lean thinking implementation process; second, bringing out a company's own production system model in the form of lean house as a critical success factor of lean implementation process success; and third, the degree of adoption (DOA) analysing model was applied to assess the results of lean implementation process of the companies studied.

Practical contribution consists in development of the lean thinking implementation process model for companies which wish or are implementing lean. Each company which is starting its lean road (or already going that road) could take the model as an instruction of what to do and how to do it. Hence the results of lean implementation in companies could be better and more successful.

2. Theoretical Framework

Every company has to have a clear vision and target of the lean thinking implementation process (Voss 1984). In other words, they have to answer the question "Why are we doing this?" Innovations and improvements create problems for the companies and thus they have to be managed (Trott 2008).

Literature gives us different strategies for the implementation of lean manufacturing principles, whereas no research on lean implementation results depending on the methodology used was identified in the literature. As examples, three main references were found (Cuatrecasas et al. 2007): Lean Thinking (Womack and Jones 1996), Going Lean (Hines and Taylor 2000) and the Procedures Manual from Lean Aerospace Initiative (Crabill et al. 2000). Those strategies provide very general steps and do not point out any critical aspects of the lean implementation process – the steps which determine the overall success of lean thinking implementation. Womack and Jones (1996), for example, offer the following path for lean thinking implementation: defining customer value; eliminating all activities which do not contribute to the customer's value; as a result of waste elimination, processes take less time, quality, safety and moral is higher; process should be continuous.

Achanga et al. (2006) in their research have brought four main key factors that are fundamental or even critical for the implementation of lean manufacturing: leadership and management, finance, skills and expertise, and culture of the organisation. Leadership stands for 50%, finance for 30%, organisation and culture for 10% and skills and expertise also for 10% of influencing the results of lean implementation. They suggest that "leadership and management commitment are the most critical ones in determining the success of a lean project. Strong leadership ethos and committed management support is the cornerstone to the success of implementing any idea within an organisation." Output of management is a correctly organised and controlled process (Slack et al. 2012). Thus, strong management of lean implementation results in a correct and effective lean implementation process. Also other authors show that management support and commitment to problem solving are the main factors for successful lean implementation (Antony and Banuelas 2001; Coronado and Antony 2002; Eckes 2000; Henderson and Evans 2000).

Oprime et al. (2011) in their study bring the summary of critical success factors of continuous improvement (Table 1). This study focuses on factors themselves and does not investigate the process of lean implementation. The factors of lean implementation are divided into three groups: organisational and operational, incentive systems and support tools. The process of lean thinking implementation is left aside and only factors facilitating the process or used during the process are considered (Table 1).

Hilton and Sohal (2012) in their investigation again relay on factors of lean itself, not on factors of the process of implementation. They find that these success factors are: leadership, communication, behaviour and awareness of Six Sigma; policies, culture and organizational support and strategy; education, training and competency of the Six Sigma experts; project improvement teams and project management; and performance evaluations based on quality criteria, information systems, data and measurement.

To conclude it is important to notice that so far studies in academic literature mostly focus either on very general lean implementation process (e.g. Womack and Jones 1996; Hines and Taylor 2000, or Crabill et al. 2000) or on general organisation's characteristics, which should facilitate the process of lean implementation (e.g. Achanga et al. 2006; Antony and Banuelas 2001; Coronado and Antony 2002; Eckes 2000; Henderson and Evans 2000, or Oprime et al. 2011). Additionally, companies are taking lean as a popular thing and do not properly study the issue. As a result, the process of lean implementation does not achieve the desired results and resources are wasted for nothing.

Table 1:   *Critical success factors of continuous improvement (Oprime et al. 2011, complemented by the authors)*

Categories	Critical factors	Cited by	Connection to the process of lean thinking implementation
Organization and operation	New behaviours and values Leadership Employees' involvement Cooperation and integration Communication system Promotion of CI activities Problem solution models and skills Organizational support	Bessant et al. (1994); Savolainen (1999); Harrison (2000); Delbridge and Barton (2002); Hyland et al. (2003) Bessant and Caffyn (1997); Caffyn (1999); Bessant et al. (2001); Terziovski (2002); Dabhilkar and Bengtsson (2004); Bessant and Francis (1999); Murray and Chapman (2003); Abrahamsson and Gerdin (2006)	*Focus on cultural aspect (both employees and companies in general) of lean thinking implementation; creates the environment suitable for the lean thinking implementation process development.*
Incentive systems	Personal characteristics Company skills for employees' involvement Motivation Formal and informal rewards	Dabhilkar and Bengtsson (2004); Delbridge and Barton (2002); Caffyn (1999) Bessant & Caffyn (1997); Atkinson (1994); Hyland et al. (2003); Davison et al. (2005); Lee (2004)	*Motivation for the process to be working on continuous circle*
Support tools	Problem solution models and skills Standardization tools Problem identification tools	Bessant et al. (1994); Delbridge and Barton (2002); Atkinson (1994); Terziovski and Sohal (2000) Bechet et al. (2000) Bond (1999)	*Techniques and methods used in the process*

A deeper investigation of the literature allows pointing out critical aspects of lean thinking implementation by different authors. First, as a basis for manufacturing process improvement many authors (Heizer and Render 2011; Voss 1998; Santos et al. 2006, etc) point out the standards. Taiichi Ohno (1988) said very clearly: "You have to have standards, even if they are bad standards". Standard process means that the same process is performed each time exactly the same way independent of who is performing the process. And if the process is performed every time the same way, we can easily predict how much time it will take and what will be the result. We can call such process also controlled or quality process (Ainosuke 1989; Slack et al. 2010; Heizer and Render 2011). It is impossible to improve the non-quality process because it is not possible to measure it and thus to define value non-adding activities. Lack of standard processes will demand hard work to improve them (Flynn et al. 1994; Crabill et al. 2000; Hilton and Sohal 2012).

Hence the process quality is a starting condition for lean thinking implementation and its status in company could be assessed by the following determinants (which are developed by the authors based on the literature review): the amount of standardised processes and working instructions related to all processes should increase; the number of deviations from the standards and real life should decrease; the amount of scrap and rework costs related to the revenue should decrease; the responsibility of standards creation should move from functional managers to the multifunctional teams; the ratio of non-value added activities in processes is constantly decreasing; the number of process improvements per employee is constantly increasing.

Furthermore, many studies show that companies do not really understand what is lean and how it could be implemented. For example, about 10 per cent or less of companies succeeds in implementing lean manufacturing practices (Bhasin and Burcher 2006). Furthermore, "only 10 per cent has the philosophy properly instituted" (Sohal and Eggleston 1994, p. 8). On the other side, new paradigms and best practices are often taken as a "black box", which has many dangers inside (Voss 2007). Also, if companies use lean initiatives almost as a fad, most of their efforts will fail to produce significant results (Repenning and Sterman 2001; Hogg 1993). Consequently, lean knowledge should be present in the company and spread around it so that each employee understands what lean thinking is and for what it is used. Lean knowledge acquisition could be done in many different ways: books, articles, trainings, consultant help, benchmarking other companies, etc. Lean knowledge acquisition assessment should be performed according to the following determinants: the number of personnel trained in lean should increase; the number of topics deeply taught to personnel should increase; the number of benchmarked companies should increase; the number of books mandatory to read by all employees should increase.

Based on the gathered lean knowledge the company has to construct their own model of the new production system it would live with – lean house: the base for the whole lean process and if it is missing, the lean implementation process will not be continuous and sustainable in long perspective (Phillips 2000; Liker 2004; Santos et al. 2006; Voss 1995b). Lean house development results are assessed in respect to five determinants: attitude toward lean implementation should move from project type (principle by principle) to company's own production system based on the lean principles approach; lean principles integrated into company values are increasing; lean principles integrated into daily work are increasing; attitude towards lean philosophy should move from waste elimination techniques to the way of working; as a result, lean house (or own production system) is created.

In lean house training a company should focus on training the way the company understands lean (Abdullah 2003). Determinants are as follows: the number of employees trained should increase; the number of employees able to train lean house to others should increase; the amount of information about lean house should increase.

As soon as lean house is created and communicated to the company, a lean implementation plan should be developed and executed. Without a long-term plan and its step-by-step execution the whole lean implementation idea becomes a short project and it is inspired by moment emotions (Sakakibara 1993). As a result, nothing is achieved and the company is not changing its nature towards being lean (Achanga et al. 2004, 2006; Bhasin 2011; Rother 2010). The current step shows the way lean is implemented in the company and the determinants are: lean implementation approach is moving from project type towards the way of doing work based on lean house; lean implementation plan is long term with clearly defined small steps and targets; continuous improvement, also improvement of the lean implementation plan is built into the lean implementation plan.

The execution of plans is one of the vital elements for the success of the process (Heizer and Render 2011; Slack et al. 2010). The determinants are as follows: lean implementation execution approach is moving from project type towards the way of doing work based on lean house; lean implementation follows the plan and is continuously improved based on the achieved targets.

An intended result of the discussed steps is successful lean thinking implementation. Several lean status or lean performance assessment methods could be identified in the literature. One of those is offered by Little and McKinna (2005). They named it Lean Assessment Tool and it is designed to investigate, evaluate and measure the key areas of manufacturing within the company. Boyer

(1996) assessed the managerial commitment to lean production. He proposed that "plants which have a high degree of commitment to lean production simultaneously support this commitment with investments in the supporting manufacturing infrastructure, as measured by QLEAD, GROUP, TRAIN, WEMP" (Boyer 1996, p. 50). QLEAD signifies quality leadership, GROUP – group problem solving, TRAIN – training, and WEMP is worker empowerment. These four criteria have determinants (each criteria have a different number of determinants) which are assessed by company's employees as 1 = strongly disagree, 4 = neither agree nor disagree, to 7 = strongly agree.

Karlsson and Åhlström (1996) have developed their own model of lean assessment and they call it Degree of Adoption (DOA). This method was also used by Soriano-Meier and Forrester (2002) for assessing the degree of leanness of manufacturing firms. Karlsson and Åhlström's (1996) method has nine criteria which allow assessing the degree of lean adoption: elimination of waste; continuous improvement; zero defects; just in time deliveries; pull of raw materials; multifunctional teams; decentralization: integration of functions; vertical information systems.

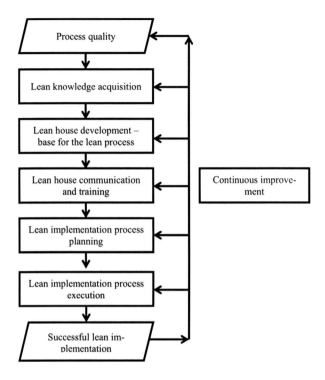

Fig. 9:   *Lean implementation process model (constructed by author)*

The conclusions and results in this point are as follows. Based on the litera-ture review the authors constructed the process of lean thinking implementation, which incorporates important steps indicated above and which leads to the suc-cessful lean implementation (Fig. 9). The steps regarded as critical are: process quality, lean knowledge acquisition, lean house development, training of lean house, lean thinking implementation process planning, execution of the plan and as a result, successful lean thinking implementation. Since implementation should never end (Crabill et al. 2000; Kobayashi 1994; Leseure 2010) the step of continuous improvement closes the loop.

3. Methodology

The purpose of the research is to define the successful lean thinking implemen-tation process in manufacturing companies. During the research the companies' approaches to lean thinking implementation were analysed. The data for this study are qualitative by nature; therefore a qualitative design is most appropriate to answer the research question of this study.

Two gaps in the theory of lean thinking were discovered: first, the lean thinking implementation process has not been studied sufficiently and thus companies are missing the standard framework for lean thinking implementation; second, lean thinking implementation is relying on critical steps which define overall success or fail of that process and respectively manufacturing companies have to be aware of those critical success factors for effective lean thinking implementation. These gaps allow continuing with the next steps of the research.

The first step of the study was the literature review based on two different approaches: domain-based for academic papers and snow-balling for the books and other sources. The main results of that step are a comprehensive theoretical framework of lean thinking and the developed successful lean thinking implementation process. The second step of the research was selecting of companies for the study based on the multiply case study method and as a result, twelve companies implementing lean were chosen. Additionally, one reference company was selected for double check of the results.

Availability of the companies allowed moving on to data collection with usage of different approaches: observation of companies' daily activities with focus on lean thinking, semi-structured interviews of companies' personnel and study of companies' documents. Finally, the collected data massive was analysed based on the content analysis method; lean thinking implementation process steps and degree of adoption of lean thinking were assessed, and finally, the critical success factors of lean thinking implementation were pointed out. A more detailed overview of the data collection and analysis methods is presented below.

The empirical study was conducted in the years 2009 and 2010 in twelve Estonian manufacturing companies. The selection of companies was based on multiple case study method. The case study method was chosen because of the qualitative nature of the study. Also, the case study method does not require control over the activity or process being studied and is focused on contemporary events (Yin 2003). The lean thinking implementation process is a contemporary event and the authors do not have control over it.

Single case study requires the use of theory, multiple case study analysis requires replication logic and benchmarking of cases from different industries (Yin 2003). Exactly the same tactics was used in the current research, where companies from different industries were benchmarked against each other and findings were replicated.

The authors chose 12 manufacturing companies from different industries for the study purposes, which were chosen based on the company's own statements that they were implementing lean practices and principles to improve their operations, and lean was not taken as a "popular thing" in those companies. Additionally, the authors used Scania as a reference company – applying the same degree of adoption assessment model and comparing the results to Estonian companies. The authors tried to test the proposed empirical model and assessment method also in other environments – since it is a common knowledge (among lean researchers and professionals) that Scania is one of the best examples of lean implementation after Toyota Corporation, then the proposed model and assessment method should prove that.

The targets of the data collection step were first to collect data in order to understand the initial (before starting lean initiative) performance of companies; and secondly to collect enough data to assess how companies' performance changes during lean implementation. Thus, the main focuses of data collection were:

- assessing process quality;
- assessing how and in what amount lean knowledge was acquired;
- assessing how lean knowledge was analysed and interpreted into lean house (and was it at all interpreted);
- assessing how interpreted (if it was) lean knowledge was communicated to the personnel;
- assessing how lean implementation was planned and executed, and
- assessing the results of lean implementation.

The main collected data types are text, narrative data and visual data. Text data were represented in the form of different company documents (Barley 1990; Becker and Geer 1957) to assess the aspects of lean thinking implementation process and its results in the company. The second data type was narrative data, which came from interviews, informal discussions and field observations. In the focus of collecting narrative data were mainly persons involved in the lean implementation process (questionnaire and discussions) and process performance (field notes). The third type of data is visual data, which could be represented in the form of photos and videos (Barley 1990; Becker and Geer 1957) and which were used to collect evidence of lean thinking implementation results. The data collection was performed in the companies during the period from 2009 to 2010. The consequent step of data collection was data analysis and assessment of the studied companies. The assessment was focused on two main areas: the process of lean thinking implementation and the result of that process.

The qualitative content (text, narrative and visual) was analysed by using the content analysis method. According to Neuendorf (2002, p.10), "content analysis is a summarising, quantitative analysis of messages that relies on the scientific method and is not limited as to the types of variables that may be measured or the context in which the messages are created or presented". The content analysis method could incorporate various kinds of analysis where communication content is categorised and further classified (Krippendorff 2004) and "it is a systematic, replicable technique for compressing many words of text into fewer content categories based on explicit rules of coding" (Stemler 2001).

During data analysis the emergent coding approach with application of recording units was used. In the emergent coding *categories* were established *following some preliminary examination of data*: material was reviewed and a set of features in the form of a checklist was created, further applied for coding (Haney et al. 1998). Recording units were defined syntactically, that is, to use the separations created by the author, such as words, sentences, or paragraphs (Stemler 2001).

Additionally, the question of validity is very important. As such, validation of the inferences made on the basis of data from one analytic approach demands the use of multiple sources of information. Meaning the researcher should try to have some sort of validation study built into the design, for example, in the form of triangulation, which is often used in qualitative research. By triangulation the credibility of the findings could be achieved by incorporating multiple sources of data (Erlandson et al. 1993). Three main types of data were used in our research.

Based on the method of content analysis, the data were naturally categorised into categories of lean thinking implementation process steps and into criteria of DOA of lean from Karlsson and Åhlström (1996), and further subcategorised into categories derived from determinants of each criterion (process steps and criteria of DOA). Next, subcategorised data were analysed and the concentrated relevant information was identified based on data types – text (company documents), narrative (questionnaire and interviews) and visual (photos, video and field notes).

Further, data in subcategories were assessed based on the model created by Karlsson and Åhlström (1996) and modified by the authors. The assessment grades used for assessing process steps and DOA are: 2 – determinant is implemented; 1 – determinant is partly implemented; 0 – determinant is not implemented. These grades were developed by the authors because Karlsson and Åhlström's (1996) model had no exact rules for the grades. The grades allow making simple assessment of the results of companies' lean thinking implementation and are suitable for Estonia due to the same simplicity. Estonian manufacturers are just starting the lean thinking implementation and hence a more sophisticated assessment degree would be hard to apply due to not so differentiated results of the companies. In general, grade 0 means that the respective determinant is not applied sufficiently in the company and has to be dealt with (subjectively representing 0–30% of possible activities and results of the determinant); grade 2 means that the determinant is applied and at the moment of study no further developments are required (subjectively representing 70–100% of possible activities and results of the determinant); grade 1 represents the wider scale (subjectively representing 30–70% of possible activities and results of the determinant) and means that the determinant is applied although further development of it is highly recommended.

Table 2: *Maximum scores of lean adoption degree criteria (constructed by authors)*

Criterion	Number of determinants	Maximum score
Elimination of waste	6	12
Continuous improvement	2	4
Zero defects	6	12
Just in time deliveries	4	8
Pull of raw materials	2	4
Multifunctional teams	5	10
Decentralization	4	8
Integration of functions	2	4
Vertical information systems	4	8
Total	35	70

Assessment is done by comparing the status of each determinant before starting the lean thinking implementation process in the company with the status at the moment of study. Collected data (text, narrative and visual data) forms and amount vary from company to company and the assessment is done partly by company representatives and partly by the authors, though final decision about the grade is done by the authors following the rules of assessment and data derived from the categories of content analysis. Since each criterion has a different number of determinants, the maximum score for each criterion is different (Table 2 and Table 3).

Table 3: *Maximum scores of starting point and five steps of the process (author's constructed)*

Starting point/step	Number of determinants	Maximum score
Process quality	6	12
Lean knowledge acquisition	4	8

Lean house	5	10
Lean house communication and training	3	6
Lean implementation planning	3	6
Lean implementation plan execution	2	4
Total	**23**	**46**

The scientific perspective considered by the authors is hermeneutic since the main focus of research is on interpretation of companies' processes of lean implementation and interpretation of their understanding of lean. The scientific approach used in the paper is inductive since the authors make the conclusions based only on companies studied in the framework of the current research, which in fact does not eliminate the possibility that the conclusions in general are false.

4. Research Results and Discussion

The assessment of lean initiative of the companies is summarised in Table 4. The main results can be formulated as:

- DOA (or success of lean initiative) depends on how well the lean implementation process steps were performed – Result 1 (R1);
- DOA depends on the existence of lean house (or own production system) – Result 2 (R2);

These results represent the main outcome of the study and prove the proposal made by the authors while introducing the empirical model of lean thinking implementation process. In general, the results show that understanding about lean thinking should be inverted into company's own language as company's own production system (or lean house, or any other form of formalisation of lean thinking principles made especially for the company) and this is possible if company has a good starting point (high process quality) together with well performed steps of lean thinking implementation process.

Result 1 – DOA dependence on process

This is the main result of the research and it proved the model of lean thinking implementation: companies with higher scores for the starting point and process steps will also have higher scores for the degree of lean adoption. This result is depicted by visual patterns of the sum of starting point and process steps

(SP&PS). DOA very much depends on how high the scores of starting point and process steps are.

This result allows stating that the constructed model of lean thinking implementation could be regarded as a standard framework for the manufacturing companies which would like to implement lean. The companies which have a good starting point (process quality) and have performed all steps within the model, or in other words, have been following the standard framework, have better results than those who have not.

Result 2 – DOA dependence on lean house

Quite the same picture as in the first result is seen by comparing the scores of lean house and DOA. From that result we get the next conclusion – the main critical success factor of all steps is the creation of lean house as the basis for the whole lean implementation process and consequent steps.

In other words, in order to have successful lean implementation and not to fail with it each company has to understand and interpret lean thinking principles into intra-company knowledge and create company's own production system in the form of lean house.

XPS – Company's X Production System (analogically to the TPS – Toyota Production System, and SPS – Scania Production System) – is the description of the general rules and values based on which the company works and implements lean.

The proposed model of lean thinking implementation process embodies the starting point – a good process quality, and five steps: lean knowledge acquisition, lean house development, lean house communication and training, lean implementation planning and execution of lean thinking implementation plan. The argumentation hereinabove has indicated that process quality is important but not a critical factor and all process steps are critical success factors. Per contra, it was clearly seen that the basis for the proposed lean thinking implementation process is lean house step. In case of missing lean house all other steps could even remain as critical, but they lose their major purpose and are insufficient for achieving successful lean implementation. The latter was shown at the example of all other companies except score leading companies (companies C4, C5 and C12). Hence, it could be concluded that the main critical success factor for successful lean implementation in the proposed empirical model is the lean house creation step and the criticality of others is driven by it.

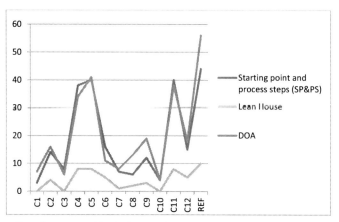

Fig. 10:   Visual patterns of SP&PS, Lean house and DOA (constructed by the authors)

Finally it could be stated that the constructed model of lean thinking implementation process is valid and could be used by companies first to analyse their
current initiative and secondly for constructing their lean implementation process and incorporating understanding of lean philosophy into it by creating their
own vision in the form of lean house. The initial idea says that the correct starting point and performing the steps in certain sequence and to the certain depth
are the critical success factors of successful and continuous lean implementation. By performing current research the authors have proved that if the above
mentioned aspects are taken into consideration and are actually implemented,
then the company has all prerequisites to achieve its desired targets in terms of
lean – meaning successful lean implementation. At last, creation of the lean
house is the central part of the model; it drives all other steps and thus is the
main critical success factor for the successful lean thinking implementation.
With this, contributions into theory, methodology and practice are made.

Table 4:   Assessment results of company's lean initiative (author's constructed)

	C1	C2	C3	C4	C5	C6	C7	C8	C9	C10	C11	C12	REF
Process quality	1	5	5	10	11	6	3	2	5	2	11	4	12
Lean knowledge acquisition	2	5	3	6	7	4	3	2	4	2	7	5	6
Lean house	0	4	0	8	8	5	1	2	3	0	8	5	10
Lean house training	0	0	0	6	6	1	0	0	0	0	6	1	6
Lean implementation planning	0	0	0	5	5	0	0	0	0	0	5	0	6
Lean implementation execution	0	0	0	3	3	0	0	0	0	0	3	0	4
Starting point and process steps	3	14	8	38	40	16	7	6	12	4	40	15	44
Elimination of waste	1	4	2	6	11	2	1	3	4	1	9	3	10
Continuous improvement	0	0	0	3	4	0	0	0	0	0	4	0	3
Zero defects	2	1	1	4	5	3	2	2	2	1	4	1	6
Just in time deliveries	0	1	1	4	5	1	1	1	2	0	5	2	8
Pull of raw materials	0	0	0	0	0	0	0	0	0	0	0	0	3
Multifunctional teams	3	3	1	8	6	1	3	3	5	1	7	5	9
Decentralisation	0	1	0	2	2	0	1	1	2	0	2	1	6
Integration of functions	0	0	0	0	0	0	0	0	0	0	0	0	3
Vertical information systems	1	6	1	7	7	2	1	2	4	1	7	6	8
DOA	7	16	6	34	40	9	9	12	19	4	38	18	56

5. Conclusions

One of the main gaps in the researched theory was the lack of certain framework or step-by-step process of implementing lean ideas in manufacturing companies. This paper proposed one of the possibilities to approach the lean implementation process by performing steps in certain sequence and assessing those steps based on the determinants of each step. The model proposed in this paper is novel, has not been implemented before, is focusing very much on the presence of lean house and provides a starting point for further development of the theory.

Also, the importance of own vision of lean philosophy for each company in the form of lean house has not been discussed widely before and hence it is another important contribution to the development of academic knowledge of the lean implementation process. Quite often companies see lean as a set of principles and start the implementation by just using these principles. In such case, the implementation of lean looks like a set of small projects: 5S, VSM, SMED and so on. Those projects by themselves might achieve the required targets, but in general they are not focused on a single target – changing the culture and philosophy of company's manufacturing.

The current research discovered the importance of looking into lean thinking principles through the prism of company nature. Each company is unique and thus the lean thinking principles might not be suitable for all within the same format. *Scania* is one good example – they went to Toyota, understood TPS, rethought it and created its own lean system. Three companies out of twelve had interpreted lean thinking into their own formats (though not in the form of lean house) and thus had achieved better results in lean thinking implementation by the date of research. Thus, lean house could be regarded as one of the main critical success factors of lean thinking implementation process. Finally, the presence of lean house is not possible without a good starting point and with the next consequent steps together with the creation of lean house itself. Such step-by-step model of lean thinking implementation approach has not been covered in theory before and thus is one of the important contributions of the current research.

References

Abdullah, F. 2003. Lean manufacturing tools and techniques in the process industry with a focus on steel. Dissertation. University of Pittsburg.

Achanga, P., Shehab, E., Roy, R. and Nelder, G. 2005a. Lean manufacturing to improve cost-effectiveness of SMEs. Proceedings of the Seventh International Conference on Stimulating Manufacturing Excellence in Small and Medium Enterprises, University of Strathclyde, Glasgow.

Achanga, P., Shehab, E., Roy, R. and Nelder, G. 2005b. Lean manufacturing for SMEs: enabling rapid response to demand changes. Paper presented at the 15th International Conference on Engineering Design, Melbourne.

Achanga, P., Taratoukhine, V., Roy, R. and Nelder, G. 2004. The application of lean manufacturing within small and medium sized enterprises: what are the impediments? Paper presented at the 2nd International Conference on Manufacturing Research (ICMR 2004), Sheffield Hallam University, Sheffield.

Achanga, P., Shehab, E., Roy, R. and Nelder, G. 2006. Critical success factors for lean implementation within SMEs. Journal of Manufacturing Technology Management, Vol. 17, No. 4, pp. 460–471.

Ainosuke, M. 1989. Preventive Maintenance. TPM Development Program: Implementing Total Productive Maintenance, Productivity Press, Cambridge, Massachusetts, pp. 219–286.

Antony, J. and Banuelas, R. 2001. A strategy for survival. Manufacturing Engineer, Vol. 80 No. 3, pp. 119–21.

Bateman, N. 2002. Sustainability. Lean Enterprise Research Centre Publication, Cardiff, April, pp. 2–24.

Barley, S. R. 1990. Images of Imaging: Notes on Doing Longitudinal Field Work. Organization Science, Vol. 1, No. 3, pp. 220–247.

Becker, H. S. and Geer, B. 1957. Participant Observation and Interviewing: A Comparison. Human Organization, Vol. 16, No. 3, pp. 28–32.

Bhasin, S. and Burcher, P. 2006. Lean viewed as a philosophy. Journal of Manufacturing Technology Management, Vol. 17, No. 1, pp. 56–72.

Bicheno, J. 2000. Cause and Effect Lean. Lean Operations, Six Sigma and Supply Chain Essentials, PICSIE Books, Buckingham.

Bicheno, J. 2004. The New Lean Toolbox towards Fast and Flexible Flow. PICSIE Books, Buckingham.

Boyer, K. 1996. An assessment of managerial commitment to lean production. International Journal of Operations & Productio n Management, Vol. 16, No. 9, pp. 48–59.

Coronado, R.B. and Antony, J. 2002. Critical success factors for the successful implementation of six sigma projects in organisations. The TQM Magazine, Vol. 14, No. 2, pp. 92–97.

Crabill, J., Harmon, E., Meadows, D., Milauskas, R., Miller, C., Nightingale, D., Schwartz, B., Shields, T. & Torrani, B. 2000. Production Operations Level Transition-To-Lean Description Manual. WP, Center for Technology, Policy, and Industrial Development, Massachusetts Institute of Technology.

Cuatrecasas, L., Cuatrecasas, O., Fortuny, J. and Olivella, J. 2007. Notes for the implementation of lean production approach in medium sized manufacturing companies. Proceedings of 14th International Annual EurOMA Conference.

Eckes, G. 2000. The Six Sigma Revolution. Wiley, New York.

Erlandson, D.A., Harris, E.L., Skipper, B.L. & Allen, S.D. 1993. Doing Naturalistic Inquiry: A Guide to Methods. Newbury Park, CA: Sage Publications.

Flynn, B.B., Schroeder, R.G. and Sakakibara, S. 1994. A framework for quality management research and an associated measurement instrument. Journal of Operations Management, Vol. 11 No. 4, pp. 339–66.

Fukuda, K. J. 1988. Japanese-style management transferred: the experience of East Asia. Rouledge, London.

Harbison, F. H., and Myers, C. A. 1959. Management in the industrial world: An international analysis. McGraw-Hill, New York.

Haney, W., Russell, M., Gulek, C., and Fierros, E. 1998. Drawing on education: Using student drawings to promote middle school improvement. Schools in the Middle, 7(3).

Heizer, J. and Render, B. 2011. Principles of Operations Management, Pearson Education

Henderson, K. and Evans, J. 2000. Successful implementation of six sigma: benchmarking general electric company. Benchmarking: An International Journal, Vol. 7, No. 4, pp. 260–81.

Hilton, R. and Sohal, A. 2012. A conceptual model for the successful deployment of Lean Six Sigma, International Journal of Quality & Reliability Management, Vol. 29 (1), pp. 54–70.

Hines, P. and Taylor, D. 2000. Going Lean. Lean Enterprise Research Centre. Cardiff Business School. Cambridge, MA.

Hogg, T.M. 1993. Lean Manufacturing. Human System Management, Vol. 12, pp. 35–40.

Karlsson C. and Åhlström P. 1996. Assessing changes towards lean production. International Journal of Operations & Production Management, Vol. 16, No. 2, pp. 24–41.

Katayama, H. and Bennett, D. 1996. Lean production in a changing competitive world: a Japanese perspective. International Journal of Production and Operations Management, Vol. 16 No. 2, pp. 8–23.

Kobayashi, I. 1994. 20 keys to workplace improvement. Productivity Press, New York.

Krippendorff, K. 2004. Content Analysis: An Introduction to Its Methodology. 2nd edition, Thousand Oaks, CA: Sage.

Leseure, M. 2010. Key Concepts in Operations Management. Sage Publications Ltd.

Liker, J. 2004. The Toyota Way: 14 Management Principles from the World's Greatest Manufacturer. McGraw-Hill.

Little, D. and McKinna, A. 2005. A Lean Manufacturing Assessment Tool for use in SMEs. Stimulating Manufacturing Excellence in Small and Medium Enterprises, SMESME 2005, SME Support Network, University of Huddersfield, UK.

Mohan A. and Sharma S. 2003. Lean approach: some insights. Journal of Advances in Management Research, Vol. 1 (1).

Moore, R. 2001. Comparing the major manufacturing improvement methods. Plant Engineering, September, pp. 1–3.

Neuendorf, K.A. 2002. The Content Analysis Guidebook. Thousand Oaks, CA: Sage Publications.

Oberg, W. (1963). Cross-cultural perspectives on management principles. The Academy of Management Journal, Vol.6, No.2, pp.129-143.

Ohno, T. 1988. The Toyota Production System: Beyond Large Scale Production. Productivity Press, Portland.

Olexa, R. 2002a. Freudenberg – NOK's lean journey. Manufacturing Engineering, January, pp. 2–8.

Olexa, R. 2002b. Manufacturing lite with lean. Forming and Fabricating, Vol. 9, pp. 1–6.

Oprime, P., de Sousa Mendes, G.H., and Lopes Pimenta, M. 2011. Continuous Improvement: Critical Factors in Brazilian Industrial Companies. International Journal of Productivity and Performance Management, Vol. 61 (1).

Pepper M.P.J. and Spedding T.A. 2010. The evolution of lean Six Sigma, International Journal of Quality & Reliability Management, Vol. 27 No. 2, pp. 138–155.

Phillips, T. 2000. Building the lean machine. Advanced Manufacturing, January.

Repenning, N. and Sterman, J. 2001. Creating and sustaining process improvement. California Management Review.

Rother, M. 2010. Toyota Kata: managing people for improvement, adaptiveness, and superior results, McGraw-Hill.

Sakakibara, S., Flynn, B.B. and Schroeder, R.G. 1993. A framework and measurement instrument for just-in-time manufacturing. Production and Operations Management, Vol. 2 No. 3, pp. 177–95.

Santos, J., Wysk, R. and Torres, J.M. 2006. Improving production with Lean Thinking. John Wiley and Sons.

Slack, N., Chambers, S. and Johnston, R. 2010. Operations Management, Pearson Education Limited.

Sohal, A. and Eggleston, A. 1994. Lean production: experience amongst Australian organizations. International Journal of Operations & Production Management, Vol. 14, pp. 1–17.

Soriano-Meier, H. and Forrester, P.L. 2002. A model for evaluating the degree of leanness of manufacturing firms. Integrated Manufacturing Systems. 13/2, pp. 104–109.

Stemler, S. 2001. An overview of content analysis. Practical Assessment, Research & Evaluation, 7(17).

Söderkist, K. and Motwani, J. 1999. Quality issues in lean production implementation. Total Quality Management, Vol. 10, No. 8.

Teresko, J. 2002. A partnership in excellence: Boeing Co.'s success in long beach celebrates a commitment to employee involvement and lean manufacturing (best plants). Reprint from Gale Group, October.

Trombly, R. 2002. Running lean running strong: lean manufacturing processes lead to a stronger, more efficient business. Reprint from Gale Group, August.

Trott, P. 2008. Innovation Management and New Product Development. Pearson Education.

White, M., and Trevor, M. 1983. Under Japanese management: The experience of British workers. Heinemann, London.

Williams, K., Haslam, C., Williams, J., Cutler, T., Adcroft, A. and Johal, S. 1992. Against lean production. Economy and Society, Vol. 21, No. 3.

Womack, J.P. & Jones, D.T. 1996. Lean thinking: banish waste and create wealth in your corporation. New York, Free Press.

Womack, J.P., Jones, D.T. and Roos, D. 1990. The Machine that Changed the World, Macmillan Publishers. The Massachusetts Institute of Technology, Woodridge, IL/Cambridge, MA.

Womack, J.P. and Jones, DT. 2005. Lean Solutions: How Companies and Customers Can Create Wealth Together. New York, Simon & Schuster.

Voss, C. A. 1984. Japanese Manufacturing Management Practices in the UK, International Journal of Operations and Production Management, Vol. 4, No.2, pp. 31–38.

Voss, C. A. 1988. Implementation: A Key Issue in Manufacturing Technology: The Need for a Field of Study, Research Policy, Vol. 17, pp. 53–63.

Voss, C. A. 1995a. Operations Management: From Taylor to Toyota: And Beyond?, British Journal of Management, Vol. 6, Special issue, pp. SI7–S29.

Voss, C. 1995b. Alternative paradigms for manufacturing strategy. International Journal of Operations & Production Management, Vol. 15 No. 4, pp. 5–16.

Voss, C. A., Blackmon, K., Hanson, P. and Oak, B. 1995. The Competitiveness of European Manufacturing: A Four Country Study, Business Strategy Review, Vol. 6, No.1, pp. 1–25.

Voss, C. 2007. The evolution of best practices in operations. Proceedings of 14th International Annual EurOMA Conference.

Yin, K. 2003. Case Study Research: Designs and Methods. Thousand Oaks CA: SAGE Publications, 2003

.

Impact of Entrepreneurship Education on Students' Metacognitive Awareness: Analysis Based on Students' Self-assessments

Hannes Ling[1]

Abstract

The importance of metacognition and the need to develop students' metacognitive abilities and their awareness of cognitive patterns through educational programs has been actively studied and encouraged by entrepreneurship scholars worldwide. However, there is not enough empirical evidence about how metacognition and cognitive adaptability could be considered in the teaching process. In order to contribute to this the aim of the current paper is to assess on the basis of empirical study the role of entrepreneurship education in the development of metacognitive awareness of students. The contribution of this study to scientific discussion involves presenting an assessment and analysis of the level of metacognitive awareness and its changes during the study of students with different backgrounds in the context of entrepreneurship education courses. The analysis revealed certain aspects of metacognitive awareness that necessitate consideration for improving the content of training courses.

Keywords: entrepreneurship education, students, metacognitive awareness

JEL classification: L26, J24, M13

1. Introduction

The question of how to prepare students for better adapting their knowledge through learning tasks in order to develop the necessary entrepreneurial skills is a focus for many scholars. Findings of past research have shown that success of a person is affected by entrepreneurial competencies (Man and Lau 2005) which, involving different skills and attitudes, can be taught (Henry, Hill and Leitch 2005a). Researchers have been advocating also for the connection between improved levels of entrepreneurial skills and both metacognition (Batha and Carroll 2007; Veenman, Van Hout-Wolters and Afflerbach 2006) and metacognitive awareness (Haynie and Shepherd 2009; Schraw 1998). It has been established that increased awareness of a person about its thinking patterns promotes greater success both in entrepreneurship (Ku and Ho 2010) and academic settings (Young and Fry 2008). Adding to this, it has been proposed that students having more metacognitive knowledge perform better in the context of critical thinking (Magno 2010).

---

1 Tallinn School of Economics and Business Administration of Tallinn University of Technology

As regards engineering education or other specialities, Hytti and O'Gorman (2004) have argued that for a successful career it is needed to have not only outstanding professional knowledge in a specific area but also more interdisciplinary skills and attitudes are of great importance. This supports the notion that in order to become successful, either as an entrepreneur or when working for someone else, it is vital to develop metacognitive abilities. Consequently, the need to develop students' metacognitive abilities and their awareness of cognitive patterns through educational programs has to be encouraged with entrepreneurship training programs worldwide.

The focus of on-going scientific discussions has been largely on uncovering impact of metacognitive issues both in educational contexts and learning (Batha and Carroll 2007; Downing, Ning and Shin 2011). However, there is only limited amount of related empirical research available thus generating uncertainty regarding the most appropriate approach for assessing the level of metacognitive abilities among students. Georghiades (2004) has suggested this could be caused by difficulties in assessing the students' metacognitive abilities or performance.

Some instruments developed for this purpose have focused on aspects of metacognition, e.g. strategy use in different contexts (Mokhtari and Reichard 2002; O'Neil and Abedi 1996; Pintrich and de Groot 1990) or task monitoring accuracy (Tobias and Everson 1996). Others have focused on the regulation and knowledge domains of cognition (Pang 2008; Schraw and Dennison 1994) in the classrooms. Haynie (2005), drawing on Schraw and Dennison (1994), adjusted the instrument for assessing metacognition also in an entrepreneurial context. Haynie's instrument incorporates goal orientation, metacognitive experiences, metacognitive knowledge, monitoring and abilities to choose between choices. Indeed, abilities related to setting the goals, adapting past cognitive experiences for present tasks, seeing different ways to solve problems and constantly monitoring the success all play a significant role for entrepreneurs in the continuously changing and uncertain business environment. The same abilities are also important for individuals within existing organisations. Allowing any entrepreneurial person to be more successful it is important to be able to identify, utilize and consciously develop all them.

Previous research works have shown that metacognitive awareness has implications for the pedagogy of entrepreneurship and teaching in general, and that these implications can be realized given that research has repeatedly demonstrated that metacognition can be taught, and cognitive adaptability enhanced (Mevarech 1999; Nietfeld and Schraw 2002; Schmidt and Ford 2003). Haynie and Shepherd have concluded that the concomitant consideration of cognitive adaptability in the design of curriculum and teaching methodologies can enhance learning (Haynie and Shepherd 2009). However, there is not enough empirical evidence about how metacognition and cognitive adaptability could be considered in the teaching process. In order to contribute to this the aim of the current paper is to assess on the basis of empirical study the role of entrepreneurship education in the development of metacognitive awareness of students. For that reason the following research questions were developed:

1) How different student groups are influenced by university entrepreneurship course programmes assessed through change of students' metacognitive awareness?
2) Which statements of metacognitive awareness are most influenced by university entrepreneurship course programmes?

The contribution of this study to scientific discussion involves presenting an assessment and analysis of the level of metacognitive awareness and its changes during the study of students with different backgrounds in the context of entrepreneurship education courses. The current study provides a possibility to extend the empirical evidence concerning students' self-assessments in terms of their metacognitive awareness, as well as to find a basis for improvement of the content of entrepreneurship courses.

Next we first define metacognition and metacognitive awareness and the importance to increase students' metacognitive awareness in entrepreneurship education. This is followed by a discussion of the chosen methodology of the study and analysis of the results. At the end both research limitations and ideas for future research are provided.

2. Theoretical Framework

Metacognition has been identified as something referring to 'the ability to reflect upon, understand and control one's learning' (Schraw and Dennison 1994: 460) or 'thinking about one's own thinking' (Georghiades 2004:365). It can be said that metacognition plays a role in how people adapt to their developing and changing circumstances that are present in any entrepreneurial processes (Haynie, Shepherd, Mosakowski and Earley 2010). It has been acknowledged that opportunities and their identification is an integral part of entrepreneurship (Sarasvathy and Venkataraman 2011) and that opportunity evaluation is always affected by risks present in an environment (Keh, Foo and Lim 2002). But the probability to recognize and interpret opportunities for success is only partially affected by environment. As addressed in past research also person's cognitive abilities play an important role in opportunity recognition processes (Baron and Ward 2004; Forbes 1999). Moreover, Hayton and Cholakova (2011) have proposed that besides cognitive also closely related affective states of mind influ-ence entrepreneurial alertness of a person. Therefore it can be assumed that in-creased levels of metacognitive abilities as a basis for person's cognitive ones serve for greater success in evaluating potential business opportunities.

Henry, Hill and Leitch (2005b) have in parallel argued for the greater need for people to have entrepreneurial skills in order to better adapt to a changing environment and becoming more self-reliant in facing the future. Supported by this there is a correlation between a person's metacognitive abilities and the lev-el of their capacity to adapt to uncertainty. In addition, it is argued that the more conscious a person is about their own adopted thinking patterns, the greater the chances to overcome the individual weaknesses in the cognitive processing that affect their behaviour under different conditions. This also correlates with the findings of Schmidt and Ford (2003), suggesting that effective engagement in metacognitive abilities is critical to enhancing learning outcomes and that per-sons who are engaged in metacognitive activities do not necessarily work longer but spend time more effectively.

The ability to consciously utilize one's own metacognitive abilities will lead to more success when faced with novel tasks. As much as being adaptable with any task is about taking advantage of your own metacognitive abilities, it is also about raising an awareness that such abilities exist and can be developed. Back-haus and Liff (2007) found a correlation between academic performance, deep, strategic learning and metacognitive awareness of students. This presents a foundation for the reasoning in this paper. Awareness of one's own strengths and weaknesses would allow students to adjust their learning in such a manner that they will become more adaptive in the context of different tasks.

Connecting to this, Efklides (2008) has uncovered the interplay between metacognition and self-regulatory skills in learning. Schraw, Crippen and Hart-ley (2006) have suggested instead that self-regulation in learning involves a combination of cognitive strategy use and metacognitive control. Findings by Cassidy (2006) add that self-assessment skills involve the ability to monitor one's own learning and performance. Moreover, by using self-regulatory pro-cesses students will become more self-aware, knowledgeable and decisive in their approach to learning (Zimmerman 1990). Indeed, metacognitive abilities of students receive great importance in developing learners who are able to adapt more easily to the demands of different tasks. However, when trying to develop such skilful students one needs to also consider the impact of learning methods and study motivation. Findings of previous research have contributed to this by establishing a link between motivation of students, their performance and the level of metacognitive practices, suggesting that greater use of metacognition adds to motivation to learn and is also affecting performance (Kramarski and

Feldman 2000; Vandergrift 2005). Vos and de Graaff (2004) have additionally suggested that students learn a wider range of abilities when being exposed to active learning instead of a more traditional approach. Furthermore, Sandi-Urena et al. (2011) have reported that collaborative intervention involving metacognitive reflection helps to increase students' ability to solve problems. They also suggest that more meaningful and purposeful social interaction facilitates metacognitive development and awareness.

Considering the statements above it is possible to conclude that being aware about one's thinking patterns ultimately affects the way one pursues towards one's goals, i.e. behaves. On the other hand, the behaviour of a person is affected by the environment. Under dynamic circumstances it is important to be able to quickly switch between multiple tasks presented by rapidly changing environmental conditions. By failing to do so the person becomes inadaptable and is eventually unable to utilize its full potential. This is important not only in the university environment and related learning processes but persons are also able to take advantage of their self-analysis skills and create awareness of thinking in career building and in personal life in general. In this regard it becomes irrelevant if a person is planning to pursue an entrepreneurial (independent) career or work for someone else. In either case they will be more successful by being able to monitor themselves and adapt any steps according to the changed environment. In relation to this, the main task of entrepreneurship education is to use a teaching approach and methods which are meant to develop students' metacognitive abilities and awareness, which would motivate students to start with their own businesses or to increase their employability at the labour market. This is especially important for engineering students to support a development of their entrepreneurial mind sets and generic skills in addition to deep knowledge in their study field, and in this way to increase the employability of graduates in the labour market.

3. Study Design

3.1 Development of research model

Empirical evidence was collected using a Measure of Metacognitive Awareness (MMA) developed by the author on the basis of Metacognitive Awareness Inventory (MAI) by Shraw and Dennisson, and Haynie's original Generalised Measure of Adaptive Cognition (GMAC) (Haynie 2005). The main proposal emitting from the theoretical concept is summarised in the research model depicted in Fig. 1.

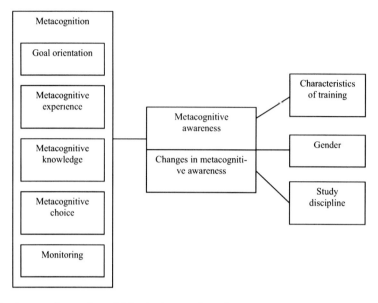

Fig. 1:   Research model (author's compilation)

It is based on the argument that metacognition involves different components (such as: goal orientation, metacognitive knowledge, metacognitive experience, metacognitive choice and monitoring as proposed by Haynie) and confirmed by the results of factor analysis based on students' self-assessments of
their metacognitive awareness (Ling et al. 2013). As a result of the analysis, the
MMA instrument was developed by the author, which includes 29 different
statements covering the above-mentioned five components of metacognitive
awareness. The research model is based on measuring the changes in metacognitive awareness and its components in students that occurred as a result of the
impact of the entrepreneurship education course.

In this paper the focus is on explaining the level and changes in the level of
metacognitive awareness of students with different backgrounds during their
study in different study programmes. Students were asked to assess the level of
their metacognitive awareness in a pre- and post-course study design configura-
tion using the MMA instrument. It is our intention to reach the results which
would allow making improvements into the programmes of entrepreneurship
education and to increase students' metacognitive awareness.

3.2. Sample characteristics

The author was working with two samples: The first sample included a dataset of 280 students of several disciplines taking part in a compulsory entrepreneurship training course over a three year period between 2008 and 2010. The courses lasted through the whole semester involving lectures, various practical exercises and solving teaching cases using the project based (business planning) learning approach. This means that a more traditional approach to teaching entrepreneurship was applied (Hytti and O'Gorman 2004). Here it is needful to consider that in parallel with the entrepreneurship course students had passed several other courses during the semester, which means that finally we measure the impact of all studies during the semester and the influence of entrepreneurship education is only partly influenced.

Table 1:   *Characteristics of the samples*

	Count N	Male (%)	Female (%)	Total (%)
1	2	3	4	5
First sample	280			
Undergraduate	118	51.7	48.3	100.0
Graduate	162	69.1	30.9	100.0
Logistics	59	61.0	39.0	100.0
Technical sciences	140	83.6	16.4	100.0
Natural sciences	81	24.7	75.3	100.0
Second sample	79			
Undergraduate	74	55.4	44.6	100.0
Graduate	5	80.0	20.0	100.0

Source: author's compilation

By the variety of the disciplines, all of the students were grouped into three categories: technical sciences (information technology, mechatronics, transportation technology, product development and production engineering), natural sciences (chemistry, physics, gene technology, geology) and logistics (with business background). In addition, students from both undergraduate and graduate studies were involved.

The second sample included a dataset of 79 respondents who participated in a short and very intensive (i.e. 24 hours without a break) entrepreneurship training during 2009 and 2010. An action learning approach was used during these courses. The purpose of the course was to write a business plan and in addition, it also provided a number of discussion hours with the aim of developing creativity, innovative thinking, self-assessment skills and supporting teamwork necessary for entrepreneurial undertakings. These courses were voluntary, thus students were more motivated to learn about and for entrepreneurship (Hytti and O'Gorman 2004), and the action learning approach was used.

The first sample contained more graduate than undergraduate students in different disciplines. At the same time, the second sampleincluded students studying mostly at the undergraduate level. Furthermore, the majority of students in both samples were male, except for the students in the first sample who were studying natural sciences, of which the majority (75.3%) were females.

3.3. Analysis

In order to answer the first research question about how different student groups are influenced by university entrepreneurship course programmes assessed through change of students' metacognitive awareness, its level and changes were calculated on the basis of students' self-assessments looking at the role of the study programme (e.g. two different approaches of learning, i.e. traditional project based and action learning approach), allowing to reveal the effect of students' study motivation. Furthermore, the role of students' gender, study level and discipline are covered as well.

The goal of analysis was to look at students more closely so that groups with different backgrounds and with different levels of metacognitive awareness would be identified. It was assumed that such groups' present characteristics allowing making recommendations regarding the design of entrepreneurship trainings to better fit with the needs of different students.

The central idea of identifying different student groups was to distinguish the ones who, based on their MMA assessments, presented either significantly high or low levels of metacognitive awareness. As a result it was possible to compare the two groups in order to check if the respective students present similar changes in metacognitive awareness before and after the course.

For the purpose of defining the above-mentioned groups of students the clustering is carried out using the *K-means* method (MacQueen, 1967). This is a combinatorial data analysis method using a partitional clustering approach, where the objective is to maximize the intra-cluster similarity and minimize the inter-cluster similarity between data points. According to the information gained from the theoretical background and considering within the cluster sum of squared errors, the students were divided into five categories, with at least 25 students in each of them. Consequently, each respondent was assigned to a group of similar students based on the scores given to statements. The analysis of changes in the statements of metacognition can help us also to solve the second research question of the study – which statements of metacognitive awareness are most influenced by university entrepreneurship course programmes.

4. Results

4.1 The assessment of the level of students' metacognitive awareness

The purpose of this analysis is to identify different groups of students for revealing the distinctive properties of development of their metacognitive awareness. Clustering of students from the first sample into five groups presents the necessary evidence for identifying different students based on the level of their metacognitive abilities before and after the training (Table 2). Despite the fact that there are five groups of students identified, the ones being most significant for the following analysis are the two extreme groups, i.e. metacognitively high- and low-achievers (clusters CL3 and CL5 respectively). By focusing more on these groups it is assumed that differences between them will be more prominent in every aspect of metacognitive awareness. In order to reveal the two significantly different groups of students among the ones who took part in voluntary entrepreneurship training, the second sample was clustered by adopting a similar approach. However, due to the size of the second sample (79 respondents) only two clusters were identified. This helps to avoid having several clusters with insufficient amount of data points for the following analysis.

The results of t-tests conducted on samples for establishing if the changes in metacognitive awareness scores are statistically significant indicate that among high-achievers in the first sample the changes remain insignificant in all five components (i.e. between –1.6% and .3%). This means that the course of entrepreneurship education did not influence the students' metacognitive abilities. At the same time, the scores given by these students were already before the training course in the upper end of the measurement scale (i.e. 80% and more). In parallel, low-achievers in the first sample present statistically significant changes in all components of metacognition. The changes in both clusters remain above the limit of statistical significance. Thus, the results indicate that the level of metacognitive awareness has been significantly increased during the training for students in all clusters except in cluster 3 (i.e. high-achievers in the first sample).

Table 2: Metacognitive awareness of students in different clusters (% on the scale of 0...100)

	First sample					Second sample	
	CL1	CL2	CL3	CL4	CL5	CL6	CL7
N	67	81	91	10	28	49	29
1	2	3	4	5	6	7	8
Goal Orientation							
Before	76.4	72.3	85.6	76.6	55.8	79.0	58.9
After	77.2	76.9	84.2	78.6	66.1	82.8	74.3
Difference	.8	4.6 *	-1.4	2.0	10.3 *	3.8 *	15.4 *
MC knowledge							
Before	69.6	66.1	82.1	60.3	54.9	76.0	56.3
After	73.6	69.6	82.0	74.4	65.1	79.7	75.0
Difference	4.0 *	3.5 *	-.1	14.1 *	10.2 *	3.7 *	18.7 *
MC experience							
Before	63.3	74.2	80.4	65.7	57.9	76.3	59.7
After	72.9	75.3	80.7	68.3	67.4	80.3	73.2
Difference	9.6 *	1.1	.3	2.6	9.5 *	4.0 *	13.5 *
MC choice							
Before	71.2	60.9	82.9	72.3	60.7	76.3	54.7
After	71.7	67.8	81.3	76.4	67.6	79.5	69.9
Difference	.5	6.9 *	-1.6	4.1 *	6.9 *	3.2 *	15.2 *
Monitoring							
Before	72.8	71.3	84.2	74.0	65.3	78.4	63.6
After	76.4	74.3	83.8	78.9	72.0	82.0	77.8
Difference	3.6 *	3.0 *	-.4	4.9 *	6.7 *	3.6 *	14.2 *

Note: (*) denotes statistically significant difference at $p<.05$;
Source: author's compilation

The study results show that for a group of high achievers (33% of the total sample) entrepreneurship education influenced less their metacognitive awareness or the teaching method did not support the development of metacognition of those students. Such a result implies also that different methods of teaching should be used for students in these cluster, or students with higher and lower metacognitive awareness should study in different groups. Comparison of the two samples suggests that the active study method and students' motivation to study support development of these metacognitive abilities.

Table 3:   Characteristics of students with high and low metacognitive awareness (% of respondents in clusters)

	First sample		Second sample	
	High-achievers	Low-achievers	High-achievers	Low-achievers
	N=91	N=28	N=49	N=29
1	2	3	4	5
Undergraduate students	35.2	35.7	89.8	100.0
Graduate students	64.8	64.3	10.2	-
Male	69.2	57.1	59.2	51.7
Female	30.8	42.9	40.8	48.3
Logistics	18.7	17.9	6.1	-
Natural Sciences	22.0	32.1	28.6	10.3
Technical Sciences	59.3	50.0	30.6	41.4
NA	-	-	34.7	48.3

Source: author's extract of first and second samples' clustering results

It is also evident that low-achieving students in both samples (clusters CL5 and CL7) present the lowest levels in all five components of metacognitive abilities before the training. After the training the same students indicate bigger than average relative increase in their assessments in all metacognitive components. For example, the scores of metacognition given to goal-orientation in the first sample increased by 10.3 per cent (from 55.8 to 66.1). In order to reveal the underlying reasons affecting the described results in relation to entrepreneurship education course, the following analysis focuses on high- and low-achieving students only (Table 3). Reasoning behind this relies on the first sample's clusters CL3 and CL5 covering altogether 40.7% of the entire sample (30.7% and 10.0% respectively). Based on this it is assumed that clusters with extreme values reflect more clearly underlying trends and provide more information about the aspects affecting the results. It is evident that in the first sample the share of graduate students is significantly higher among both high-achievers and low-achievers compared to undergraduate ones. Furthermore, the percentage of students studying natural sciences is significantly lower among metacognitively high-achievers compared to low-achievers (22.0% against 32.1%). In addition, the share of female students is smaller among the high-achievers (30.8%) compared to the ones with low awareness (42.9%). Adding to this, most of the students in the second sample are studying at the undergraduate level. But at the same time there are also more male than female students in both samples and significantly more students have been classified into the group of high-achievers. The latter suggests that regardless of the characteristics of entrepreneurship training, students on average tend to assess their abilities at a higher level.

Table 4:   *Statistical significance of differences in magnitude of entrepreneurship training effect between samples (% on the scale of 0...100)*

	Goal Orientation	MC knowledge	MC experience	MC choice	Monitoring
1	2	3	4	5	6
Low-achievers (1st sample/2nd sample)					
Male	11.5/13.0 *	9.0/17.3 *	8.3/15.0 *	4.5/12.7 *	8.1/13.6 *
Female	8.6/18.0 *	12.0/20.3 *	11.1/11.8 *	10.0/18.0 *	4.7/14.9 *
Undergraduate	10.0/15.4 *	13.8/18.8 *	4.7/13.5 *	7.0/15.2 *	7.0/14.2 *
Graduate	na	na	na	na	na
High-achievers (1st sample/2nd sample)					
Male	-1.5/2.5	-.4/1.9	-.3/1.3	-3.2/4.2	-1.0/4.3
Female	-1.3/5.7	.6/6.2	1.5/8.0	2.1/1.8	1.0/2.7
Undergraduate	-2.3/4.1	1.0/4.0	1.4/3.9	-.6/3.0	-.1/3.7
Graduate	-.9/1.1	-.7/.8	-.3/5.3	-2.1/5.2	-.6/2.7

Note: The scores represent changes transferred to the initial measurement scale between 0%...100%; (*) denotes statistically significant difference at p<.05; "na" denotes "not available"
Source: author's extract from the test output

However, the next step is to check whether the impact of entrepreneurship trainings on metacognitive awareness of different groups of students is statistically significant. For this purpose t-tests are conducted on students' gender and study levels (Table 4). It is evident that entrepreneurship training has produced relatively bigger changes in every component of metacognition among low-achieving students compared to high-achieving ones. More specifically, the metacognitive knowledge component has presented the biggest increase among low-achieving students in terms of females and undergraduates both from the second (20.3% and 18.8%) and the first sample (12.0% and 13.8% respectively). Based on this the students in above-mentioned groups have become significantly more aware about how to make tasks cognitively more understandable and to break them down into smaller pieces regardless of the type of training (mandatory or voluntary) or learning approach (traditional or action learning) used.

It is also interesting that low-achievers present only positive changes in metacognitive awareness scores in all categories of students in both samples. This suggests that the training has affected low-achieving students to become significantly more structured and systematic in their thinking. Looking at high-achievers in the first sample, it is essential that based on magnitude these changes are statistically insignificant. However, although the magnitude of changes remains below the limit of statistical significance and in some metacognitive components it gets even lower it is probably not indicating negative impact on high-achieving students' metacognitive awareness and their potential success. Instead it is possible that students have become more aware about the level of their metacognitive abilities after the training. It is reasonable to expect there exists additional variable(s) which has(ve) not been covered in the frame of the current study. It might be the case that high-achieving students start assessing their cognitive processes more realistically after the course. Such an explanation is supported by findings of Ehrlinger et al. (2008) and Langendyk (2006) suggesting that there is a tendency of under-estimation among high-achieving persons. In this case it is justified that the scores got lower.

However, it should not be forgotten that students in the first sample took the mandatory entrepreneurship training course (incl. traditional learning method) when the second group was involved with a voluntary one (incl. action learning method). In this context the study motivation of students could be of significant importance in an attempt to explain the changes in metacognitive awareness. This is supported by the findings of Kramarski and Feldman (2000) and Vandergrift (2005) who established that study motivation is likely to have an impact both on the degree students' metacognitive practices and also their performance. At the same time Kleitman and Stankov (2007) have proposed that metacognitive awareness correlates with the level of self-confidence. If this is correct, then based on the results of entrepreneurs' psychological portrait the level of students' metacognitive awareness in different clusters differs substantially. In the first sample the rate of students classified as self-confident is much larger among high-achievers than among low-achievers (71% and 57% respectively). Similarly, in the second sample there is 82 per cent of self-confident students among high-achievers, compared to 72 per cent among low-achievers. This indicates that students in the second sample have become more confident about their metacognitive processing than the ones in the first sample. Such a difference can be explained by higher motivation among students in the second sample as well as by using the active method of study compared to the first sample where the students' motivation was lower and traditional methods of study were used.

Concerning the magnitude of change among males and females the analysis suggests that females, especially in the second sample, rate their metacognitive abilities significantly higher than males. A similar trend is also available in the first sample, although the differences are not as big and they are not statistically significant in terms of goal-orientation and metacognitive choice. Therefore the effect of entrepreneurship training is bigger on females than males suggesting that the gender of students is an important factor. Still, these results are unexpected as they contradict with theoretical evidence of both Memnun and Akkaya (2009) and Stewart, Cooper and Moulding (2007) who proposed that gender of students does not have a significant influence.

In this context it is interesting to look at the differences between study-disciplines of students. Interestingly, the effect on students studying logistics and natural sciences remains largely below the criteria of statistical significance between both samples.

Additionally, it is important that on the basis of students' self-assessment, the influence of courses is different by different components of metacognitive abilities. For example, goal-setting skills have been significantly changed by the training among low-achievers in all different groups of students. Indeed, related skills have been a focus of educators, in terms of teaching, for many years and scholars have identified goal setting as one of the critical abilities for everyone. Therefore it has been assumed that effects of entrepreneurship training are also prominent in the goal orientation component. Comparing low- and high-achieving students in both samples based on the magnitude of change in all metacognitive components after the training, a similar trend is apparent, as seen from Table 5.

Table 5:   Difference between high- and low-achieving students' metacognitive awareness by components (% on the measurement scale of 0...100)

Metacognitive component			Second sample	
	before	after	before	after
1	2	3	5	6
Goal Orientation	34.8	21.5	25.4	10.2
MC knowledge	33.2	20.6	26.0	5.8
MC experience	28.0	16.4	21.7	8.9
MC choice	26.8	17.0	28.3	12.0
Monitoring	22.4	14.1	18.9	5.1

Source: author's compilation

Students' metacognitive abilities in two different groups (i.e. high- and low-achievers) have become closer to each other after entrepreneurship training, suggesting that low-achieving students' reasoning has become more comparable to high-achieving ones. In addition to goal orientation, abilities related to making new information more understandable (i.e. metacognitive knowledge) has also received a substantial change (difference decreasing by 12.6 and 20.2 per cent among samples respectively). In parallel, students' metacognitive choice and monitoring abilities in the first sample have changed less (9.8% and 8.3%) with the training compared to other components. The fact that self-monitoring abilities have been affected less by the training suggests that students might not consider such abilities equally important compared to others or these aspects have not been considered sufficiently in the study programmes.

Until now the focus of this analysis has been on attempting to explain the changes in high- and low-achieving students' metacognitive abilities by exploring the respective components on a more general level. But the actual reasons of the changes and their impact on entrepreneurship training have still not been sufficiently uncovered. Consequently, for the purpose of explaining in more details what might be causing the presented changes it is necessary to look into the dynamics of individual statements (Table 6). Based on the average values calculated for each of the five metacognitive components, the magnitude of changes among low-achievers is relatively higher than those of high-achievers also in all individual statements in both samples. Besides this, the changes among high-achievers in the first sample remain below the limit of statistical significance. The impact of training among low-achievers extends from 2% up to 21% depending on the component of metacognitive awareness. The fact that the rate of change poses such a positive consistency over all the five components allows suggesting that the training had higher impact on low-achieving participants in all aspects of metacognitive awareness. Positive correlation between training outcome and increased metacognitive awareness also supports the theoretical assumptions by which the metacognitive training has positive impact both on decision-making capabilities (Batha and Carroll 2007) and critical thinking (Magno 2010).

Based on the evidence that the magnitude of changes in students with low metacognitive awareness in both samples is (as expected) significantly higher in all five components of metacognition it is needful to analyse the statements which were most influenced. On the basis of the results of analysis it will be possible to identify the need for the improvement of the entrepreneurship course programme. Looking at the table in Appendix it becomes evident that there are 2–3 statements in every component where comparably significant changes have occurred.

The goal-orientation statement "I ask myself how well I have accomplished my goals once I have finished" present significant increases, especially among low-achievers in both samples (20% and 15% respectively). Also the statement „When performing a task, I frequently assess my progress against my objectives" has changed among students in both samples (17% and 21% respectively). The statements "I set specific goals before I begin a task" and "I organise my time to best accomplish my goals" has changed most among students of the second sample (19 and 21% respectively). These results show that study programmes support the goal orientation development among students, and this is supported more strongly through the type of teaching method (i.e. action learning) and motivation of students (i.e. voluntary study programme). The same conclusions can be made also when analysing the impact of study programmes on other components of metacognition.

Looking into the aspects related to metacognitive knowledge, this involves both students' skills to focus on the most important aspects of new information, questioning their own assumptions when confronted with novel tasks and having more knowledge on how to disassemble bigger problems into more manageable smaller tasks. Related to this, the scores of the first sample's low-achieving students given to the statements "*I challenge my own assumptions about a task before I begin*" and "*I ask myself questions about the task before I begin*" show significantly increased values (by 13% and 11% respectively). Among the second sample's students the trend is almost the same with the exception of the statement "*I try to break problems down into smaller components,*" which presents the highest level with a 26% increase. Low-achieving students seem to perform better in already familiar conditions or put high value into the information reviewing practices, allowing to suggest that students possess a certain level of metacognitive awareness already prior to the training. In terms of skills involving awareness about finding different ways to solve a problem and analysing itself about the rate of learning after the task has been finished the statement "*I ask myself if I have learned as much as I could have after I finish the task*" provides the magnitude of change as large as 14% (first sample) and 21% (second sample) among low-achievers. Supported by that it seems to be the case that metacognitively low-achieving students initially possess only limited cognitive skills in analysing the results and taking the best of them for improving the performance in the future tasks. Considering the rate of change, they are nevertheless improving themselves significantly within a limited timeframe.

Among metacognitive experience the statement "*I consciously focus my attention on important information*" presents significant increases, especially among low-achievers in the first and second sample (14% and 12 respectively). This supports the suggestion that students with a lower level of metacognitive awareness are more likely to have bigger impact and take greater advantage of the courses. On the other hand, a large magnitude of change coupled by a low level of initial scores suggests the students become more cognitively aware through learning, although lower levels of awareness before the course indicate that they know only moderately the best cognitive strategies for any given task. Only the changes in the metacognitive experience component in the second sample are bigger than in the first sample. Increase is available in the task-specific awareness of strategy-use, i.e. statement "*I am aware of what strategies I use when engaged in a given task*" (16%). On the other hand, skills related to prioritizing information "*I know what kind of information is most important to consider when faced with a problem*" have increased also most among students of the second sample (21% compared with 12% in the first sample). Consequently there is evidence available suggesting that entrepreneurship trainings in general affect students from multiple disciplines in a different manner.

Among the component of metacognitive choice bigger changes have occurred among students in the second sample, e.g. in the statements: "I ask myself if I have considered all the options when solving a problem" (20%), "I ask myself if there was an easier way to do things after I finish a task" (13%) and "I ask myself if I have considered all the options when solving the problem" (13%). Therefore the motivation of students and action learning method are supporting most the metacognitive choice of students.

The impact of study programmes on the monitoring statement "*I find myself analysing the usefulness of a given strategy while engaged in a given task*" experienced the biggest increase among the students of the second sample (20% compared with 10% of the first sample). The impact is considerable also on the statement "*I find myself pausing regularly to check my comprehension of the problem situated at hand*" (10% in the case of first and 16% of second sample). But the statement "*I stop and go back over information that is not clear*" has been highly assessed by students of the second sample (18%), but around six times less by the students of the first sample (3%). From here a conclusion is that traditional teaching methods do not support development of students' monitoring abilities.

Based on the results of analysis above, it has been successfully shown that high- and low-achievers have properties that make them different from each other. Therefore it comes out that various groups of students should be approached differently during entrepreneurship training in order to benefit from the courses to the fullest extent. Hence the results should be taken into account for the improvement of students' performance.

5. Conclusions and Discussion

The purpose of this research was to contribute to the assessment practices of students' metacognitive awareness by presenting and testing empirically a model that contributes to existing theory by exploring the link between five inherent components of metacognition and different types of entrepreneurship training. On the basis of empirical research including two individual samples consisting of students participating in entrepreneurship training courses with different configurations and students with varying backgrounds, the research contributes to the impact of entrepreneurship education in the development of students' metacognitive awareness. Among student groups gender, the effect of study discipline and study motivation were explored. Also, the impact of study programmes on different statements of students' metacognitive awareness were deeply analysed with the aim of finding a basis for improvement of the content of entrepreneurship courses.

The current research shows that the research model based on measuring of the changes in the metacognitive awareness of students with different backgrounds makes it possible to verify the impact of entrepreneurship education courses on students' metacognitive awareness. The use of MMA (Measure of Metacognitive Awareness) instrument brings out the most critical aspects in metacognition, which are needful to consider in planning the study programmes. This suggests that the current study contributes by filling a gap in existing entrepreneurship research by extending the empirical evidence concerning students' self-assessments in terms of their metacognitive awareness.

Considering that the metacognitive awareness of students was calculated before and after the course and students in both samples were classified as metacognitively high- and low-achieving ones, the analysis of the results indicated certain differences between students in the degree of change in metacognitive abilities as a result of entrepreneurship training. Although the reasons affecting such an outcome are not revealed to its full extent in the frame of this study, the fact that the training courses had positive impact on students' self-analysis and assessment skills supports the findings of Henry et al. (2005b).

The results clearly indicate that the impact of entrepreneurship training courses on different student groups is bigger for metacognitively low-achieving ones. However, it is necessary to remember that the changes to high-achieving students' metacognitive processing were statistically insignificant. It might be that high-achieving students already employed metacognitive processing skills to a greater extent before the training even began, making it difficult to make a substantial impact on their skills. In parallel, low-achieving students present evidence suggesting that they are more successful in adapting their cognitive patterns according to the environment. This is supported by additional findings showing that the differences between high- and low-achieving students' metacognitive awareness scores decreased substantially after the training. Therefore it is evident that the skills of metacognitive information processing have grown similar between two clasters of students after the trainings on the account of increasing level of metacognition among low-achievers. The fact that there were minimal changes in metacognition among high-achievers directs to the idea that these two clasters of students require separate study programmes according to the specific needs of both groups of students.

Following this it is possible to influence and develop students' awareness about their own cognitive patterns through university courses. Nevertheless, there were also differences in training programs. For the students in the first sample the training program was mandatory (with traditional learning approach) as opposed to the second sample taking a voluntary (with action learning approach) one. This is likely to have an effect on the results in terms of students' study motivation supplemented with the use of different learning approaches. The findings of this study correlate with the theoretical assumption by which the study motivation affects the students' metacognitive abilities and performance.

In addition, the results indicate there is a significant difference between male and female students' self-reported levels of metacognitive abilities. The changes are present among all the components, although on average they are greatest among high-achieving students in goal orientation. For low-achieving students, on average, the biggest differences are instead in metacognitive knowledge. More importantly, regardless of the exact components the results contradict with the theoretical underpinnings of Memnun and Akkaya (2009) and Stewart, Cooper and Moulding (2007) who proposed that the gender of students does not have significant influence.

The findings of the current study suggest that entrepreneurship training courses should be designed by keeping greater focus on specific needs of different students. Supported by Anderson (2011), there is a stronger need to focus more on the contents of the courses for different groups of students in order to utilize the strengths of universities. By designing the training course so that students' attributes are considered the overall usefulness of the training is likely to be increased. The detailed analysis of the different statements of the measurement tool revealed certain aspects of metacognitive awareness that necessitate consideration for improving the content of training courses, e.g. in supporting development of students' metacognitive awareness, especially in metacognitive choice and monitoring, but also considering specific statements across all different components of metacognitive awareness.

Based on the results of the research, the contribution of this study to scientific discussion involves presenting an assessment and analysis of the level of metacognitive awareness and its changes during the study of students with different backgrounds in the context of entrepreneurship education courses. The current study provides a possibility to extend the empirical evidence concerning students' self-assessments in terms of their metacognitive awareness, as well as to find a basis for improvement of the content of entrepreneurship courses.

6. Research Limitations and Ideas for Future Research

There are several aspects that should be taken into account when interpreting the findings of this research. It is important to utilize the instrument empirically also in other environmental contexts. This makes it possible to compare and better generalise the results of the surveys. Moreover, the contribution can be made by extending the diversity of study disciplines, i.e. by involving students studying business administration and economics, arts and design and others. The findings of the current research also suggest that the gender of students is an important factor influencing metacognitive awareness. As this contradicts with earlier research evidence, it is expected that the effect of students' gender will be studied more in future research.

In addition, the use of only a quantitative measurement tool does not allow explaining the evidence in full detail, a qualitative survey is needed as an additional tool. It is likely that there exist more latent variables affecting the results than covered in this study.

It is the author's hope that the contribution into the theory of metacognition assessment by presenting a model will generate more research in the future aiming to elaborate the relationship between the success of different students and the level of their metacognitive abilities.

References

Backhaus, K. and Liff, J. P. (2007). Cognitive Styles and Approaches To Studying in Management Education. *Journal of Management Education, 31*(4), 445–466. doi:10.1177/1052562905284674

Baron, R. A. and Ward, T. B. (2004). Expanding Entrepreneurial Cognition' s Toolbox : Potential Contributions from the Field of Cognitive Science. *Entrepreneurship Theory and Practice, winter,* 553–573.

Batha, K. and Carroll, M. (2007). Metacognitive training aids decision making. *Australian Journal of Psychology, 59*(2), 64–69. doi:10.1080/00049530601148371.

Cassidy, S. (2006). Learning style and student self-assessment skill. *Education + Training, 48*(2/3), 170–177. doi:10.1108/00400910610651791

Downing, K., Ning, F. and Shin, K. (2011). Impact of problem-based learning on student experience and metacognitive development. *Multicultural Education & Technology Journal*, *5*(1), 55–69. doi:10.1108/17504971111121928

Efklides, A. (2008). Metacognition. Defining Its Facets and Levels of Functioning in Relation to Self-Regulation and Co-regulation. *European Psychologist*, *13*(4), 277–287. doi:10.1027/1016-9040.13.4.277

Ehrlinger, J., Johnson, K., Banner, M., Dunning, D. and Kruger, J. (2008). Why the Unskilled Are Unaware: Further Explorations of (Absent) Self-Insight Among the Incompetent. *Organizational behavior and human decision processes*, *105*(1), 98–121. doi:10.1016/j.obhdp.2007.05.002

Forbes, D. P. (1999). Cognitive approaches to new venture creation. *International Journal of Management Reviews*, *1*(4), 415–439. doi:10.1111/1468-2370.00021.

Georghiades, P. (2004). From the general to the situated: three decades of metacognition. *International Journal of Science Education*, *26*(3), 365–383. doi:10.1080/0950069032000119401

Haynie, M. J. (2005). *Cognitive Adaptability: The Role of Metacognition and Feedback in Entrepreneurial Decision Policies*. University of Colorado.

Haynie, M. J. and Shepherd, D. A. (2009). A Measure of Adaptive Cognition for Entrepreneurship Research. *Entrepreneurship Theory and Practice*, *33*(3), 695–714.

Haynie, M. J., Shepherd, D., Mosakowski, E. and Earley, P. C. (2010). A situated metacognitive model of the entrepreneurial mindset. *Journal of Business Venturing*, *25*(2), 217–229. doi:10.1016/j.jbusvent.2008.10.001

Hayton, J. C. and Cholakova, M. (2011). The Role of Affect in the Creation and Intentional Pursuit of Entrepreneurial Ideas. *Entrepreneurship Theory and Practice*, *May*(39), 1–27. doi:10.1111/j.1540-6520.2011.00458.x

Henry, C., Hill, F. and Leitch, C. (2005a). Entrepreneurship education and training: can entrepreneurship be taught? Part I. *Education + Training*, *47*(2), 98–111. doi:10.1108/00400910510586524

Henry, C., Hill, F. and Leitch, C. (2005b). Entrepreneurship education and training: can entrepreneurship be taught? Part II. *Education + Training*, *47*(3), 158–169. doi:10.1108/00400910510592211

Hytti, U. and O'Gorman, C. (2004). What is "enterprise education"? An analysis of the objectives and methods of enterprise education programmes in four European countries. *Education + Training*, *46*(1), 11–23. doi:10.1108/00400910410518188

Keh, H. T., Foo, M. Der and Lim, B. C. (2002). Opportunity Evaluation under Risky Conditions: The Cognitive Processes of Entrepreneurs. *Entrepreneurship Theory and Practice*, (Winter), 125–148.

Kramarski, B. and Feldman, Y. (2000). Internet in the Classroom: Effects on Reading Comprehension , Motivation and Metacognitive Awareness. *Educational Media International*, *37*(3), 149–155.

Ku, K. Y. L. and Ho, I. T. (2010). Metacognitive strategies that enhance critical thinking. *Metacognition and Learning*, *5*(3), 251–267. doi:10.1007/s11409-010-9060-6

Langendyk, V. (2006). Not knowing that they do not know: self-assessment accuracy of third-year medical students. *Medical education*, *40*(2), 173–179. doi:10.1111/j.1365-2929.2005.02372.x

Ling, H., Kyrö, P. and Venesaar, U. (2013). Entrepreneurship Education and Metacognitive Awareness: Development of a Tool to Measure Metacognitive Awareness. Conceptual Richness and Methodological Diversity in Entrepreneurship Research, edited by A. Fayolle, P. Kyrö, T. Mets and U. Venesaar, Edward Elgar, 132–164.

MacQueen, J. (1967). Some methods for classification and analysis of multivariate observations. In L. LeCam and J. Neyman (Eds.), *Proceedings of the Fifth Berkeley Symposium on Mathematical statistics and probability* , 281–297.

Magno, C. (2010). The role of metacognitive skills in developing critical thinking. *Metacognition and Learning, 5*(2), 137–156. doi:10.1007/s11409-010-9054-4

Man, T. W. Y. and Lau, T. (2005). The context of entrepreneurship in Hong Kong: An investigation through the patterns of entrepreneurial competencies in contrasting industrial environments. *Journal of Small Business and Enterprise Development, 12*(4), 464–481. doi:10.1108/14626000510628162

Memnun, D. S. and Akkaya, R. (2009). The levels of metacognitive awareness of primary teacher trainees. *Procedia – Social and Behavioral Sciences, 1*(1), 1919–1923. doi:10.1016/j.sbspro.2009.01.337

Mokhtari, K. and Reichard, C. a. (2002). Assessing students' metacognitive awareness of reading strategies. *Journal of Educational Psychology, 94*(2), 249–259. doi:10.1037//0022-0663.94.2.249

O'Neil, H. F. and Abedi, J. (1996). *Reliability and Validity of a State Metacognitive Inventory : Potential for Alternative Assessment,* Vol. 1522, 1–29, Los Angeles.

Pang, K. (2008). *The Metacognitive Expertise Assessment Tool: A Predictive Scale for Academic Achievement Across Disciplines*. Texas A&M University-Commerce.

Pintrich, P. R. and De Groot, E. V. (1990). Motivational and self-regulated learning components of classroom academic performance. *Journal of Educational Psychology, 82*(1), 33–40. doi:10.1037//0022-0663.82.1.33

Sandi-Urena, S., Cooper, M. M. and Stevens, R. H. (2011). Enhancement of Metacognition Use and Awareness by Means of a Collaborative Intervention. *International Journal of Science Education, 33*(3), 323–340. doi:10.1080/09500690903452922

Sarasvathy, S. D. and Venkataraman, S. (2011). Entrepreneurship as Method: Open Questions for an Entrepreneurial Future. *Entrepreneurship Theory and Practice, 35*(1), 113–135. doi:10.1111/j.1540-6520.2010.00425.x

Schmidt, A. M. and Ford, J. K. (2003). Learning Within a Learner Control Training Environment: the Interactive Effects of Goal Orientation and Metacognitive Instruction on Learning Outcomes. *Personnel Psychology, 56*(2), 405–429. doi:10.1111/j.1744-6570.2003.tb00156.x

Schraw, G. (1998). Promoting general metacognitive awareness. *Instructional Science, 26* (1-2), 113–125.

Schraw, G., Crippen, K. J. and Hartley, K. (2006). Promoting Self-Regulation in Science Education: Metacognition as Part of a Broader Perspective on Learning. *Research in Science Education, 36*(1-2), 111–139. doi:10.1007/s11165-005-3917-8

Schraw, G. and Dennison, R. S. (1994). Assessing Metacognitive awareness. *Contemporary Educational Psychology, 19*(4), 460–475.

Stewart, P. W., Cooper, S. S. and Moulding, L. R. (2007). Metacognitive Development in Professional Educators. *The Researcher, 21*(1), 32–40.

Tobias, S. and Everson, H. T. (1996). *Assessing Metacognitive Knowledge Monitoring*, 1–41. New York.

Vandergrift, L. (2005). Relationships among Motivation Orientations, Metacognitive Awareness and Proficiency in L2 Listening. *Applied Linguistics*, *26*(1), 70–89. doi:10.1093/applin/amh039

Veenman, M. V. J., Van Hout-Wolters, B. H. a. M. and Afflerbach, P. (2006). Metacognition and learning: conceptual and methodological considerations. *Metacognition and Learning*, *1*(1), 3–14. doi:10.1007/s11409-006-6893-0

Vos, H. and De Graaff, E. (2004). Developing metacognition: a basis for active learning. *European Journal of Engineering Education*, *29*(4), 543–548. doi:10.1080/03043790410001716257

Young, A. and Fry, J. D. (2008). Metacognitive awareness and academic achievement in college students. *Journal of the Scholarship of Teaching and Learning*, *8*(2), 1–10.

Zimmerman, B. J. (1990). Self-Regulated Learning and Academic Achievement: An Overview. *Educational Psychologist*, *25*(1), 3–17.

Appendix 1. Changes in metacognitie wareness among high- and low-achieving students (% on the measurement scale of 0…100 %)

1	First sample			Second sample		
	HA	LA	Total	HA	LA	Total
	2	3		4	5	
Goal Orientation						
I often define goals for myself		6.8	3.8	3.9	11.0	7.5
I understand how accomplishment of a task relates to my goals	-3.2	8.2	2.5	3.9	11.0	7.5
I set specific goals before I begin a task		9.3	4.9	3.9	18.6	11.2
I ask myself how well I have accomplished my goals once I have finished		19.6	9.6	4.3	14.8	9.6
When performing a task, I frequently assess my progress against my objectives		16.8	7.8	4.9	21.2	13.0
I think about what I really need to accomplish before I begin a task			0.7		10.7	5.8
I organise my time to best accomplish my goals	-4.9	8.2	1.6	5.1	21.0	13.1
Average	-1.4	10.3	4.5	3.8	15.4	9.6
Metacognitive knowledge						
I challenge my own assumptions about a task before I begin	2.6	12.9	7.7	3.5	15.9	9.7
I ask myself questions about the task before I begin	3.0	11.1	7.0	7.6	21.0	14.3
I try to translate new information into my own words		7.1	4.1	3.1	13.1	8.1
I try to break problems down into smaller components		10.4	4.5	3.1	25.9	14.5
I focus on the meaning and significance of new information	-5.6	10.0	2.2		17.9	9.5
I ask myself if I have learned as much as I could have after I finish the task		14.3	6.7	4.3	21.4	12.8
I periodically review to help me understand important relationships		5.7	3.2	3.3	18.3	10.8
Average	-0.1	10.2	5.1	3.7	18.7	11.2
Metacognitive experience						

I use different strategies depending on the situation		6.8	2.6		10.7	5.8
I am good at organising information		10.0	5.6	5.3	14.8	10.1
I know what kind of information is most important to consider when faced with a problem		11.4	6.6	5.7	20.7	13.2
I consciously focus my attention on important information		13.9	6.5	3.3	12.1	7.7
I am aware of what strategies I use when engaged in a given task		8.9	5.4	8.4	15.5	11.9
Average	**0.3**	**9.5**	**4.9**	**4.0**	**13.5**	**8.8**
Metacognitive choice						
I think of several ways to solve a problem and choose the best one			-0.6		8.6	5.1
I ask myself if I have considered all the options when solving a problem	-1.6	5.7	2.0	5.3	13.1	9.2
I ask myself if there was an easier way to do things after I finish a task	-3.3		-0.4	2.4	13.1	7.8
I ask myself if I have considered all the options after I solve a problem		12.1	5.3	2.4	20.0	11.2
Average	**-1.6**	**6.9**	**2.7**	**3.2**	**15.2**	**9.2**
Monitoring						
I perform best when I already have knowledge of the task		3.9	1.4		4.8	2.9
I try to use strategies that have worked in the past		6.1	2.7		6.9	3.7
I stop and go back over information that is not clear		8.2	3.2		17.6	9.7
I find myself analysing the usefulness of a given strategy while engaged in a given task		10.4	5.7	2.2	20.0	11.1
I find myself pausing regularly to check my comprehension of the problem situated at hand		10.0	4.9	10.8	15.5	13.2
I ask myself questions about how well I am doing while I am performing a novel task. I stop and re-read when I get confused			0.3	2.4	9.0	5.7
Average	**-0.4**	**6.7**	**3.2**	**3.6**	**14.2**	**8.9**

Source: author's compilation;
Note: HA denotes high-achievers and LA low-achievers

International Trade Fairs for Facilitating the Internationalisation of Enterprises

Rünno Lumiste[1], Gunnar Prause[1], Christian Feuerhake[2], Urve Venesaar[1], Ann Vihalem[1] and Marianne Kallaste[1]

Abstract

Trade fairs have historically been a key marketing tool. Learning more about the choice, use and evaluation of fairs benefits industry as much as it interests academic researchers. The aim of the current study was to assess the impact of trade fairs for facilitating the internationalisation of enterprises in Estonia and Germany, i.e. to investigate whether companies exhibiting are different with respect to their internationalisation compared with other enterprises who have not participated in international trade fairs.

A structured questionnaire was used and a survey was conducted among enterprises in the federal state of Mecklenburg-Vorpommern in Germany. The Estonian questionnaire was developed partly covering the German questions. All together around 800 German and Estonian companies were included in the survey. The opinion of entrepreneurs about the issues of trade fair participation and marketing activities in Estonia and Germany were compared. The study revealed certain similarities and differences between Estonian and German companies in respect to goals of participation in trade fairs, and satisfaction with trade fair results.

Keywords: internationalisation, trade fairs, marketing, small and medium-sized enterprises

JEL: M3

1. Introduction

International trade fairs are important events which support processes of interactive learning, knowledge creation and the formation of international networks (Batheld and Schuldt 2008) for those who participate via exchanging information about new market developments, presenting new products, monitoring the innovations of others and establishing contacts with new partners.

Initially trade fairs emerged as marketplaces where sellers had a chance to demonstrate their goods and buyers had a chance to get price information and buy goods. With growth and concentration trade fairs acquired a stronger price and quality settlement function. They started to act as places for learning, trend-setting and informing (Bathelt and Zakrzewski 2007).

---

1   Tallinn School of Economics and Business Administration, Tallinn University of Technology

2   Wismar Business School, Wismar University of Applied Sciences

Hence, researchers have been aware of the importance of trade fairs as a marketing tool several decades already (Kerin and Cron 1987; Tanner and Chonko 1995). There are three principal actors in trade fairs: organizer of trade fairs, exhibitor companies presenting their output, and visitors. In the current paper attention is paid to the two latter actors. The literature review shows that the investigations in trade fair industry (Mu 2010, Schaper 2010) cover the organizational factors of trade fairs and trade fairs as a temporary cluster for learning and interaction (Aspers and Darr 2011). The literature about exhibitors covers participation strategies (Bathelt and Schuldt 2008), trade fairs as a marketing tool (Meffert 1993; Bathelt and Schuldt 2010), participation in trade fairs as a tool for learning (Prüser 1997; Schuldt and Bathelt 2011), knowledge spillover agents in regions (Ramirez-Pasillas 2008), trade fairs as locations of information exchange and a good marketplace for face to face contacts (Bathelt and Schuldt 2010; Schuldt and Bathelt 2011), trade fair communication (Blythe 2009; Ahola 2012). The motivations and behaviour of visitors (Blythe 2009; Ahola 2012) have been less studied.

A major goal for the participation in trade fairs is to inform existing and potential clients about your products and/or services (Bathelt and Schuldt 2008). For peripheral countries and firms from peripheral countries trade fairs offer an opportunity to introduce their products for oversees customers and clients. Media coverage, number of other exhibitors and big number of visitors give a chance to get known for big and focused audience. There is not yet so much literature linking trade fairs and internationalization. In the biggest European Trade Fair, Hannover Messe in 2010, from 4695 participating firms 2215 were of non-German origin from 64 different countries (Euro Fair Statistics 2010). Big trade fairs have often an additional programme with lectures and social life. In addition, trade fairs invite state officials like ministers to give an opening speech. All those factors show that trade fairs serve as a platform for internationalization.

The aim of the current study is to assess the impact of trade fairs for facilitating the internationalisation of enterprises in Estonia and Germany, i.e. to investigate whether companies exhibiting are different with respect to their setting of goals and satisfaction with results of trade fair participation in two countries compared with other enterprises not participating in international trade fairs. We will then be able to draw conclusions about the role and possible influence of the promotion of trade fair exhibiting by government.

One starting point for the paper was a study about fair participation of SMEs in Mecklenburg – Vorpommern, which Wismar Business School developed together with the Association of the German Trade Fair Industry (AUMA) and the regional Ministry of Economics and which has been transferred meanwhile to other European countries (WM MV 2009).

The structure of the paper includes the theoretical framework of internationalisation of enterprises and trade fairs. Next, data and method are described and the results of analysis are brought. Finally the survey results are concluded.

2. Theoretical Framework

2.1 Internationalisation of enterprises and trade fairs

The internationalisation process can be explained by multiple approaches. The Nordic gradual internationalisation approach (Johanson and Vahlne 1977), the network approach (Johanson and Mattson 1988) and born-global approach (Oviatt and McDougall 1994) are most commonly used. Until the born-global approach the internationalization literature was mainly concerned about big firms (MNC). Internationalization of small and medium-sized enterprises (SME) was small and relatively unobserved (Jansson and Sandberg 2008). Compared to big and established firms SMEs lack resources and resource management is crucial for them. A major factor preventing SME internationalization and export is uncertainty, which is caused by cultural, time and geographical distance.

SMEs tend to have less contacts, good single relationships are more important for them than for MNCs. Different networks play a big role in internationalization. Those networks can be networks of suppliers, customers, banking and other type networks (Jansson and Sandberg 2008). Methods and places through which firms start network building in foreign countries are called *entry nodes*. SMEs select entry nodes that can be used at low costs and offer flexibility.

A study made among South-Sweden firms in 2004–2005 showed that the entry process is critical in network creation (Jansson and Sandberg 2008). The study showed also that SME internationalization is a cumulative process where firms step-by-step accumulate target market knowledge and based on that knowledge adjust/increase their operations.

A link between international trade and trade fairs was established already long time ago (Brown and Duguid 1991). The study conducted by Bathelt and Schuldt (2008) identified the trade fair goals like making new customer contacts, dealing with existing customers, presentation of innovations, conducting sales and orders and assessing new markets. Interaction with existing and potential customers was seen as the most important goal. Seeing of competitors and suppliers was seen as less important.

Support for trade fair participation is in many nations a major component in their promotion programmes for internationalisation assisting companies learning to cope and to build their competence in a global business environment. Supporting systems for international trade fairs are developed in both countries and are important for facilitating internationalisation of enterprises.

2.2. Trade fairs as a global marketplace and marketing tool

Different firms from different countries value fairs as a marketing and international trade tool. Industrial fairs or tradeshows have developed into a global industry. Trade fairs offer a unique opportunity to get an overview of all industry. Biggest trade fairs in Hannover, Milan, Düsseldorf, Paris and Cologne have well over thousands of exhibitors and tens of thousands visitors (Euro Fair Statistics). Economic growth in the Far East and Middle East has created new trade fair locations, among them Hong-Kong, Shanghai, Singapore and Dubai. It is physically almost impossible to get such a focused and global audience of visitors and exhibitors in other ways. Big concentration of participants serves as an audience for further trendsetting. Companies can assess future technologies and trends.

There were 1973 trade fairs in 2010 organized by the European Trade Fair Association. At these events, organized by 434 organizers, a total of 575,597 exhibitors, 52.2 million visitors and 21.04 million square metres of rented space were registered (Euro Fair Statistics). 46% of the exhibitions were addressed to trade visitors, 39% to public visitors and 15% to both target groups. Major topics of trade fairs were leisure, hobby, entertainment, general fairs, construction, infrastructure, engineering, industrial, manufacturing, machines, instruments and hardware.

Different trade fairs bring together participants from all over the world and help to create the environment for learning and business. Temporarily, enterprises and visitors have a chance for face to face interaction and interviews are tools for effective short-time communication (Schuldt and Batheld 2011). Within a short period entrepreneurs can acquire key information and identify similar thinking patterns. Those patterns are difficult to identify in advance.

Trade fairs can be also considered as market models geographically concentrated on one spot where firms that are competitors meet and so they serve as information dissemination places. There are anecdotal evidences about actively photographing Asian carmakers from Geneva and Frankfurt Car Fairs. Seeing the competitors allows comparing own products to the competitors ones.

Trade fairs serve as an informational tool for wider audience than only exhibitors themselves or visitors (Skov 2006). People whose task is to create information environment for particular industry use fairs as a focal point of information. Industry journalists and opinion leaders spend a lot of time on covering the novelties and predicting the trends for next years (Deg 2006; Bruhn, Esch and Langner 2009). Technology trends and novelties identified in trade fairs serve as guidance for development of industrial sectors in the next period.

Trade fair industry is not only global trade fairs. Between big international trade fairs and local countryside market fairs there are different regional organizers and events. Regional trade fairs have a double role for exhibitors. They can be the first step for market penetration for importing foreign firms and, secondly, they can serve as a marketing tool for local firms to introduce novelty products and increase awareness about the company and brands.

Since the study is based on a comparison between the German Federal State of Mecklenburg –Vorpommern and Estonia it should be mentioned that the biggest trade fair organizer in Mecklenburg, Vorpommern, is Hansemesse Rostock, which is organizing 10–12 fairs yearly. Smaller, more locally oriented fairs are organized in other cities like Schwerin, Greifswald, Wismar and other locations.

Estonian trade fairs are relatively small and regionally oriented. Two major companies organizing trade fairs are *Estonian Fairs* in Tallinn and *Tartu Fairs* in Tartu. Estonian Fairs Ltd is a major organizer of general fairs. The yearly number of trade fairs is between 7 and 9. Tartu Fairs tends to organize fairs oriented to agro-food industries in South-Estonia. The other fairs are rather smaller events mainly concentrated to agriculture, gardening, forestry and other local activities.

2.3. Data and method

Based on the existing questionnaire of the Wismar Business School in Mecklenburg, Vorpommern, an Estonian questionnaire was developed, partly covering the German questions (WM MV, 2009). The German survey was carried out by mail among enterprises in the federal state of Mecklenburg-Vorpommern in Germany; the Estonian survey was conducted mostly by telephone. Potential respondents in Estonia were pre-screened randomly from the large database for the type of exporting enterprises and one third of the sample were selected from the list of those who had participated at the trade fairs and received support during the last five years from the government for marketing activities. The opinions of entrepreneurs about the issues of trade fair participation and marketing activities in Estonia and Germany were compared.

The sample group had a total of 795 enterprises from Germany and Estonia. All German enterprises were from the federal land of Mecklenburg-Vorpommern. 303 enterprises were members of the Chamber of Craft (*Handwerkskammer*), 328 were members of the Chamber of Industry and Trade (*IHK*).

Members of the Chamber of Craft were self-employed persons and smaller firms with more local or regional scope for their business activities whereas members of the Chamber of Industry and Trade represented all kind of SMEs and even larger companies with a scope of their business operations between regional and international level depending on the branch and size of the company. 164 enterprises in Estonia were interviewed.

Multivariate method of analysis is used to first validate the grouping of companies into those exhibiting and those not participating at the trade fairs. Second, the analysis is applied to the multi-measure international trade fair performance construct to reveal differences between the groups. T-tests are used to compare different activities of the exhibitors.

3. Results

3.1. Participation in trade fairs

In order to understand better the economic environment of German and Estonian enterprises the export rates in Germany and Estonia are compared. In Estonia about 75% of the GDP is generated by exports, in Germany it is only about 40% and the contribution of SME sector to exports is about 30%. It is important to underline that the export figures in Eastern Germany, i.e. also in Mecklenburg-Vorpommern, are about half as high as in Western Germany (Prause and Kramer 2006). An internationalisation study conducted in Western Mecklenburg identified that about 20% of the SMEs enjoy international turnovers and that only 10% of all regional turnovers are generated by international operations due to the small company size of the SME sector in Mecklenburg-Vorpommern (Beifert and Prause 2006). The results of the current study draw a more positive picture of Western Mecklenburg, but it has to be stated that the study is not representative due to the small sample.

In order to make the results better to compare, the sample was split into two groups containing non-exporting enterprises and enterprises exporting more than 10% of their sales. The number of companies exporting more than 10% was 6% among the members of the Chamber of Crafts (HW), 29% among the members of the Chamber of Commerce and 74% among Estonian enterprises (Table 1). A closer look at the field of activity showed that 33% of enterprises in the sample group were manufacturing firms, 6% wholesale and trade firms and 49% service firms.

So the first observation of the data revealed that the German SMEs were more focused on domestic business activities compared to the Estonian companies, which is due to the small size of the Estonian market. Furthermore, the data showed that German member companies of the Chamber of Trade and Industry are more active in foreign business operations than the members of the Chamber of Crafts, stressing the different regional scope and different business strategies of German enterprises.

Table 1: Export sales and fair participation

	MV-IHK	%	MV-HW	%	EE	%
Number of firms in the survey	328	100	303	100	164	100
With export sales	156	48	37	12	153	93
With export sales more than 10% of sales	96	29	17	6	122	74
Participating in trade fairs	179	55	66	22	51	31

When it comes to the importance of trade fairs as a marketing tool for the considered sample companies it turned out that only for the German members of the Chamber of Industry and Trade fairs play a significant role. Members of the Chamber of Industry and Trade (179 firms) participated in 338 fairs. Among the destinations were 52 foreign fairs and 287 German fairs. Major foreign destinations were Dubai (6) and Russia (8). Companies participating in Dubai and St. Petersburg fairs were also eligible for public support funds. Major destinations in Germany were Berlin (30), Düsseldorf (28), Hamburg (29), Hannover (30), Cologne (20), Leipzig (12), Munich (15) and Nuremberg (19). 63 fair participations happened in federal land Mecklenburg-Vorpommern. Major local fairs happened in Rostock.

Estonian sample group companies (51 firms) participated in 29 Estonian trade fairs and 63 foreign trade fairs. Major destinations of the foreign trade fairs for Estonian companies were Finland (12), Germany (9), Russia (8 incl. 7 in Moscow), Sweden (9), Riga (4), Lithuania (4) and Paris (4). The Chamber of Craftsmen firms (66 firms) participated in 91 fairs. 49 fairs were local Mecklenburg-Vorpommern fairs. Other major locations were Berlin (14), Hamburg (6), Düsseldorf (4) and Sweden (4).

All three groups show different patterns for fair participation. Estonian firms participate in different foreign fairs with a focus on neighbouring countries. The Chamber of Crafts firms participate according to their regional scope mainly in Mecklenburg-Vorpommern and nearby Berlin and Hamburg trade fairs. The Chamber of Industry and Trade participants participate mainly in big international trade fairs happening in Germany.

When it comes to the fair activities of Germany SME the results are fitting well to the expected company strategies. Due to small average company size in Mecklenburg-Vorpommern trade fair participations are underdeveloped because of lack of knowledge and resources. Even the fair active companies are focussing on fairs which are in-line with their strategies, i.e. members of the Chamber of Craftsman are mainly present in local and regional fairs whereas members of the Chamber of Industry and Trade concentrate on regional, national and partly also on international fairs. And fair participation is merited by the market since fair active companies have significantly higher growth rates and higher export rates than other companies.

3.2. Reasons for not participating in trade fairs

A large number of enterprises did not take part in trade fairs during the last five years. There could be several reasons for that. One reason of not participating in trade fairs is linked to the corporate structure. Local Estonian entities are responsible for the manufacturing and subcontracting part and often do not have marketing capabilities.

Size of company and therefore limited resources and competencies were the biggest reasons for not participating in trade fairs (Table 2). Two basic problems are lack of resources and capabilities and non-reach of target customers. Deficit of resources and capabilities could be in the form of too high charges for fairs, lack of marketing capabilities and appropriate personnel. Considering the most significant differences between German and Estonian companies it can be stated that for Estonian SME finance related reasons for not taking part in trade fairs play a more important role than for German companies. In this context the Estonian companies are less satisfied with the public support system for trade fairs than their German counterparts since insufficient public state grants were mentioned nearly 3 times more often in Estonia than in Germany (Table 2).

Reasons for not participating in trade fairs were also limited competences, i.e. skills, experiences and knowledge. Here the Estonian companies revealed weaknesses which are about twice as high as in Germany. These lacks in the skills can only be fixed by further qualification and consulting services for the Estonian SME sector.

Not taking part in trade fairs doesn't mean that enterprises are not able to export goods and services. Two cheaper and better focused marketing tools are personal selling and internet selling. Internet allows technically easy communication and in the case of standardised products it is a good alternative for smaller and less resource rich firms.

Table 2: Reasons for not participating in trade fairs, % of respondents

Reasons for not participating	IHK	HW	EE
	N=148	N=244	N=167
Size of our company	34	41	38
Lack of experiences as an exhibiting company	9	13	27
No qualified staff in the company	9	11	22
Excessive costs of participation	21	21	43
Excessive requirements of the organizer of a fair	3	7	18
Too large distances to the location of the exhibition	6	9	33
Inappropriate target groups	11	12	25
We can obtain our target groups with other sales instruments better	18	11	30
There is no trade fair appropriate to our choice of products	7	7	17
Our choice of products is not suitable for trade fairs	14	14	22
Lack of knowledge of foreign languages	8	13	17
Insufficient state grants	8	8	23
Insufficient organizational support	3	6	17
Insufficient results (Turnover/contracts)	6	9	17
Initiation of co-operations is not possible	3	5	13
The identification of tendencies of development is not possible	1	4	14
There is no possibility to meet competitors	3	5	13
Insufficient information about customer wishes	1	3	14
It is not possible to get to know new markets	1	5	12
It is not possible to explore new export opportunities	1	5	12

Note: IHK – Chamber of Industry and Trade; HW– Chamber of Craft; EE- Estonia

More than half of the companies who did not participate in trade fairs sent employees as visitors to trade fairs. In addition to the participation in trade fairs as exhibitors three of four enterprises sent their employees to trade fairs as visitors.

3.3. Selection of trade fair and goals of trade fair participation

Preparatory work for trade fairs starts from the selection of appropriate trade fair. There are a number of same sector trade fairs and companies have to choose. Trade fair selection is also affected by path dependency. Regular visiting of same trade fairs helps to see same partners again and therefore create more sustainable networks and to get attention of others (Power and Jansson 2008). Two major sources to get information about trade fairs in Mecklenburg-Vorpommern (both Chamber of Commerce and Chamber of Craft) were internet searching and special media (professional journals). Several firms also got information from the Chambers and their suppliers and customers. In Estonia most important sources for information were suppliers, customers, fair organizers and search from internet.

Different aspects play a role in the selection process of the right trade fair. Like any other investment it should be feasible, practical, matching with company strategy and cost effective. It is hard to estimate benefit factors related to trade fairs in advance. Booth costs in Tallinn fairs starts from several hundred euros and in German trade fairs several thousand euros (Estonian Trade Fairs). Budget of participation in international trade fairs can extend to tens of thousands euros. In international trade fairs it is possible to meet sector professionals who are very difficult to contact with other means.

Among the importance factors firms considered internationality (number of customers from foreign countries) and number of professional visitors. Public support was important for smaller firms but in case of medium sized firms it did not play a crucial role.

Although increase in the degree of awareness of the company was frequently mentioned by firms in both countries, Estonian firms had shorter and more concrete goals compared to German firms (Table 3). Estonian firms wished more to get concrete sales negotiations instead of rising general awareness and introducing of novelty products. A significant difference between German and Estonian firms is in the field of exchanging and collecting information during fair participations, which is for Estonian companies much more important than for German SMEs. One reason for that could be related to the small national market in Estonia making it complicated to get a full overview about product and product development in Estonia.

Table 3: Importance of different goals of trade fair participation, % of respondents

	IHK, n=182			HW, n=66			EE, n=52		
	1	2	3	1	2	3	1	2	3
Increase in degree of awareness of the company	80	19	1	76	22	2	77	21	2
Refreshing existing customer contacts	65	30	5	54	40	6	71	23	6
Extraction of new customers	86	12	2	87	13	0	71	27	2

Opening up new markets	52	39	10	51	43	6	58	35	8
Demonstration of presence in the market	59	33	8	52	38	10	69	21	10
Launch/presentation of new products	52	28	20	49	38	13	54	38	8
Increase in awareness of products	65	25	11	64	24	11	63	27	10
Exchange/collection of information	45	44	11	37	46	17	77	21	2
Identification of product trends	44	40	16	49	38	13	42	46	12
Identification of customer wishes	60	32	8	78	20	2	71	25	4
To influence customers' decisions	39	44	17	40	53	6	50	42	8
Completion of sales or contracts	27	38	35	40	34	26	38	44	17

Notes: 1–important; 2 – partially important; 3– unimportant

Common methods of preparation for trade fairs were communicating with customers, building special stands, advertising campaigns and training of stand personnel. There were four tools requiring certain time or financial resources: sending letters to potential customers, calling to potential and existing customers, designing the trade fair stand and preparing special advertising materials like booklets and souvenirs for the trade fair.

3.4 Satisfaction with trade fair results

Major goals for the Estonian firms participating in trade fairs were similar to the firms in German (Bathelt and Schuldt 2008) trade fairs. Among those goals was interaction with potential future customers, interaction with existing customers, learning from innovations and just being presented. It can sound trivial but companies who did perceive a fair as an important marketing tool prepared relatively well for those events and also had a relatively high satisfaction rate. Companies perceived trade fairs as places for searching of information about new trends, competing products and emerging technologies (Table 4). Presenting themselves, demonstration of own existence and of own products were also assessed at a good level. At least in some aspects there was partial satisfaction.

Table 4: Opinion of entrepreneurs about the satisfaction with trade fair goals

	IHK	IHK firms in international fairs	IHK in regional fairs	Crafts	EST
N	161	63	50	49	52

Increase in degree of awareness of the company	1.58	1.35	1.68	1.27	1.48
Refreshing existing customer contacts	1.51	1.26	1.75	1.52	1.44
Extraction of new customers	1.98	1.72	2.12	1.13	1.81
Opening up new markets	2.01	1.79	2.13	1.55	1.92
Demonstration of presence in the market	1.62	1.56	1.77	1.58	1.54
Launch/presentation of new products	1.67	1.49	1.84	1.64	1.69
Increase in awareness of products	1.73	1.59	1.96	1.47	1.50
Exchange/collection of information	1.65	1.65	1.80	1.80	1.48
Identification of product trends	1.75	1.70	1.89	1.64	1.67
Identification of customer wishes	1,67	1,55	1,87	1,24	1,56
To influence customers' decisions	1.99	1.96	2.07	1.66	1.75
Completion of sales or contracts	2.15	2.02	2.32	1.85	1.92

Note: Scale 1-3

Finding new customers was important for approximately three fourth of the firms. However, the satisfaction rate of finding new contacts was approximately one fourth. There could be several reasons like insufficient preparation, unattractive business offers and small recognition. Uncertainty about small firms and their products is a major factor preventing materialization of business deals (Aspers and Darr 2011). The difficulties of finding new customers could be caused by the fact that single fair visits have limited effect on trade. Investing into recognition is a longer process.

Quite satisfied with trade fair results were the Chamber of Craft firms. They have participated mainly in local trade fairs and the gap between expectations and real results is relatively small. There are different expectations for Estonian and German participants in international trade shows (Bathelt and Schuldt 2008). German firms participating in fairs stress more on recognition and raising awareness about their firm. Estonian companies participating in trade fairs have big expectations for finding of new customers, but this goal seldom materializes during the first trade fair visit.

Analysis of the statistical correlation between the answers concerning satisfaction with trade fairs between different groups leads to the observation that the German craftsmen companies are only weakly related to the Estonian SME and German members of the Chamber of Industry and Trade whereas the answering patterns of the Estonian SME and the German Chamber of Industry companies show high values where the Estonian answers have the closest correlation with the German SME focusing on regional fairs. This leads to the statement that due to the small Estonian market international trade fair participation of Estonian companies is comparable to the regional fair participation for German trade and industrial SME.

A statistical ANOVA test reveals significant differences among the groups of SME with a significance level of more than 99.9%. The German Craft companies have the lowest satisfaction level related to fairs with a value of about 1.55. The highest satisfaction level has been reported by German SME of the Chamber of Industry and Trade about regional fairs with a value of about 1.96. The Estonian SMEs share nearly the same satisfaction level of about 1.66 with German SMEs which are active in international fairs.

4. Discussion and Conclusions

Trade fairs help companies with limited time to create sustainable networks that could be even considered as temporary clusters (Aspers and Darr 2011). Trust between companies maintains the environment that is the basis for interaction between companies and consequential internationalization. In trade fairs participants adjust their behaviour, inform each other for the reduction of uncertainty. Furthermore, trade fair participation is a natural part of the enterprise development process and participation in trade fairs is considered as a usual marketing and internationalisation tool by a number of firms. Selection of trade fair and participation method depends on several factors like: existing customer base, support from public sources and price/benefit ratio of particular trade fair.

The survey conducted among the firms in Mecklenburg-Vorpommern and Estonia showed that creation of networks in trade fairs is essential for internationalization. The biggest obstacles to participation in trade fairs are company size and lack of appropriate resources as well as competences.

On the other hand, the success of trade fair participation is linked to the existence of a company strategy and an appropriate fair participation strategy and corresponding operational targets, which has to be accompanied by professional preparation, after fair work and controlling. Here a fair consulting project at Wismar Business School proved that SMEs can be effectively supported in their fair activities.

Trade fair as tool of communication and marketing is expected also to grow among Estonian companies. Short development time forces companies to focus on marketing and quick overview of the markets. The easiest way to do it is to participate in trade fairs. At the same time, building of brand is a time, effort and resources consuming process.

In Estonia, Enterprise Estonia (main enterprise support agency), Estonian Agricultural Registers, Information Board (agro-food industries) and Tallinn City Government offer support schemes for enterprises for participating in trade fairs. Several foreign enterprises participating in Estonian trade fairs come to Estonia with the support of their government. Similar support schemes are available in Mecklenburg-Vorpommern. Still a lot of research work has to be done in order to understand the success factors of trade fair participation. A clear link between company strategies, internationalisation and trade fairs is still missing. Furthermore, the definition of fitting fair strategies and activities depending on the company stage is still open. Finally there is still research to be done to define the commonly accepted success and key performance indicators for trade fair participation.

References

Ahola, E.-K. (2012) Towards an understanding of the role of trade fairs as facilitators of consumer creativity. Vol. 18, no. 5, pp. 321–333.

Aspers, P. and Darr, A. (2011) Trade shows and the creation of market and industry. *The Sociological Review*, vol. 59, no. 4, pp. 758–778.

Bathelt, H. and Schuldt, N. (2008) Between Luminaires and Meat Grinders: International Trade Fairs as Temporary Clusters. *Regional Studies*, vol. 42, no. 6, pp. 853–868.

Bathelt, H. and Schuldt, N. (2010) International Trade Fairs and Global Buzz, Part I: Ecology of Global Buzz. *European Planning Studies*, vol. 18, no. 12, pp. 1957–1974.

Bathelt, H. and Zakrzewski, G. (2007) Messeveranstaltungen als fokale Schnittstellen der globalen Ökonomie. *Zeitschrift für Wirtschaftsgeographie*, vol. 51, no. 1, pp. 14–30.

Beifert, A. and Prause, G. (2006) Internationalization Services for SMEs. An empiric Study. in J. Batog (eds.) *Baltic Business Development - Regional Development, SME Management and Entrepreneurship*, Szczecin: University of Szczecin, pp. 239–257.

Blythe, J. (2000) Objectives and Measures at UK Trade Exhibitions. *Journal of Marketing Management*, vol. 16, no. 1–3, pp. 203–222.

Brown, J.S. and Duguid, P. (1991) Organizational Learning and Communities of Practice. Toward a Unified View of Working. *Organization Science*, vol.2, no.1.

Bruhn, M., Esch, F.-R. and Langner, T. (2009) *Handbuch Kommunikation Grundlagen — Innovative Ansätze — Praktische Umsetzungen*, Gabler.

Deg, R. (2006) 'Basiswissen Public Relations. Professionelle Presse- und Öffentlichkeitsarbeit. VS Verlag Für Sozialwissenschaften, Kapitel 3, pp. 127–132.

Estonian Trade Fairs. Retrieved from http://www.fair.ee [accessed 15 Apr 2013].

Euro Fair Statistics (2011) Global Association of the Exhibition Industry. Retrieved from http://www.auma.de/_pages/d/16_Download/download/FKM/EuroFairStatistics2010.pdf [accessed 19 March 2013].

Fairlink (1999) *Swedish Trade Fairs organization*. Retrieved from http://www.fairlink.se/web/Swedish_manufacturing_companies_1999.aspx [accessed 23 Apr 2013].

Jansson, H. and Sandberg, S. (2008) Internationalization of small and medium sized enterprises in the Baltic Sea Region. *Journal of International Management*, vol 14, no. 1, pp. 65–77.

Johanson, J. and Vahlne, J.-E. (1977) The internationalization process of the firm – a model of knowledge development foreign commitments. *Journal of International Business Studies*, vol. 8, no. 1, pp. 23–32.

Johanson, J. and Mattson, L.G. (1988) Interorganizational relations in industrial relations in industrial systems: A network approach compared with the transaction cost approach. *International Journal of Management and Organization*.

Kerin, R. A. and Cron, W. L. (1987) Assessing Trade Show Functions and Performance: An Exploratory Study. *Journal of Marketing*, vol. 51, no. 3, pp. 87–94.

Meffert, H. (1993) Messen und Ausstellungen als Marketinginstrument. in Goehrmann, K. E. (eds.) *Polit-Marketing auf Messen*, Düsseldorf: Verlag Wirtschaft und Finanzen, pp. 74–96, http://openarchive.cbs.dk/bitstream/handle/10398/7883/druid_05_20.pdf?sequence=1

Mu, G. (2010) The Yiwu Model of China's Exhibition Economy. *Provincial China*, vol. 2, no. 1, pp. 91–115.

Oviatt, B. M. and McDougall, P.P. (1994) Toward a theory of international new ventures. *Journal of International Business Studies*, vol. 25, no. 1, pp. 45–64.

Power D. and Jansson, J. (2008) Cyclical Clusters in Global Circuits: Overlapping Spaces in Furniture Trade Fairs. *Economic Geography*, vol. 84, no. 4, pp. 423–448.

Prause, G. and Kramer, J. (2006). Internationalisierung und Netzwerkbildung im Mittelstand. in Sepp, J.; Hennies, M. & Raudjärv, M. (eds.) *14th scientific conference on economic policy: reports-papers of the XIV scientific and educational conference: (Tartu - Värska, 29 June – 1 July 2006)*, Berlin: Berliner Wissenchafts-Verlag, Mattimar, pp. 543–567.

Prüser, S. (1997) *Messemarketing: Ein netzwerkorientierter Ansatz*. Wiesbaden: Deutscher Universitäts-Verlag.

Ramirez-Pasillas, M. (2008) Resituating Proximity and Knowledge Cross-fertilization in Clusters by Means of International Trade Fairs. *Europan Planning Studies*, vol. 16, no. 5, pp. 643–663.

Schaper, E. (2010) Efficient IP Enforcement at Trade shows in Germany. Licensing Journal. Sep. 2010, Vol. 30 Issue 8. http://web.ebscohost.com/ehost/detail?vid=7&sid=a2249241-3eb7-4cd1-a360-c45741834541%40sessionmgr11&hid=14&bdata=JnNpdGU9ZWhvc3QtbGl2ZSZzY29wZT1zaXRl#db=bth&AN=53490683

Schuldt, N. and Bathelt, H. (2011) International Trade Fairs and Global Buzz, Part II: Practices of Global Buzz. *European Planning Studies*, vol. 19, no. 1, pp. 1–22.

Skov, L. (2006) The role of Trade Fairs in the Global Fashion Business. *Current Sociology*, vol. 54, no. 5, pp. 764–783.

Tanner, J. F. jun and Chonko, L. B. (1995) Trade Show Objectives, Management and Staffing Practices. *Industrial Marketing Management*, vol. 24, no. 4, pp. 257–264.

WM MV (2009) Empirische Studie zum Messeverhalten von Unternehmen der Industrie- und Handelskammern und der Handwerkskammern in Mecklenburg-Vorpommern. *Ministry of Economics and Tourism of the German State of Mecklenburg*, Vorpommern: Schwerin. http://www.google.com/url?sa=t&rct=j&q=&esrc=s&source=web&cd=1&ved=0CC8QFjAA&url=http%3A%2F%2Fservice.mvnet.de%2F_php%2Fdownload.php%3Fdatei_id%3D7924&ei=iD-wUZm_LsPaswaF1YD4Aw&usg=AFQjCNFtH5bpo3ZE2rhK6Qt-UhwPBJOP0w&sig2=WKfVSoFS_9hA03i5YGhnvw&bvm=bv.47534661,d.Yms&cad=rja

Consumer Behaviour in Social Media: Patterns of Sharing Commercial Messages

Iivi Riivits-Arkonsuo[1] and Anu Leppiman[2]

Abstract

The online word-of-mouth is a powerful marketing force and social media present both challenges and opportunities for marketers. Why online word-of-mouth takes place and how it is generated and shared is not fully known. This empirical paper investigates the factors affecting Estonian consumers' willingness to pass on commercial messages and to share online word-of-mouth information in a consumption context. First, an exploratory qualitative study was designed to determine consumer behaviour in social media channels. As the next step, statistic evidence was collected for the online consumer behaviour. The data were analysed using the explorative factor analysis. The representative online survey sample consisted of the responses of 418 respondents. Based on the results of both studies, a consumer decision-making model was developed regarding forwarding of online word-of-mouth.

JEL classification codes: M3, D1

Keywords: online word-of-mouth (WOM) communication, consumer behaviour, social media platforms, word-of-mouth (WOM) marketing, experience marketing

Publication of this paper is granted by the Doctoral School of Economics and Innovation created under the auspices of the European Social Fund.

1. Introduction

The emergence of the phenomenon known as social media (also consumer-to-consumer communication, consumer-generated media) is a hybrid of mixed technology and media origins that enable real-time communication. It utilises multi-media formats (audio and visual presentations) and numerous delivery platforms (Facebook, YouTube, and blogs) with a global reach. These formats and platforms that can be considered an extension of traditional word-of-mouth communication enable consumers to communicate with each other (Mangold and Faulds 2009).

The online WOM communication, an essential part of online consumer interaction, is generating interest in business disciplines, such as marketing, consumer behaviour, economics, and information systems. In order to communicate effectively and efficiently, marketers have to go where the consumers are, and that is online (Keller 2009). The intentional influencing of consumer-to-

---

1   Tallinn University of Technology, PhD student, e-mail: Iivi.Riivits@.ttu.ee
2   Tallinn University of Technology, Professor of Marketing, e-mail:Anu.Leppiman@ttu.ee

consumer communication by professional marketing techniques is called word-of-mouth marketing (WOMM), known also as viral marketing, buzz, or guerrilla marketing (Kozinets et al. 2010, Kaplan and Haenlein 2011). It expands the ability of marketing to move consumers from awareness to engagement, consideration, and loyalty (Hanna et al. 2011). The social media channels give their users a possibility to advocate or sabotage brands. A satisfied and committed consumer can become a distributer of a brand message and can create the brand advocacy. A disappointed consumer can start working against the brand and may hurt brand equity by distributing negative messages (Ward and Ostrom 2006, Keller 2007).

Thus, the online WOM is undoubtedly a powerful marketing force and social media create a marketplace that attracts a wide range of users. Social media present both challenges and opportunities for companies and marketers. While companies cannot directly control consumer-to-consumer messages, they still are in the position to influence the conversations between consumers. In that case, control is in the hands of the consumers, they define the rules. Communication on the social media platforms involves a trust-based dialogue between a consumer and a company (Diffley et al. 2011, Keller 2009). Marketers should try to identify 'social influencers' in social media by encouraging users to spread positive online WOM regarding selected brands and discouraging them from sharing negative information within their personal networks (Chu and Kim 2011).

On the other hand, consumers prefer interacting online with each other rather than directly with marketers (Campell et al. 2012). Evidence has been found that social media users value activities with marketing purposes in social media applications negatively. Based on their studies, professional research companies (Millward Brown 2010, Strativity Group 2010) claim that consumers' attitude towards marketing communication in the social media is rather dismissive since they consider social media to be a communication, not an advertising platform. Consumers do not wish to see social media as a place where aggressive business disturbs their communication flow. In the social media, consumers expect a dialogue, in which brands listen to what they have to say rather than simply pushing promotional marketing messages without considering what consumers think, feel, and want (Akar and Topçu 2011, Fogel 2010, Keller 2009).

Why and how online WOM takes place in the online social sphere is not fully understood (Chu and Kim, 2011, Cheung and Lee, 2012). Most of the research addresses the impact of online WOM communication, while research on the reasons why consumers engage in WOM in online consumer-opinion platforms has remained rather limited (Cheung and Thadani 2010). Cheung and Lee (2012) agree that online WOM studies focus primarily on the impact of online

WOM consumer purchasing decisions, while there is a lack of understanding of how and why consumers are willing to spend their time sharing their purchasing experiences with other people in the online environment.

The present study analyses the consumer behaviour in social media channels. The aim is to find the patterns of generation and sharing of online WOM.

The Internet is a global medium, yet its content is local to each country. Chu and Kim (2011) and Henning-Thurau et al. (2004) have highlighted the need for exploring consumers' online articulation in different cultural contexts. The aim of this research is to study the online behaviour at the Estonian example. According to Eurostat (2011), 73% of the Estonian population aged 16–74 are regular Internet users. Thus, Estonia ranks as one of the countries with the highest Internet penetration rates in Europe today, making it a suitable market to study online issues.

Against this background, the following research questions can be formulated:

RQ 1: Which factors affect the way Estonian consumers pass on commercial messages and share positive and negative online WOM?

RQ 2: What is the consumer decision making model while forwarding online WOM?

2. Theoretical Considerations

Online WOM differs from traditional, offline WOM in many ways. Online WOM communication possesses unprecedented scalability and speed of diffusion. It is more persistent and accessible and more measurable than traditional WOM (Cheung and Lee 2012). Traditional WOM emanates from a sender who is known to the receiver of the information, thus the credibility of the communicator and the message is known to the receiver. The electronic nature of online WOM eliminates the receiver's ability to judge the credibility of the sender and his/her message in most applications (ibid). When the conversation moves online, the number of participants increases dramatically and the potential impact of the conversation is magnified exponentially. Moreover, the transmission messages related to a brand, company or product can occur in an exponentially growing way (Kaplan and Haenlein 2011, Fogel 2010).

Hennig-Thurau et al. (2004) report that due to the conceptual closeness of online WOM and traditional offline WOM communication, consumer motives that have been identified in the literature as relevant for traditional WOM can also be of relevance for online WOM. Brown et al. (2007) disagree and insist that existing offline theory may be inappropriate to describe online WOM and its influence on consumer behaviour. In our paper we support the view of Brown and colleagues. They offer a conceptual model of the online interaction and information evaluation process. The three key constructs driving the social online relationships are tie strength, homophily and source credibility. The tie strength refers to the intensity of an interactive relationship between an individual and a Web site. The homophily means the congruence between a user's psychological attributes and Web site content. The source credibility is the perceived competence of the Web site and its membership.

The study by Chu and Kim (2011) extends the conceptual model of the online interaction created by Brown and colleagues. They identify social factors that influence consumers' engagement in online WOM 'in the online hangout places' (Facebook and MySpace and other social media platforms). They point out that consumer conversations in social media involve a high level of voluntary self-discourse among users, for instance profile data such as names and affiliations. Consumers can associate themselves with brands by becoming a friend or fan. A conceptual model developed and tested by Chu and Kim identifies tie strength, homophily, trust, normative and informational interpersonal influence as important drivers of online WOM behaviour.

According to Cheung and Thadani (2010), factors related to a receiver's psychological state, such as purchase intention, attitude, information adoption, and trust, are the most commonly investigated outcomes of online WOM communication, especially purchase intention. The online WOM behaviour is primarily explained from individual rational perspective with the emphasis on cost and benefit (Cheug and Lee 2012). Hennig-Thurau and colleagues (2004) provide insight into a variety of different motives for online WOM communication and their impact on consumer behaviour. The resulting analysis suggests that consumers' desire for social interaction, desire for economic incentives, their concern for other consumers, and the potential to enhance their own self-worth are the primary factors leading to online WOM behaviour. Nambisan and Baron (2007, 2009) list four benefits that consumers gain from their interactions in virtual consumer environments: cognitive or learning benefits, social integrative benefits, personal integrative benefits, and hedonic benefits.

Kietzmann et al. (2012) make the difference between intrinsic and extrinsic consumer motivation. Intrinsic motivation is driven by an intense interest and involvement in the activity itself, curiosity, enjoyment, peer recognition, a personal sense of challenge, accomplishment or belonging, whereas extrinsic motivation is driven by the desire to achieve some external reward.

The results of Cheung and Lee's study (2012) show that sense of belonging to the community, reputation, and enjoyment of helping others are the most critical factors that encourage consumers to share their experiences with others in the context of online consumer-opinion platforms. All above factors are related to the spread of positive WOM. Sen and Lerman (2007) expect the negativity effect that has been so frequently observed in offline behaviour to exist in online consumer behaviour as well. In this case, consumers are more likely to consider negative than positive online WOM for their decision-making.

Online consumer behaviour is explained with Csikszentmihalyi's theory of flow. In online environments it means that first a consumer's activity is goal directed (for instance, searching for a book at Amazon.com) but then it shifts into an experiential activity. Thus, the flow occurs for both goal-directed and experiential activities. The flow is acknowledged as a useful construct. Nevertheless, it is difficult to conceptualise and measure since the impact of the flow on online consumer behaviour is not fully known (Lee and Chen 2010, Hoffman and Novak 2009).

Consumer behaviour is mostly modelled as a cognitive process, an intellectual sequence of thinking, evaluating, and deciding. The inputs to the process are the most basic bits of data available to the consumer, stimuli from the environment in the form of marketing messages, and conversations with friends and relatives (Foxall 2005). In the context of our paper a marketing message can, for example, be a viral video shared via YouTube, a campaign in Facebook or new product information in Twitter. It is a positive and memorable former consumption experience and an established relationship with the brand act as stimulus. According to Foxall (ibid.), the cognitive process itself consists of the mental treatment of this data as consumers store the data, links it with existing ideas and memories, and evaluates its relevance to their personal goals. The outputs are the attitudes the consumer forms toward an advertised brand, an intention to buy and if the attitude and intention are positive, the act of purchase. Our analysis is based on the consumer decision-making model described above.

In order to measure the online behaviour of consumers, we carried out an extensive literature search and review that focuses on the following concepts: the conceptual model of offline and online social networking (Brown et al. 2007), the model of online WOM in social networking sites (Chu and Kim 2011), and the typology for motives of consumer online articulation (Hennig-Thurau et al. 2004).

3. Research Methods

3.1. Qualitative study

First, an exploratory qualitative study was planned to determine consumer behaviour in social media channels. The study was designed in two stages because of the consideration that the qualitative content analysis would offer useful insights to construct items for a quantitative survey.

The media users (n=16) were asked to answer the questions how they pass on commercial messages and share positive and negative online WOM. The age of the informants ranged from 21 to 35, and 8 females and 8 males were involved, their education varying from high school to postgraduate degrees. The interviewee group was composed of students, IT-specialists, health professionals and bank employees as well as high-level managers. The sample was selected with an attempt to concentrate on heavy or at least medium users of various social media channels (such as Facebook, Twitter, LinkedIn). Face-to-face in-depth interviews were carried out in a semi-structured manner by MBA students participating in the Marketing Research course during the spring semester 2012. Every student chose an interviewee from his/her own social network.

An interview guide was developed from existing consumer behaviour concepts and discussed within the group under the supervision of one of the authors, the professor of the Marketing Research class. An interview lasted on average about 60 minutes and all the interviews were recorded. The transcripts of the recorded interviews were produced by each of the interviewing student. The interviewees were asked to describe their social media channel usage and habits, to explain their motives to pass on messages, to share positive and negative opinions; they were also asked to describe their opinion about campaigns and to explain their relationship with brand related online sites. Each interviewer analysed the text he/she had produced and portrayed the behaviour of the respondent in the class. The interviews were initially analysed by the students, later the codes and categories were created by the authors of this paper.

3.2. Quantitative survey

In the next step, our goal was to collect statistic evidence for the consumer online behaviour. Since only a few established scales for measuring the willingness to share commercial messages are known, we used the results of the qualitative study to construct the items of the scale as well as items identified in (Brown et al. 2007, Chu and Kim 2011, Hennig-Thurau et al. 2004), modifying the latter to suit the context of the present study. In order to generate scale items, first we refined the scales from the *Marketing Scales Handbook* (Bruner et al. 2005), using individual semi-structured interviews as well as input from a marketing research supplier *Turu-uuringute AS* (Estonian Surveys Ltd). The qualitative content analysis of the interview material provided useful insights into defining a list of items. Our 7-point measurement scales included both behavioural and attitudinal indicators[3].

The data were collected from a representative sample of Estonian Internet users. A self-administrated online survey was conducted, using the online panel of a professional research agency *Turu-uuringute AS* (Estonian Surveys Ltd). An e-mail was sent to 1,350 panellists inviting them to fill out a web questionnaire. In four days, responses of 542 panellists were returned. These data were weighed in order to correct the results of the sample so that they would match the model of the whole Estonian Internet users as close as possible. Information about the demographic profile of the sample is presented in Table 1. The table shows those Facebook user profiles who completed the questionnaire.

Table 1. The demographic profile of the sample, n=418

The variable	Categories	Percentage of the sample
Age (M=35.55; SD 12.68)	15-19	4.5
	20-29	37.9
	30-39	25.4
	40-49	16.1
	50-59	10.7
	60+	5.5
Gender	Female	54.8
	Male	45.2
Education	Primary or basic	6.6
	Secondary (high school)	44.0
	College or University	44.3
	Other	5.1
Place of residence	Capital	31.7
	City > 50,000 inhabitants	18.4
	Town, 5,000-50,000 inhabitants	23.8
	Smaller town < 5,000 inhabitants	11.6
	Village, rural area	14.5

After answering 'no' to the question 'How often do you use social media network sites (such as Facebook, Twitter, Youtube)?' the questionnaire was closed for 56 (10.3%) panellists. The question about Facebook account usage

---

3   The original Estonian wording of each item is available upon request from the authors

screened out another 68 panellists (13.9%) who responded that they do not use Facebook. First of all, our focus was on Facebook users and their motivations to share both positive and negative content. Facebook is the superpower of the social media world, thus offering a tempting platform for marketers to build a viral-driven, multidirectional communication with consumers (Chu 2011; Holzner 2008). Likewise, Facebook is the most popular social network site in Estonia According to current Estonian Facebook Statistics, there are **459,860 Facebook users in Estonia. Facebook penetration rate** is **35.62%** of the country's population and **47.42%** of all Estonian Internet users (Socialbakers.com 2012).

Deriving from the above, the next items directly addressed Facebook users since this network platform allows users to build up a list of 'friends' and interact with them by sharing personal information, pictures and other self-presentational items. First, 32 items characterising behaviour and attitudes were entered into an analysis of principal components to examine the dimensionality of the entire set of items. Since the correlations of some items were too low and thus the Cronbach's α was too low, we abandoned the initial matrix containing 10 components.

A principal component analysis (PCA) was conducted on 27 items with orthogonal rotation (varimax). The Kayser-Meyer-Olkin measure verified the sampling adequacy of the analysis, KMO=0.832 ('great' according to Field 2009), and all KMO values for individual items were > 0.7, which is well above the acceptable limit of 0.5 (Field 2009). Barlett's test of sphericity $\chi^2(351)$ = 5,591.121 $p < 0.001$ indicated that correlations between items were sufficient for the PCA. An initial analysis was made to obtain eigenvalues for each component in the data. Seven components had eigenvalues over Kaiser's criterion of 1 and in combination explained 67.20 % of the variance. Given the large sample size and the convergence of the scree plot and Kaiser's criterion on seven components, a number of components were retained in the final analysis. Table 3 shows the factor loading after rotation.

4. Results and Discussion

The key issues and categories that emerged from the qualitative stage are presented in Table 2. Typical answers are categorised so that the sex of the respondent (F – female, M – male) as well as his/her age and field of activity are visible. This enabled us to open the social-demographic structure of our interviewees in relation to their arguments. The comments of one and the same respondent can be found in rather contradictory categories, thus illustrating how ambivalent respondents' attitude towards WOM marketing is.

Participants like and share only the brands they really like, and only if they have had a very positive experience. They hope to promote the welfare of the company as well as that of the people working there by sharing brands and posting on the wall of the latter. The common denominator for those answers would be 'An outstanding experience brings along sharing'.

The interviewees are not generous when it comes to liking and sharing brands in Facebook. They see clicking the like button as equal to giving an opinion, thus they will not do that without considering it first, in order not to devaluate the like button in their own eyes. At the same time they are of the opinion that other users misuse the like button by clicking it too fast. If no trust has immersed between the brand and the consumer, there is no liking and no sharing. The users understand that if they like and share, they promote WOM marketing. Yet, they do not want to do that, they dislike it – this was mentioned several times in the interviews. We interpret that as unwillingness to co-operate, keeping distance. The category labelled 'direct distrust' includes even more distrust. Brand communication is not perceived as true and honest, thus a conscious distance is put between brand communication and oneself.

Table 2. Categorizing the results of the in-depth interviews

Categories	Typical examples
A good experience creates a wish to help	F, 25, a health professional: *Good service in real life has earned a virtual praise* F, 31, architect: *I thought I'll help them and write a positive comment, maybe it promotes their sales* M, 23, assistant: *I gave feedback about the service person, hoping to influence the salary in a positive way*
Unwillingness to co-operate since the brand is not worth it	M, 28, a soon-to-be student in the USA: *Well, all companies that think something about themselves are represented there, but it is seldom that a company makes me share something.* F, 31, an architect: *I find sharing ads bothersome. I do not want to be turned into a mediator of advertising ... Even if this is the ultimate aim of Facebook and that's how they earn money. But I do not want to offer them the satisfaction of me sharing that stuff.* F, 28, a health professional: *'Liking' is the expression of my opinion. Some click the like button all the time. But me, I use it only if I really like something.*
Direct distrust	M, 34, a civil servant: *The brand is not interested in me; it only cares for my money. The person writing for the brand, he [she] does not actually care for me.* F, 31, an architect: *There are companies that launch one-time campaigns and get their money and after that don't care for the client anymore. It bothers me a lot if a brand writes in the first person.*

One-time exploitation	F, 35, a financier: *I have written what I have 'had to write', in order to play a game. But I am a fan only in the Facebook, only because of the consumer games. Not in real life. Once the campaign is over, I delete the company from my like-list.* F, 27, a health professional: *I personally do it like that: once the campaign is over, I remove myself from that page. The settings enable that. I am there only to get something. Yes, and yet I never get anything. So unfair!*
Mutual benefit: I help you, you help me	M, 28, a programmer: *There should be discounts for those who become friends with a brand in Facebook.*
Expectations that the brand would care	M, 21, a student: *If I have questions and I get answers from there, it is great. ... We all try hard to produce the best things in the world but it does happen once in a while that something fails ... Nokia is good at communicating and helping. There are many other companies that help in a very friendly manner in Twitter.* F, 29, a freelancer: *The brand takes my comments and feedback into consideration. It is important that I get a reaction to a comment of mine. It is as if someone were interested in what I think, as if someone cared.* F31, architect: *... those who really care about their sales and clients, they have a very personal approach to all clients and thus we can say, they care.*
An outstanding experience brings along sharing	M, 28, bank employee: *That was years ago, but one of the most genius things I have seen in my life was the way an advertisement was built up (an alcohol brand, Pisang). ... Multidimensional, I shared that with all my friends since it was really – wow!* F, 29 product manager, describes an advertising campaign of a bike store: *A bike in an ice cube was put up in front of the store towards the end of winter. Then they let the people estimate when the bike would melt out of the ice. The one whose estimate was the closest, became a prize. It was a very popular campaign and the consumers constantly demanded new information (new pictures on Facebook) in order to see how much ice was left.*
Unwillingness to share negative online WOM	F, 31, PhD student of gene technology: *I definitely won't post a thing like that neither in Facebook nor anywhere else in social media. Even if I were really angry with them. I could send the company an e-mail but I would not tell others about it. Maybe if it had something to do with someone else, á la watch out – maybe then I would.* F, 27, health professional: *I do not want to use my one name in that case because then everybody would check out who she is.*

Some interviewees are willing to co-operate with the activity of the brands in the social media, calculating the benefit they personally can gain. Participation in consumer games in order to win a prize would be one of those acts of co-operation. The interviewees acknowledge that they do not care for those brands in real life. Consumer games are seen as unemotional and flat; the respondents are of the opinion that the brands organise those games in order not to be forgotten since the competition uses the games as well. After the game is over, the brand is removed from the list of things liked. This can be categorised as 'onetime exploitation'.

The category labelled 'Mutual benefit: I help you, you help me' means that the users are willing to co-operate with brands if they expect more personal gain. In that case they perceive it as an exchange: those who share brands and post on the wall of the latter get discounts or good offers.

A brand is perceived as caring (category 'Expectations that the brand would care') if every consumer post signalling a problem or dissatisfaction receives an immediate answer; besides, a solution is offered that satisfies the consumer – that is exactly what shows interest in the consumer. In that way the brand can even become a friend.

Both consumer games and general online brand communication are expected to be extraordinary, one-time, enabling an experience. If those preconditions are fulfilled, the users are willing to share the brand, to co-operate with the brand since the exchange that takes place is perceived as fair: the brand offers a memorable experience and in return the consumer shares that. In other words, consumers participate in WOM marketing. A mutually beneficial co-operation takes place: the brand invests in the consumer and thus the consumer is willing to invest in the brand. It is expected that, in a dialogue, the brands answer fast to consumers' questions and help to find solutions to consumers' problems.

The interviewees reported that mostly they do not want to share a negative consumption experience in Facebook – they prefer to share it in offline WOM. Negative information is distributed only if it is serious enough to be a threat to others who, thus, need to be warned. Several interviews revealed that since negative comments are bound to the name of the person who posted it, the users prefer to avoid negative posts since these are public.

Kaplan and Haenlein (2011) suggest that only messages that are both memorable and sufficiently interesting to be passed on to others have the potential to spur a WOM marketing phenomenon. Effective messages often contain an element of surprise, combined with other emotions that can be either positive (joy) or even negative (fear). Effective messages should be memorable, extraordinary and contrasting. On the other hand, even the most successful buzz cannot compensate for a bad product, a bad service, an inappropriate price, or insufficient distribution (ibid.). Thus, prior consumption experience is a factor that may determine whether and in which tone a message is forwarded.

Consumers may or may not trust marketing messages. The results of the analysis of our qualitative data show that consumers do notice whether a brand and the marketing personnel are dishonest, and they take no actual interest in the consumer. If the message is exciting, contrasting and catching; the brand communication is credible and the former experience is good, the message is shared. Therewith the consumer becomes a message conveyor for the brand – something that some of the participants claimed to avoid.

Next, the results of the quantitative stage of the research will be discussed. Table 3 summarises the exploratory factor analysis.

We call Factor 1 'opinion seeking, opinion giving and opinion passing' after Chu and Kim (2011). Online WOM can be discussed using those three aspects, whereby the consumer often unites all the three roles. Thus, multidirectional communication takes place: from consumer to consumer, from brand to consumer, from consumer to brand.

Table 3   Summarised exploratory factor analysis results of consumer behaviour in online questionnaire[4], n=418

		Components						
FACTORS	Item	1	2	3	4	5	6	7
opinion seeking, opinion giving and opinion passing α=0,848	If brands ask for my opinion about how to improve their services/products for the consumers, I readily share that	0.72						
% of variances 14.82	It is important that brands ask for the consumer's opinion about how to improve their services/products for the consumers	0.70						
	I readily read the posts and comments of those who have tried the product/services before me and recommend them	0.69						
	The posts and comments makes it easier for me to purchase a product/service	0.68						
	If a company/brand reacts to a post, it is a sign of caring for the consumers	0.61						
	I consider it helpful and necessary that brands that are my friends send posts about their new products and services to my wall	0.58						
	One should write comments/send posts about really good brands	0.56			0.52			
	I find it the right thing to do to warn others about a bad service/product or a negative experience	0.54						
An outstanding experience α=0.884	There are brands whose message in the social media is so different from others that I have clicked the like button and become a fan		0.88					
% of variances	There are brands whose message in the social me-		0.87					

---

4   Factor loadings are generated by a principal component analysis; those loading < 0.4 are not included.

13.05	dia is so different from others that it has led me to write a comment or send posts				
	There are brands whose message in the social media is so different from others that it has led me to share them since I want my friends to see the message as well	0.86			
	There are brands whose message in the social media is so different from others that it has led me to consume the services or products of that company	0.83			
	If a service/product is especially good, one just has to click the like button and share it	0.43			
Expected mutual exchange α=0.858	Those who like and share a brand, should be made special offers		0.91		
% of variances 12.21	Those who write comments on a brand and send posts, should receive special offers		0.87		
	I were ready to be a fan, to like and share, if I expected more personal benefit		0.81		
A wish to help α=0.782	A sales/service person who served me well can be helped by writing positive comments or sending posts			0.81	
% of variances 8.56	A company can be helped by writing positive comments or sending posts			0.80	
	About companies who really care for their clients positive comments should be written/posts should be sent		0.44	0.67	
Ignoring consumer games α=0.778	I find sharing campaign ads and consumer games bothersome				0.85
% of variances 8.37	I do not even open the consumer games my friends share				0.83
	I never press the like button or share something in order to get a prize				0.73
Being picky about sharing α=0.667	'Liking' and sharing – I am very picky about the brands I like and share				0.82
% of variances 7.07	If I like and share, then only because I really like something				0.80
	Many companies offer good service/good products but in order to share and like them, it must be at least outstanding				0.67
Unwillingness to write negative comments if one's name is visible α=0.777	I do not want to post negative comments so that everybody can see them				0.89
% of variances 6.33	I do not want to post negative comments using my own name				0.88

Using the speed and the large size of the communication network of social media, the consumers can express their positive and negative opinions, read positive and negative opinions of other users and if necessary, extend and edit them. Brands are expected to give information about new products or services, and the consumers are willing to co-operate with them by expressing their opinion. Brands are expected to give feedback, to react, once the consumer has contacted them either to consult them or to tell about a problem. The consumers are willing to promote brands by sharing their positive opinion if asked by the brand.

We named Factor 2 'Outstanding experience'. A special, extraordinary experience emerges if a brand has used something in its communication that the receiver perceives as interesting, memorable, impressive, and contrasting (aka different from what one has experienced before). Meaningful experience is one of the keywords in experience marketing and according to the experience marketing conception, constructing experiences is one of the important additional values as well as a competitive advantage for a consumer (Pine and Gilmore 1999). An element of the experience-based product or service, and in the present online context that of constructing experience-based communication, is contrast, i.e. a difference from the perspective of the consumer. The experience based product or service should be different with respect to consumer's everyday life (Tarssan and Kylänen 2009, 2007).

Factor 3 is the expected mutual exchange. In the qualitative part of our survey we called that mutual benefit, 'you help me, I help you'-logic. The consumers are willing to co-operate, to create content and to forward messages but only if a beneficial exchange is offered, for instance by sending them special offers. The quantitative survey empirically confirms that motive. Therefore we include a rational criterion 'how do I benefit from that' in our consumer decision-making model.

Factor 4, labelled as a wish to help, conveys thankfulness, a wish to give the company something in return for a good experience (Hennig-Thurau 2004). The attitude towards the brand is positive and the consumers do not think of direct benefits. Rather, they think of promoting the brand.

Factor 5, ignoring consumer games, shows that there is a group of users that finds such games bothersome. On the other hand, our qualitative research revealed descriptions of some emotionally strongly loaded consumer games that were constructed so that consumers perceived them as different, original and contrasting – thus, the games were in accordance with the elements of experience-based design model that the organizers had applied either consciously or subconsciously.

In the factor analysis we removed questions that were asked from those who had participated in consumer games. Those who had never played consumer games made up 15% of our sample. The factor analysis is based on calculating innumerous correlations. The missing 15% (n=63) of respondents' values meant that the size of the sample that the factor analysis started with decreased by more than a half. In order not to reduce the size of the sample n=418, we neglected that. We claim that the impact of the games on the consumers' decision-making process should not be underestimated.

Factor 6, 'Being picky about sharing', shows that the so-called sharing threshold is high. The consumers do not acknowledge brands heedlessly, even if the brands expose themselves and just one mouse click is needed to 'like' and share in Facebook. Thus, liking and sharing have a certain meaning for the consumer that presupposes a certain decision process.

Factor 7, 'Unwillingness to write negative comments if one's name is visible': the qualitative study showed the position of the interviewees when it comes to negative WOM: they prefer not to forward negative WOM since these posts are not anonymous. One of the items we constructed was *'I do not want to post negative comments so that everybody can see them'*, which we hoped to test empirically. The quantitative data collected from consumers and analysed by the methods we chose confirmed that distributing negative WOM is thwarted by the fact that the negative content is bound to the name of the person distributing it, and the consumers would like to remain anonymous while doing that.

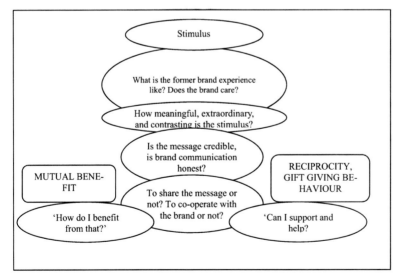

Fig. 1.   *Consumer decision-making model while forwarding online WOM composed by the authors*

Results of the quantitative research and explorative factor analysis enabled us to work out a consumer decision-making model presented in Figure 1. We complement the model also with theoretical and conceptual approaches that support the model.

Here we introduce the reciprocity discussion. It does not involve the brand committed consumer who considers forwarding online WOM only if mutual benefit is included. A very positive consumption experience creates a consumer's true wish to help and promote the company. The consumer is motivated in online communication to give the company something in return for a good experience (Hennig-Thurau et al. 2004).

Reciprocity is the norm that we should do to others as they do to us, calling for positive responses to favourable treatment and negative responses to unfavourable treatment (Hewstone et al. 1996). In reciprocity, while striving towards promoting and being promoted, the aim is a balance, that is the more one promotes the more he/she expects to receive in return, and vice versa, the more one has to receive, the more he/she can give to the other party (Antonucci and Jackson 1990; Leppiman 2010). A different point of view is expressed by Chakrabarti and Berthon (2012) who call the wish to help a brand with positive online WOM 'gift giving behaviour' that they treat like a social emotion. According to them, the triad of social emotions, social media and gift giving are key driving forces of Web 2.0. For this reason, a criterion 'Can I support and help' is included in our consumer decision-making model.

According to our consumer decision-making model, extraordinariness, contrast and meaningful experience are an important step on the way to the decision whether to forward the message or not. Experiences may occur as a result of online and offline activities. Current technologies and the growth of the Internet have both enabled and strengthened the opportunities for experience-oriented offerings beyond limitations of time and place (Chang et al. 2010). Digital technology enhances any individual's capability to perform. Being a technology of experiences, it can dramatically boost communication immediacy and effectiveness. According to Korn and Pine (2011), almost all companies can benefit from experience-designed digital innovation, if not for their offerings, then for their internal processes. Digital technology enables new-to-the-world possibilities for the delivery of emotion-evoking experiences by an ever-broadening array of methods that engage our human senses through endless sights, sounds, and other sensations. Experience marketing is usually broadly defined as any form of consumer-focused marketing activity that creates a connection to consumers. Most experiences occur directly when consumers shop, buy and consume products. Experiences (such as feelings, fantasies and fun) can also occur indirectly, when consumers are exposed to advertising and marketing communications, including Web sites (Brakus et al. 2009).

Chakrabarti and Berthon (2012) argue that the key to the experience economy is that the experience is something the companies produce for the consumer. With the rise of Web 2.0 and social media, just as consumers are becoming producers of products and services, they are also becoming producers of experiences both for each other and for companies. In the opinion of Chakrabarti and Berthon, the primary experience of value in the social media is emotion. Whereas consumption on Web 1.0 was mostly goal-oriented, rational, and functional, consumption on Web 2.0 is exploratory, idiosyncratic, and social. Thus, the newly emerging category of emotions is 'social emotions'. All emotions can be experienced in a social setting (hope, fear), however only social emotions occur specifically in relationship with others (pride, admiration). Social emotions have become the experiences that are collectively produced by consumers in social media.

5. Conclusions

The results of this study enabled us to work out a consumer decision-making model while forwarding online WOM. The model was confirmed empirically conducting a quantitative survey. The results of both the qualitative and the quantitative study show that consumers are guided by a set of rational, emotional, cognitive and experience-based factors when passing on commercial messages and sharing positive and negative online WOM. Extraordinariness, contrast and meaningful experience are an important step towards the decision whether to forward the message or not.

Our research gives several marketing implications. The respondents' attitude towards WOM marketing is ambivalent. In order to lead the consumer to cooperate with the brand in the social-media, and to motivate the consumer to promote a company with positive WOM, certain stimuli are needed. The stimulus has to be special, arousing attention, and memorable. It can be a campaign that arouses the attention of the consumer, but it can also be a positive brand experience. The brand that has not earned consumers' trust cannot be helped with smart marketing messages, including consumer games. If the consumers are not committed to the brand, they consider forwarding online WOM only if mutual benefit is included. A very positive consumption experience, especially if it is long term and based on trust, is leading to a consumer's true wish to help and promote the company. Since social media marketing is two-way, it means that a brand (including company's marketing staff) has to be constantly ready to answer consumer's questions, to apologise, if necessary, and to solve problems. If the brand does not behave like that, the trust for that decreases immediately. The results of the present study show that (Estonian) consumers are rather unwilling to distribute negative WOM. In our cultural context, a bad experience, communication perceived as neither honest nor true rather leads to ignoring the marketing activities of the brand.

This study has some limitations that are important to be discussed for the benefit of future research. The qualitative interviews and the social media user portraits of the respondents were completed by students. Since it was an MBA course and the students had a free choice of interviewees, the latter tended to be similar to the MBA students – they were graduate professionals aged about 30. This group, though, is in their social media usage more careful and decent than some other groups. We especially miss the arguments of young people aged below 20, as well as those of real brand ambassadors who would have been able to describe the mechanism that has turned them from users to brand ambassadors and distributors of the message. Collecting target group-centred qualitative data from the youth and from brand ambassadors will be the task of future research.

A drawback of the quantitative method was that we had to dismiss many exciting items since the correlation between these items and with other items was too low. Some emerged components also had too low Cronbach's α, being useless for scientific purposes. As a good value for α is taken around 0.8 or higher (Field 2009), these items were omitted from our questionnaire.

Items associated with attitudes towards consumer games created so much missing value that it disturbed the analysis and these items had to be removed. Since for many brands organising of consumer games is an opportunity to introduce their products and services and to include consumers, the impact of such games on the consumers' decision-making process cannot be underestimated. As mentioned above, we are searching an appropriate way to analyse the data as well in the future.

In the future, qualitative input should be collected from more variable target groups. A new quantitative survey should be conducted and the data analysed using the confirmative factor analysis and structural equation modelling. The experience-based marketing conception also offers an attractive research perspective. As far as we know, no empirical research has been conducted on the aspect of consumer behaviour of that conception. The conception of designing experiences has been used mainly in creating tourism, culture and entertainment services (Korn and Pine 2011; Tarssanen and Kylänen 2009).

Certainly experience-based marketing can be used in a multitude of additional areas (including in the digital environment) that will be focused on in our next studies.

References

Akar, E. and Topçu B. 2011. An Examination of the Factors Influencing Consumers' Attitudes toward Social Media Marketing. Journal of Internet Commerce, 10:1, pp. 35–67.

Antonucci, A. and Jackson, J. S. 1990. The Role of Reciprocity and Social Support. John Wiley & Sons. New York.

Brakus, J. J., Schmitt, B. H. and Zarantonello, L. 2009. Brand experience: what is it? How it measured? Does it affect loyalty? Journal of Marketing, 73, pp. 52–68.

Brown, J., Broderick, A.J. and Lee, N. 2007. Word of mouth communication within online communities: conceptualizing the online social network. Journal of Interactive Marketing. Vol. 21 Issue 3, pp. 2–20.

Bruner, G.C. II, Hensel, P.J. and James K.E. 2005. Marketing Scales Handbook, Vol. III. Chicago: American Marketing Association.

Campbell, C., Piercy, N. and Heinrich, D. 2012. When companies get caught: The effect of consumers discovering undesirable firm engagement online. Journal of Public Affairs. Volume 12 Number 2, pp. 612–169.

Chang, W.L., Yuan, S.T. and Hsu C.W. 2010. Creating the Experience Economy in E-Commerce. Communications of the ACM. Vol.53. No 7, pp.122–127.

Chakrabarti, R. and Berthon, P. 2012. Gift giving and social emotions: experience as content. Journal of Public Affairs. Volume 12 Number 2, pp. 154–161.

Cheung C.M.K. and Lee M. K.O. 2012. What drives consumers to spread electronic word of mouth in online consumer-opinion platforms. Decision Support Systems 53, pp. 218–225.

Cheung C.M.K. and Thadani, D.R. 2010. The Effectiveness of Electronic Word-of-Mouth Communication: A Literature Analysis. 23rd Bled eConference eTrust: Implications for the Individual, Enterprises and Society. June 20-23, Bled, Slovenia, pp. 329–345.

Chu, S.-C. and Kim, J. 2011. Determinants of consumer engagement in electronic word-of-mouth (eWOM) in social networking sites. International Journal of Advertising, 30(1), pp. 47–75.

Diffley, S., Kearns, J., Bennett, W. and Kawalek, P. 2011. Consumer Behaviour in Social Networking Sites: Implications for Marketers. Irish Journal of Management, Vol. 30 Issue 2, pp. 47–65.

Eurostat 2011. Accessed June, 18, 2012 available at epp.eurostat.ec.europa.eu.

Field, A. 2009. Discovering statistics using SPSS. Sage Publication Ltd.

Fogel, S. 2010. Issues in Measurement of Word of Mouth in Social Media Marketing. International Journal of Integrated Marketing Communications. Vol. 2 Issue 2: pp. 54–60.

Foxall, G.R., 2005. Understanding Consumer Choice. Palgrave Macmillan.

Hanna, R., Rohm, A. and Crittenden, V.L. 2011. We're all connected: The power of the social media ecosystem. Business Horizonz.54, pp. 265–273.

Hennig-Thurau,T., Gwinner, K.P., Walsh. G. and Gremler, D.D. 2004. Electronic word-of-mouth via consumer-opinion platforms: what motivates consumers to articulate themselves on the Internet? Journal of Interactive Marketing. Vol. 18/No 1, pp. 38–52.

Hewstone, M., Stroebe, W. and Stephenson, G. M. 1996. Introduction to Social Psychology. Blackwell Publishers Ltd. Oxford, UK.

Hoffman, D.I. and Novak, T.P. 2009. Flow online: Lessons learned and future prospects. Journal of Interactive Marketing 23, pp. 23–34.

Holzner, S. 2008. Facebook Marketing: Leverage Social Media to Grow Your Business. Que Publishing.

Kaplan, A.M., and Haenlein, M. 2011. Two Hearts in Three-quarter Time: How to Waltz the Social Media/Viral Marketing Dance. Business Horizons. Vol. 54, Issue 3, pp. 181–288.

Keller, E. 2007. Unleashing the Power of Word of Mouth: Creating Brand Advocacy to Drive Growth. Journal of Advertising Research. December, pp. 448–452.

Keller, K.L. 2009. Building Strong Brands in a Modern Marketing Communications Environment. Journal of Marketing Communications Vol. 15, Nov. 2–3, pp.139–155.

Kietzmann, J.H., Silvestre, B.S., McCarthy, I.P., and Pitt, L.F. 2012. Unpacking the social media phenomenon: towards a research agenda. Journal of Public Affairs. Volume 12 Number 2, pp. 109–119.

Korn, K.C. and Pine II J. B. 2011. The Typology of Human Capability: a new guide to re-thinking the potential for digital experience offerings, Strategy & Leadership, Vol. 39 Issue 4, pp. 35–40.

Kozinets, R. V., de Valck, K., Wojnicki, A. C, Wilner, S.J.S. 2010. Networked Narratives: Understanding Word-of-Mouth Marketing in Online Communities. Journal of Marketing, March, Vol. 74 Issue 2, pp. 71–89.

Lee, S.M. and Chen, L. 2010. The impact of flow on online consumer behavior. Journal of Computer Information Systems. Summer, pp. 1–10.

Leppiman, A. 2010. Arjen elämyksiä – Leiri- ja elämyspohjainen Arkipäivät-perhepalvelu sosiaalisen kokemuksen tuottajana/ Everyday Experiences: Camp- and Experience-based Weekdays Family Service as a Producer of Social Experience, Rovaniemi:Lapland University Press.

Mangold, W.G. and Faulds, D.J. 2009. Social media: The new hybrid element of the promotion mix. Business Horizons. 52(4), pp. 357–365.

Millward-Brown. 2010. Putting social media in context. Accessed June, 18, 2012 available at http://www.millwardbrown.com/Insights/Articles/Default.aspx

Nambisan, S. and Baron, R. A. 2009. Virtual Customer Environments: Testing a Model of Voluntary Participation in Value Co-Creation Activities. Journal of Product Innovation Management (26:4), pp. 388–406.

Nambisan, S. and Baron, R. A. 2007. Interactions in Virtual Customer Environments: Implications for Product Support and Customer Relationship Management. Journal of Interactive Marketing, (21:2), pp.42–62.

Pine, J.B. II and Korn K. C. 2011. Infinite Possibility: Creating Customer Value on the Digital Frontier. Berrett-Koehler Publishers, Inc.

Pine, J. B. II and Gilmore, J. 1999/2011. The Experience Economy. Boston: Harvard Business School Press.

Sen, S. and Lerman, D. 2007. Why are you telling me this? An examination into negative consumer reviews on the web. Journal of Interactive Marketing. (21:4), pp. 76–94.

Socialbakers.com. 2012. Accessed 30 May 2012, available at http://www.socialbakers.com/facebook-statistics/

Srtativity Group. 2010. Social media engagement study. Accessed June 18, 2012 available at http://www.strativity.com/media/2010%20Social%20Media%20Study.pdf.

Tarssanen, S. and Kylänen, M. 2007. A Theoretical Model for Producing Experiences – A Touristic Perspective, in Kylänen, M. (Ed.), Articles on Experiences 2, Lapland Centre of Expertise for the Experience Industry, Rovaniemi: Lapland University Press, pp.134–154.

Tarssanen, S. and Kylänen, M. 2009. Handbook for experience stagers. In Tarssanen, S. 5th ed. Lapland Center of Expertise for the Experience Industry, Rovaniemi: OY Sevenprint Ltd.

Ward, J.C. and Ostrom, A. L. 2006. Complaining to the Masses: The Role of Protest Framing in Customer-Created Complaint Web Sites. Journal of Consumer Research; September, Vol. 33 Issue 2, pp. 220–230.